Paulina Olowska

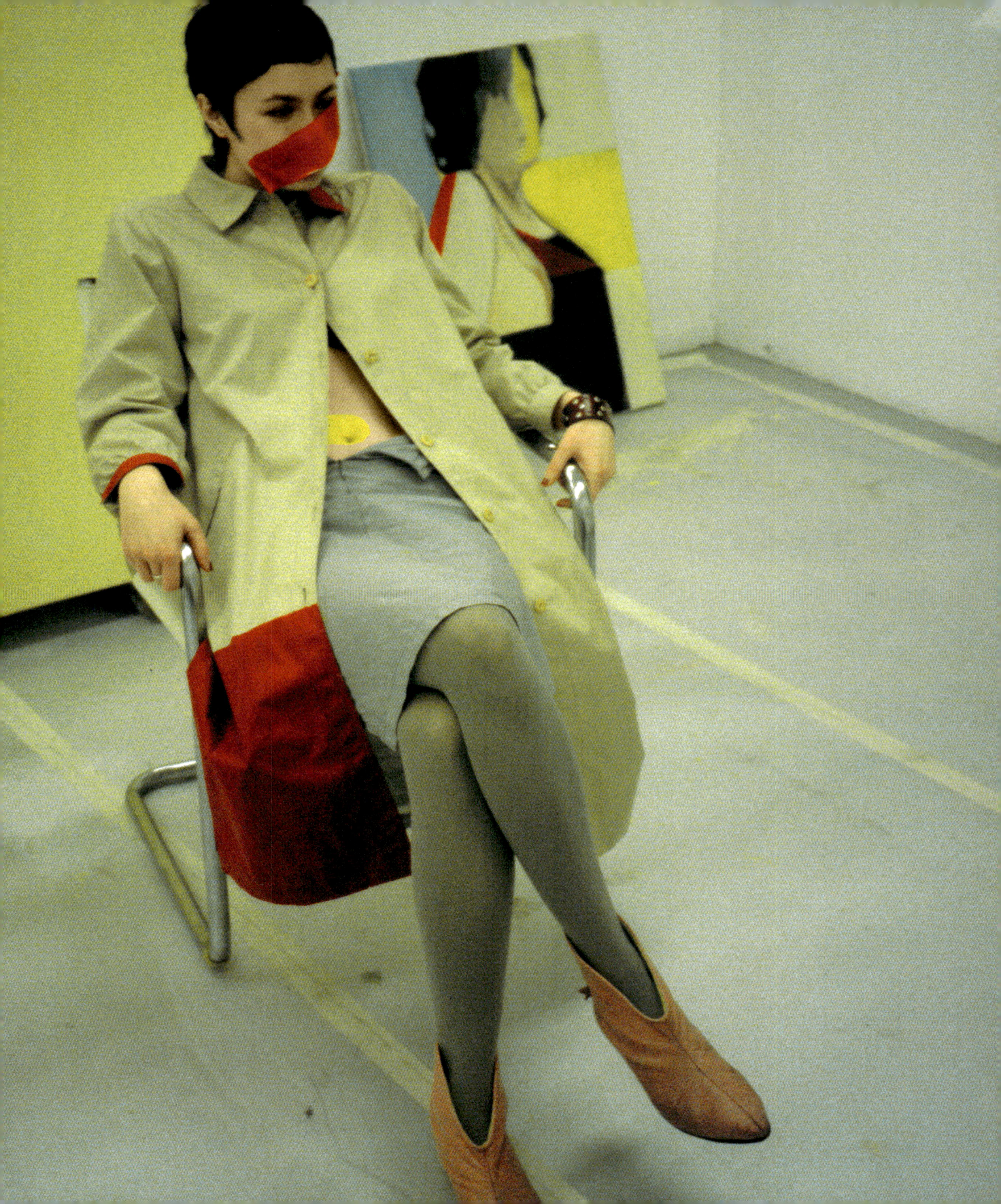

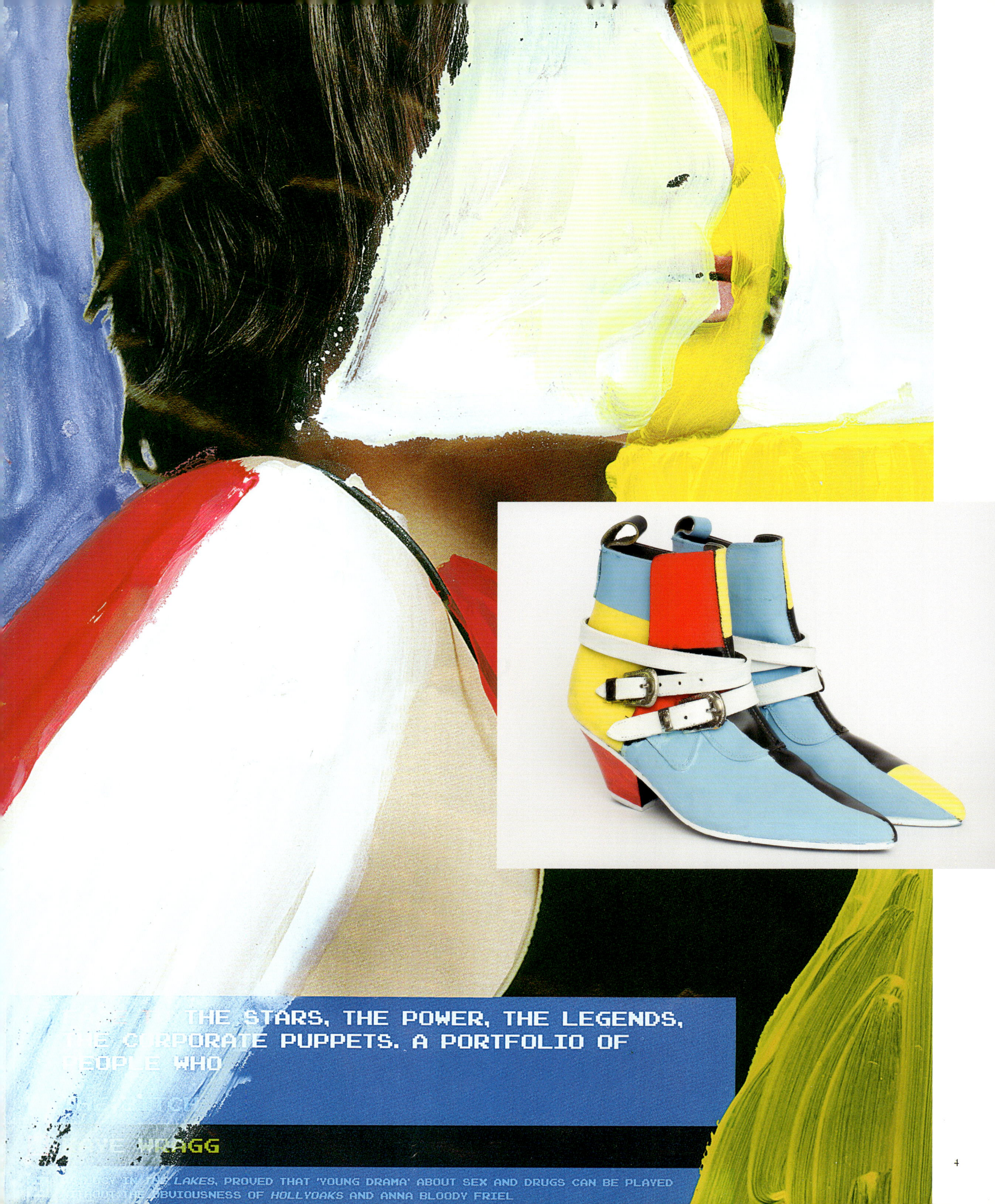
THE STARS, THE POWER, THE LEGENDS,
PUPPETS. A PORTFOLIO OF
WHO
RAGG
LAKES, PROVED THAT 'YOUNG DRAMA' ABOUT SEX AND DRUGS CAN BE PLAYED
BVIOUSNESS OF *HOLLYOAKS* AND ANNA BLOODY FRIEL

←
"Construction First-Collages from Japan" series, 2000
Modernist Rockabilly Shoes, 2000

Painted Dress, 2000
"Asymmetric Women" series, 2000

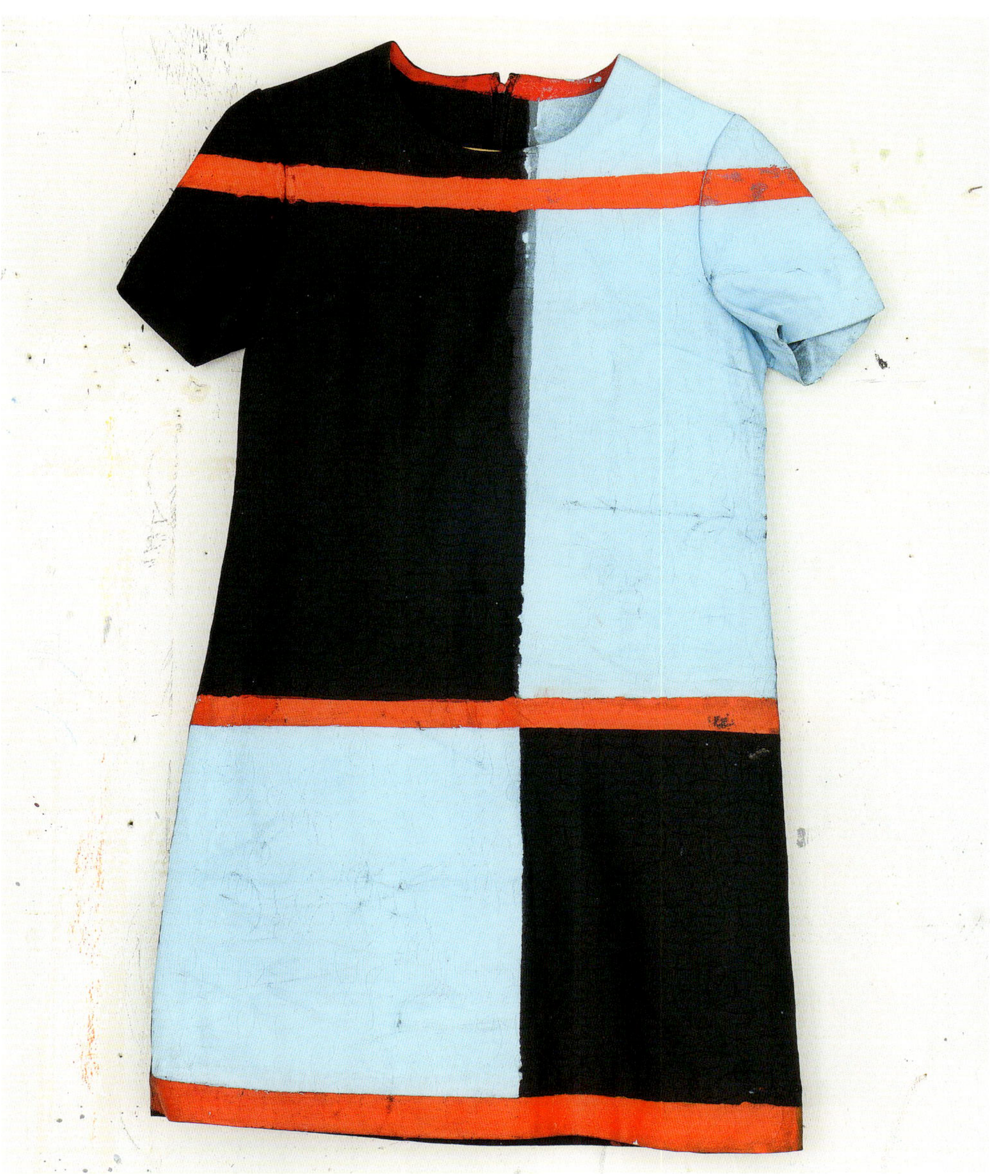

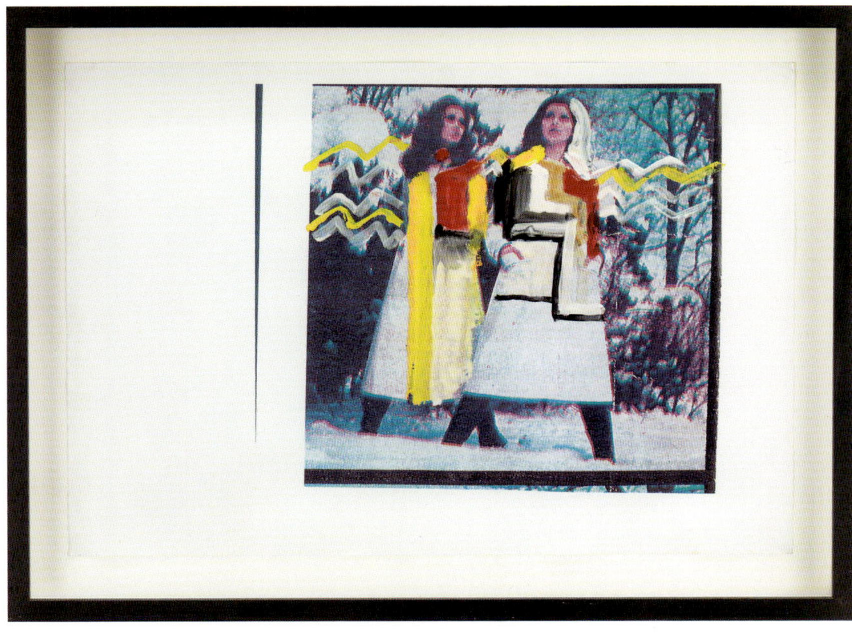

From left to right
Bridget–1964, 2001
Big Pollock, 2001
X, 2002

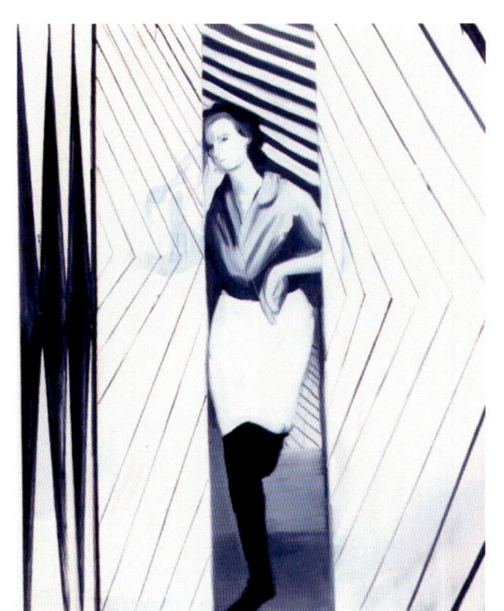

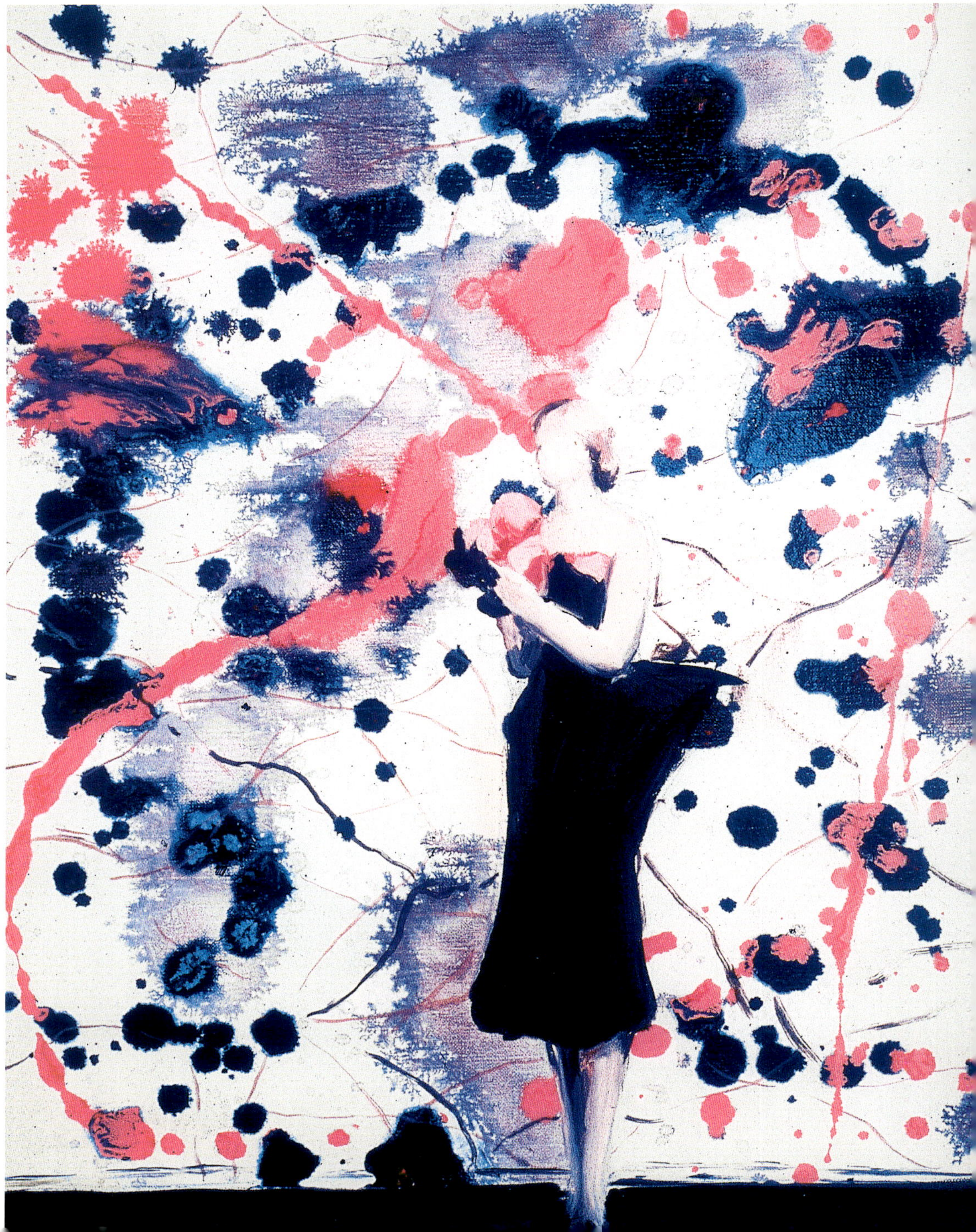

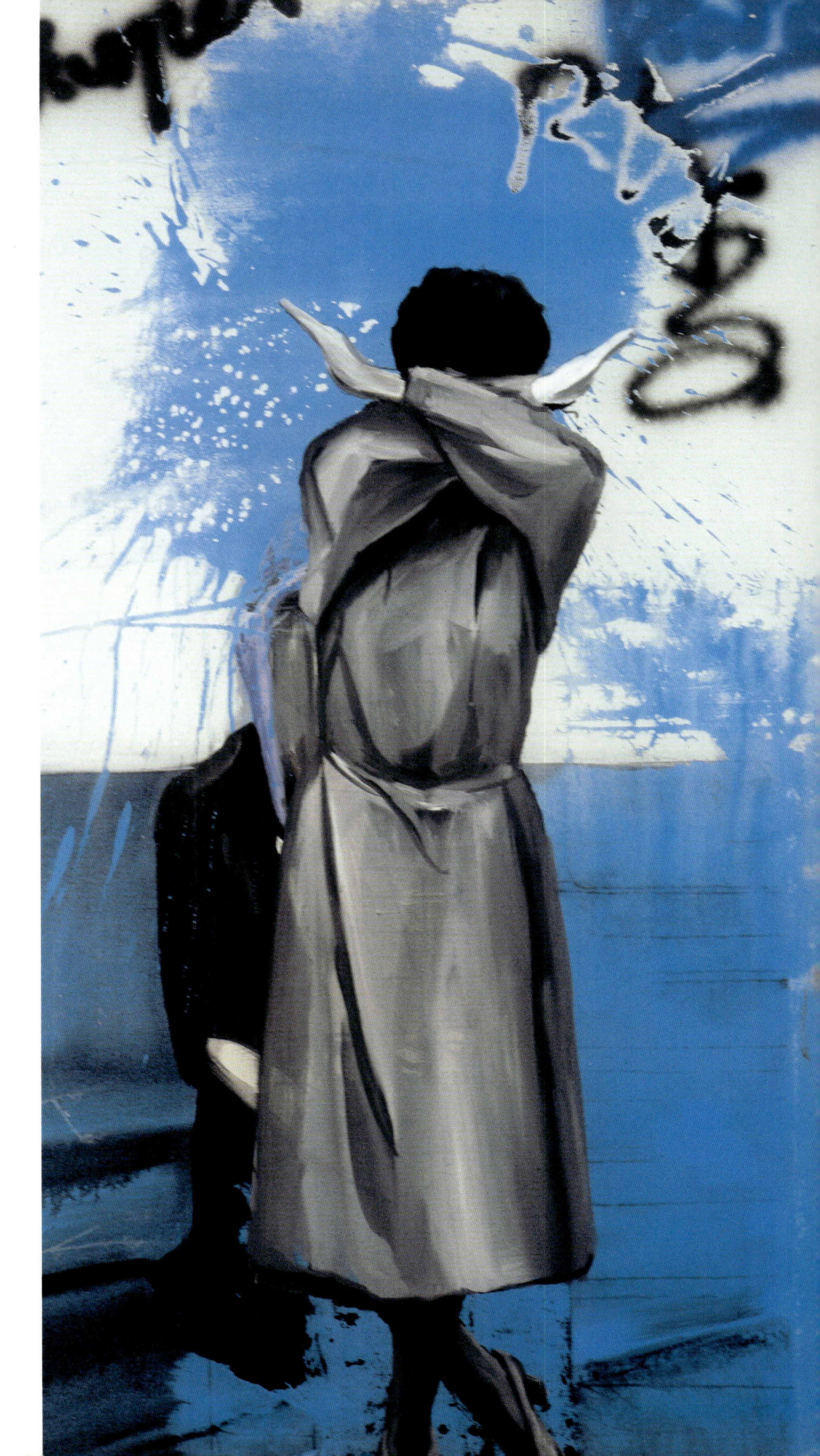

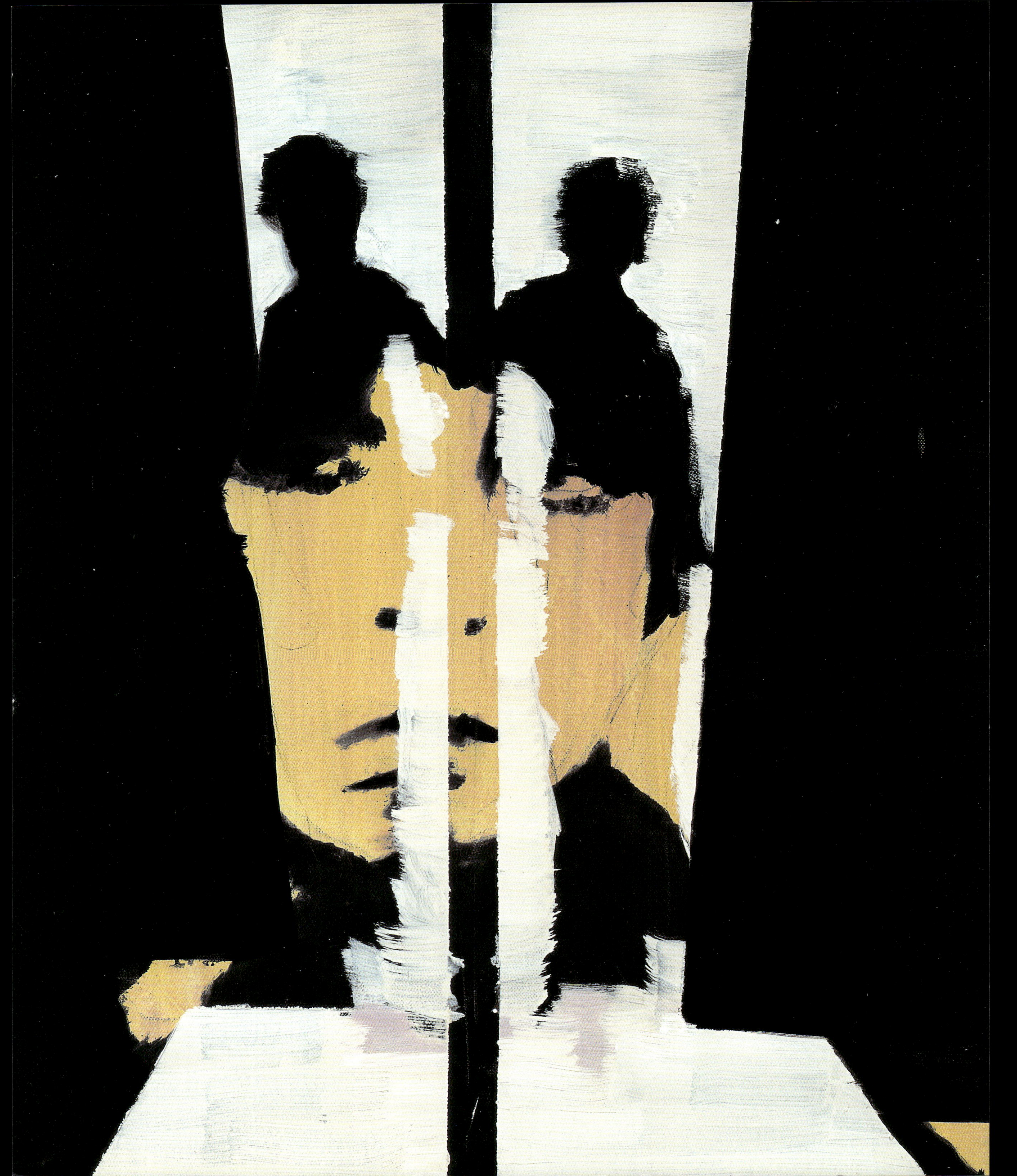

Table of Contents

The Observer, 2000

Lucy McKenzie and Paulina Olowska, *Nova Popularna*, Warsaw, 2003

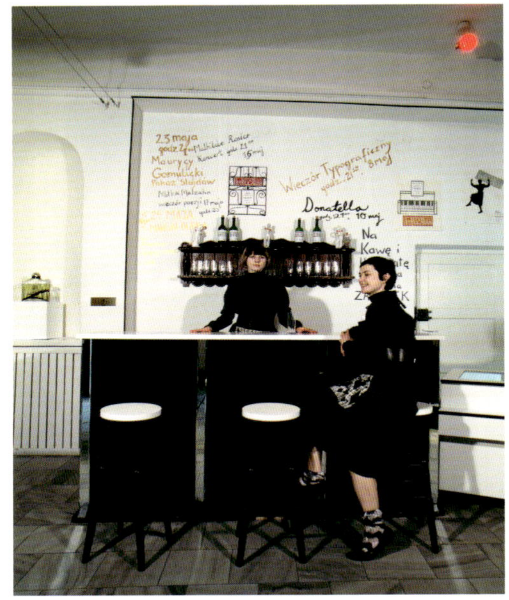

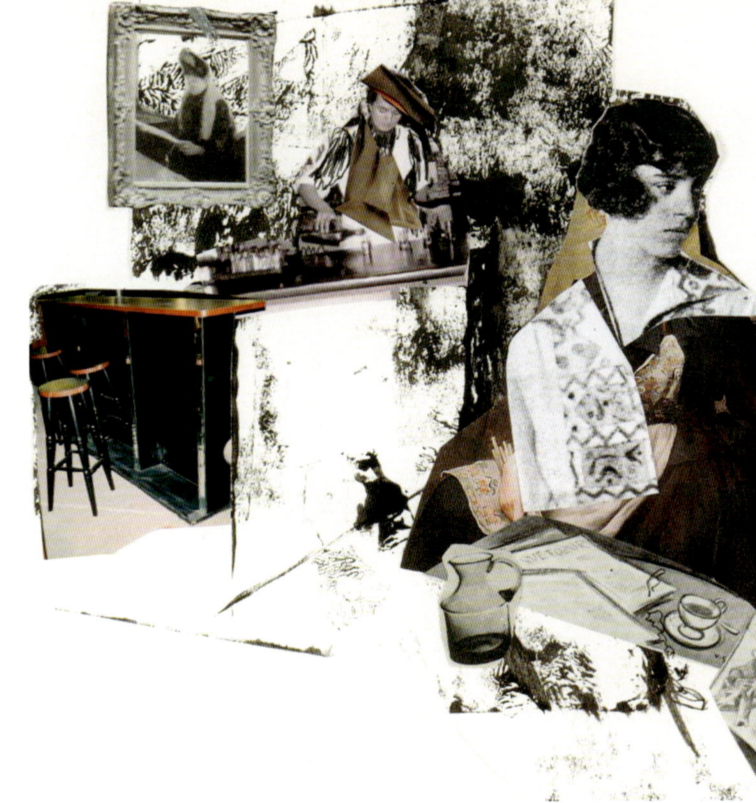

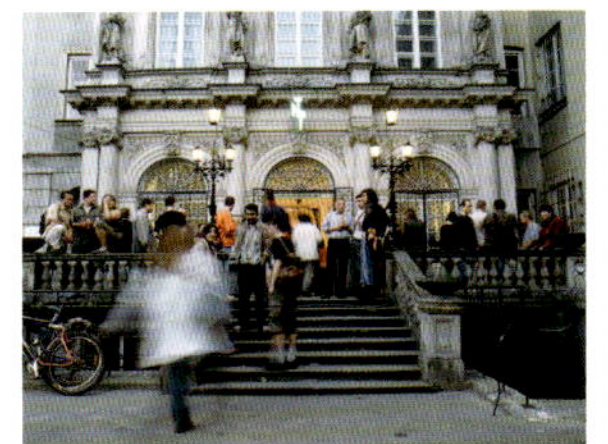

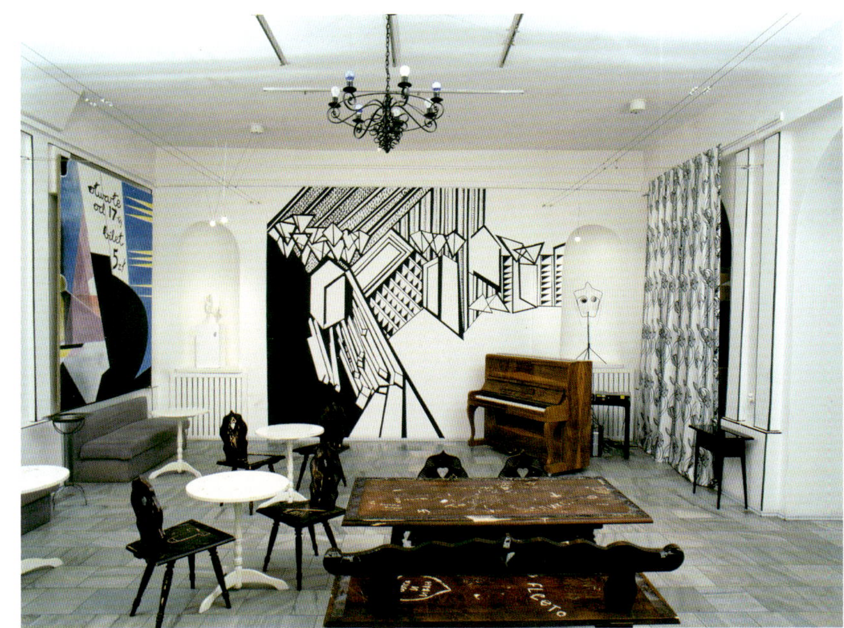

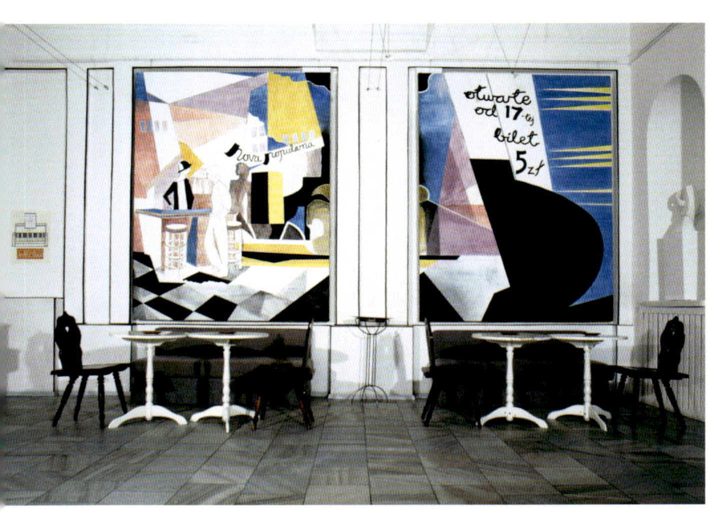

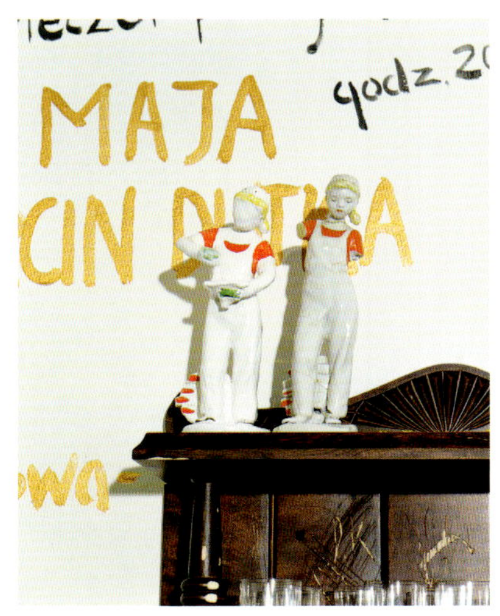

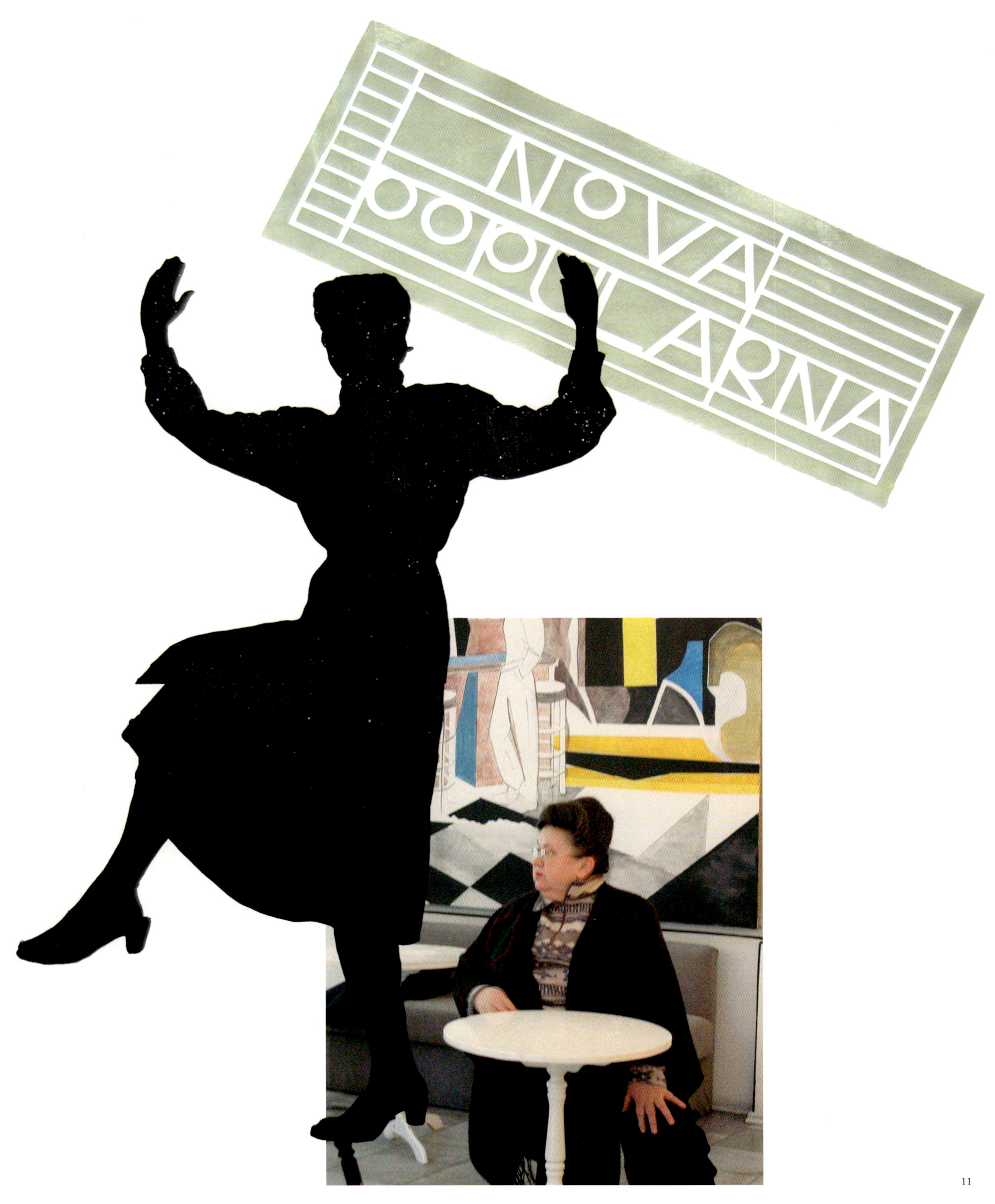
NOVA
POPULARNA

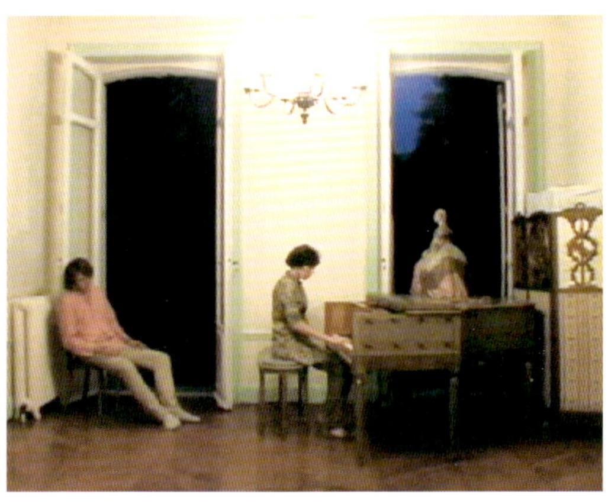
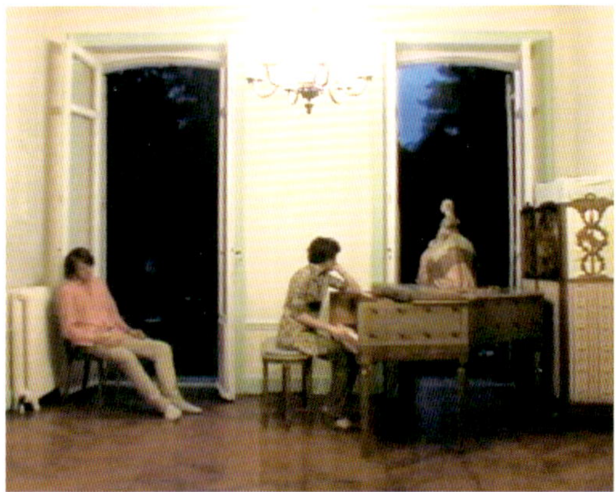
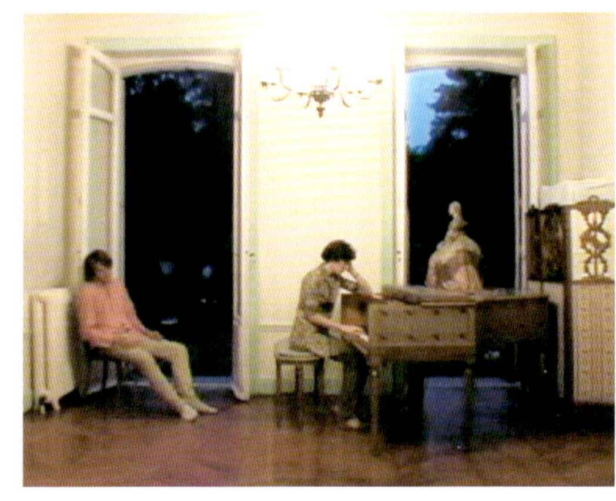
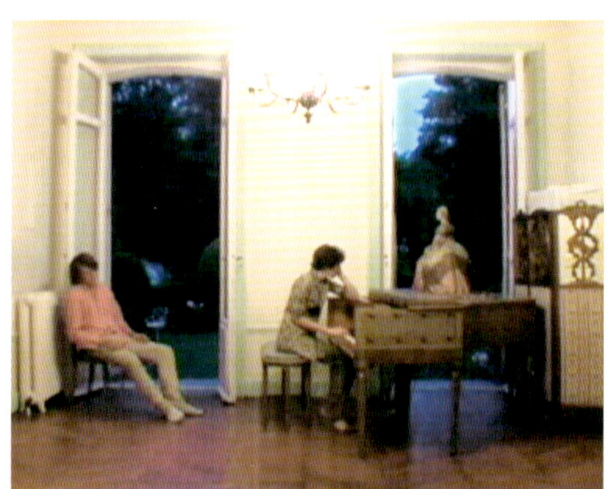
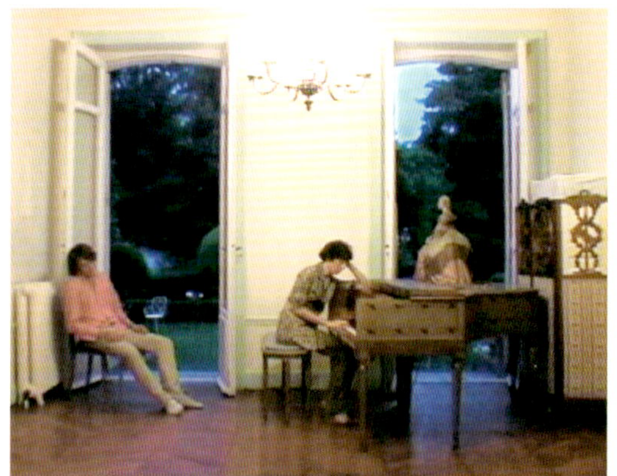
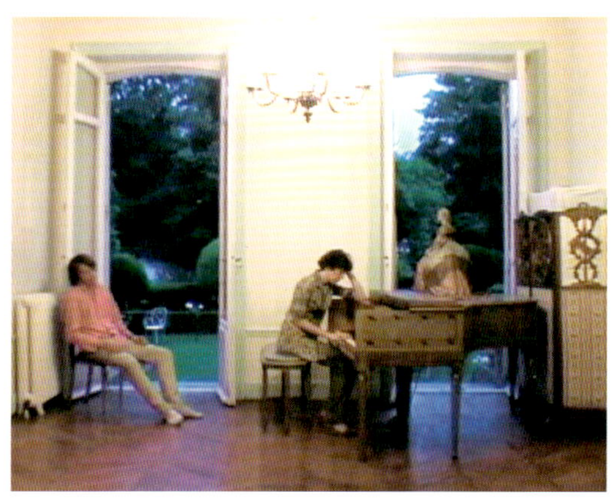

Paulina Olowska and Mathilde Rosier, *Entr'acte*, 2003

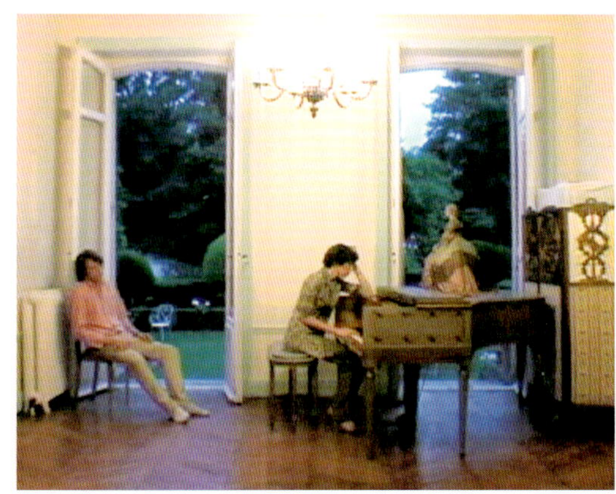

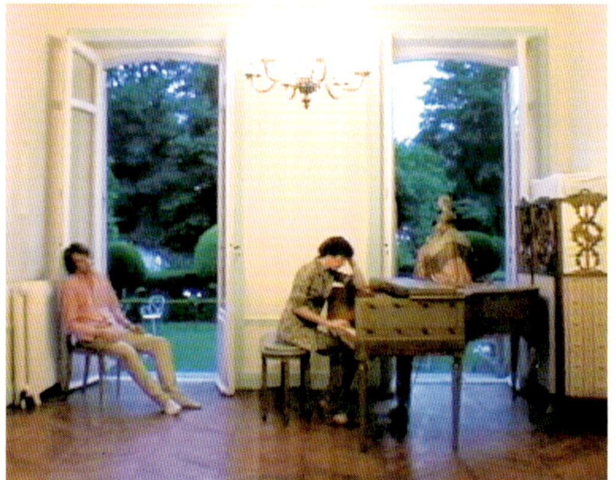

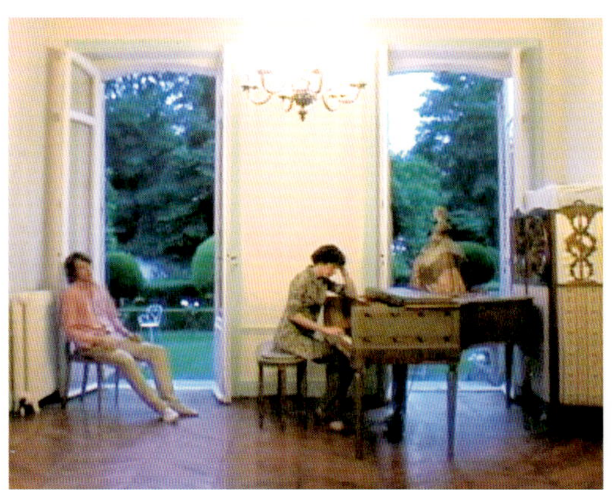

→
Paulina Olowska and Mathilde Rosier, *Entr'acte*, exhibition view, Cieszyn, 2003

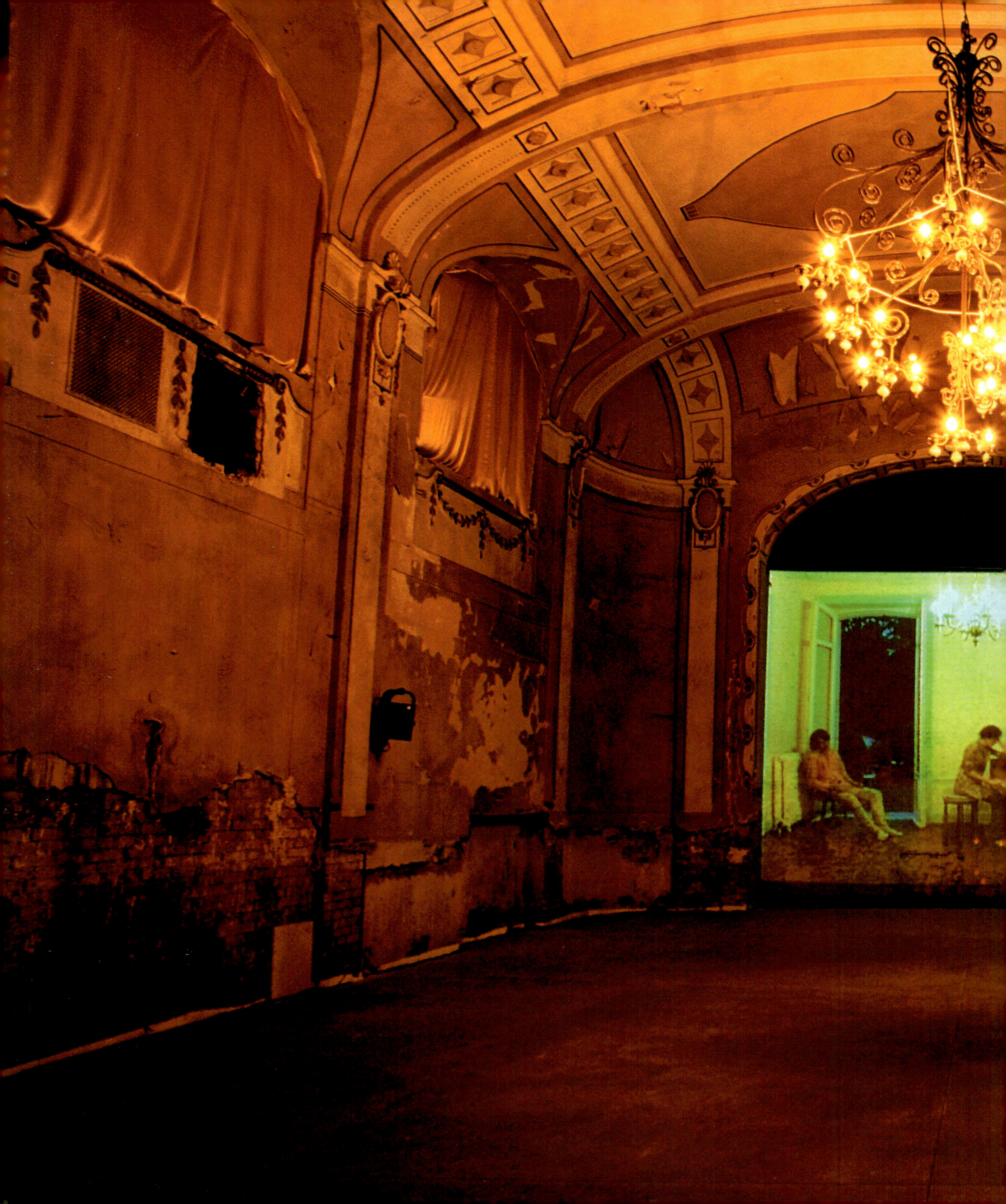

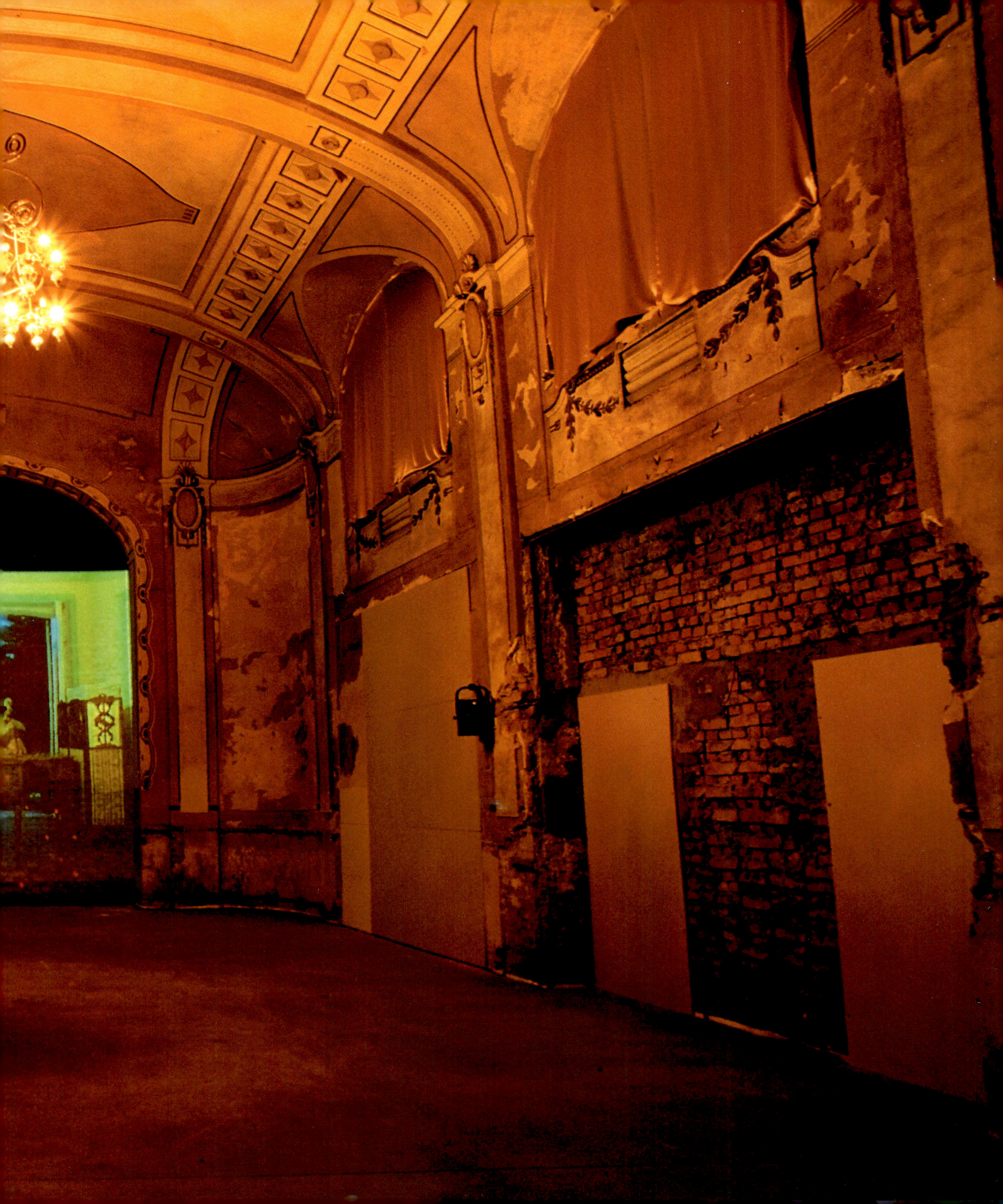

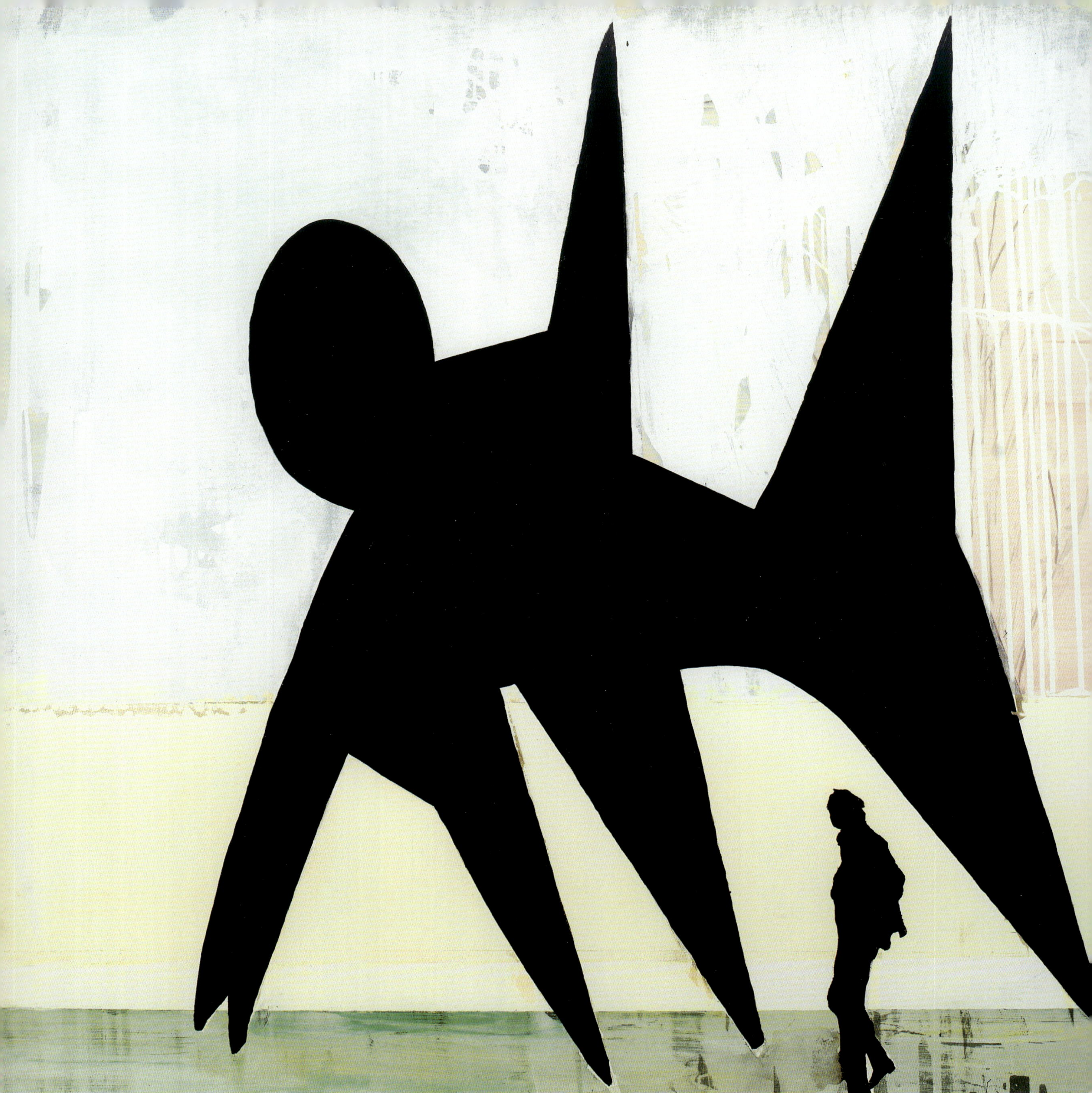

From left to right
Calder, 2003
Arriviste (XZ), exhibition view, AKINCI Gallery, Amsterdam, 2004
Library of Spoken Books/Spoken Library, wallpaper, 2003

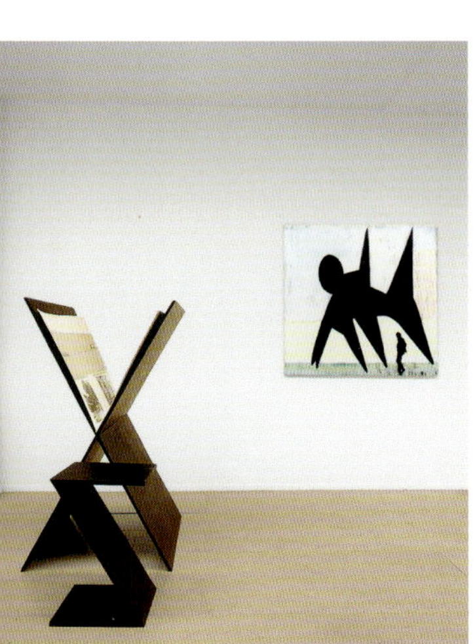

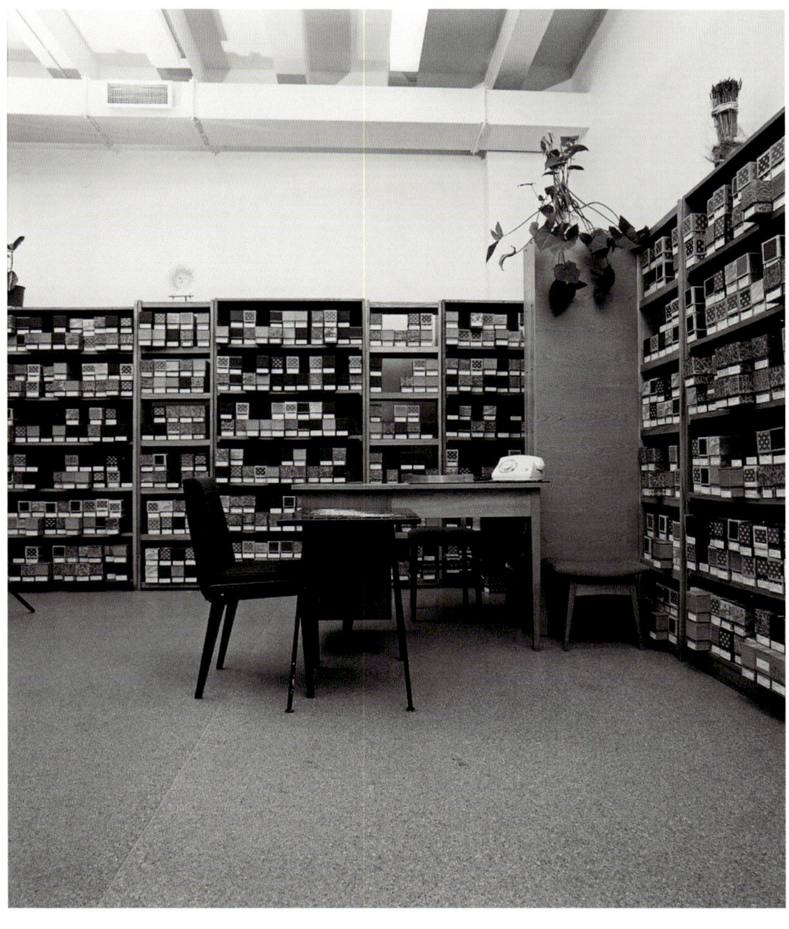

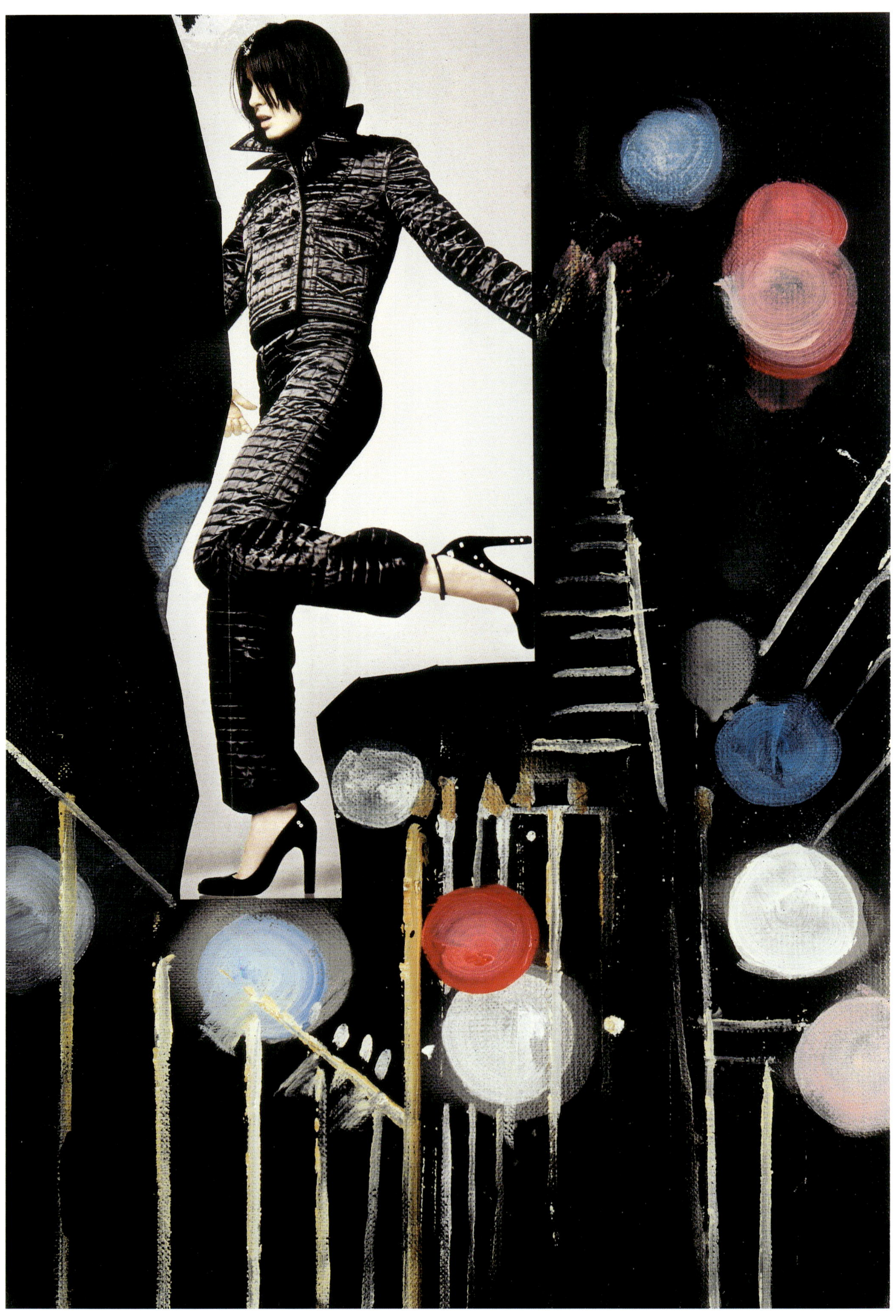

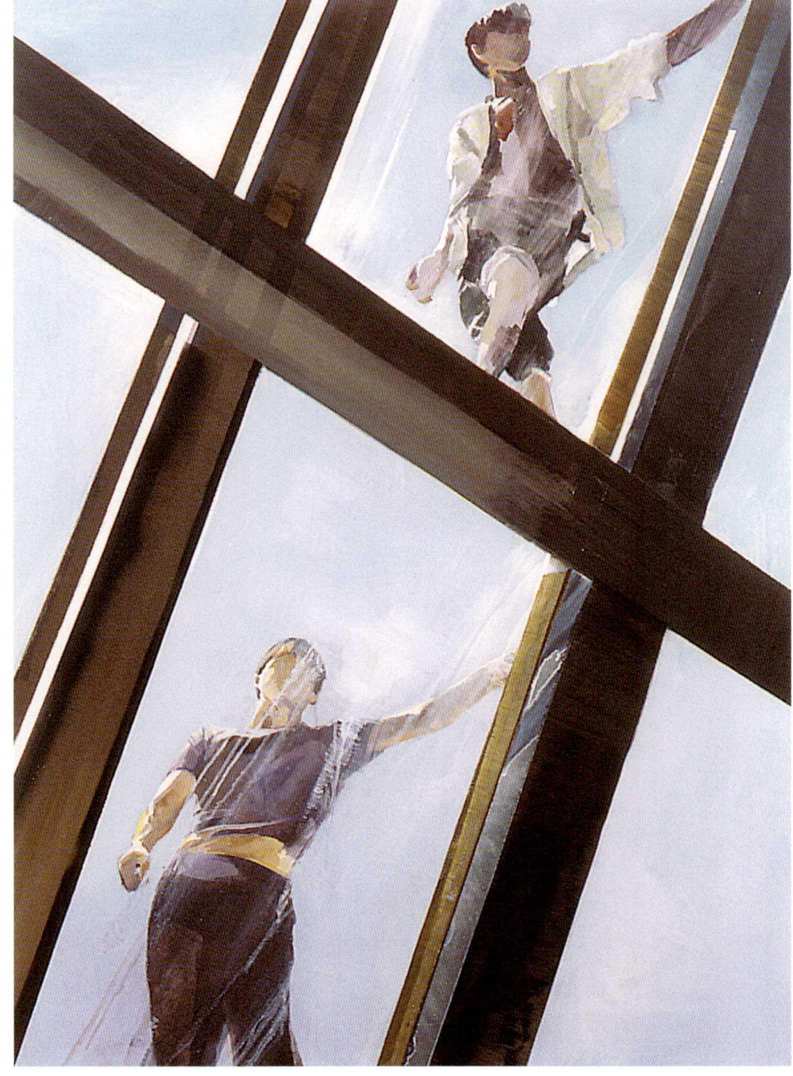

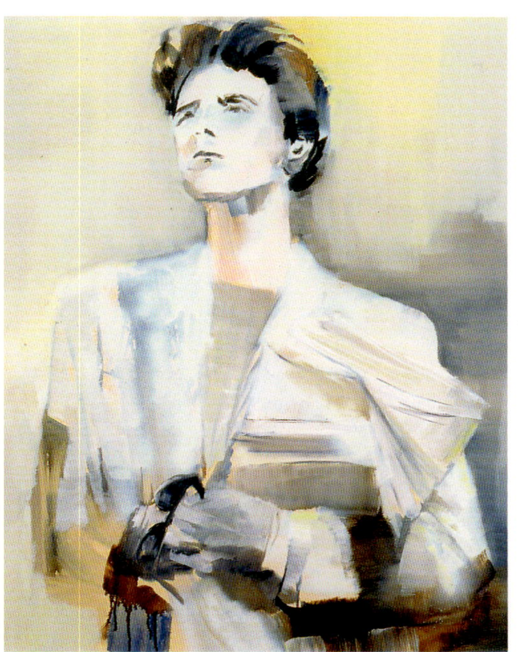

From left to right
America, 2003
Diesel, 2003
Fall 1984–85, 2003

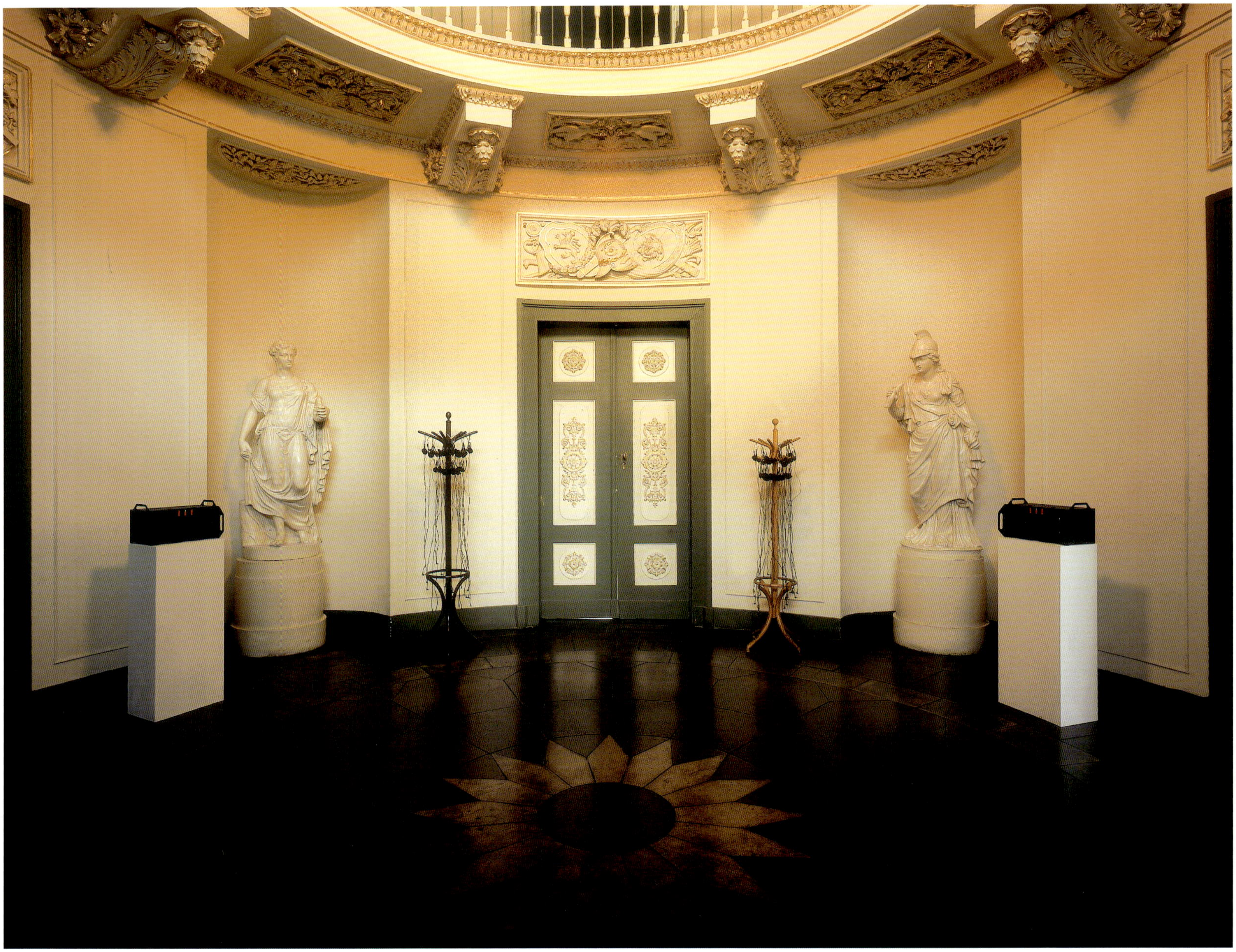

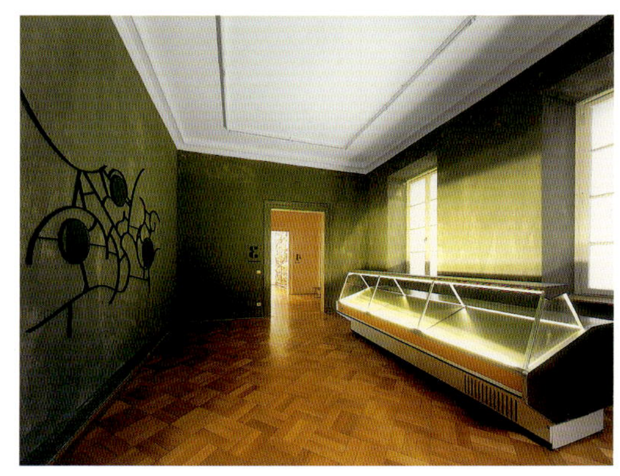

Sie musste die Idee eines Hauses als Metapher verwerfen, exhibition views,
Kunstverein Braunschweig, Brunswick, 2004

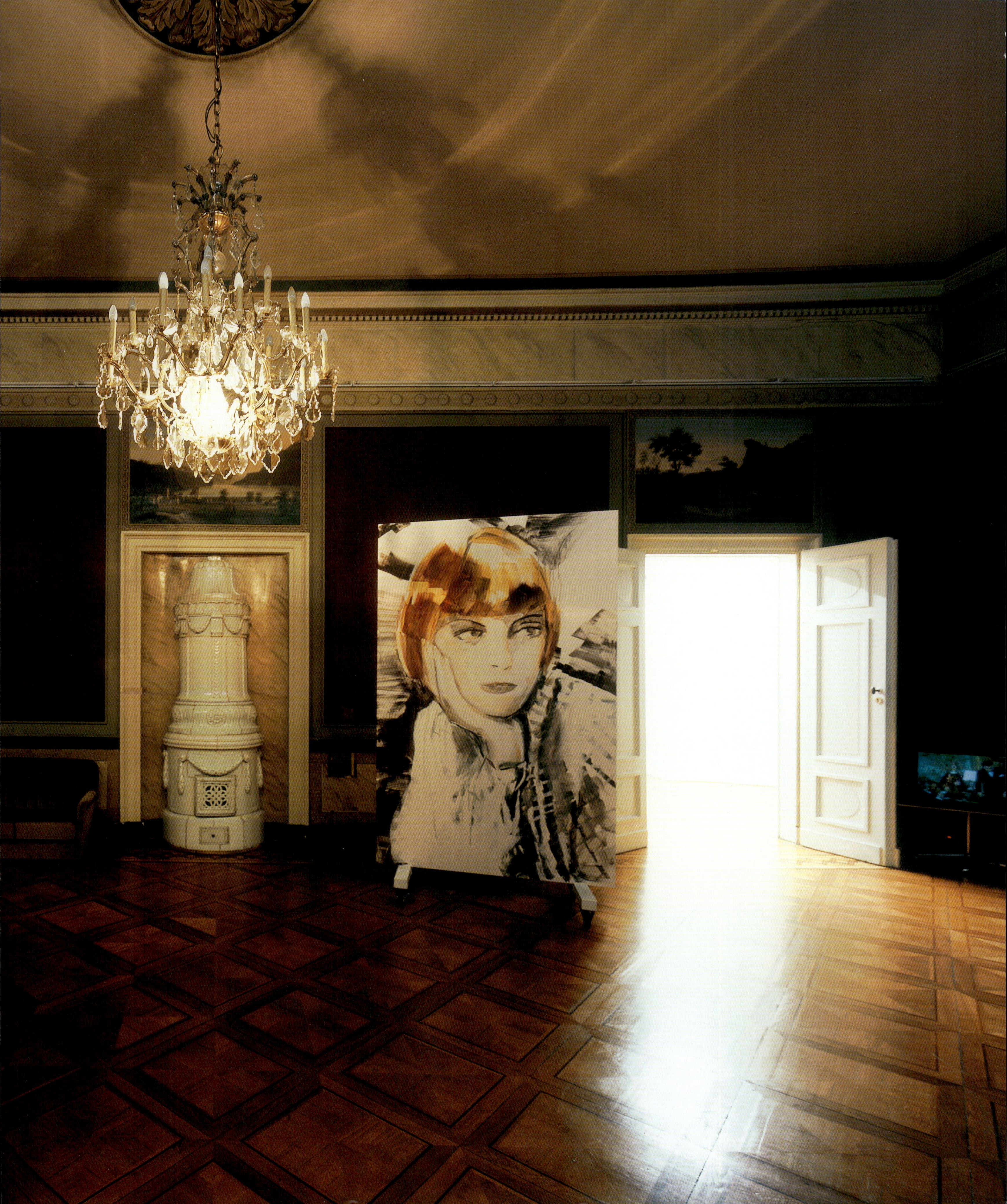

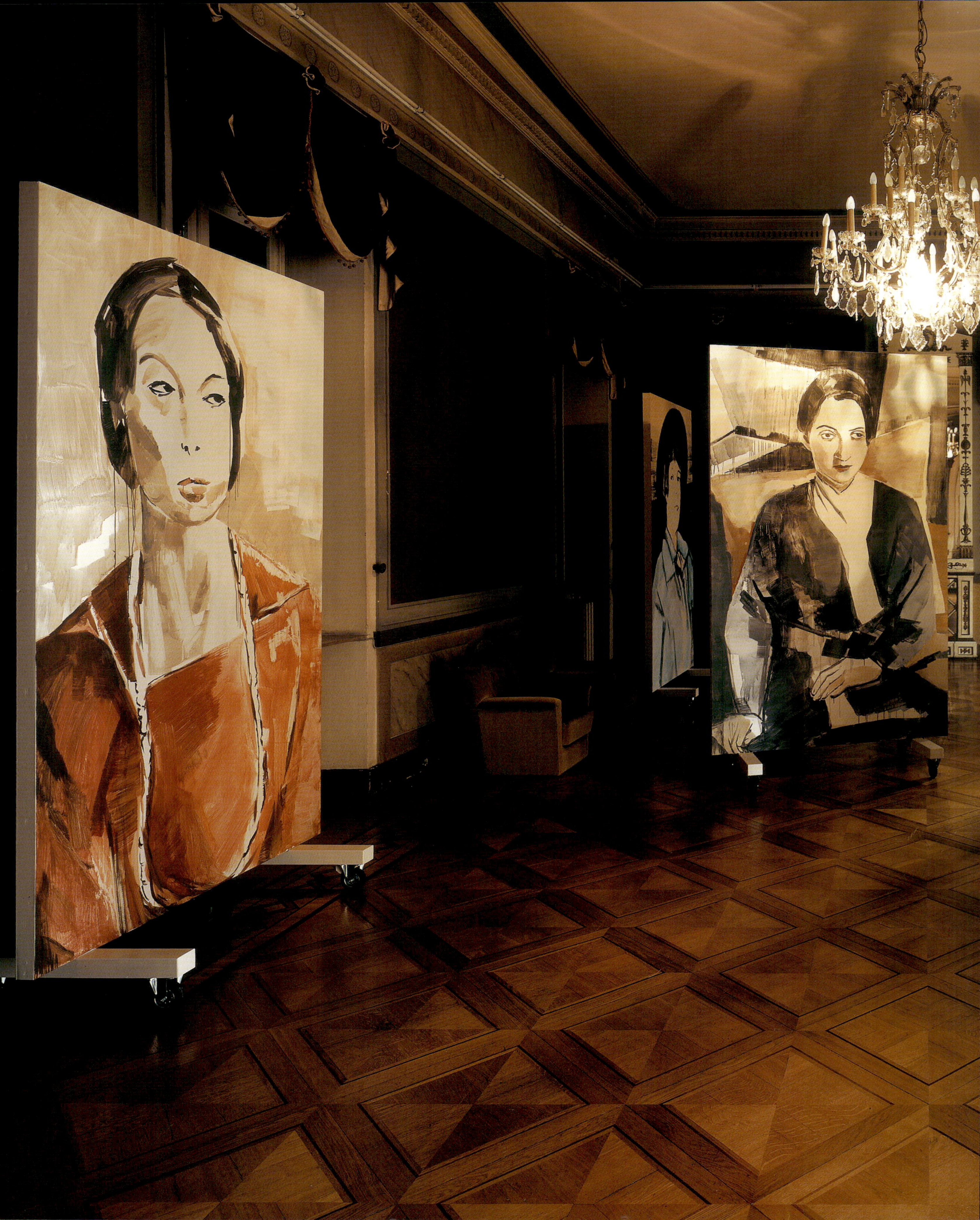

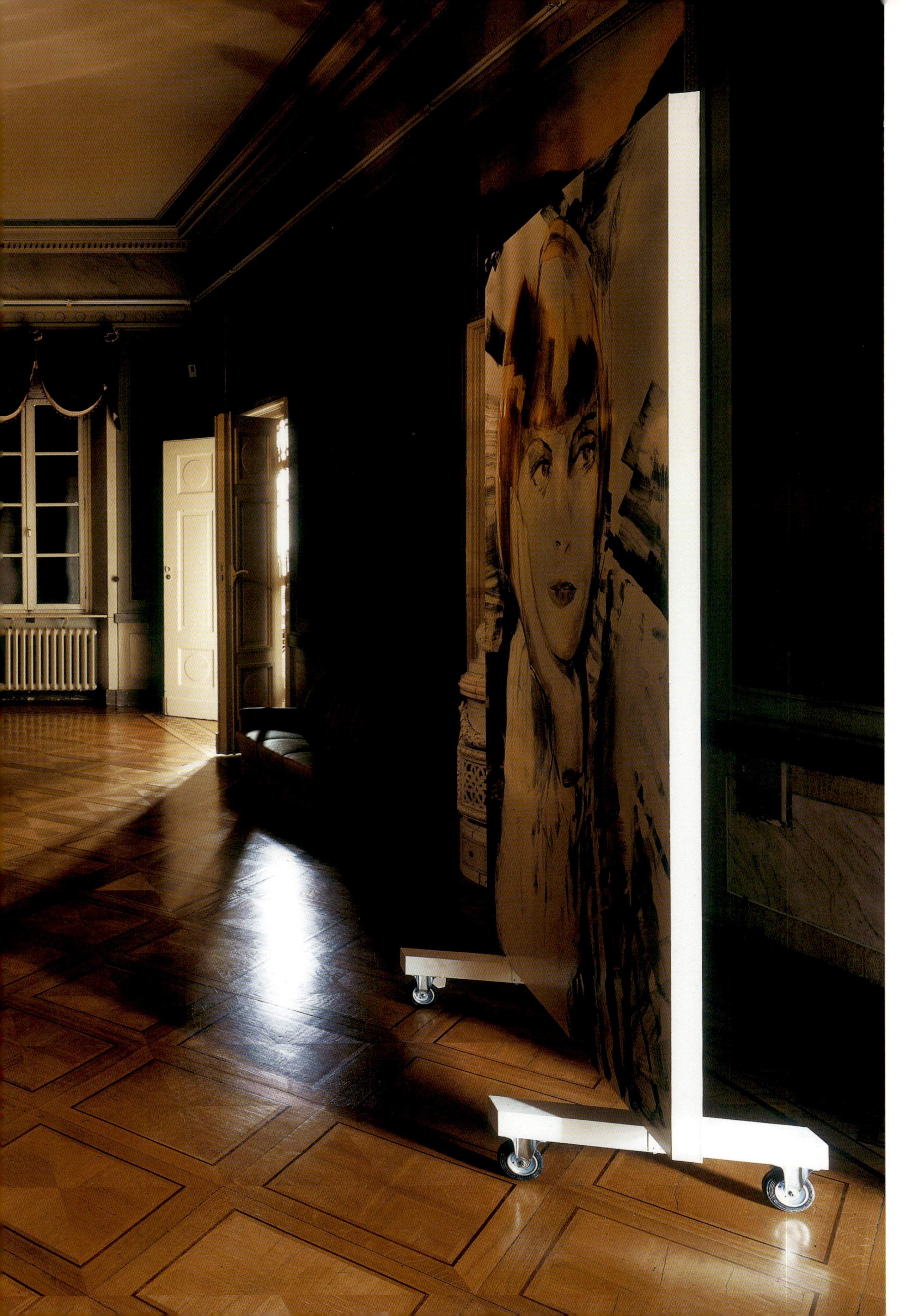

Asymmetric Display, installation view, Galerie Buchholz, Art Cologne, 2004

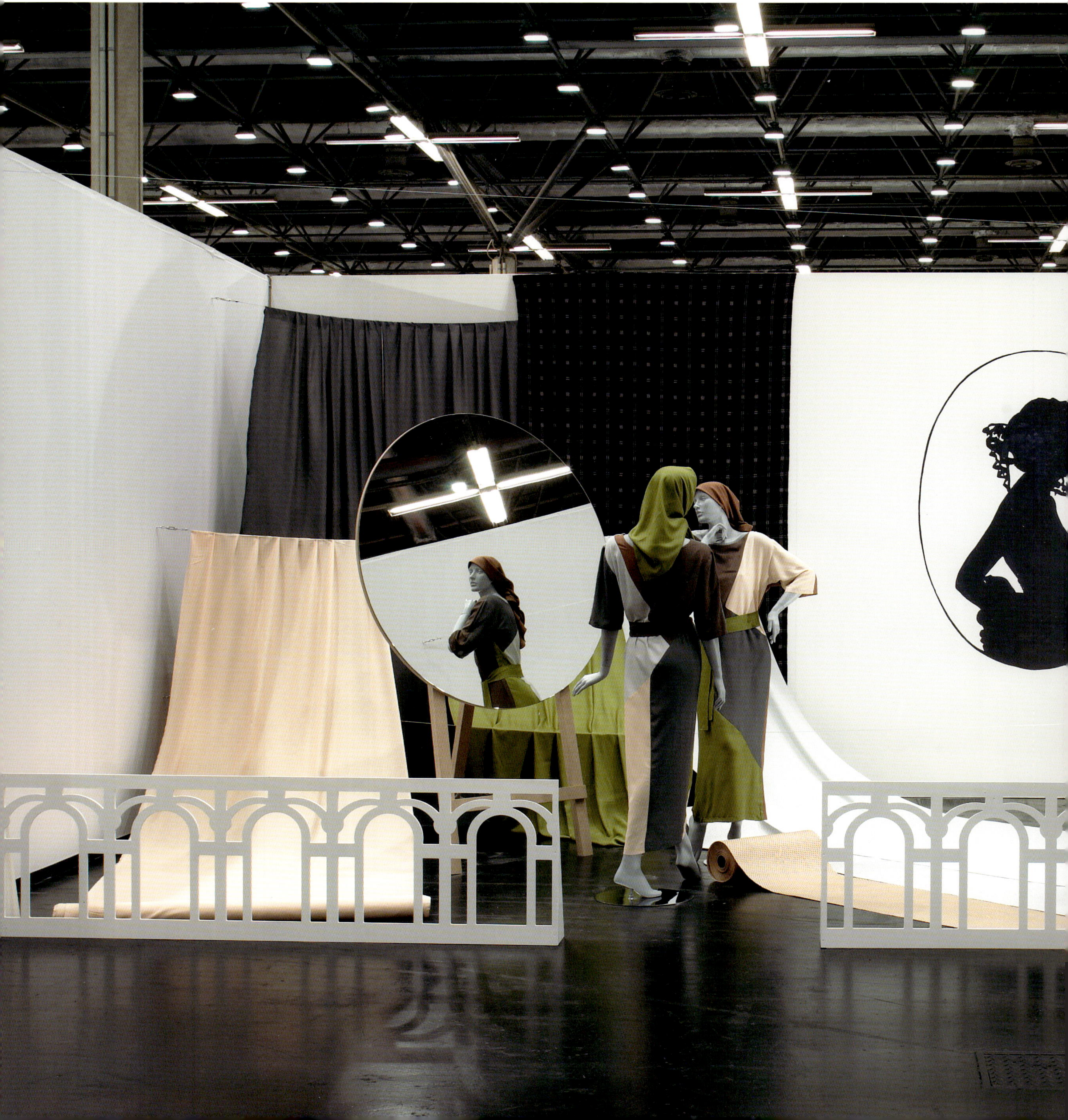

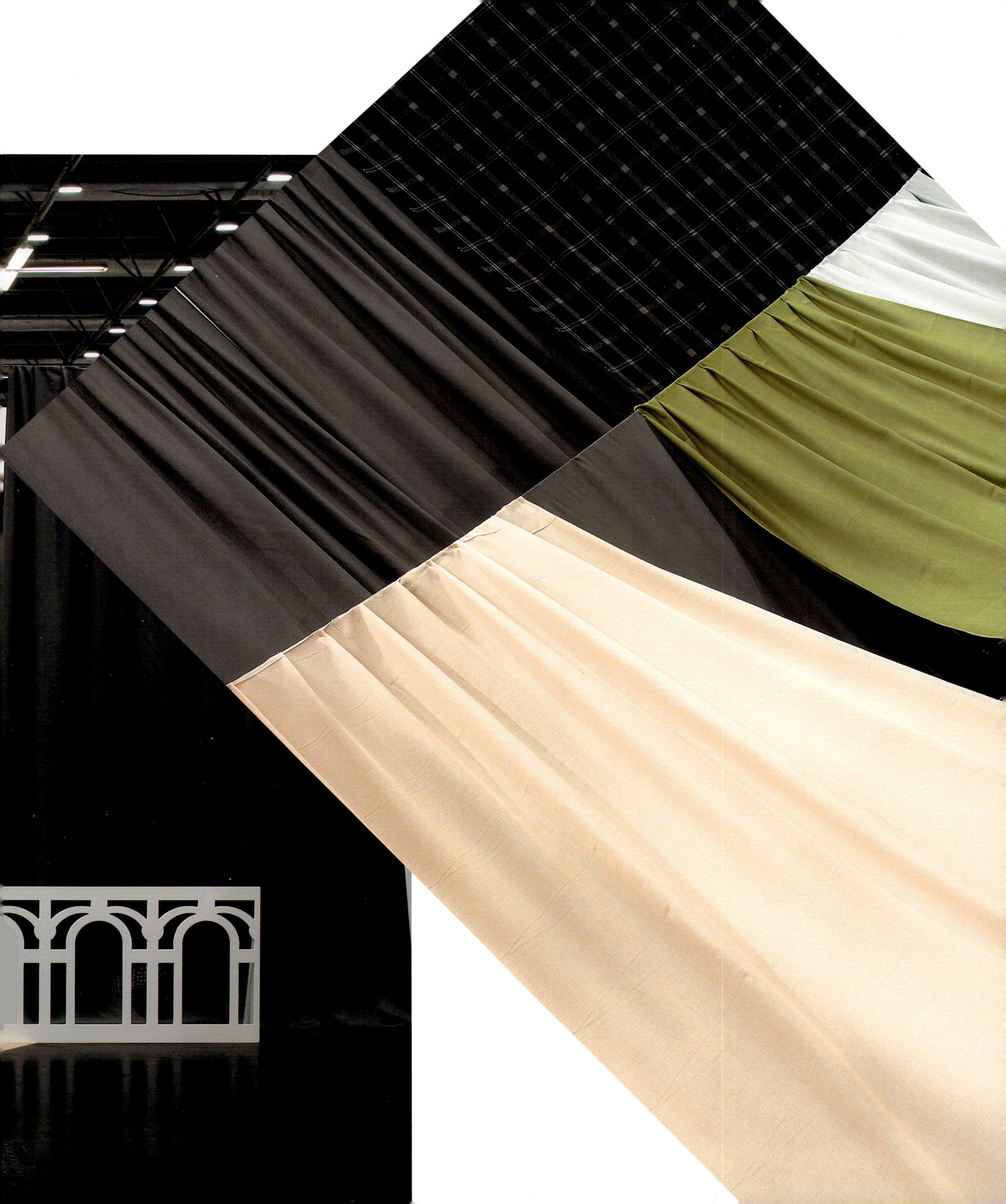

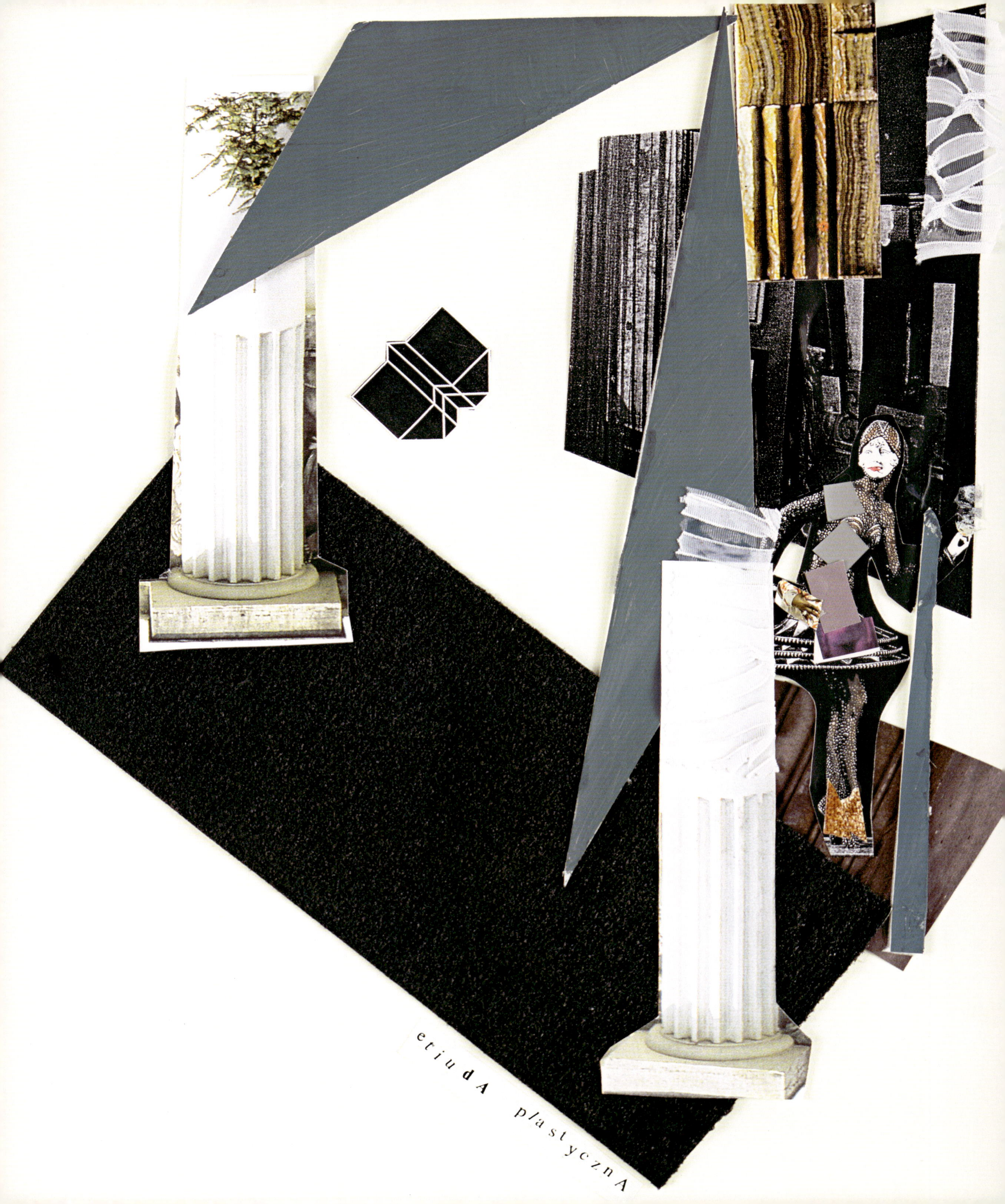
etiudA plastycznA

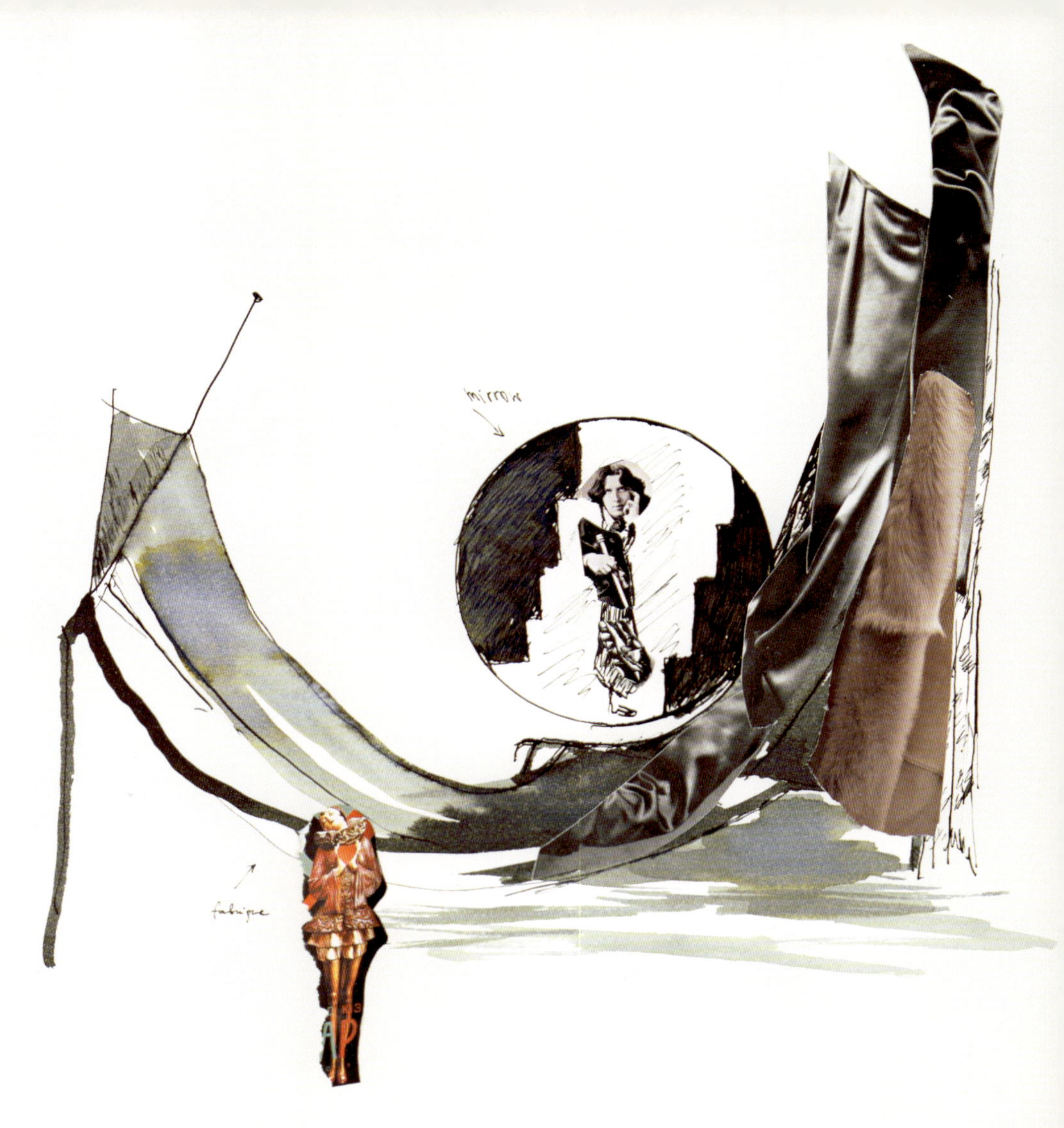

Etiuda Plastyczna, 2004
A Study with Oscar Wilde, 2004

→
Suspicious?, site-specific billboard, Chicago, 2004

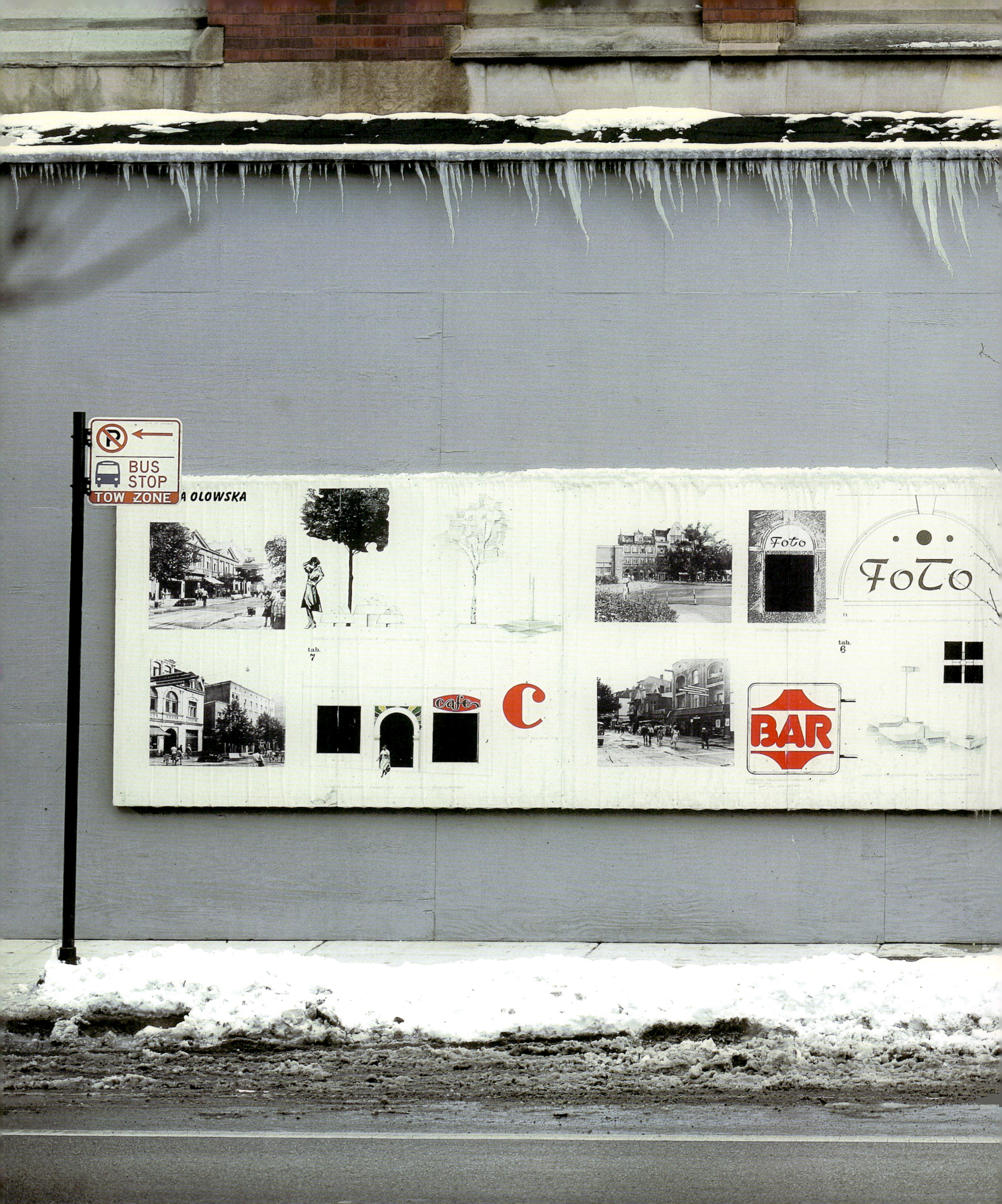
BUS
STOP
TOW ZONE
A OLOWSKA
Foto
FoTo
tab.
7
tab.
6
cafe
C
BAR

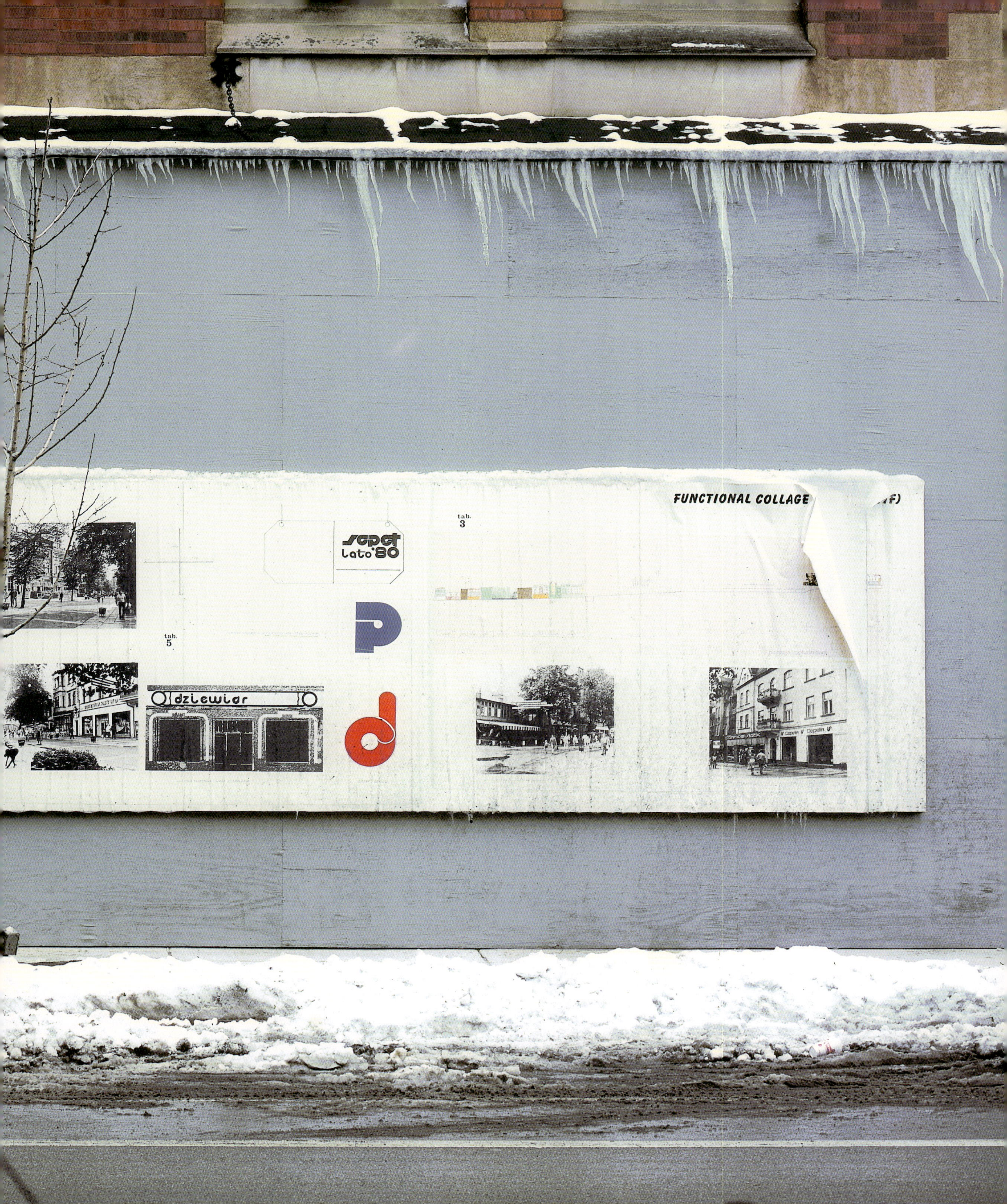

FUNCTIONAL COLLAGE
tab. 3
sopot
lato'80
tab. 5
dziewiar

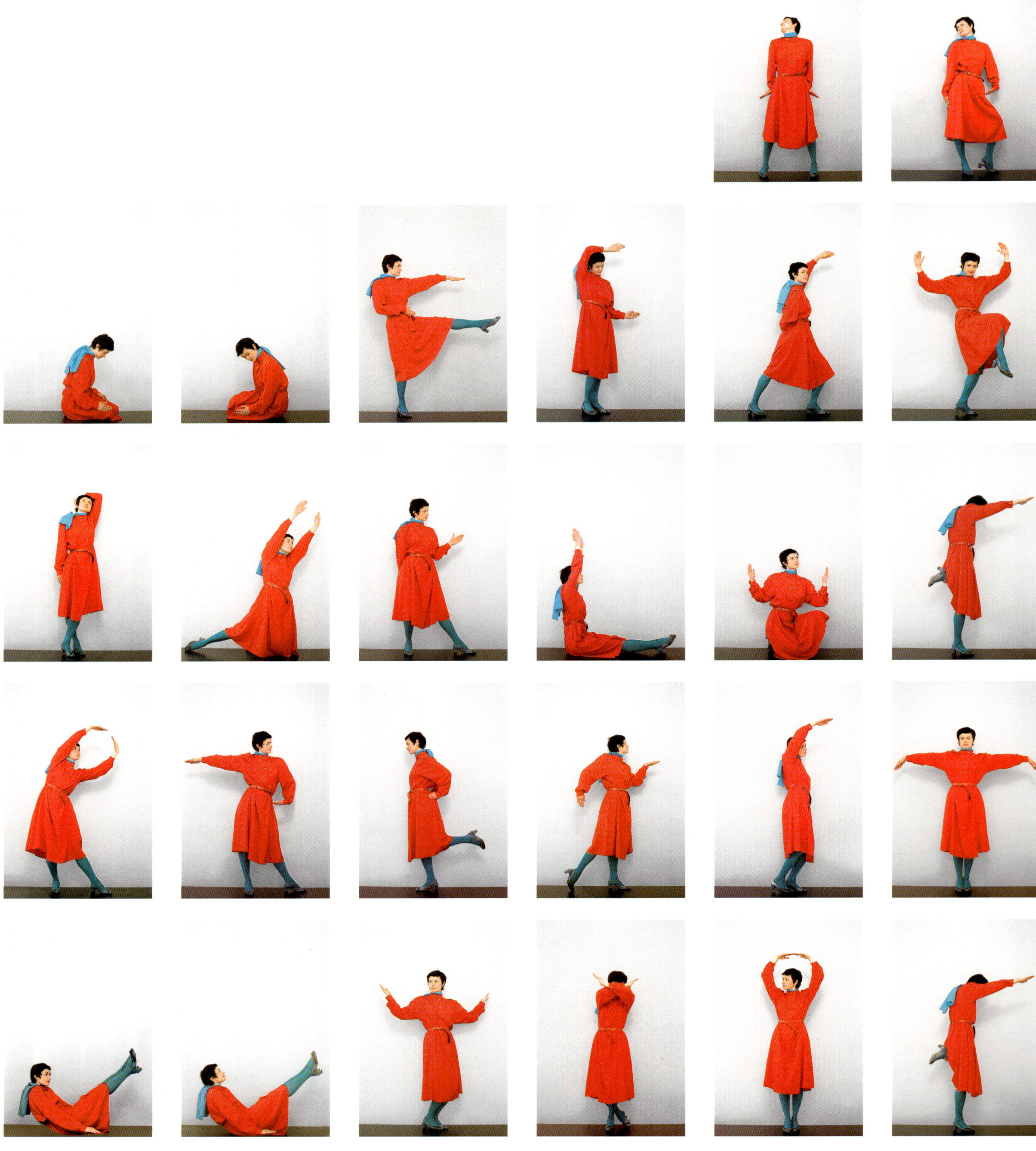

Alphabet, 2005
Alphabet, performance, The Museum of Modern Art, New York, 2012

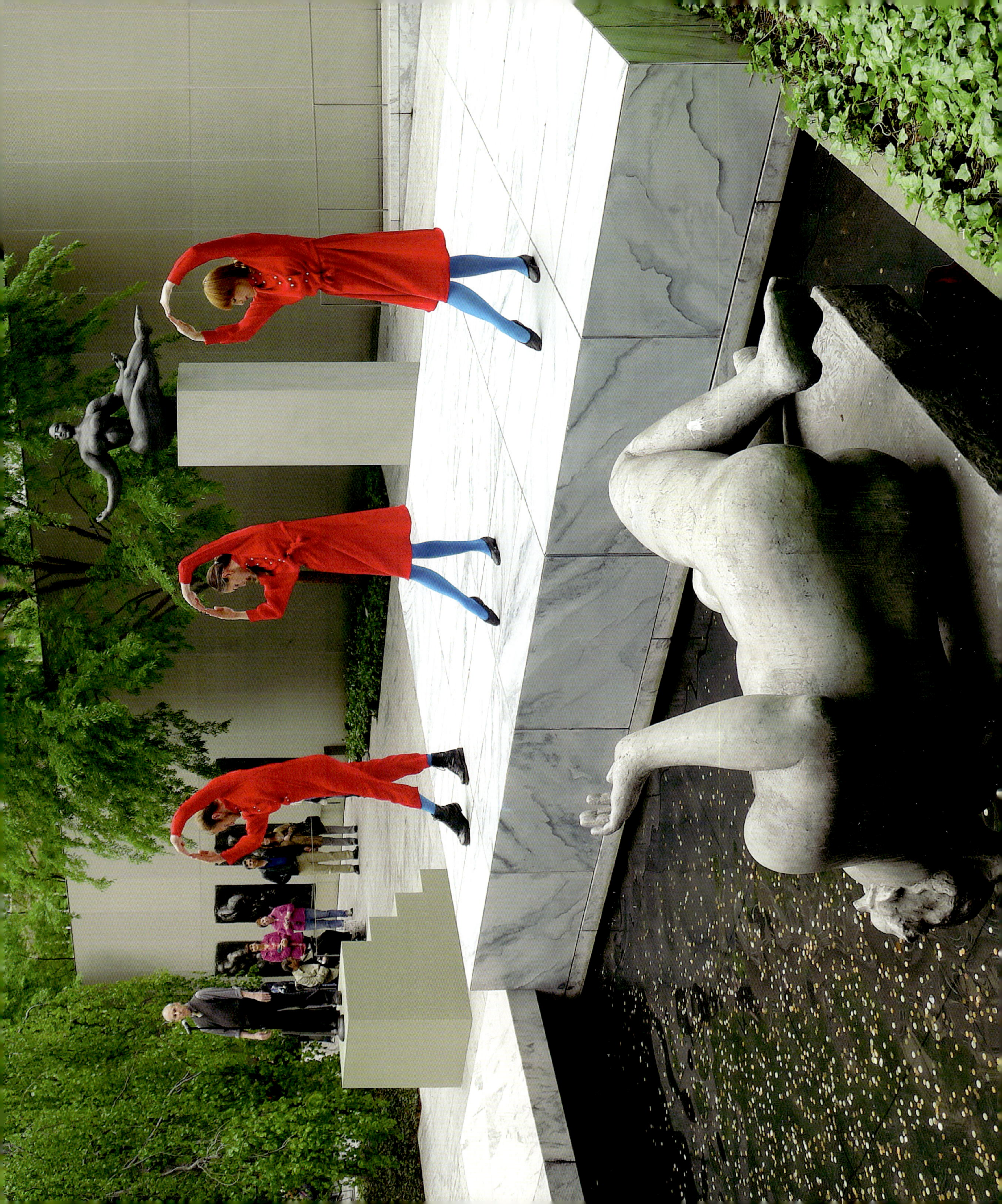

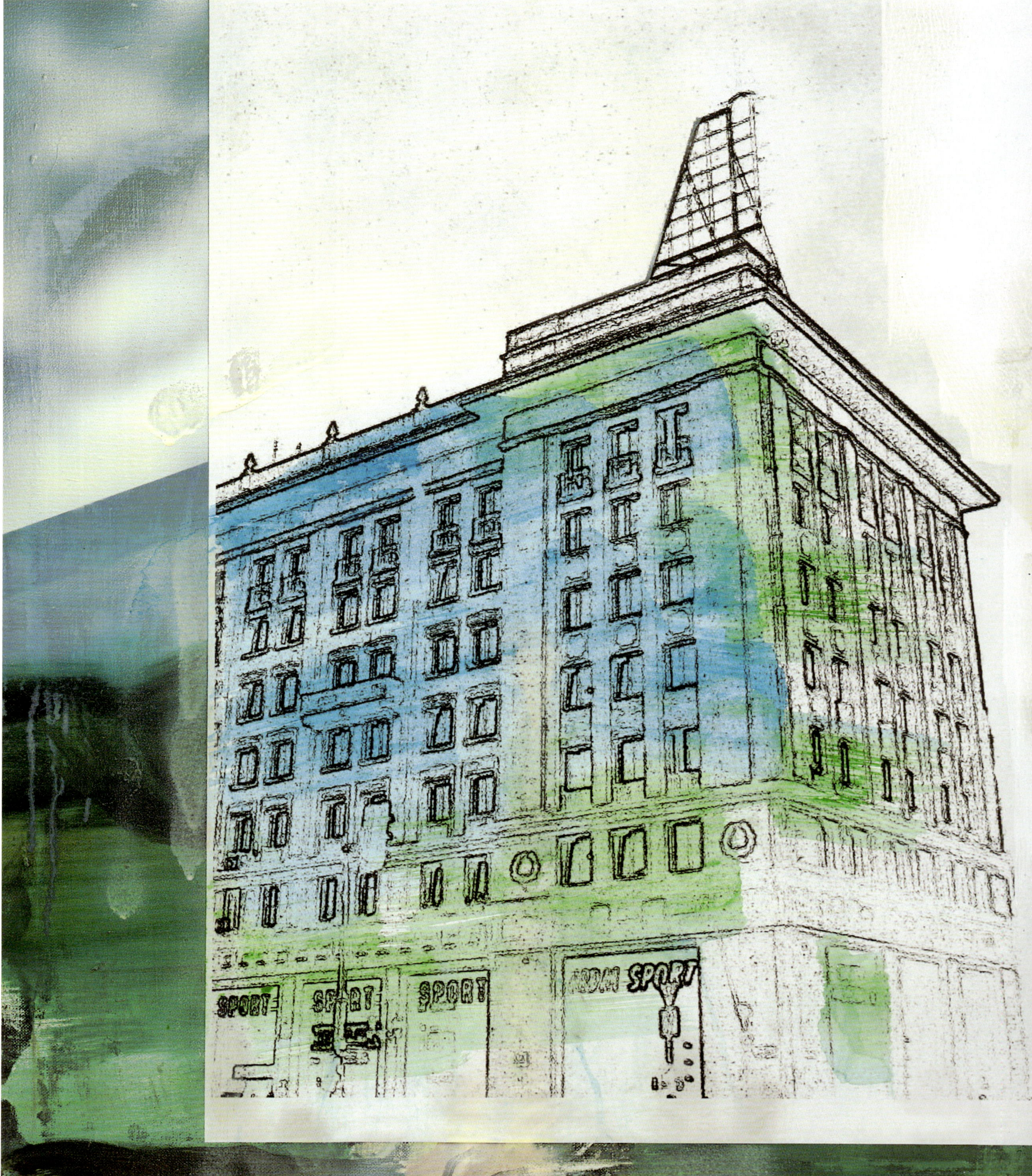
SPORT
SPORT
SPORT
SPORT

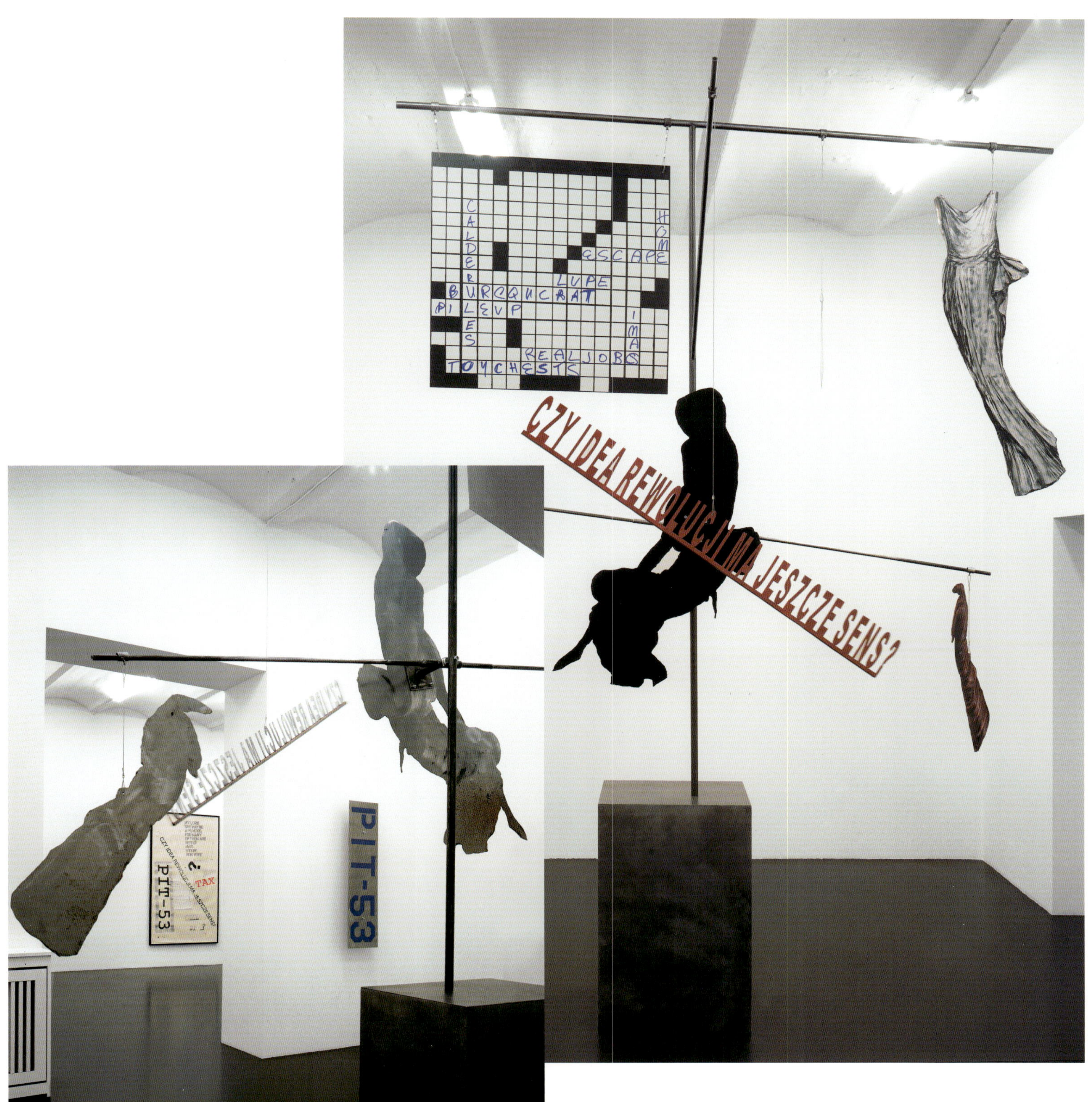

Metaloplastyka III, 2005
Metaloplastyka, exhibition views, Galerie Buchholz, Cologne, 2005

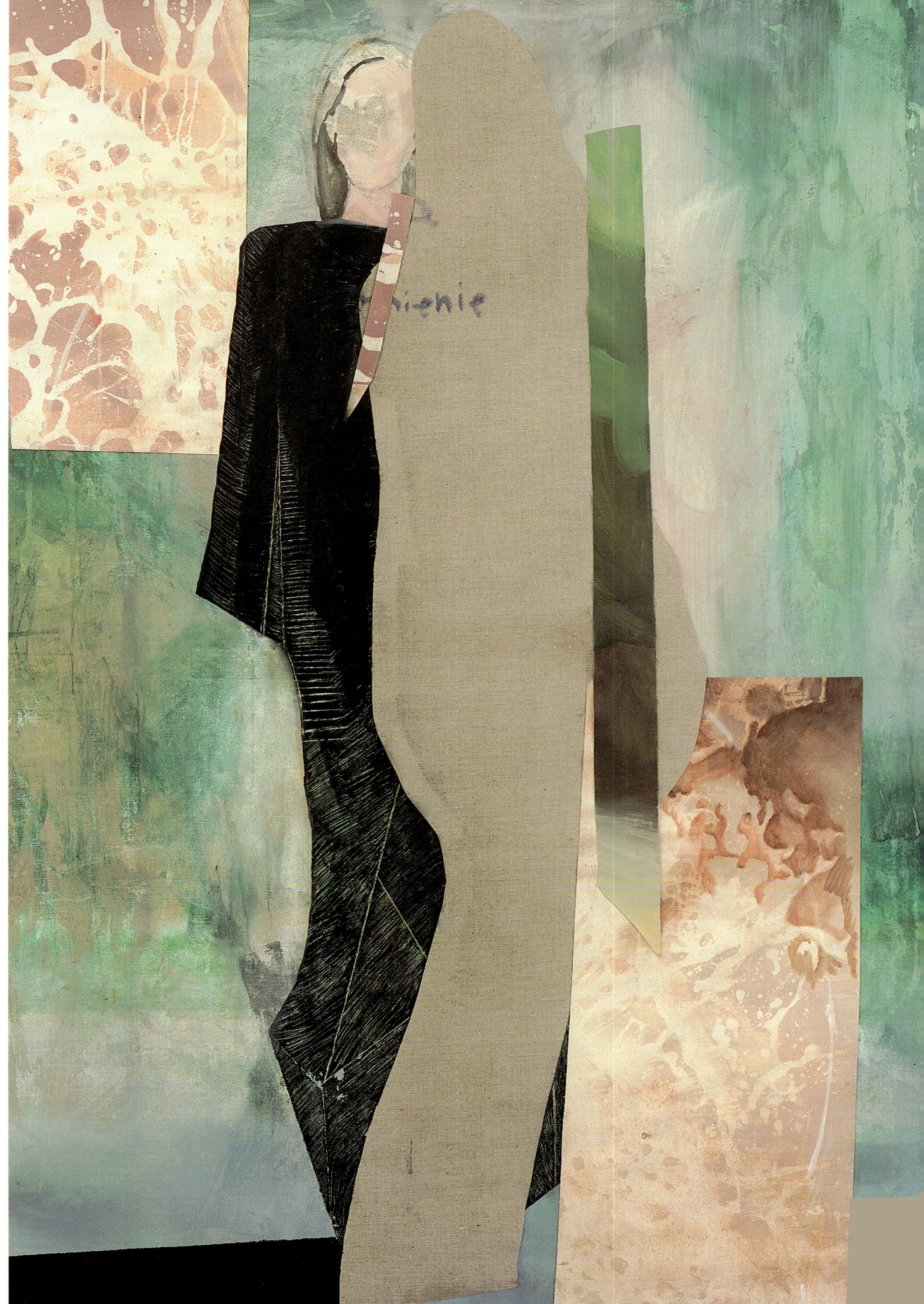

Metaloplastyka VI, 2005
Verena, 2004

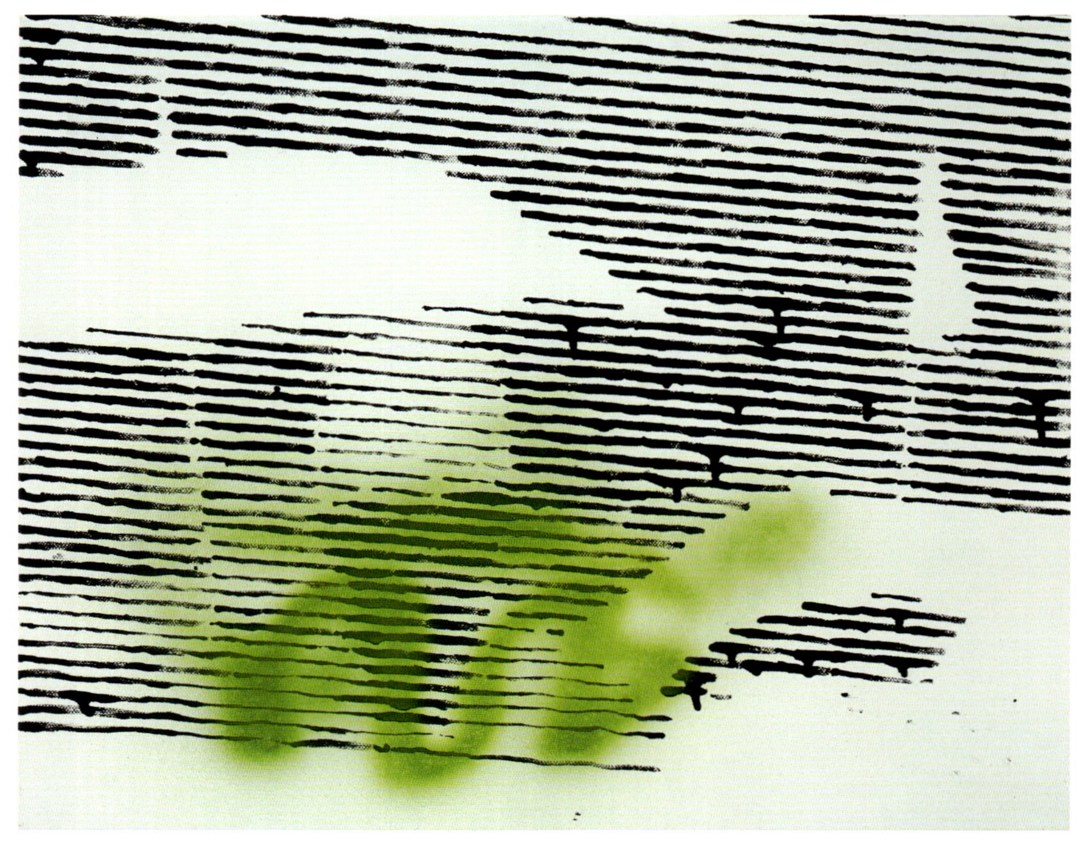

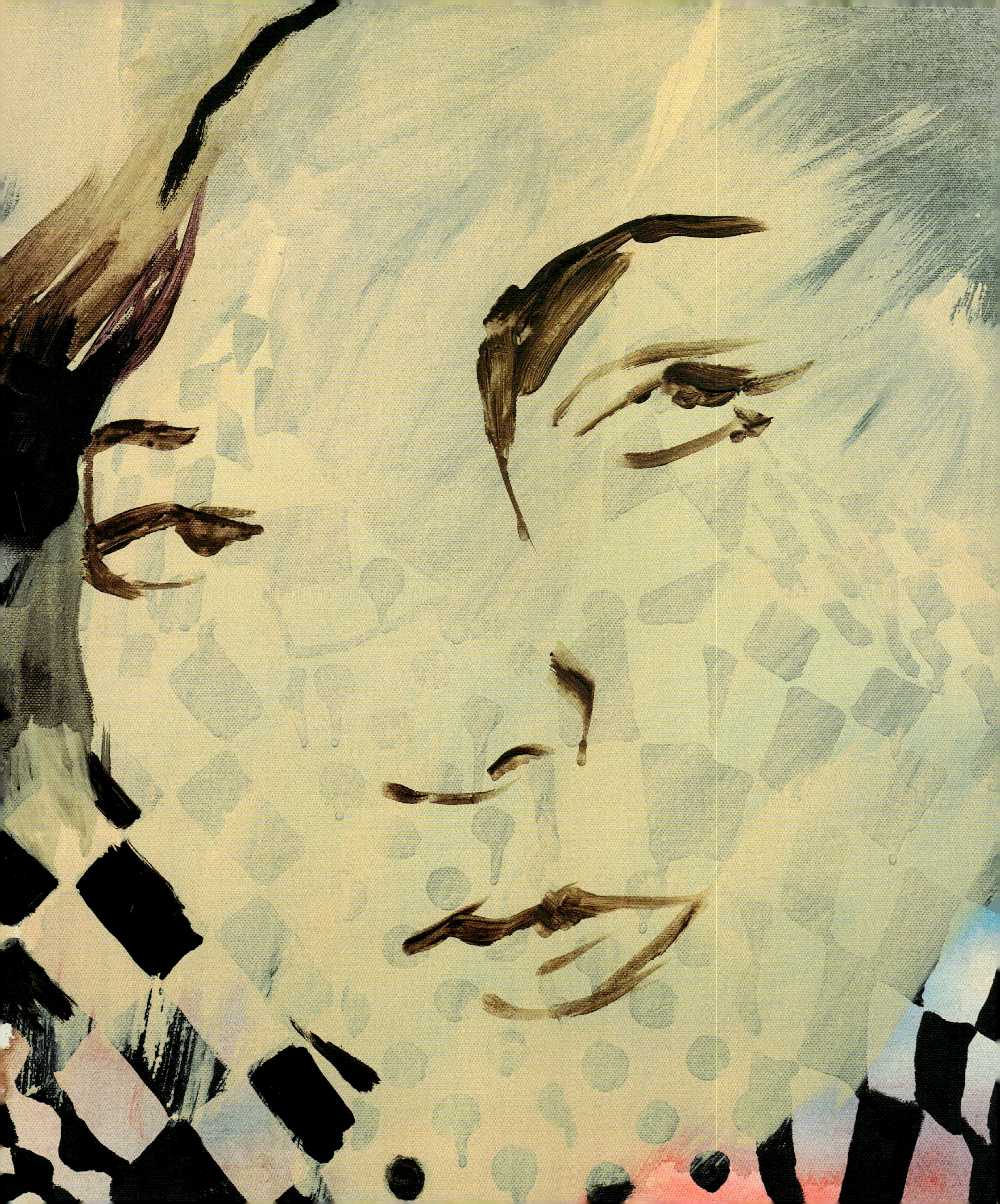

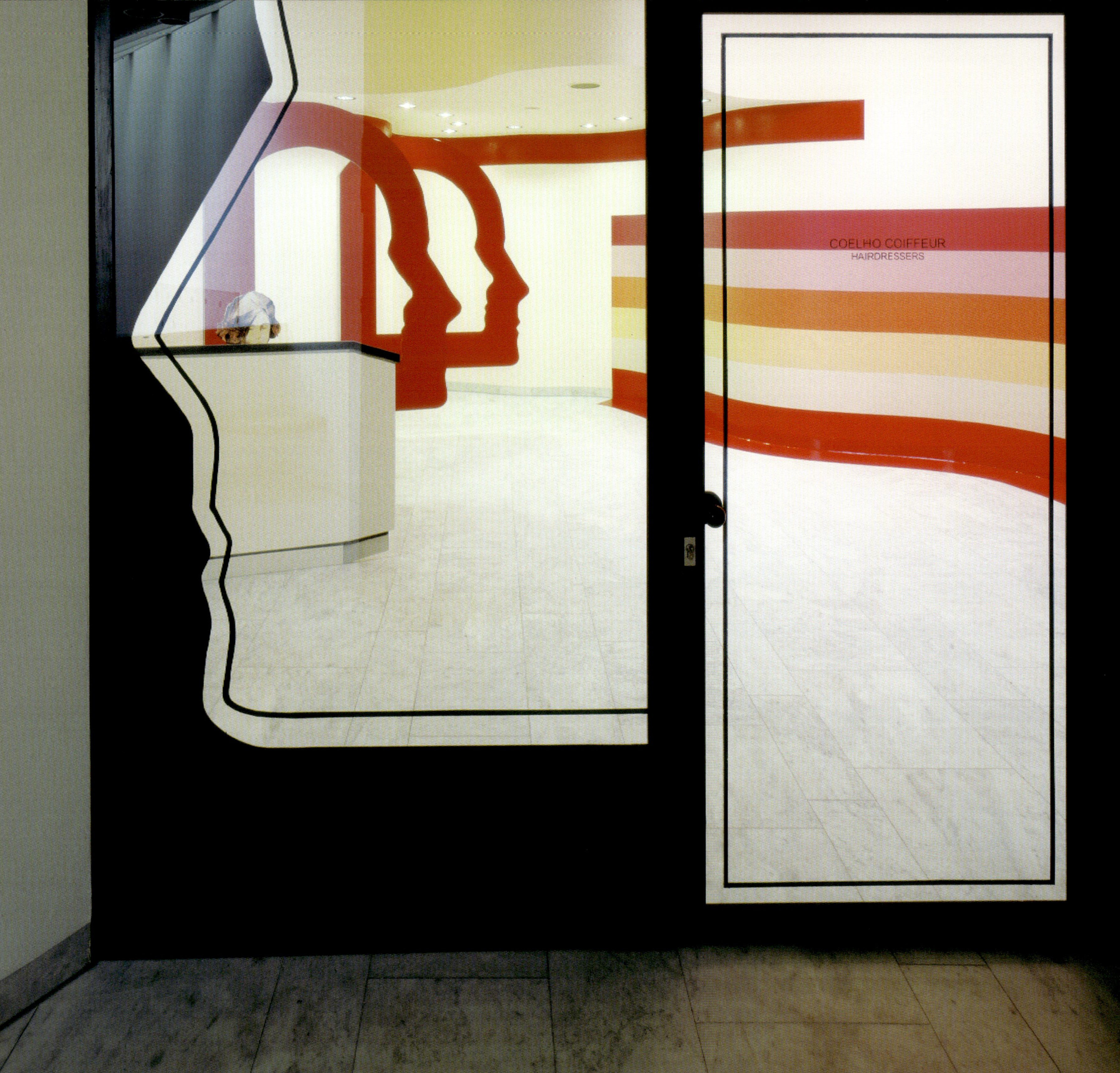
COELHO COIFFEUR
HAIRDRESSERS

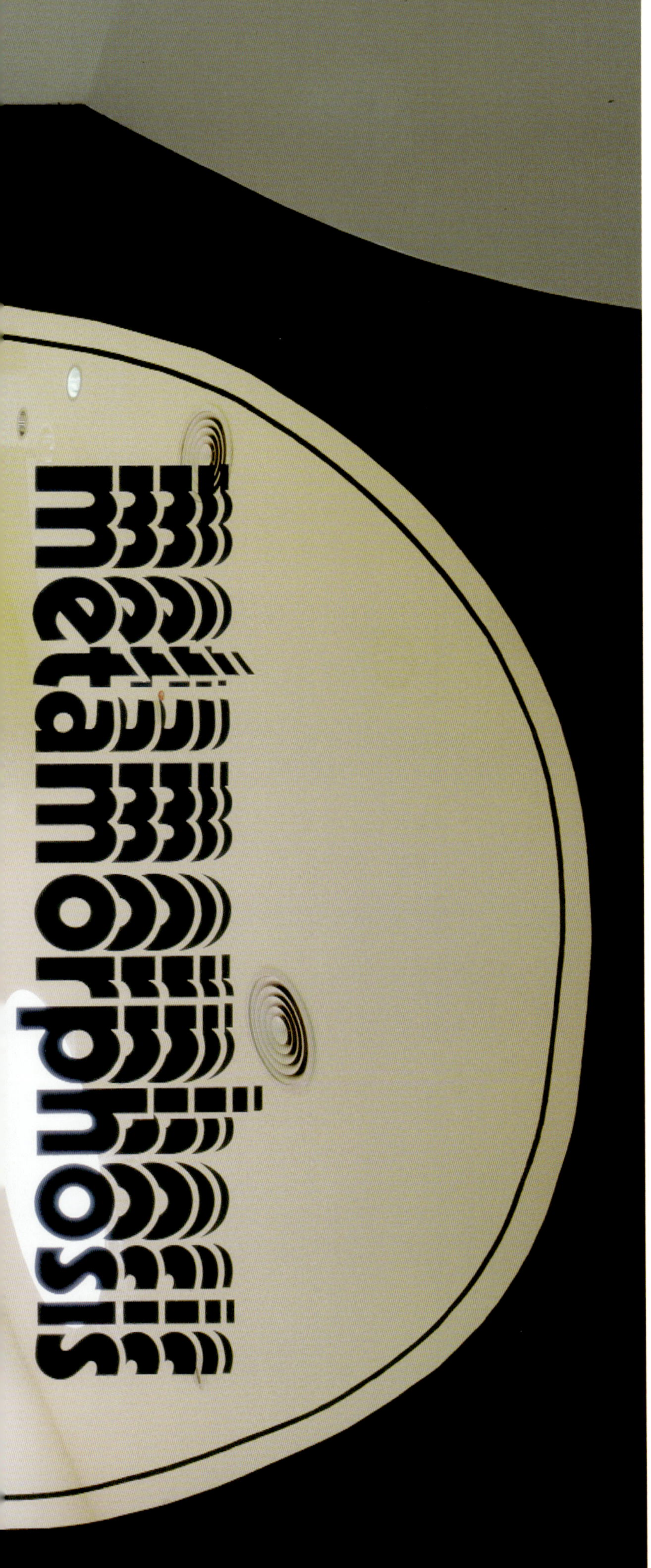

Metamorphosis, permanent installation, Museum Abteiberg Mönchengladbach, 2005

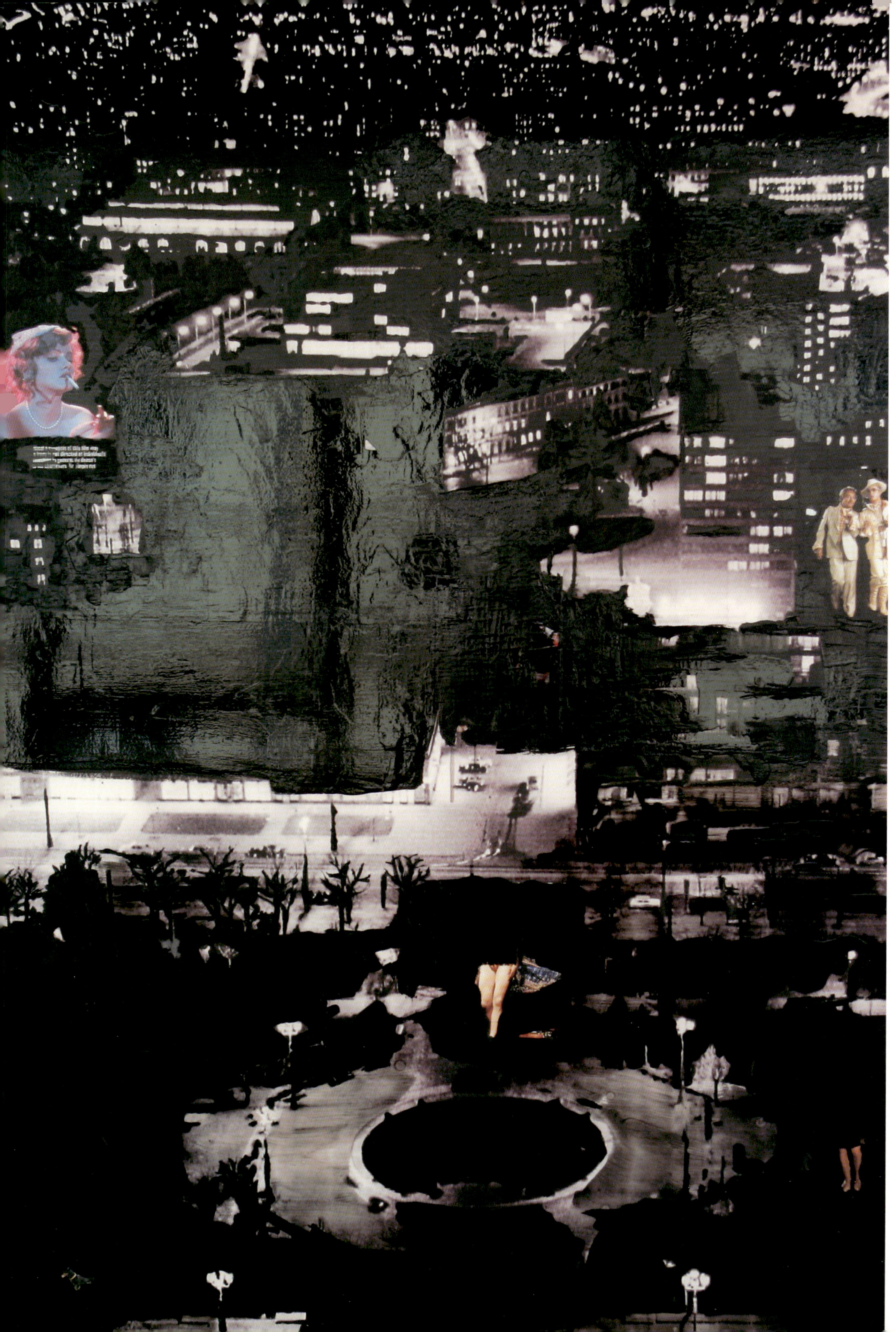

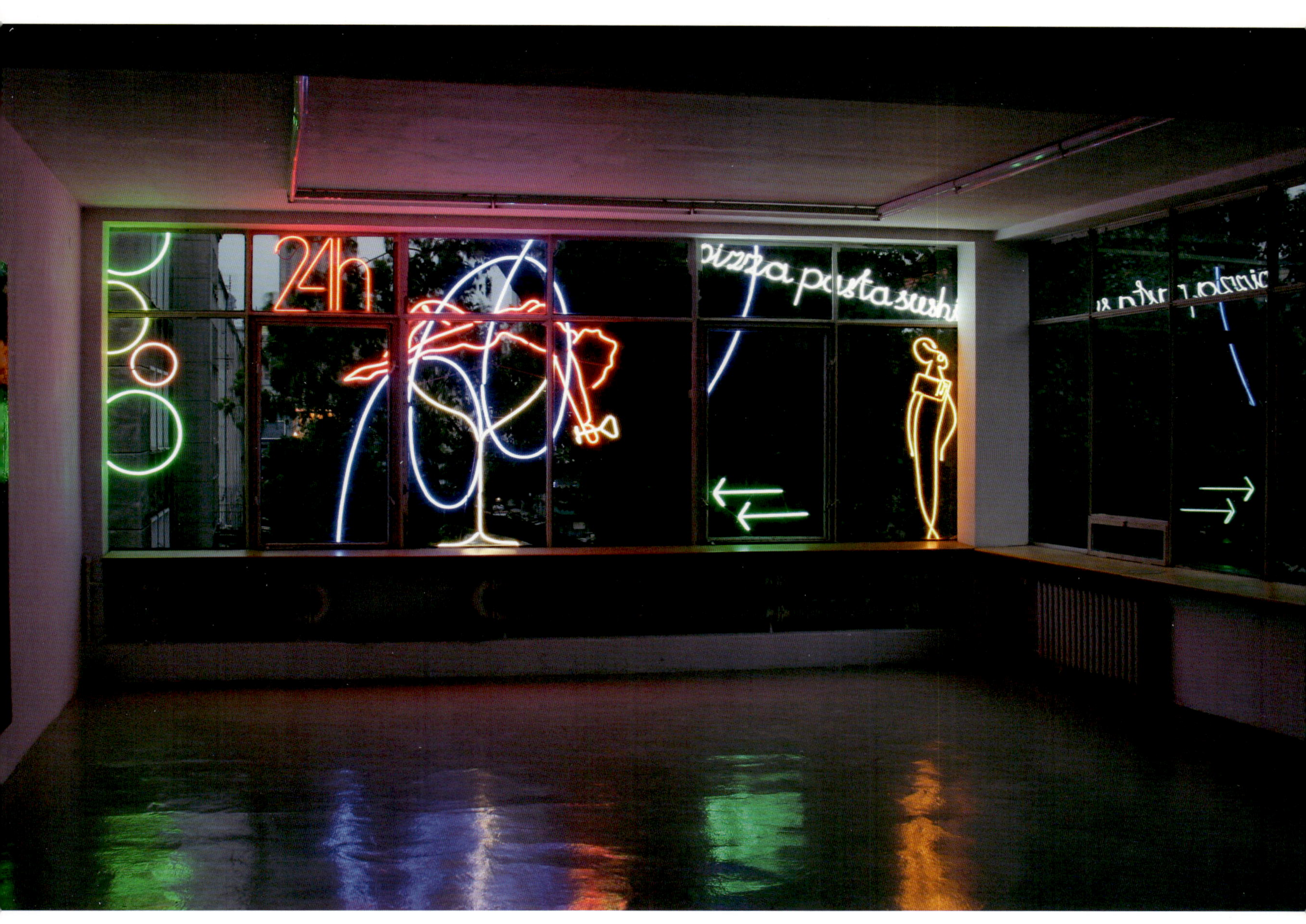

Warsaw Belongs to Bourgeoisies, 2006
Painting–Exchange–Neon, exhibition view, Foksal Gallery Foundation, Warsaw, 2006

Lighting up of the renovated neon sign *Siatkarka (Volleyball Player)* [1962] in Warsaw, 2006

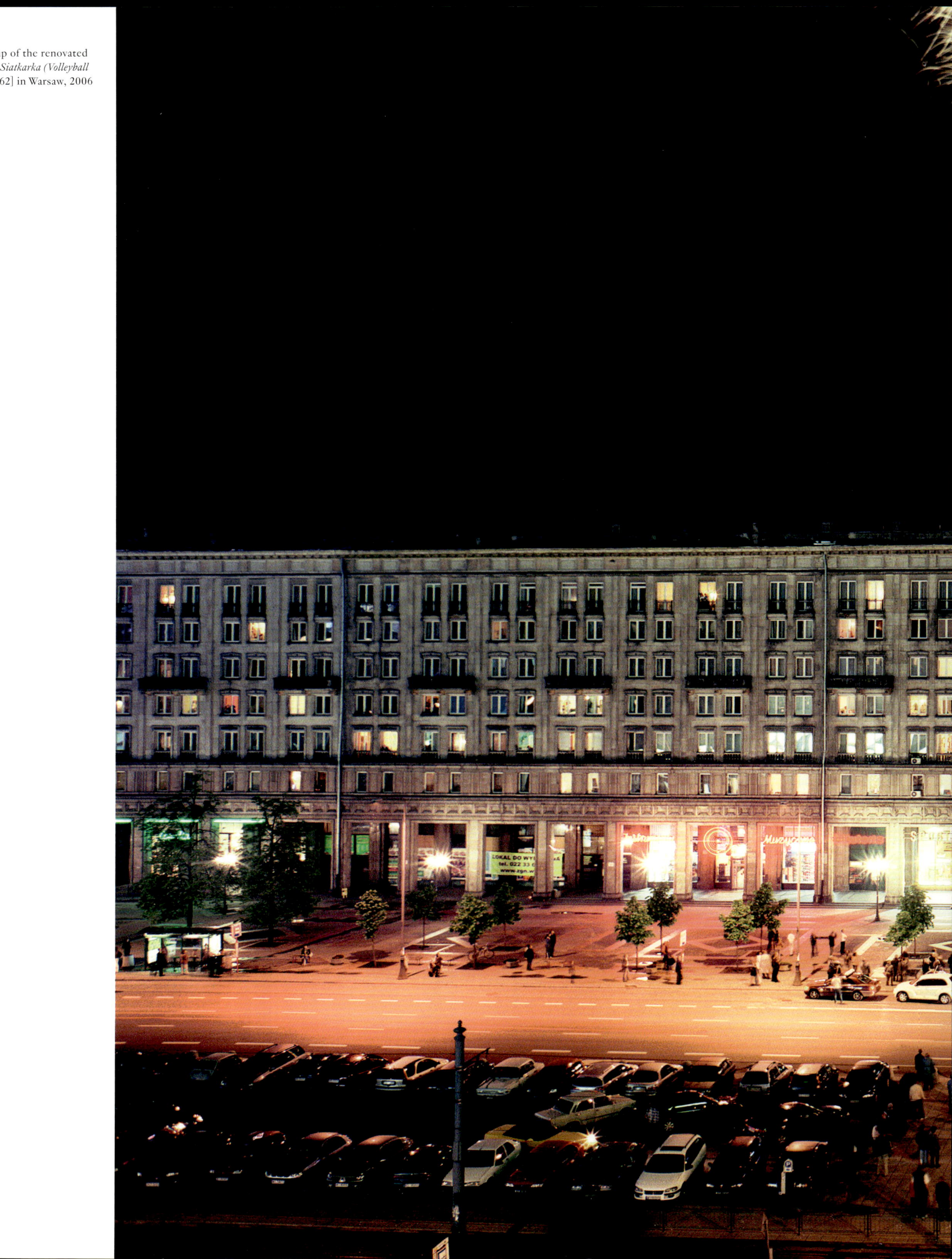

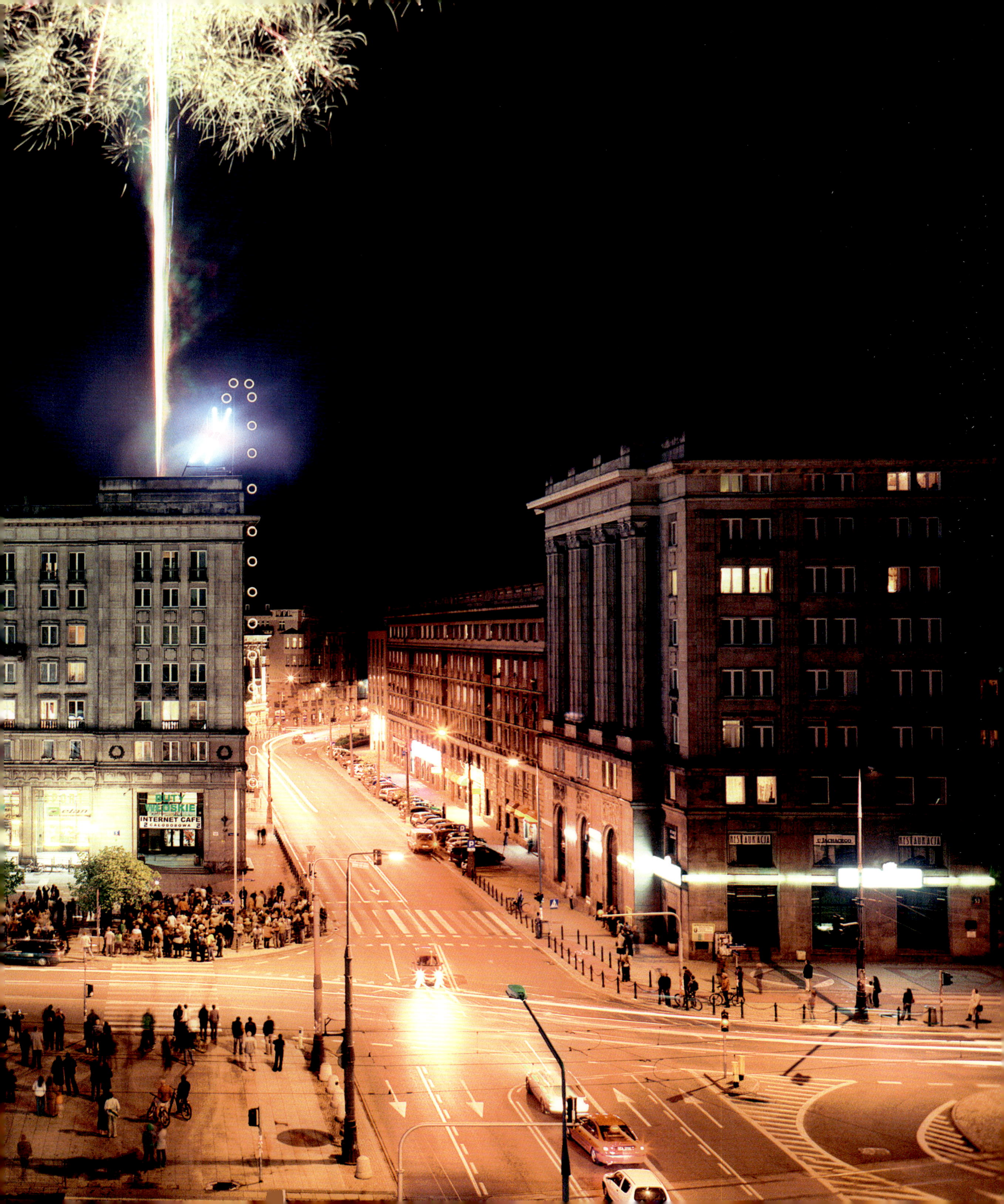
BUTY
WŁOSKIE
INTERNET CAFE
2 CAŁODOBOWA 2
RESTAURACJA
RESTAURACJA

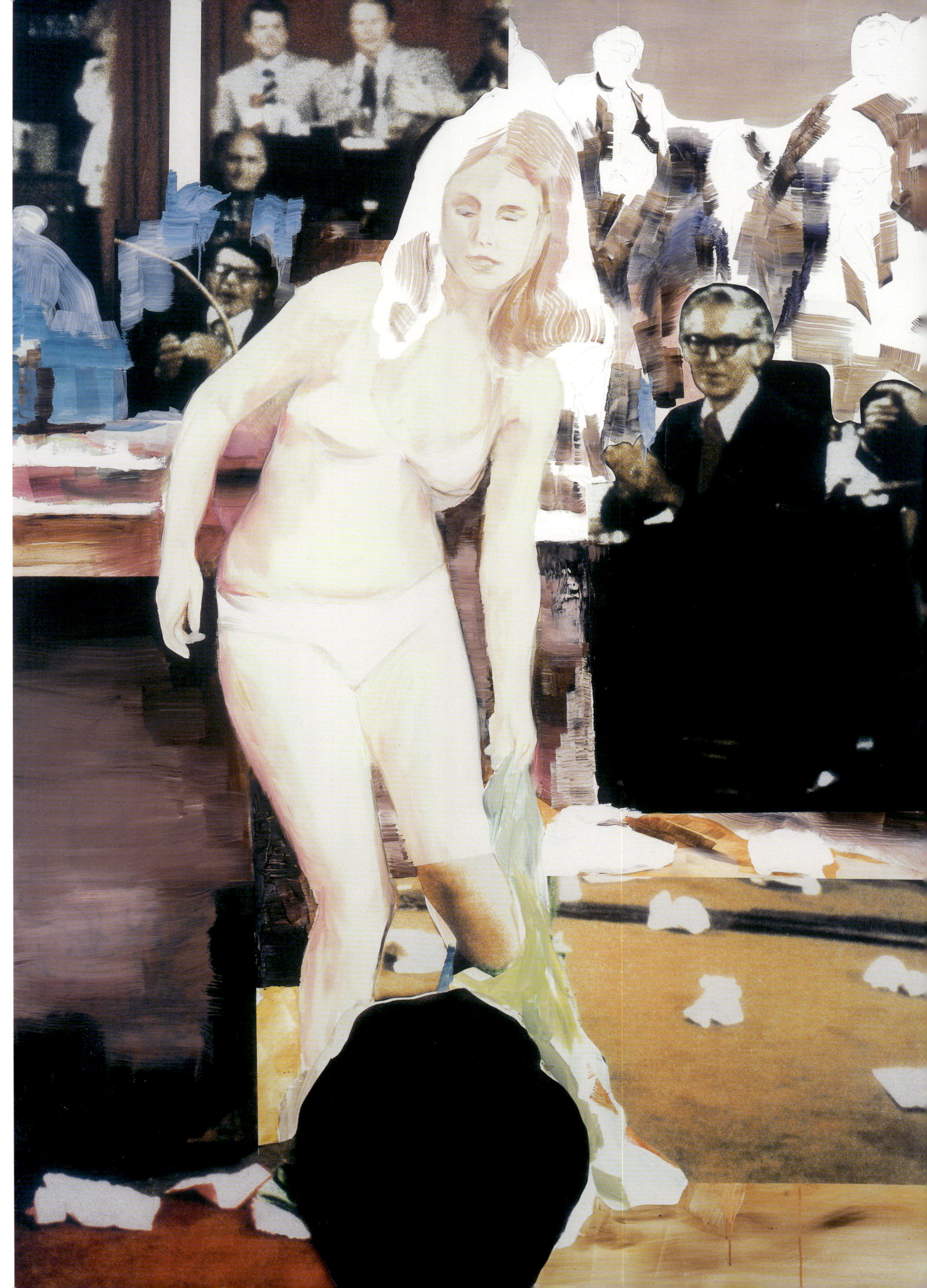

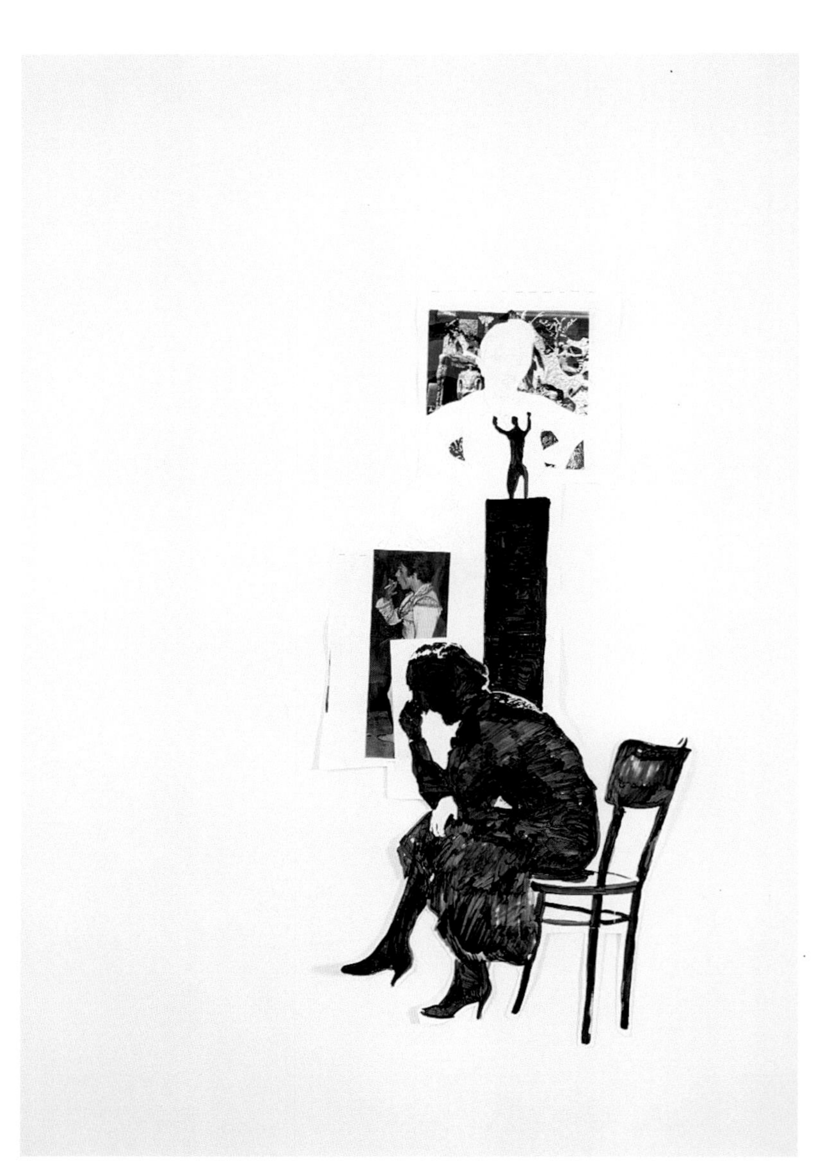

From Idea to Szapocznikow, 2006
Achievement (Black Cheerleader), 2006

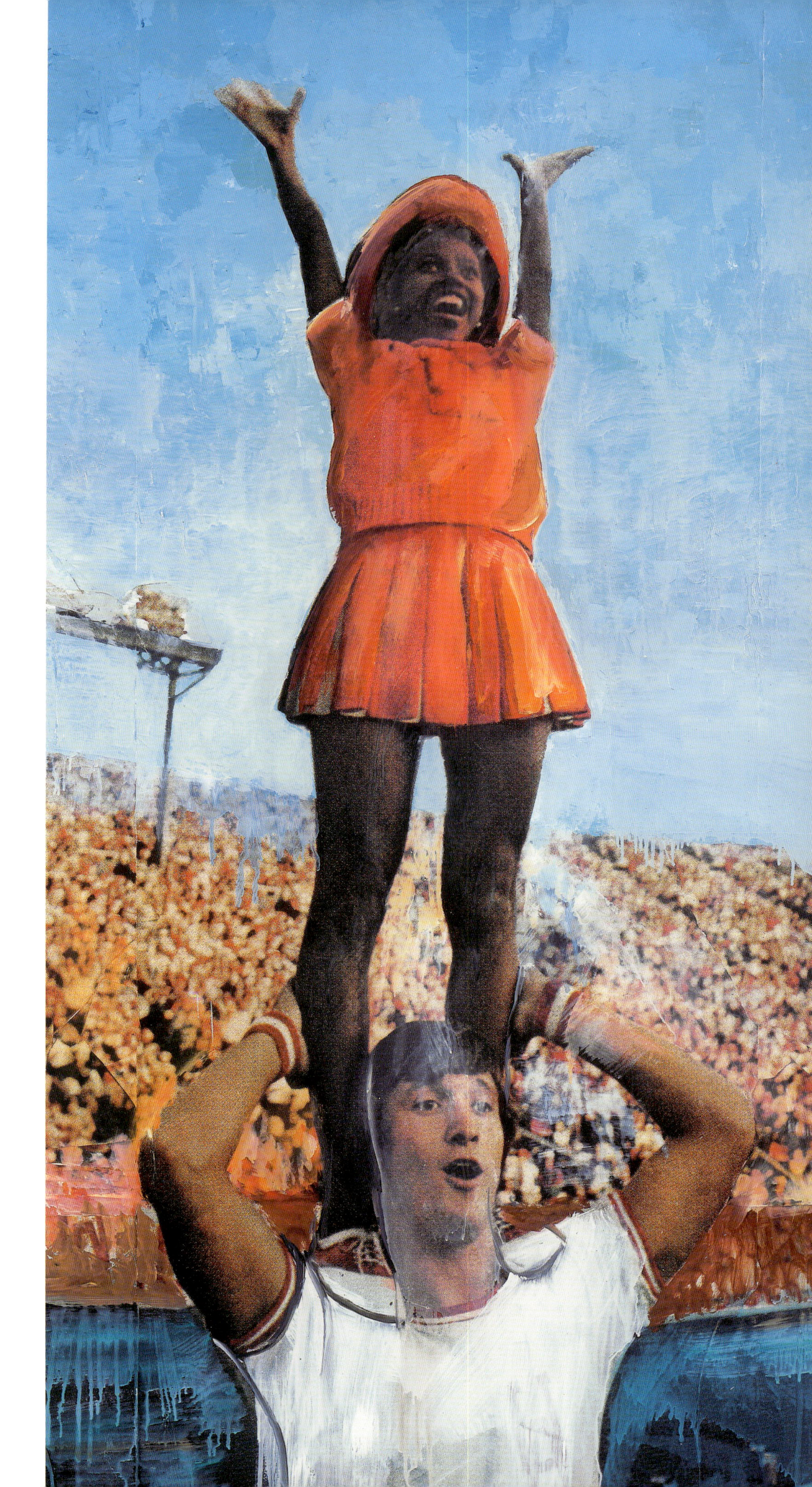

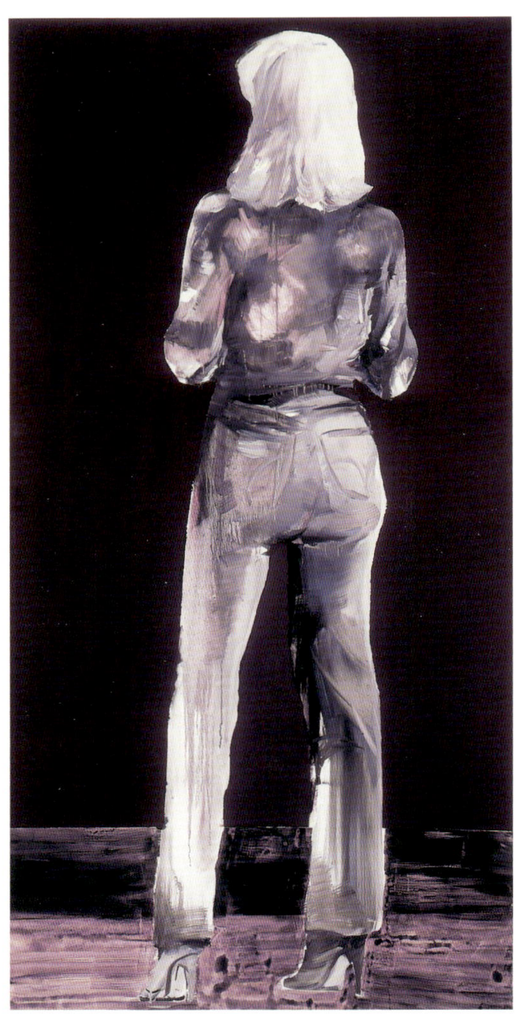

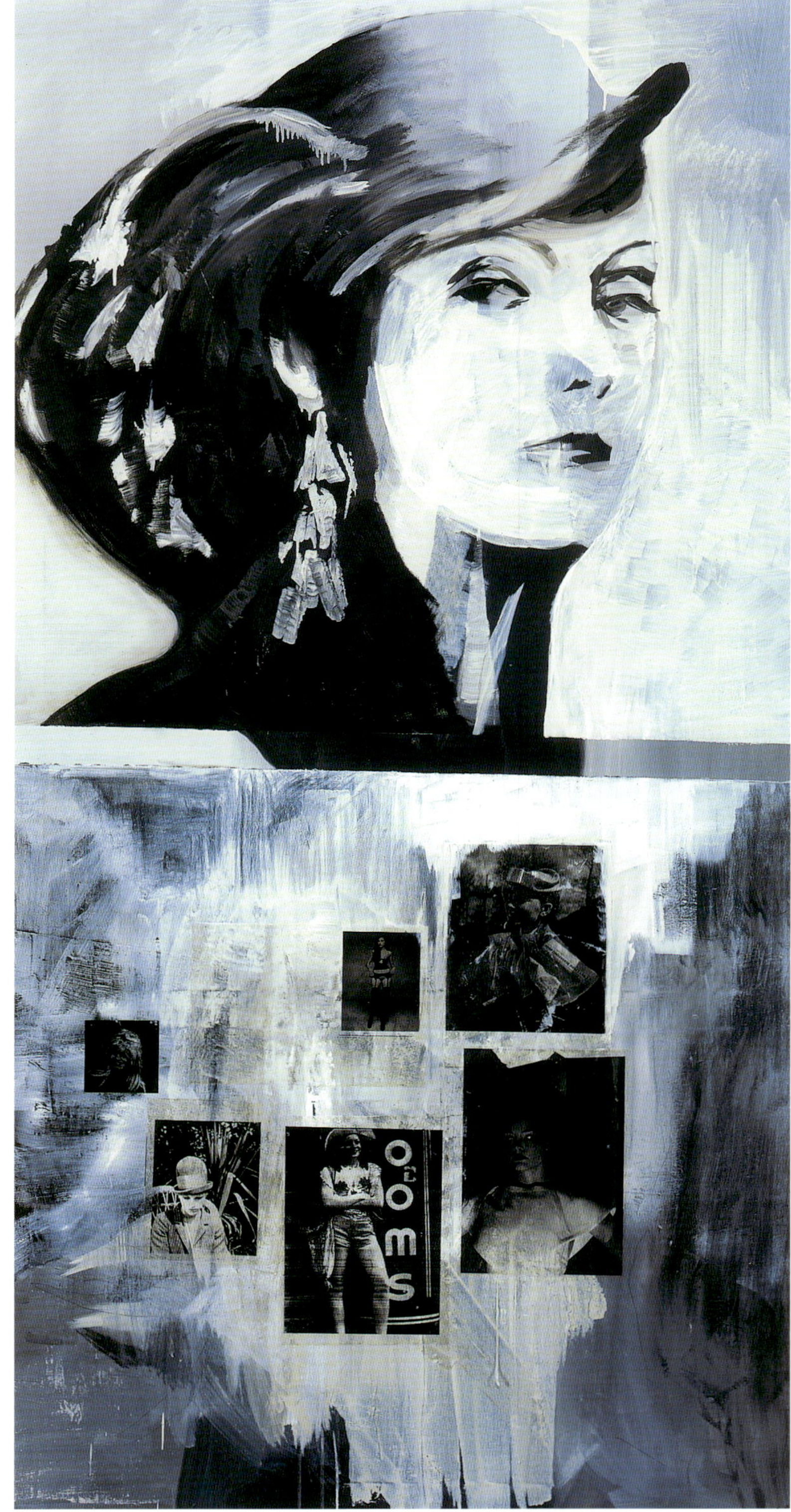

Olivia Newton-John, 2005
About Her, 2005
Pauline Boty Acts Out One of Her Paintings for a Popular Newspaper, 2005

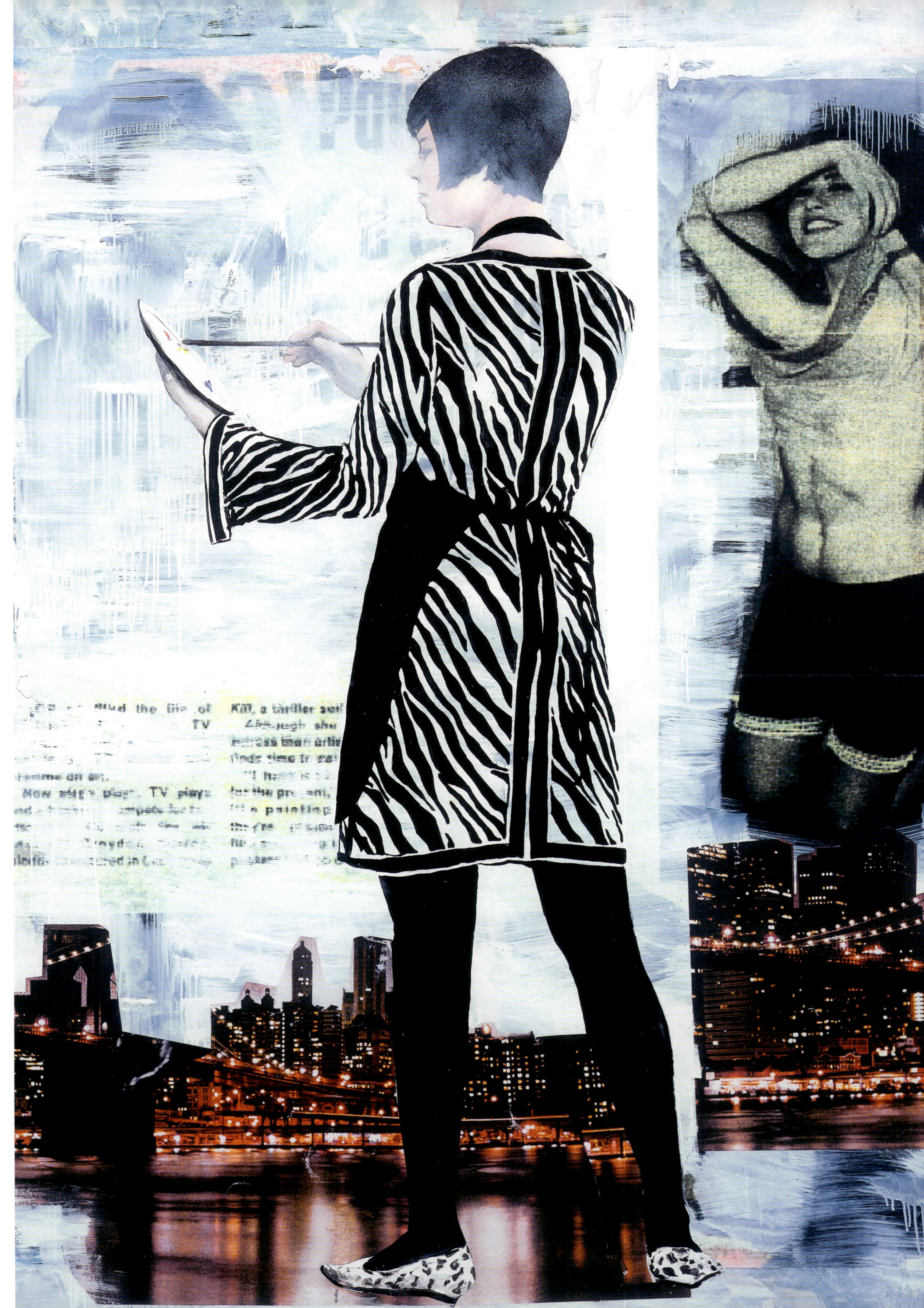

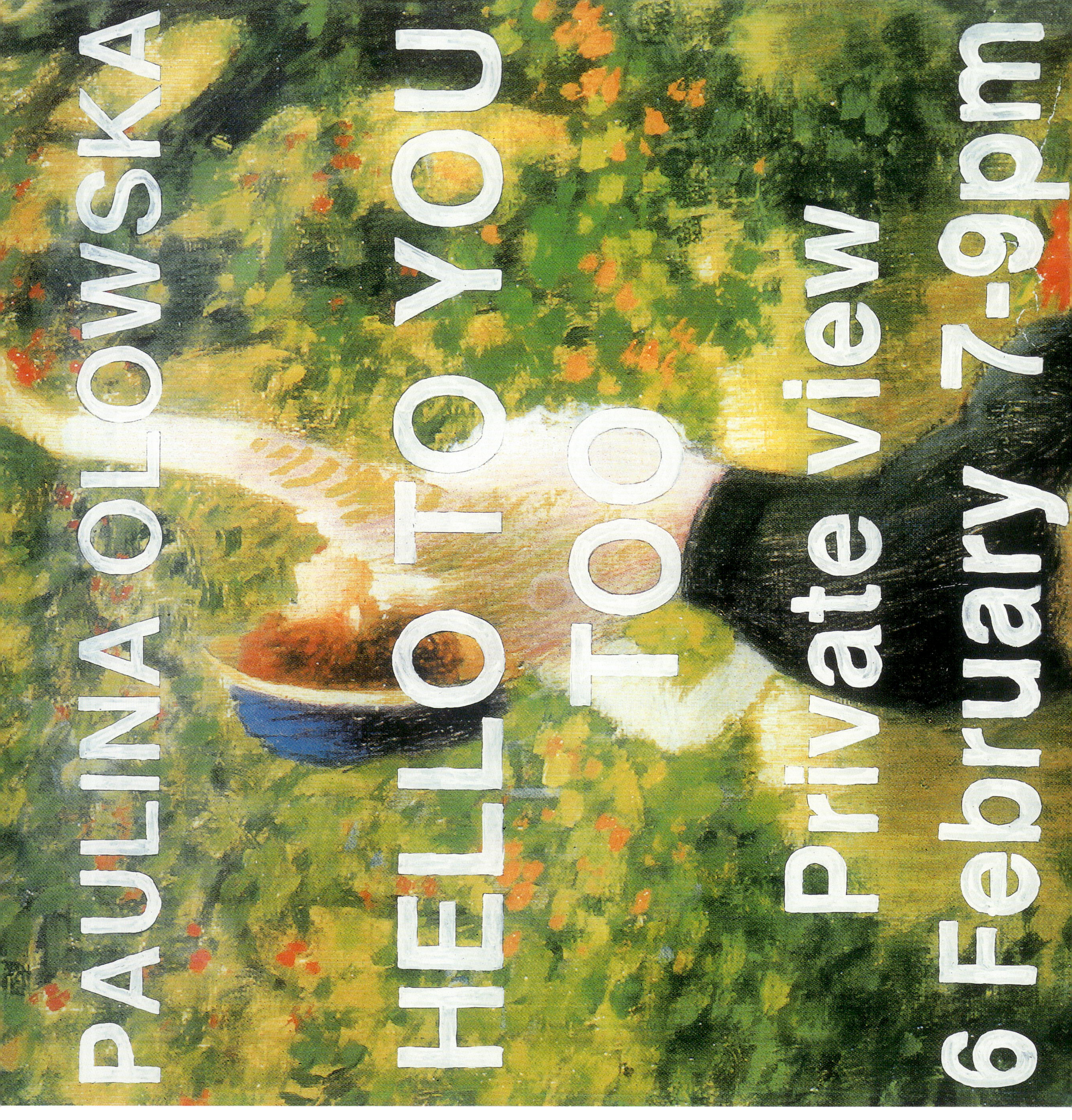
PAULINA OLOWSKA
HELLO TO YOU
TOO
Private view
6 February 7-9pm

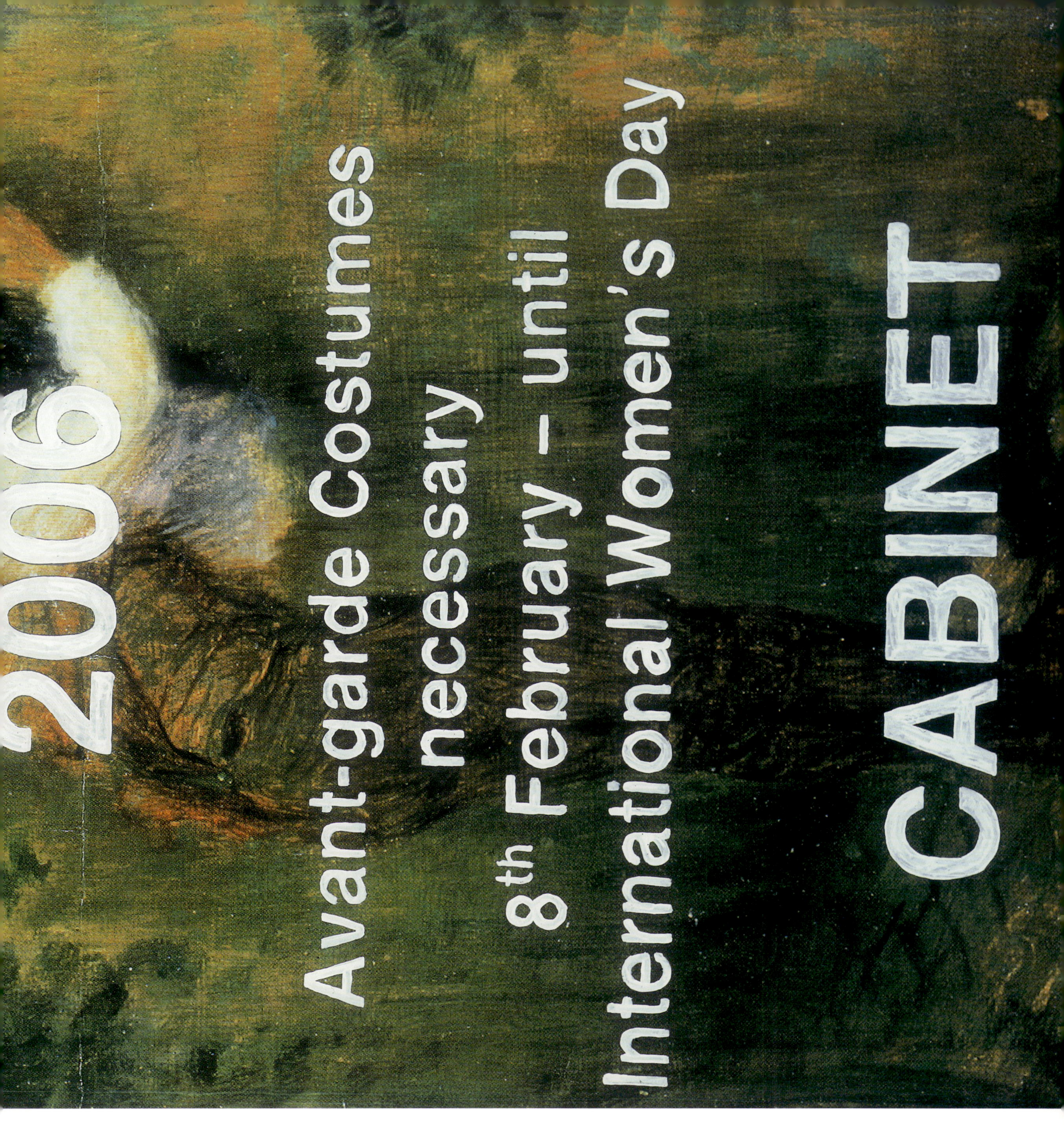

Hello to You Too/Impressionist–Cherry Picking, 2006

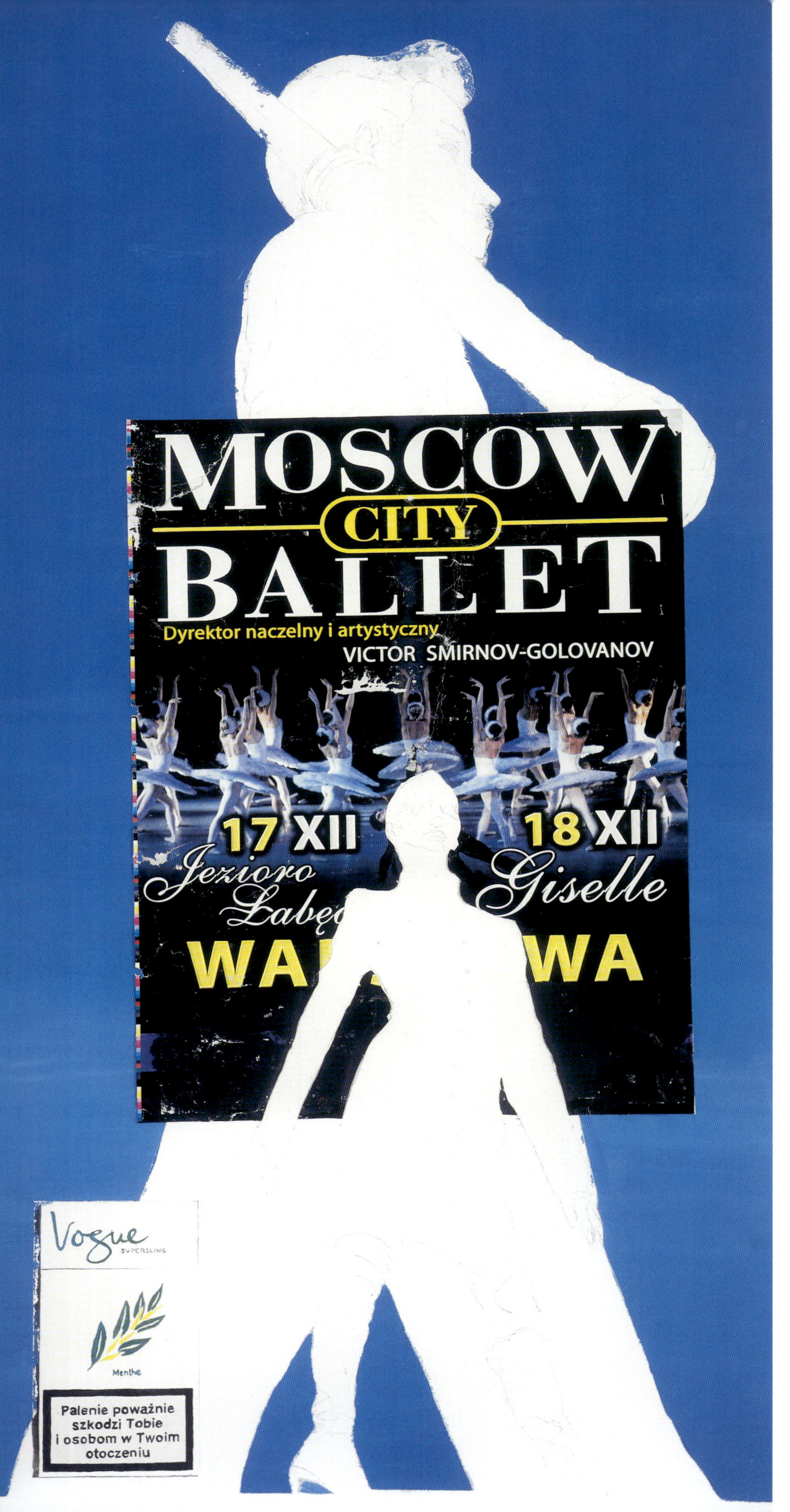
MOSCOW
CITY
BALLET
Dyrektor naczelny i artystyczny
VICTOR SMIRNOV-GOLOVANOV
17 XII
Jezioro
18 XII
Giselle
WA
WA
Vogue
SUPERSLIMS
Menthe
Palenie poważnie szkodzi Tobie i osobom w Twoim otoczeniu

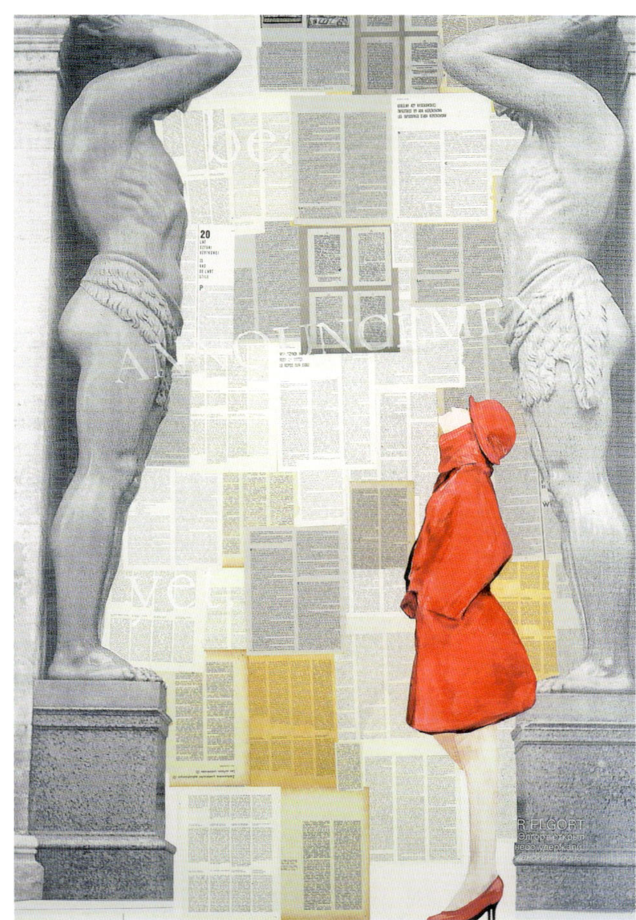

From left to right
Cigarette Break, 2005
Announcement Yet, 2005
Mieszkanie 626-83-36, 2005–2006

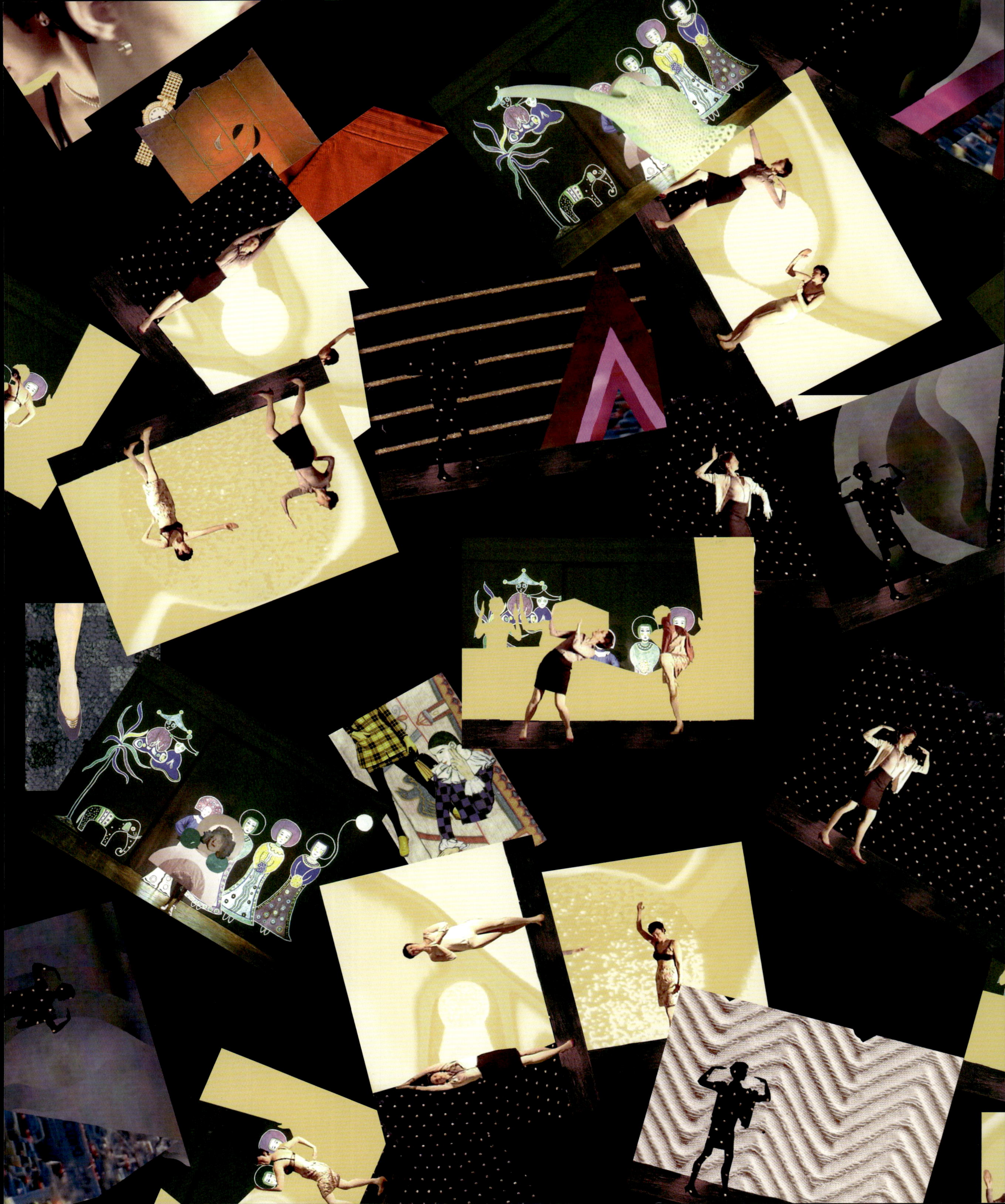

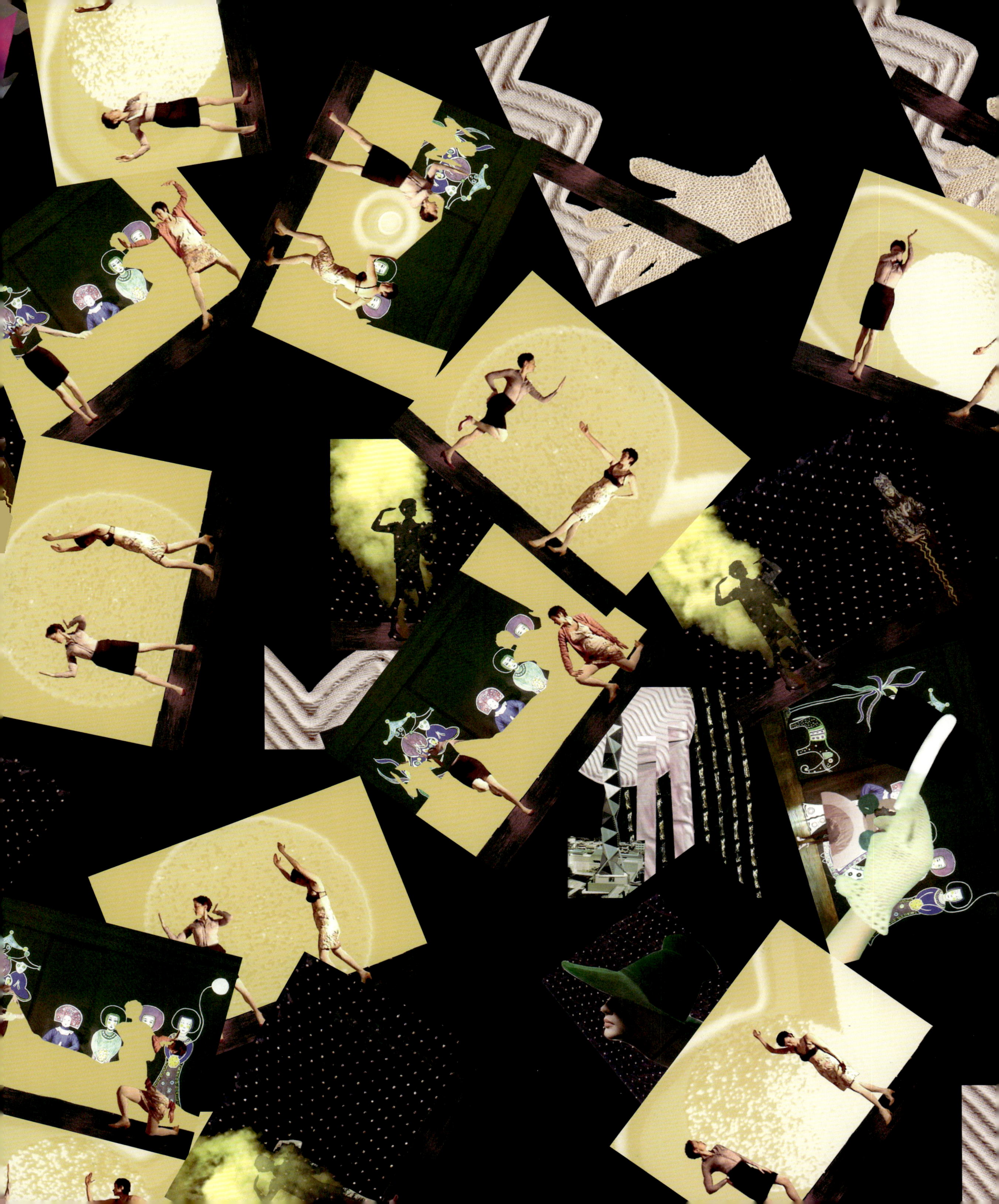

←
Bonnie Camplin and Paulina Olowska, *A Like Akarova*, film, 2007

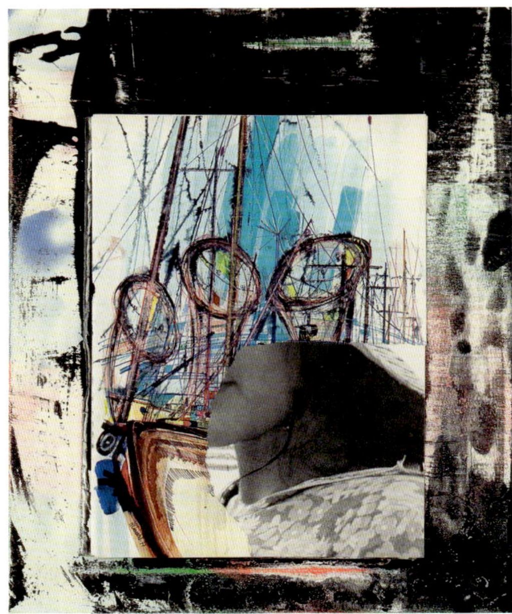

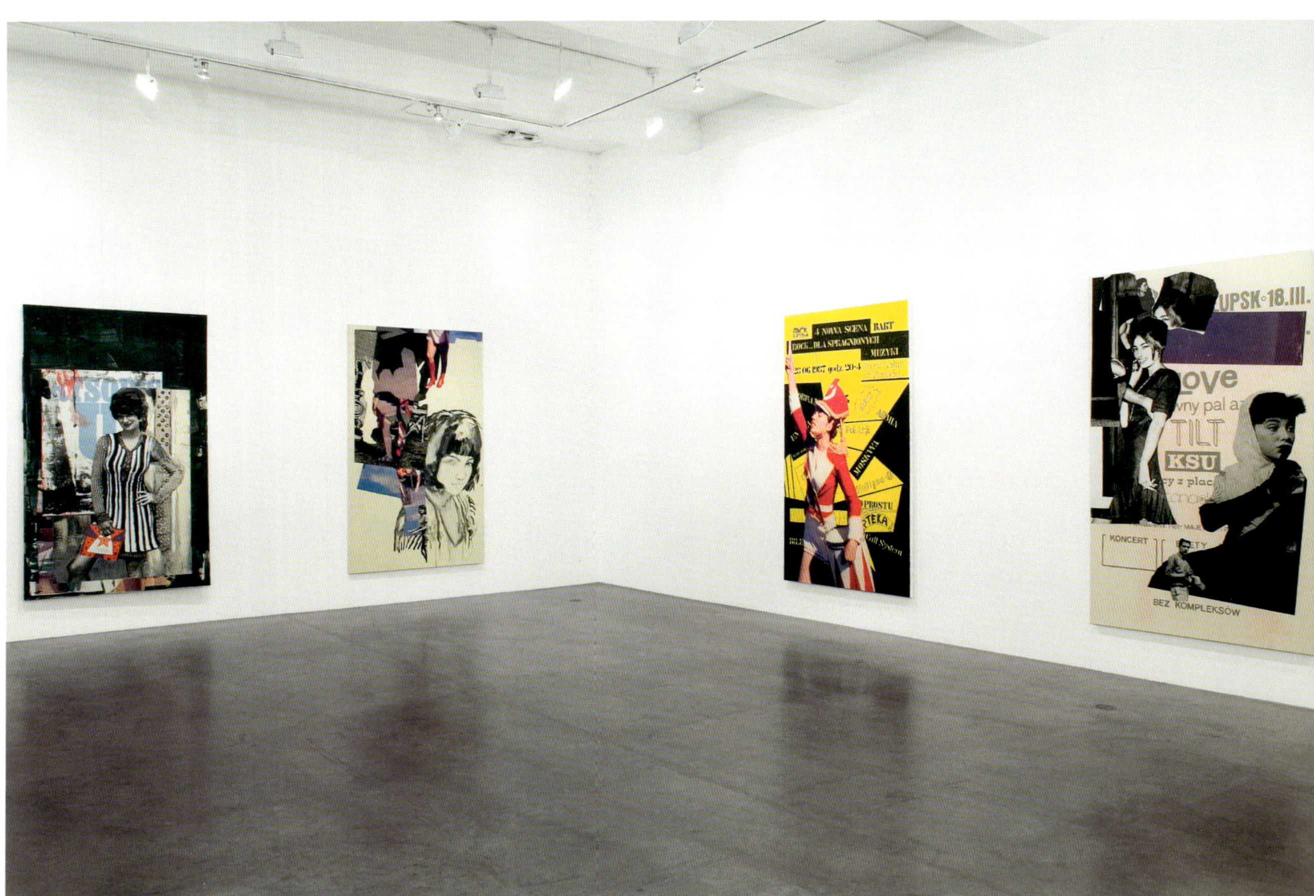

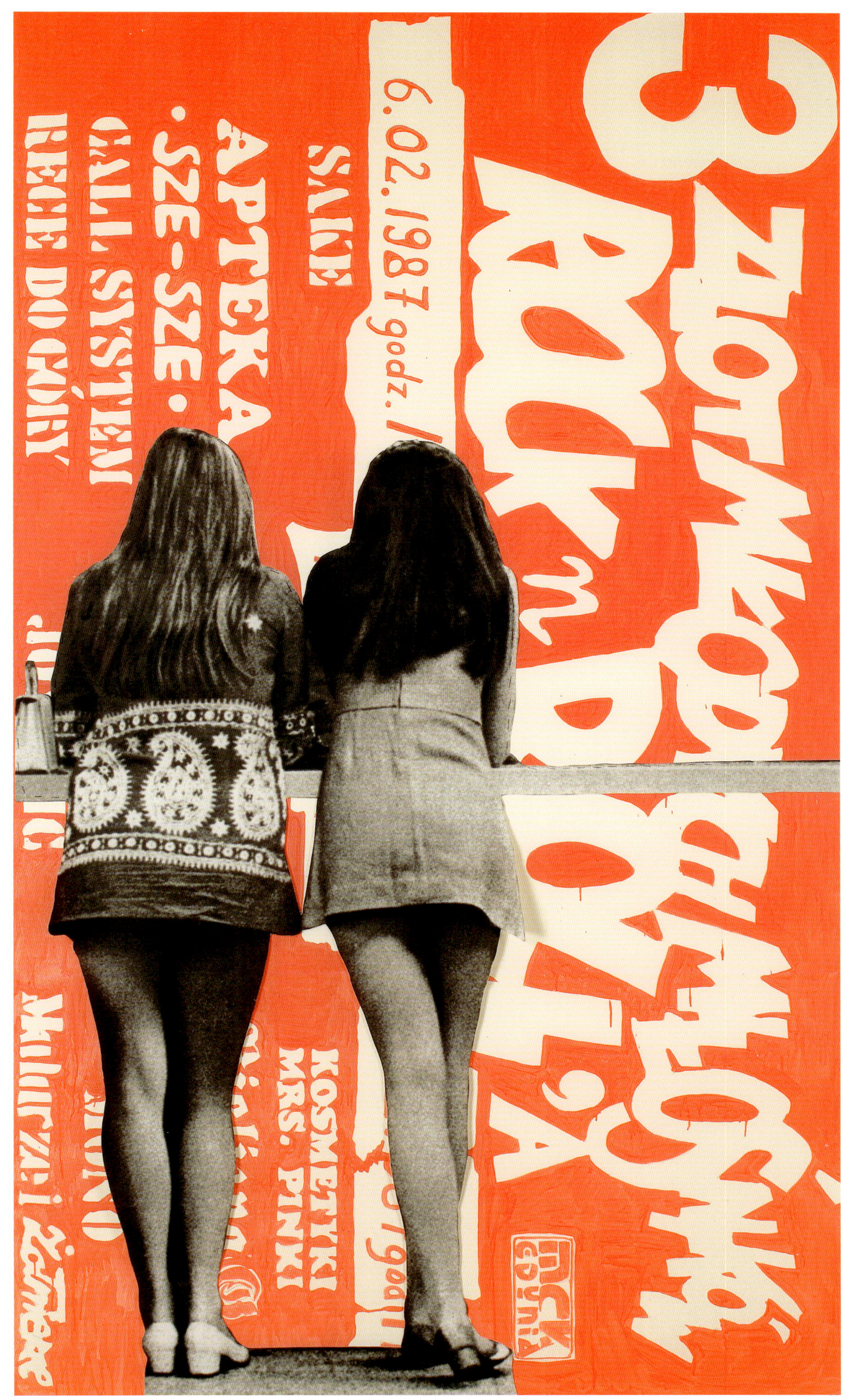

From left to right
Ship Modern Girl, 2006
Nowa Scena, exhibition view, Metro Pictures, New York, 2007
Rock and Rolla, 2006

Tree, 2006
Pantomime, 2006

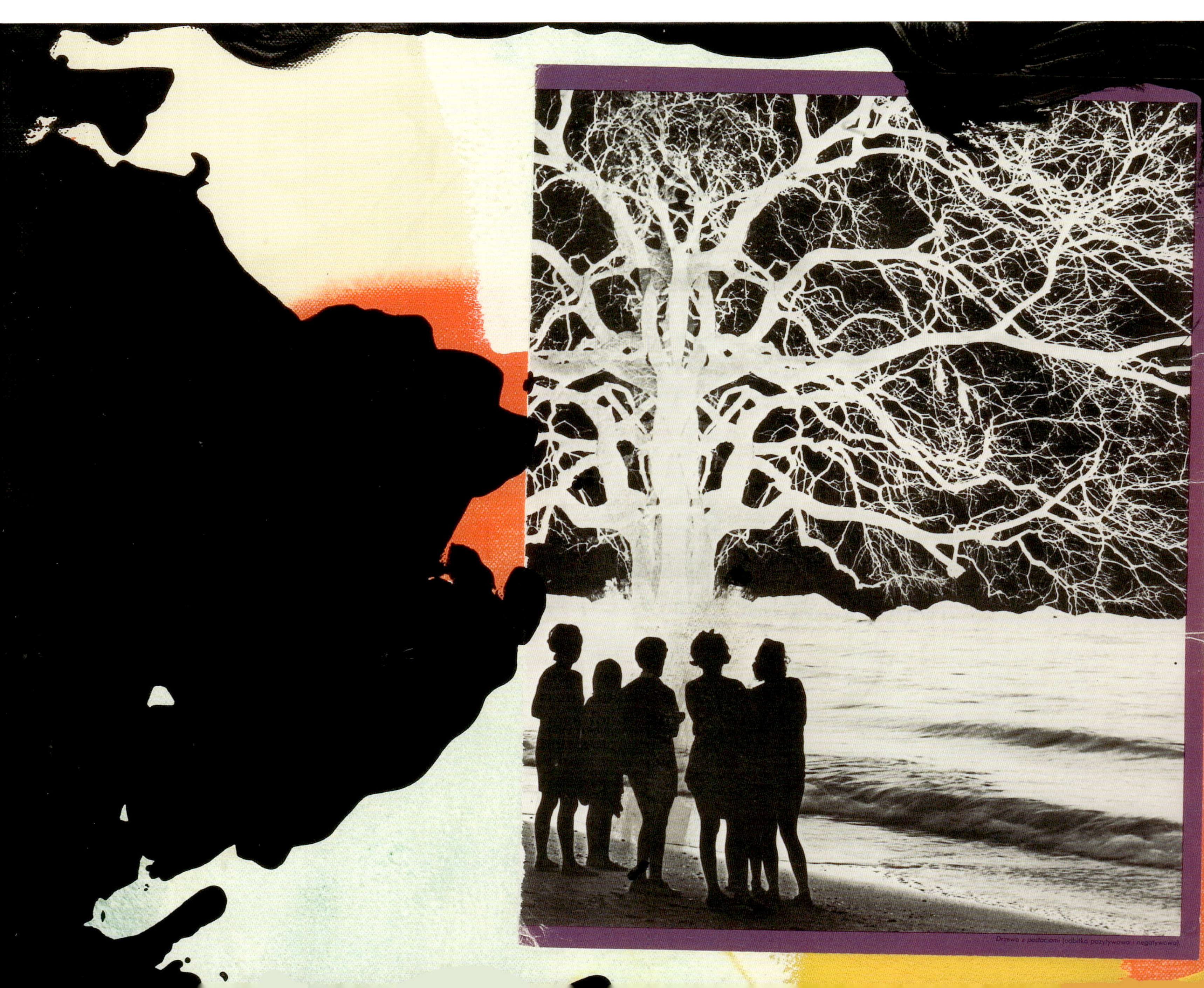

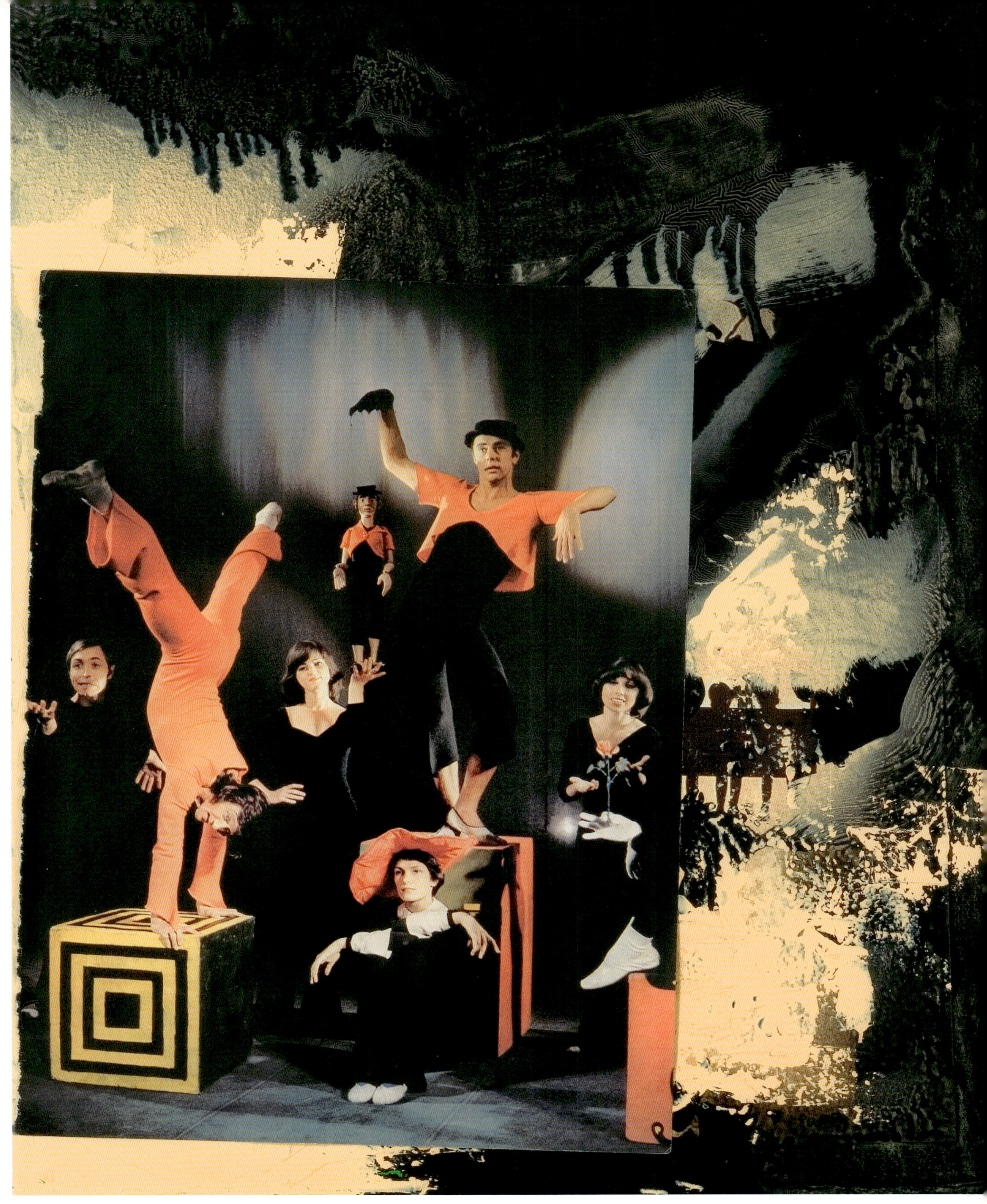

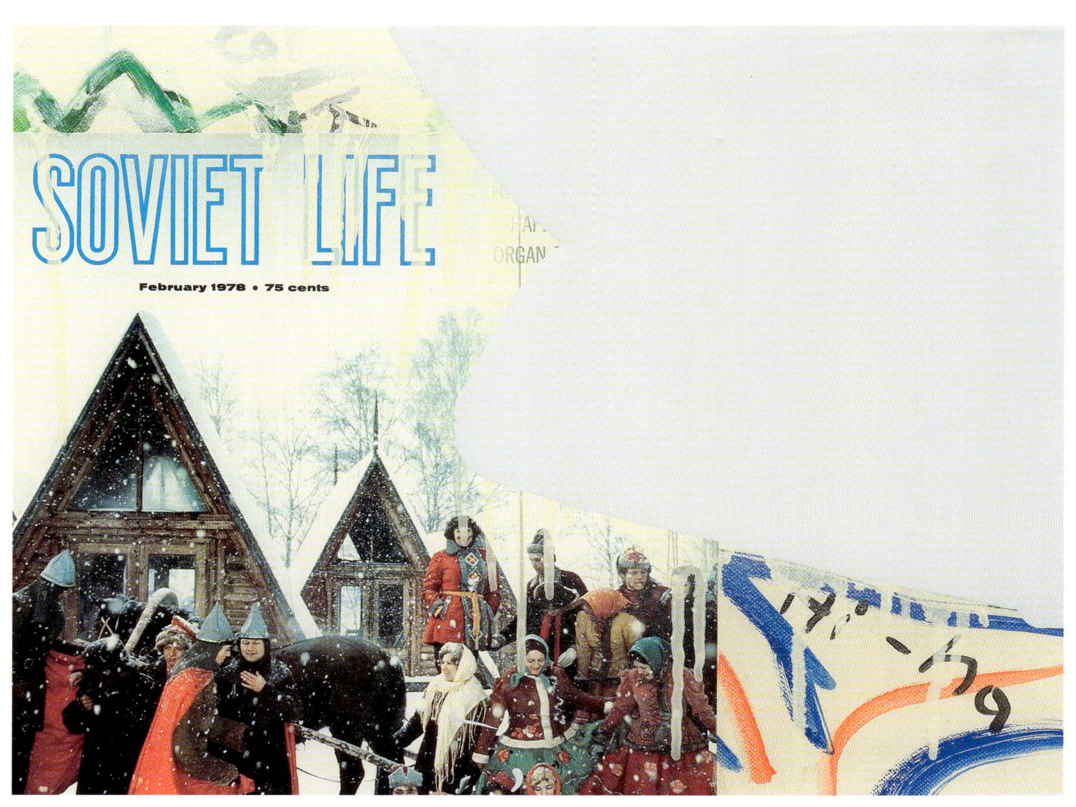

Soviet Life, 2006
Ameryka–California, 2006

AMERYKA

LIPIEC 1970 NR 138 CENA 15 ZŁ

ŚWIAT SZTUKI

Młodzież na wczasach: ocean słońce plaża

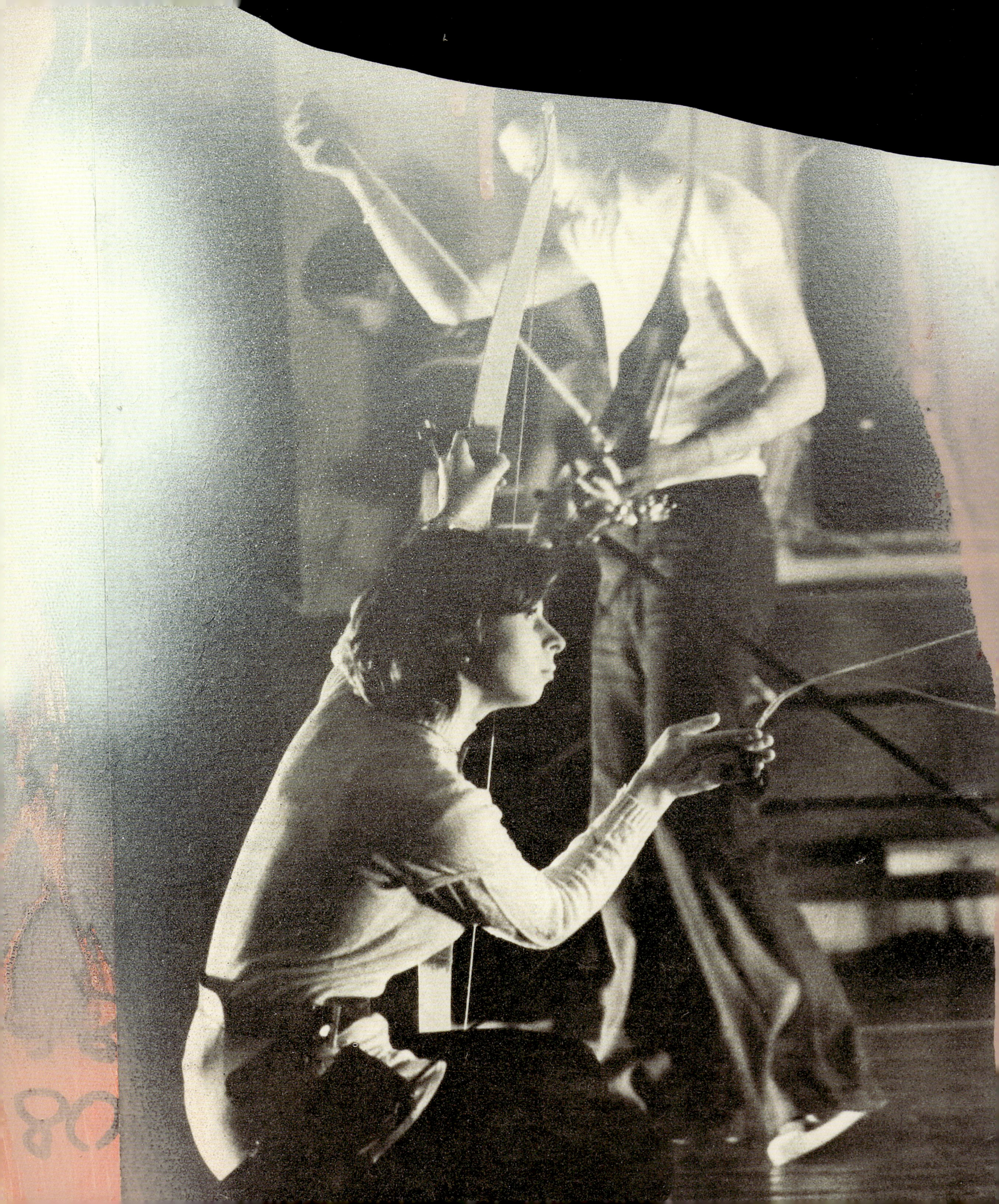

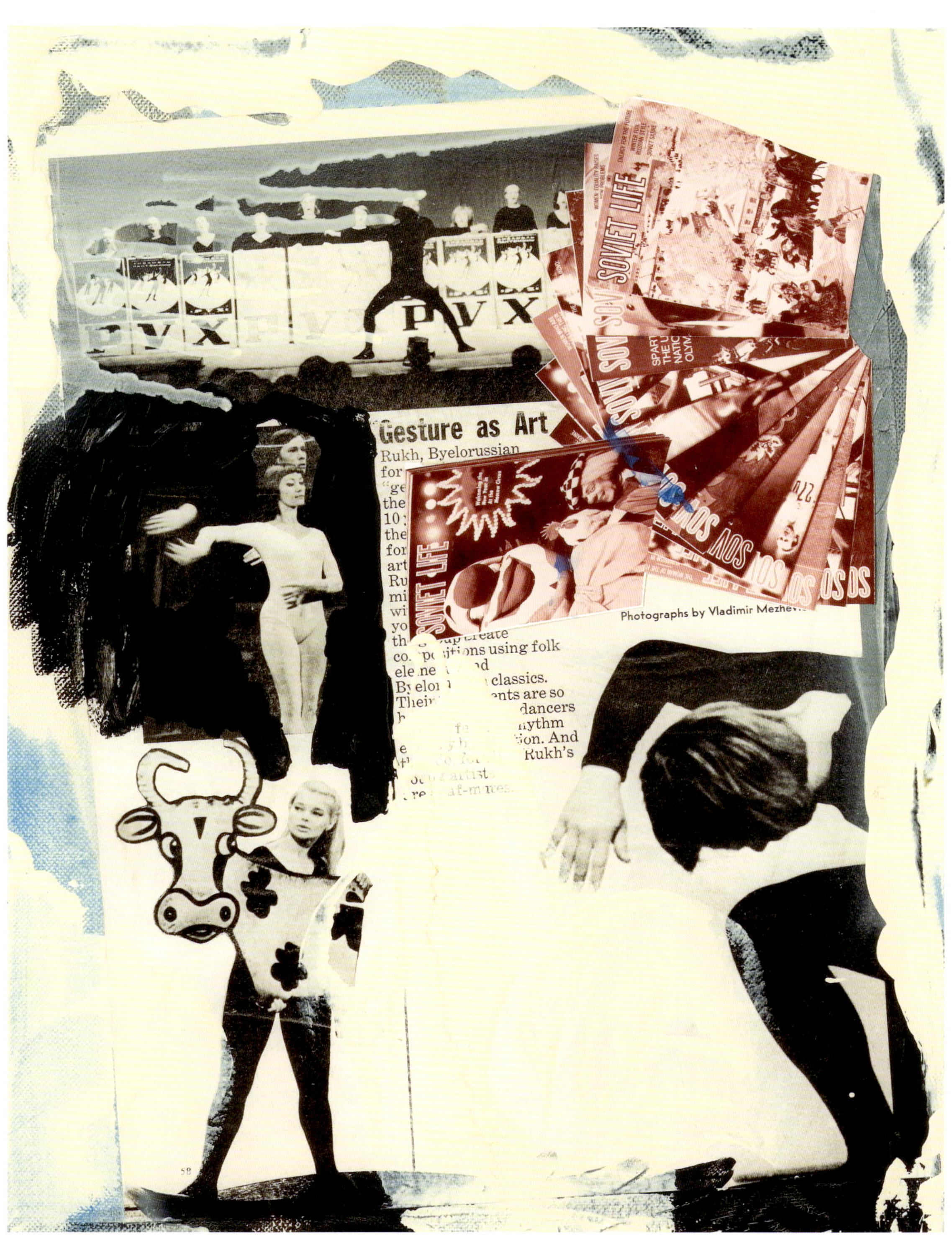

Musicians, 2006
Gestures as Art, 2006

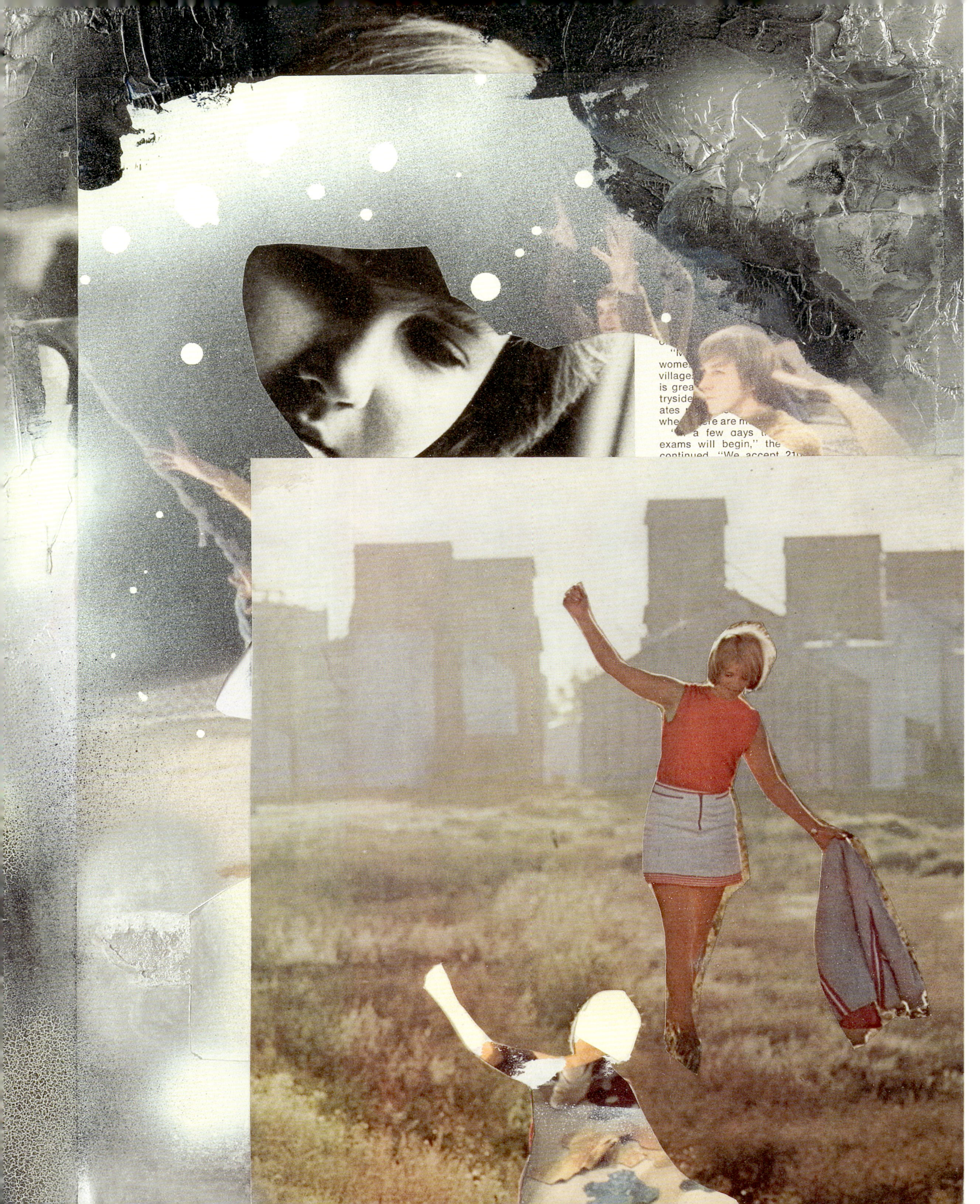
women
village
is grea
tryside
ates
where are
a few days
exams will begin," the

Historic Desire Unbound
On the Work of Paulina Olowska
Jan Verwoert

1. Dressing Up, Not Down

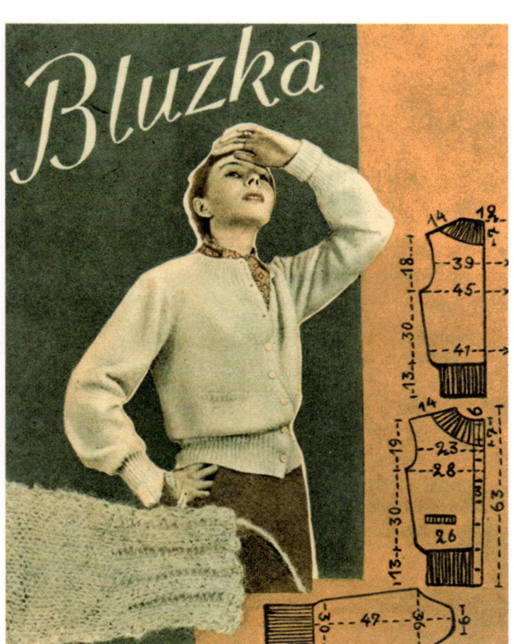

Moda i Życie, Polish magazine, circa 1950

It's time to go into town. Consider what you'll wear. It matters. When what you put on makes you feel good about stepping out of the house and meeting people, they're less likely to spoil the day for you. Dressed in a manner that makes them see who they'll be dealing with—you!—in the mood you choose to be in today, a good mood most likely, you'll be prepared to: 1. join the endless queue at the post office and retrieve a letter you had no interest in receiving; 2. pick a fight with the clerk at the tax office who hates the world at large and likes to make life harder for anyone who enjoys living; 3. teach the slob at the print shop to take orders from a woman and to do your prints properly, like you told him to, no other way. After that you may want to treat yourself to a chat with your allies, the ladies at the travel agency on Constitution Square, who book your flights and, like you, started the day dressed for battle, smiling. Their blouses have their shoulders padded so as to lift the silk fabric up at its ends, stretch it, let it fall more majestically across their chests, and convey a clear message: "Watch what you say, son, we run this place, so you'd better be on your best behavior if you want us to book you a trip out of here. For we can."

The ladies at the agency are the true heirs to the modernist cause: they've been around in the city for a long time, keeping the doors open and the lines of flight going out into the horizon of possibility, holding the fort day-to-day behind varnish-coated desks, and facing the world with a smile. The cuts, colors, and patterns on their blouses are designed to fight the dreariness of reality as we know it with the ultimate weapon: *style*—and a love for the possible look of things that beats the rhetorics of many a manifesto to the punch, because it doesn't need to be spelled out. No, the ladies rather wear it all on their sleeves.

Consulting future travel destinations with them, you pick up speed and get inspiration for taking the battle elsewhere, from the streets to bars and restaurants. You're passionate about abstraction? You talk to people about it, no matter where you are. So when the owner of the place you dined at with friends comes to your table as the digestifs are served after deserts (because he likes the idea of sitting with the artists), you have a word with him and make sure he grasps the importance of thinking about abstraction! Seriously, the city is the school and any place will do, when the conditions are right, to pass on contagious ideas or receive inspiration as easily as a radio picks up frequencies, or people contract flu when someone near them sneezes. *Achhooo!* Bless you. For the influences.

But the fight won't stop there. It continues after dinner when the powers that be retreat to the mansion library or smoking room where, throughout modernity, what's going to pass for the big picture will have been concocted. With curtains closed, drinks poured, and cigars lit, maps of the continents are rolled out and the architects of modernity go to work, pen in hand, to redraw the borderlines, distribute the real estate, divvy up territories, and recast them as modern nation-states. Thereby they also fix the brief for how the (art-)histories of the new countries afterward are to be written by diligent scholars, whose wish to be peers to potentates redrawing maps will translate into ostentatiously rigorous prose.

Few Days, 2006

To arrest time and make it seem as if all were said and done by the great men who took a position and made their move on the grand chess board of history is the use to which many words are now put. They serve but one function: to sustain the logic of Cold War thinking that we are safe as long as we keep time at a standstill. Stay dug in your trenches and count your remaining bullets, again and again: Marcel 1–2–3–4–5, Kazimir 6–7–8–9, Gerhard 10–11–12–13, Ad, Frank, Bob, Bruce, and Jeff … Wait, we're still counting and as long as we are, this war can't be over yet! How come then no shot is ever fired? It's a Cold War, stupid, so cool it! With positions taken and territories claimed, contenders can stare each other down from the depths of their armchairs for decades making sure that no one moves before they do. And they won't.

Power knows time to be on its side; it takes its time—it has a lot. People have little time. Busy, working hard for the rewards power offers, they run out of time, more so each day, until they've no time left to remember what's been lost along the way: the shoulder pads, the good chats, and all the tricks, techniques, and teachings that make up the craft of living with the joy and pain of life. This craft is born out of improvisation, it's the art of finding ways to make a day better (than it would have been, had one not tried turning it around). Changing with the times, the seasons, the fashions, the economic, social, and political conditions, the *arts and crafts of daily improvisation* can't be claimed by nations as heritage. They escape the grip of organized tradition. That's why they fall into oblivion easily. Things get faster. People forget. And techniques become supplanted by new technologies. If we could remember each single moment in which the arts and crafts of improvisation saved the day, and add those moments up, their sum total would show us the actual face of modern life as it was and is lived. One look into this face should suffice to discredit big picture theories of modernity (and all the bullet-counting) as the delusions of power-brokers (who never had to save a day in their lives). But since neither comedy nor tragedy lends itself to quantification, the world of modern joys and pains can hardly be made to compute in terms of grand historical checks and balances.

But that's no reason to admit defeat. Just get yourself an invitation. When you dress up, not down, and improvise, remember: there is a way to enter the smoking rooms and libraries—right through the front door. Walk in, and with a sunny *dzień dobry pani*, make them look up from their maps. Those fellows need to be taught some *appreciation* for all that passes them by below the radar, but that shapes the styles and politics of survival each day that the modern world is being built. Instead of master plans for putting future and past in order, the lesson to learn, *mon général*, is how to delve into *nostalgia*! Not for the good old times that never were, heaven forbid, that's big-picture thinking again! No, nostalgia for the fruits garnered by the arts and crafts of daily improvisation! What they can offer may be irrecuperably particular, oblique, crooked, and skewed, yes, *Herr Professor*, but so infinitely more potent than maps. Because each art or craft has its very own mode, manner, key, and fashion for changing realities.

On your way out, you bring the point home by brushing by a glass of red wine, gently tipping it over. The liquid pours out over the map on the table to form a blotch of color with fluid outlines, a crimson country with no name and erratic borders in a place where only who knows how to spill stuff too will know how to find it. No need to clean it up. Learn to live in it. Good night for now. See you in there later.

2. Carrying It Out, Not Back

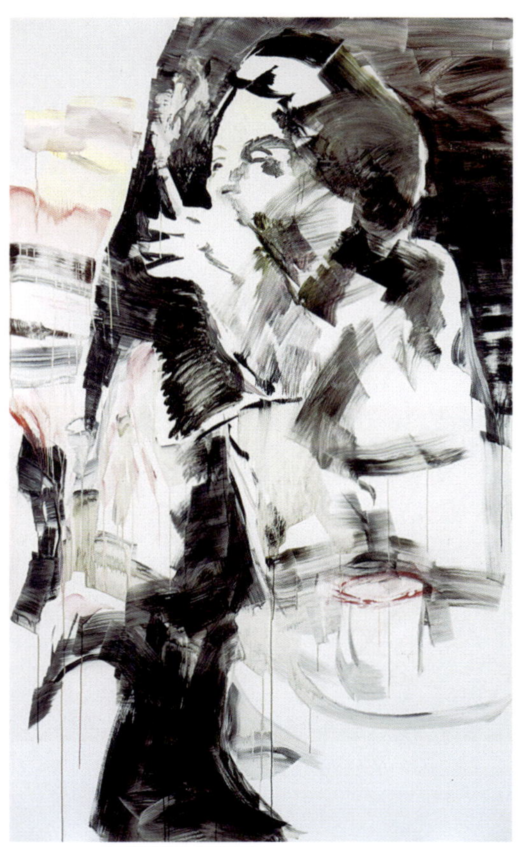

Djuna, 2004
Acrylic on wood, wheels, 250 × 150 cm
Private Collection

Paulina Olowska is not alone in her work. She turns her art into a medium for cultivating affinities and solidarities—with specific realities, memories, and styles, and with particular women, and ways of going through the day creating lives, cities, groups, which are particular to these women, and to her. Where she ends and they begin doesn't matter much. Olowska's work is a milieu unto itself, a materialized mental space in which spirits meet and influences are allowed to play themselves out. Her studio is like an urban salon frequented by the living as much as by revenants from the past. In her work, however, channeling spirits is not a one-way affair. Many souls speak through her, but she is most distinctively present in all her articulations. For this is part and parcel of the craft of urban hosting: no need for authors to die—they are invited, brought to life, and arrive, alive and kicking, to enjoy a night that the host authorizes. It is her night, all night, but precisely because of this, guests in her house can enjoy the house as theirs. By hosting many souls in the mind-space of her work, Olowska authors collective intelligence.

Look at the room she created to host Virginia Woolf, Vanessa Bell, and more Shakespearian sisters—*Virginia, Charlotte, Dolores, Jean, Mary, Nina, Djuna, Vanessa*—for her exhibition *Sie musste die Idee eines Hauses als Metaphor verwerfen* (She Had to Discard the Idea of the House as a Metaphor) (2004). She made big portraits of the modernists, painted them rapidly, and put them on wheels, so they could be moved around the gallery like theater set pieces or mobile divider walls. Their design both did and did not match the space they were made for—the grand salon at the Kunstverein Braunschweig, a former mansion, with ornate stucco, mirrors, and chandeliers. Indeed the space became a salon again, prepared as it now was by Olowska for the séance-like invocation of the mothers of modernism. Yet the rough and ready look of the props also made it clear that there was no intention here to stage a period drama and turn Braunschweig into Bloomsbury. With a few quick concise gestures, the space was instead practically repurposed for the ceremony in the manner in which one redesignates a space for a party by decorating it for that special night only.

And the spirits came. In the room it felt as though a collective of souls had convened in an inspirational urban mind-space to dress up, debate, struggle, joke, and party together. What indeed matters most in the convocation of spirits is the very spirit in which they are summoned. The tone of the invitation shapes the feel of the event. And the tone Olowska sets in environments like *Virgina, Charlotte, Dolores…* (as in many if not most of her works) is defined by a very particular mix of full dedication and devil-may-care improvisation. To put rapidly painted portraits up on wheels intuitively communicates that checking dates and footnotes is no priority here. Throwing the doors to history open so that guests can come on in, is. The genius of a good salon host lies in creating a space where the laws of normative social role-play are temporarily suspended, so that guests feel free to engage with their guard down. Olowska hits that note. Right from the outset, the rapidly-done, improvised makeup of the mise-en-scène debunks false anxieties about having to seem sophisticated, and instead tunes the space to the key of a quick-witted, truly urban, intuitive exchange. Intuitions don't abide by the rule of instant pricing (Good? How much?) with which economic rationality kills thought. To keep an intuitive exchange flowing, one needs instead to listen closely and respond quickly. This is why many of Olowska's works have the air of gifts received in inspired moments of internal or external conversation and rapidly passed on to the viewers, so that they don't lose the key quality of things shared through intuition: you can't be sure whether they are silly or wise, or both, profoundly so.

The act of passing on inspirations from the past is usually understood in terms of making "references." This term already prescribes the direction that things are meant to take. "Refer" comes from the Latin *referre*, which means to carry something back (home). So to call something a reference is to imply that the one making it has an interest in restoring something to its proper place. What if history had no home to which it could be returned? What if history was the very force that irreversibly eroded "proper" places of return? Then it would indeed be pointless to think in terms of "re-ference." In creating affinities and solidarities with particular people, works, styles, and moments in time, Olowska battles the restorative attitude to history. Her work is animated by a tangible defiance of the very notion of the proper. She takes care of her affinities and solidarities with a dedicatedly carefree spirit. Those whom she meets are, after all, the mothers of invention. So she engages them without the anxieties that paralyze artists and scholars who act as if they had to go home to a punishing father and ask him permission to speak about the past.

The house Olowska is building in her work is not a place of imaginary returns, but a site for gathering sister spirits. She indeed becomes a carrier but, instead of going *back* in history, she carries it *out*. Incubation leads to action, as she channels the style, spirit, or humor of a person, a period, a magazine, a movie, or a movement in her work. And she always carries some history *around* with her, from work to work, in the manner in which one may take a book for (and on) a journey or carry some change in one's pocket. So much maybe that some is bound to fall out. Spilling stuff is an art form. In treating inspiration as a currency to be squandered, Olowska rejects harboring it as exclusive capital to be jealously protected. She makes no difference between obscure and popular sources. Poses from *Vogue*, dresses from Burda, neons from the street, New Wave movies with hot actors in strange interiors, biographical hints, black-and-white textbook picture plates, publicity photographs of artists in their studio, journals from socialist Poland of the 1960s and 1970s like *Ameryka*, a periodical promoting an imaginary version of the USA, or *Ty i Ja*, officially a women's league magazine, effectively one of the best-designed fashion magazines ever released ... It's all in. (And so is she.)

To draw on the known as much as the unknown is a decisive choice: Olowska refuses to play the sphinx for an audience that expects riddles from the East. Her provocation lies in making you see that you *can* see what her work is about, even if you might not know right away what it means. Her artistic language is direct. She makes the work talk about very particular experiences. But in so doing, she freely mixes global and local idioms. If you wanted to locate her practice, you could probably say that Olowska has set up shop on the median strip of the main street dividing the city. Between the west and east sides, this strip is the line that runs across the center. To follow that strip, making art, is to claim the center, but to claim it as a line of flight, from city to city, a road movie shot all across town.

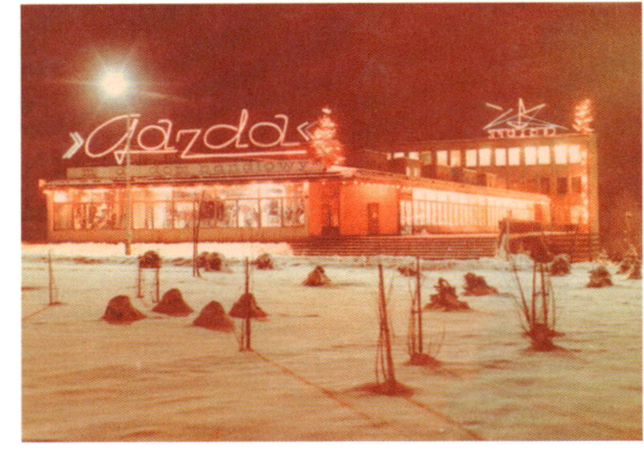

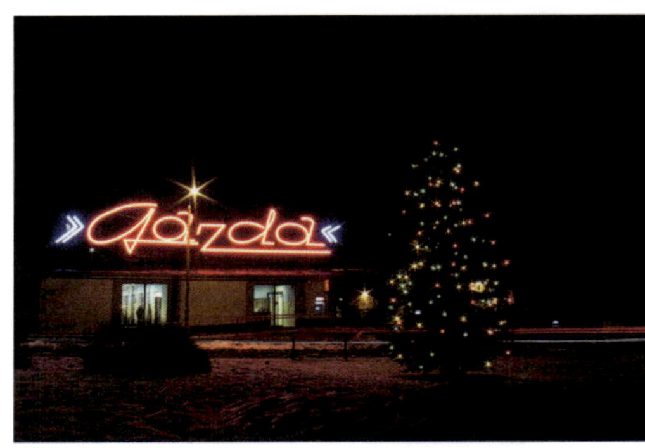

Gazda neon in Rabka Zdrój, Poland, postcard, 1970
Lighting up the reconstructed Gazda neon in Rabka Zdrój, Poland, February 1, 2013

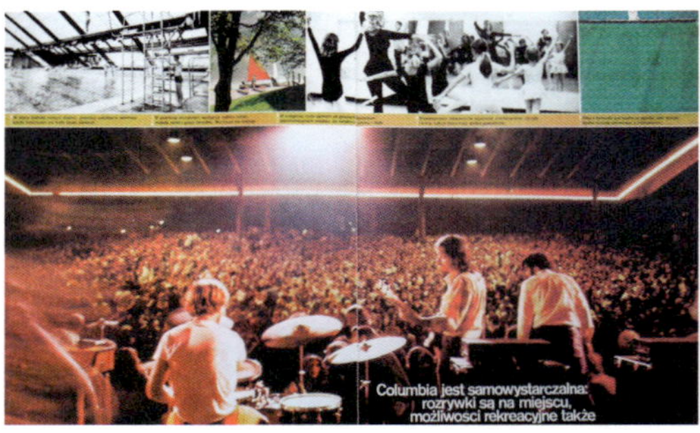

Ameryka, Polish magazine, circa 1970

3. Exile on Mean Street

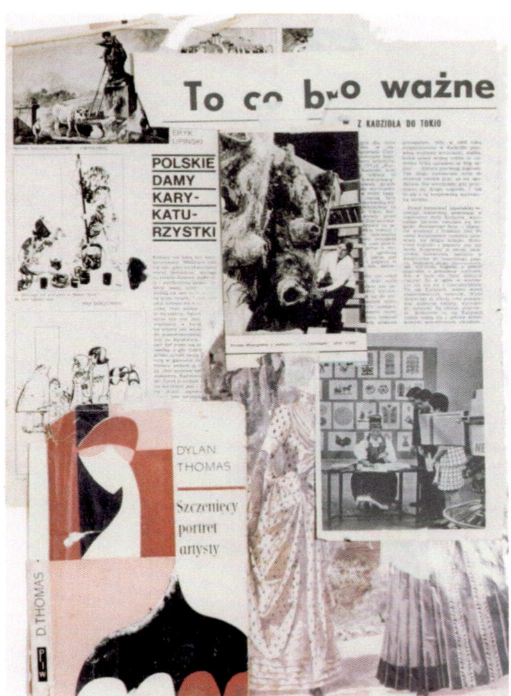

Untitled, 2004
Collage on paper, 56 × 42 cm
The Craig Robins Art Collection, Miami

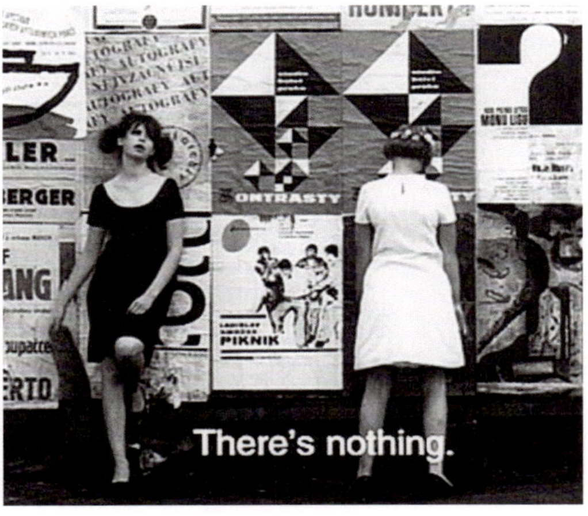

Věra Chytilová, *Sedmikrásky (Daisies)*, 1966

But it's a fight to stay out on this road and keep the future in sight. Because Main Street today is turning into *Mean* Street. Neo-nationalism is on the rise. Turbo-capitalism demands it. When only money counts but money divides people, society falls apart unless you fake it and fabricate something to believe in for everyone: the idea of a strong nation (bolstered by xenophobia and homophobia, sexism and racism). This Mean Street is the road to the social norm, not only in the former member states of the Eastern bloc, but pretty much everywhere around the globe. Yet, lest we forget, it was but a few years ago that the main street still appeared to lead somewhere else. For a brief moment after 1989, it felt genuinely possible to throw the talk of East and West onto the scrapheap of Cold-War-speak and imagine what Europe could be now. No one knew. But this is precisely why we were free to picture a different (geo-political, social, historical, biographical) horizon for the future, present, and past: an horizon in which the iron curtain drawn across the map had been lifted, to reveal what the lie of the land could have been, had art, humor, culture, and knowledge been able to spread, spill over, and mix fluidly and freely. They did a couple of times, didn't they? The mutual-inspiration societies of international avant-gardist improvisation after all showed that a free, fluid Central Europe was within reach at the beginning of the 20th century and during the thaw period of the 1960s.

To see a horizon of historic potentiality open up is a visceral experience. Which can inform a practice. Sensing the chance to see past, present, and future in a different light, you dress, act, paint, write accordingly—differently. The optimism that Olowska wears on her sleeve, in her work, testifies to the visceral experience of a sense of historic potentiality. Her stylistic exuberance is a time portal. Through it, sister spirits of the 1920s and 1960s enter and chime into the improvised tune of desire unbound by the liberation of the historical imagination.

Consider, for example, her iconic painting *Looking Up Not Down*. Two girls in colorful clothes—one in red and white, the other in blue, red, and white. They pose to show what they wear. So it must be a shot for a fashion magazine. Yes, but there is something peculiar about the girls' look and posture. Viewed slightly from below, their bodies seem dramatically elongated. Their faces carved out against an agitated sky, they look up, not down, like visionaries or heroines facing the future. Yet the challenge they rise to is not to fight enemies, but to find things to wear, days to enjoy, people to meet. The feel of the picture is distinctively 1960s. There's a touch of Soviet partisan glamour to the way the girls interpret their pose, so most likely the picture stems from *Ty i Ja*. Amplifying its rich colors and heroicism, Olowska most vividly renders the particular verve that the girls exhibit. They radiate the revolutionary promise of *being fashionable* in a country where capitalism doesn't exist, but the wild desire for consumption does, enhanced by the near absence of market structures to channel and contain it. Two girls. But they could unhinge history with their desire. For their craving for consumer joy is a weapon against the colorless world of old men, run by the secretaries and bureaucrats of Soviet-style patriarchy. It's the same anarchic desire that the heroines of Věra Chytilová's 1966 New Wave movie masterpiece *Daisies* (Czech: *Sedmikrásky*) act out: with their surreal exuberance, Marie and Marie (Jitka Cerhová and Ivana Karbanová) set the functionaries' heads spinning, defuse the social norm and, in its place, create their own reality of ingenious pleasures. Olowska makes the presence of their spirit tangible with every brushstroke here.

The spirit is one of historic desire unbound. It goes beyond the realities imposed by the given status quo in pursuit of yet unknown, future pleasures to be had. To invoke this spirit today is a provocation. It is to contest the false fatalist consensus propagated in the former West and East alike: that an alternative to the new world order of neo-nationalist turbo-capitalism did not, does not, and will not ever exist. As it articulates opposition to such global repressive fatalism, optimism today is a tactical means of resistance. At odds with the decree that the present conditions are history's only conclusion, a witness to the experience of historic desire unbound might find herself an exile in her own country. In endorsing this position, Olowska chooses to work in exile on a main street turned mean street.

It is not a peaceful situation. There is a war being waged on memory lane. Svetlana Boym describes the frontlines in her book *The Future of Nostalgia*. In the moment of transition after 1989, when the identity and history of the newly independent countries emerging from the Eastern bloc (and its world view) were to be renegotiated, the dominant force, according to Boym, was what she calls "restorative nostalgia"—the wish to resurrect the times before the recent past, restore the country to its putative former glory, and reinstate its "true" identity (whatever that may be, in current popular belief)—a rebirth of the old as the new nation. Yet this is not the only kind of nostalgia there is. Boym points to a long tradition in art and thinking that she portrays as "reflective nostalgia." She associates this perspective with the life of the cosmopolitan artist or writer in exile who, like Nabokov for example, feels equally "homesick and sick of home" and, via his nostalgia, articulates a deep love-hate relationship to the country he left behind.[1]

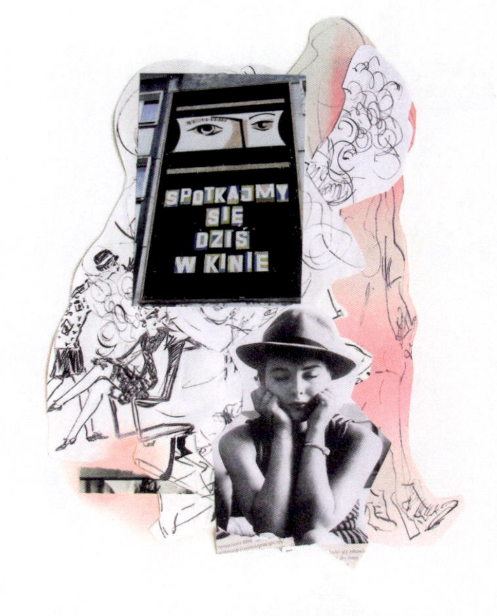

Spotkajmy się dzisiaj w kinie
(Let's Meet in a Cinema Tonight), 2008
Collage on paper, 42 × 30 cm
Private Collection

As well as harboring mixed feelings, Boym writes, reflective nostalgics are fully aware that the place they feel nostalgic for is irretrievably lost. This may be because the place is "in ruins or, on the contrary, has been just renovated and gentrified beyond recognition."[2] Or maybe because it only ever existed as a tangible, yet unrealized possibility (e.g. a Central Europe born out of art and ideas shared across borders). No talk of a return to mythic splendor or unbroken identities here: "Reflective nostalgics see everywhere the imperfect mirror images of home, and try to cohabit with doubles and ghosts."[3] In exile, this practice of cohabitation, living with ghosts, is part and parcel of an "art of survival."[4] Nostalgia becomes a medium for protecting memories of what is lost and communicating a sense of "shared longing without belonging" to fellow exiles.[5] Since contact with kindred spirits is to be made under unfavorable conditions—as most locals neither know nor care too much about what you seek to share—the act of reaching out to the like-minded has to rely on codes and innuendo understood by those whose feelings are similarly mixed. So reflective nostalgia becomes an "art of intimation, of speaking about the most personal and intimate pain and pleasures through a 'cryptic disguise.'"[6]

Many of the urban material mind-spaces that Olowska has created over the years could indeed be described as sites of reflective nostalgia: sites of longing for places that perhaps once existed, or perhaps never did, but could and should have somewhere; places that are where they aren't and aren't where they are, built from a wild assemblage of memories from—and innuendos to—very different environments and people. *Virginia, Charlotte, Dolores, Jean, Mary, Nina, Djuna, Vanessa* is but one example, a Britain in Braunschweig, with more genius on wheels than your average pantheon can hold. Another example is a collaboration with Lucy McKenzie, *Plastic Integration* (2003). The two artists

1 Svetlana Boym, *The Future of Nostalgia*, Basic Books, New York 2001, p. 50.
2 Ibid.
3 Ibid., p. 251.
4 Ibid., p. 256.
5 Ibid., p. 252.
6 Ibid.

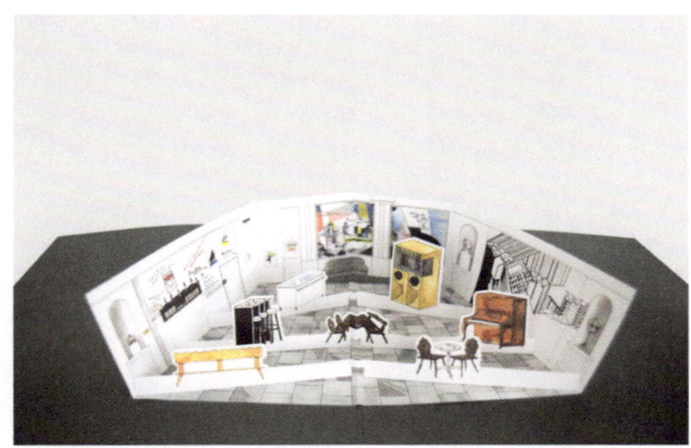

Various Artists, *Nova Popularna*, 2004
Unfolded LP sleeve, 8.5 × 63 × 31.5 cm
Label: Decemberism
Graphic design: Lucy McKenzie and Paulina Olowska

painted murals on the walls of the Gdańsk shipyard, marrying Constructivist color-field patterns to decorative motifs that would have been much to the taste of Chytilová's Marie and Marie. It is most unlikely that the workers' councils back in the day would have approved of this marriage of geometric rigor and decorative play. But just imagine if they had! (Maybe the Pope then would not have had the last word on life after the revolution.)

Deeply nostalgic for the kind of bar that artists' unions may have run, *Nova Popularna* (2003) was both a reconstruction and a full-on deconstruction of the traditional bohemian hangout. Together with McKenzie, Olowska redecorated a disused space in Warsaw and, for the duration of the month of May, ran it as a club, open to the public, with readings and concerts by many guests. Distinctively avant-gardist in its overall feel, the interior design was a candid mish-mash of styles from various times and places: Vorticism rolled up in a Polish version of Parisian elegance and smoked by a teenage offender sitting on a wooden bench covered in graffiti carvings. Each guest left further traces behind in the bar, adding their own nostalgias to the overall assemblage. Manning the bar in dresses by Beca Lipscombe that looked like costumes Natalia Goncharova could have made for a ballet of female engineers, Olowska and McKenzie decidedly undermined the macho air of the bohemian waterhole, while keeping it suitably smoky.

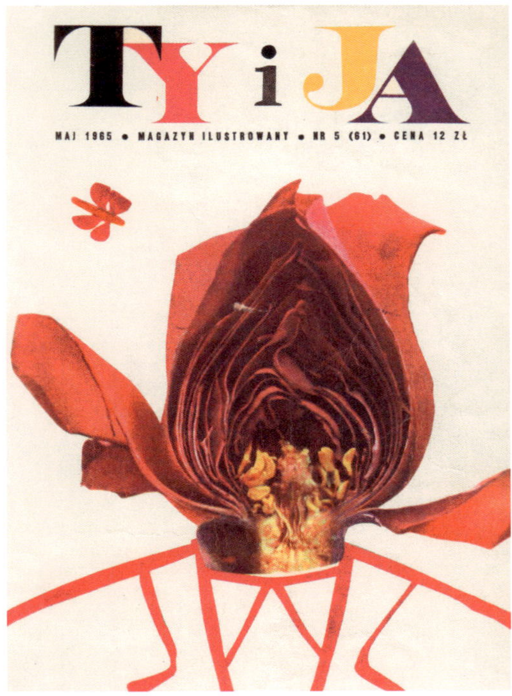

Ty i Ja, Polish magazine, 1965

Experienced as a whole, *Nova Popularna* became a collage of nostalgias. Instead of claiming a clear-cut identity for the place or selling it as a faithful reconstruction of a historical locale, Olowska and McKenzie welcomed you to a house happily assembled from parts of different ruins. Designed in the spirit of different historical styles, the bar was nonetheless clearly designated for present and future use. It was the kind of bar people open in order to have a bar to go to and to show to others: look, this is what we need to have in this town because so far this kind of place is missing! Drawing on the past, creating in the present what you would want for the future, is what Boym calls "prospective nostalgia."[7] For reflective nostalgics it offers a way of renegotiating the limits of the city they live in, "an alternative way of reading and inhabiting their own urban space."[8]

As a technique for collaging times and places, reflective nostalgia becomes a weapon against the machinery of capitalist modernization formatting life according to identical standards everywhere. Consider *Obraz—wymiana—neon/Painting—Exchange—Neon* (2006). Here, Olowska put together one big neon composition from different elements, mixing universally recognizable motifs with particular local shapes. The cocktail bar classic of a nude reclining inebriated in a cocktail glass at its center, and a 24-hour sign signaling the non-stop availability of whatever you want in a city that never sleeps, the neon evoked the promise of ecstatic urban consumption in the visual shorthand of American-style global pop. All around the world such signs say: your town is a love machine. At the same time these ciphers were offset by neons with a specific local history: four interlacing green and red circles, a blue spiral encircling the nude, two pointy arrows, and a yellow girl with a curious square collar (a TV?) observing the cocktail action from the side were all based on neons installed in Polish cities in the 1960s. Most neons of this time did not advertize anything in particular. They were strictly decorative, illuminated ornaments, magic sprinkles designed to transform streets into avenues and make them sparkle just like the Champs-Elysées.

Born out of much the same spirit as *Ty i Ja* magazine, these neons were products of the desire to celebrate fashion and consumption outside of—and independently from—the workings of the capitalist system. In an essay on *Ty i Ja*, David Crowley

7 Ibid, p. 168.
8 Ibid, p. 221.

poignantly described the manner in which this desire breached the protocols of the capitalist world and found a peculiar form of fulfillment in its sheer formulation, as the "applied fantastic."[9] And it is true, these old neons rejoice in their own form. Pleasure demands no purchase. It is already given through the very design of a neon (or a collage on a magazine cover). But when capitalism came, so did the "proper" billboards and, in no time, rooftops across town were studded with illuminated advertisements for Samsung, Siemens, and whatever company moved in first. The old neons were not dismantled. They were just no longer taken care of, and became given over to decay through sheer neglect. One sign language overwritten by another: the self-reflective language of decorative neons that gratify desire for the urban through their urban look alone silenced by the full speech of huge adverts promising something (big), but giving you nothing.

With *Obraz—wymiana—neon* (2006) Olowska entered the scene of the signs of desire being rewritten in the present historical moment. Instead of the full speech of current product advertising, she deliberately chose ciphers from American pop vocabulary: the "24h" and the cocktail girl that, as generic universals, have come to acquire the same self-reflective glow (of desire gratified in its sheer formulation) as the Polish ornaments. *Ameryka* is taken by the hand to a place and time when its name still had the same radiance as Paris. But not to consolidate value. Both the "24h" and the cocktail girl are more at home on the mundane, if not seedy, side of the neon spectrum. The nod to the new in Olowska's piece then also takes on the form of a sign derived, not from the big adverts, but from street-level, wild entrepreneurial thinking. In the upper right corner glows the line *pizza pasta sushi*—the visual equivalent of a raspy voice crooning "anything you want you got it" from inside the Asian fusion pizza parlor some genius recently opened on the corner of Main and Mean Street where, for better or worse, totally wrong is still just right, somehow.

The whole composition was mounted onto the panorama window of the Foksal Gallery Foundation overlooking the skyline of Warsaw with Stalin's "gift"—the monumental Palace of Culture—towering over the newly erected office buildings. Like a filter put before a camera lens, the neon made you see the city in a different light, as if it had been fast forwarded back into the science-fiction history of its own dreams, rewritten and fulfilled in a perplexingly erotic jumble of signs and offers.

The final twist in the battle over Main Street was still to follow. With the proceeds of the sale of the work, Olowska had one of the historic neons that had fallen into disrepair restored—an exemplary and very beautiful one. On the corner of a rooftop overlooking Warsaw's Constitution Square, a set of neons shows a girl hurling a ball into the air, and the ball dropping down the side of the house neon by neon by neon by neon by neon, only to be thrown out into the sky again by the girl a second later. Jubilant, exuberant, and very Marie and Marie too. Designed in 1961 by the graphic artist Jan Mucharski, *Volleyball Player* was her name. Getting the neon on the square to work put the story in the press and gave the question *whatever happened to Main Street?* wide public resonance—not in the name of some grand notion of lost values, but under the sign of a particular girl on a roof enjoying what you can neither buy nor sell: the joy derived from the endless revolution of time during the course of a ball being hurled, retrieved, and hurled again.

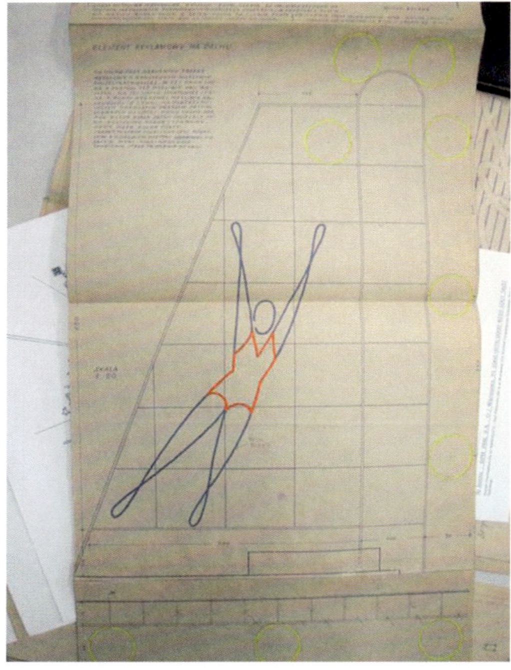

Ja Mucharski's project, *Siatkarka (Volleyball Player)*, 1961, from *Firma Reklama*, a neon studio and archive run during the 1950s in Warsaw

9 David Crowley, 'Applied Fantastic,' *Dot Dot Dot*, no. 9 (2005).

4. Meet the Mothers of Invention (Moving Sideways)

Building houses from parts of ruins is a technique for creating spaces, but also a way of moving through time. Each part added to the assemblage-architecture of memories becomes a chamber visited by the historic imagination. You cannot walk straight through a house like this. You inevitably move *sideways*, from one chamber to the one adjacent to it, and on to the one adjacent to that, and so on. *Adjacency*, not linearity, is the principle that defines the way that memories fall into place. They all somehow exist *next to* each other, like realities in a dream, or experiences in life. They relate to one another on many different levels. It is a multidimensional labyrinth with passages connecting in peculiar ways. To find your way around you need to know how to move in oblique directions. It is the set of skills for historical orientation that Boym associates with the perspective she favors: "[Reflective] nostalgia is never literal, but lateral. It looks sideways."[10] This approach, obviously, is no good if big history pictures are what you want to paint. Instead of moving sideways through its adjacent chambers, big picture advocates will portray (art) history as a series of territories claimed and conquered, one after the other, by influential men, modernizers marching onward, from questions to answers, on the road to success.

But this is not only a matter of how history is told. It is very much also a question of how we assume it is made. Hannah Arendt sharply criticized the manner in which we habitually speak about historic developments as if they were created by a single actor like a craftsman produces a table—not to claim that the forces of change were impersonal, but to stress that they emerge from *multi-lateral* human relations.[11] Only when people conspire to create commotions, do things get moving. Agents of change, in the light of Arendt's critique, would need to be portrayed not as individual makers, but as influential conduits, communicators, and connectors in the force field of human relations out of which history emerges. They are the leads to the trajectories of lateral motions that lead to historic commotion. (And one should not be surprised to find more women moving history in this manner than men hooked on the idea of being big makers.) To engender history in these terms is to move in a particular manner. Susan Hiller once remarked that dealing with the territorial growls of her male contemporaries in the Conceptual art arena of the 1960s led her and her female colleagues to the realization that, rather than play the same game (of drawing room claim-staking), one could also, as she put it, "move sideways," expand the map, and discover parallel spaces to inhabit through your work.[12]

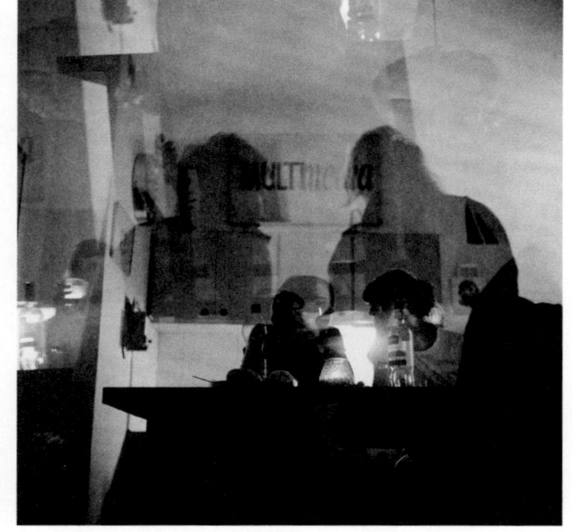

Paulina Olowska's private *Salon des Herbes*, Warsaw, 2004

The directions that Olowska's work takes are indeed set by the dynamics of (multi-)lateral motion—from adjacent places to neighboring topics and related people, and from one medium to the next: painting, fashion, performance, poetry, and environments that she moves through in a sideways motion, traversing one on the way to the other. For her, painting becomes a space that opens up onto fashion; poetry becomes a conduit for performance; environments become the connection between people, spirits, and artifacts ... Pictures never stop configuring themselves in the course of this movement. So there is always a trace of home, an echo of painting, which Olowska *holds onto* as a medium of reflection and *departs from*, leaving it behind, in a sideways motion. Painting for her is equally the kind of space you might *long for*—as the room of one's own in which to make up one's mind—and *be sick of*—when its walls close in on you and it is time to go out and see your neighbors. Fashion is always a good neighbor. It gives Olowska the grammar and vocabulary for the body language of style and attitude in her paintings. And it is one of the first chambers to stop by on the way out.

10 Boym, *The Future of Nostalgia*, p. 354.
11 Hannah Arendt, *The Human Condition*, University of Chicago Press, Chicago 1958, p. 181–188.
12 Susan Hiller in conversation with Jörg Heiser and Jan Verwoert in *Romantic Conceptualism*, Kunsthalle Nürnberg and BAWAG Foundation, Vienna 2007, p. 150–163; p.152.

To summon the spirit of Elsa Schiaparelli, for instance, and learn from her what it was like to cut dresses while spending time with the Surrealists—as Olowska did in her exhibition *Attention à la Peinture* (2008) dedicated to the exceptional designer, turning a pun of hers into a veritable double entendre. The title translates as "Beware of Wet Paint," a warning that Schiaparelli had printed on different garments when premiering her collection of 1938. Watch out for what painting can do, is what it is made to say by Olowska who, for the exhibition, teamed up with the fashion designer Min Stiller. Shapes painted by Olowska were cut out from the canvas and put together by Stiller to become skirts, blouses, dresses, and robes with multi-colored abstract patterns. Some looked light, ready to wear for late spring, early summer, others turned out quite sculptural and dignified, dresses the lady of the house may want to wear to a Fauvist country wedding. Yet others could have served as body armor for a Ming dynasty warrior or urban traveler today. The canvases from which the parts had been taken were displayed beside the dresses (stretchers showing through the cut-out bits) like used paper patterns hung on the wall when the dress is done. It made you wonder: why did angry avant-gardists of yore settle for slashing the canvases, when they could have gone all the way and cut themselves shirts from their art!

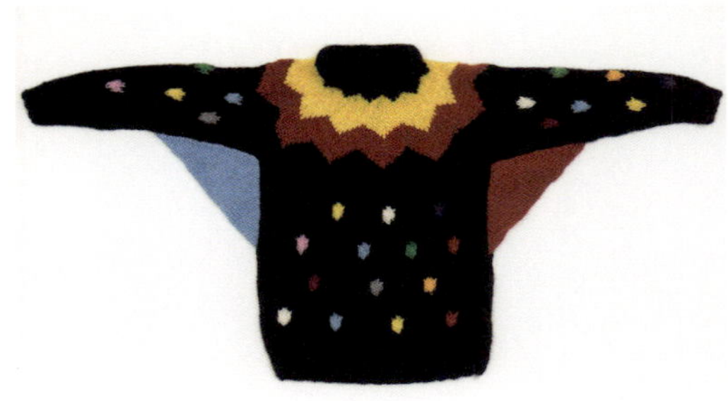

Klaun/Clown, 2010
Wool and appliqué handmade by Min Stiller for the exhibition *Applied Fantastic*, Metro Pictures, New York, 2010

From here the walk painting takes through fashion continues into the show *Applied Fantastic* (2010). Close to paper patterns in their practical logic, here it was suggestions for how to knit your own extravagantly fashionable pullovers that Olowska took from a Polish women's magazine as a starting point. Judging by the jumble of brightly colored patches and patterns, sloping shoulders, and wide sleeves, this is late 1970s, early 1980s. A postmodern look delivered with the modernist punch of existential autonomy asserted through your own creative labor—which is the spirit Olowska channeled in her large-scale repaintings of the original magazine photographs showing the knitwear worn by models. Rendered in strong, ominously glowing colors that heightened the cool, proudly defiant poses of the models, the pullovers look like they are designed for battle on the streets—genuine products of the arts and crafts of daily improvisation in the fight over how to turn a day around. The actual pullovers were there too, knitted, completed, in frames adjacent to the canvases. More paintings showed knitwear worn in action, for example *Crochet Coat* (2010), where a young girl is kept warm by a cuddly coat, and concocts mischief as her wandering eyes suggest. Or in *Woolmark* (2010), where two girl friends in knitted coats take a winter walk through a birch forest talking, by the look on their faces, about life and how to live it.

These are stories told. And vital intuitions expressed. For the connection that Olowska articulates in her works between dressing up and painting is existential. Fashion and painting are two arts of using the medium of textiles (which is what canvases are first of all) for *making an impression* on others: for letting a body appear and a self take shape in the eyes of a beholder attracted by the look of colors and patterns displayed.

In this regard, a key artist whom Olowska brings into play as a mother of invention is Pauline Boty. A first generation British Pop artist, Boty painted unabashedly strong, colorful, funny, and overtly libidinously-charged pictures. Much more pronouncedly than her contemporaries, she engaged the idea that, when you live a pop life, you become who you are by channeling how you feel through popular songs, pictures, and styles. Tongue in cheek, no doubt. But, as Sue Tate has pointed out, Boty chose *not* to adopt the air of the smooth'n'cool man of modern tastes that most of her male colleagues cultivated as their pop persona.[13] She instead took the risk of showing that she moved into the candy store of pop culture to try to inhabit it. Boty understood publicity photographs of herself as an artistic medium in its own right. An extensive series of images exist of her next to her works, striking poses or wearing clothes that match or offset the paintings, being as pop as they are and, in some cases, as provocatively erotic. Boty connects the body and the canvas in the act of making pictures that talk about the joys and pains of living life in a new age of billboard chart hits and hot new actors from France. However, first the press, then art history took a distance from Boty's rigorous embrace of pop. First she was sold to the public as a starlet, then she was written out of the picture. In one symptomatic instant, magazine editors cropped a photograph of Boty stripping next to a painting of a girl stripping—kept her but cut away her work. In denying her the status of an image-maker, they killed her joke of claiming the pose and the painting as connected forms of action.

In her painting *Pauline Boty Acts Out One of Her Paintings for a Popular Newspaper* (2006), Olowska put the maker back into her picture. The notorious shot of Boty stripping is copied, blown up, and collaged onto the canvas next to the figure of a painter (a self-portrait of sorts) in a short dress with a Bridget Riley-style pattern, visibly concentrating on her work, with bits of the New York skyline looming behind her. She gazes at the patch besides Boty's face, where fragments of newspaper print have been whitened out, waiting for a new image to be painted on top. Hosted in the super-urban painterly space that Olowska draws around her, Boty receives her proper stage. And you see: she is laughing. A tribute to this exuberance, the painting, however, performs an alchemical synthesis of Boty's hot and Riley's cool pop equally, as if to say: having to choose between one or the other is a false choice imposed by the cruel gaze of those who want to see you strip just so they can dismiss you for it. Another painting in the same body of work (shown at Cabinet Gallery, London, in the 2006 exhibition *Hello to You Too*) emphasized this point. *Stripteaser [Nashville]* (2006) shows a scene from the eponymous Robert Altman movie in which the aspiring singer Sueleen Gay (Gwen Welles) is coaxed into taking her clothes off before a crowd of leering gents in a country club.

Together the paintings launch an attack against the pressure on women to perform their sexuality and against the readiness of a patriarchal public to reduce women to their own image. At the same time, however, Olowska fully embraces the play with the visual power and pleasures of eroticism. Boty laughs. And Welles is painted with her eyes closed, dancing with herself, in proud defiance of the gaze that is on her. Taking sides with her, the painting itself is performing a striptease of sorts. Cut-out fragments of photographic print are glued onto the canvas and the brushwork around them is loose, fast, and furious. So the work is energetically stripping its visual layers off, in fact, down to the skin of the white primer showing through in many patches.

The line that Olowska walks in these and other works is to point both to the pressure to bare oneself (in the art circus and other power games) *and* to the possibility of owning the choreography of desire, so as to twist it. This double edge also characterized her collaboration with Bonny Camplin, *Salty Water/What of Salty Water?* (2007). In the exhibition, a small old cabin boat stood on a low platform, framed on either side by a tall plinth carrying the bust of a young girl with artfully braided hair. A spotlight slowly

13 Sue Watling (later renamed Sue Tate) and David Alan Mellor, *Pauline Boty: The Only Blonde in the World*, AM Publications, London 1998; and Sue Tate, "Forward via a Female Past: Pauline Boty and the Historiographic Promise of the Woman Pop Artist," in Alexandra M. Kokoli (ed.), *Feminism Reframed: Reflections on Art and Difference*, Cambridge Scholars Publishing, Newcastle upon Tyne 2008, p. 177–205.

wandered through the space like the beam of a lighthouse. At intervals it would pass over drawings by Camplin and Olowska on one wall. They showed women waiting, some in suggestive poses, dressed and undressed, drawn with the quick lines and casual style of a painter of modern life jotting down his urban experiences. In the light of the mood set by the boat and the beam, the feel of the drawing series was that of a museum graphics collection displayed in a harborside tattoo parlor. Continuing this scenario, the exhibition catalogue included photographs of the artists dressed in high boots, short skirts, and thick furs, waiting by harbor piers. As if for clients. Perhaps. Or seafaring friends. Or no one in particular really. Maybe they were just *keeping each other company*. As they did during the opening performance of the show, sitting inside the boat, dressed as sailors on a leisurely cruise, one filing her nails, the other searching the airwaves on the radio for news of upcoming weather. Playing all the roles in the power game, professional girls *and* their potential customers (sailors and flâneur artists), Olowska and Camplin appropriated the *entire* choreography of desire, and twisted its inherent logic of supply and demand: as tides go out and come in, time runs away and it remains open if anyone ever got what they thought they came for.

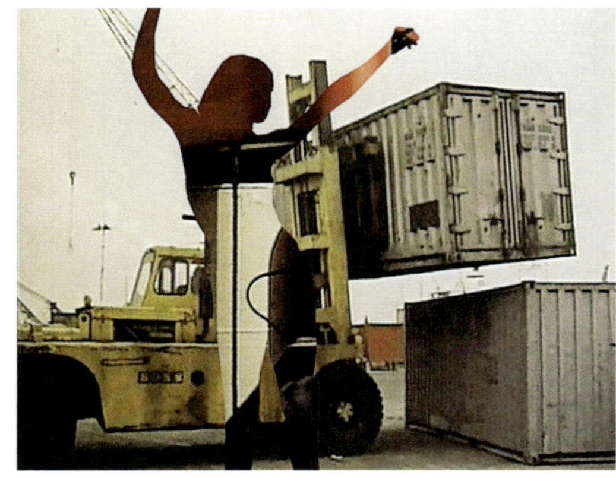

Bonnie Camplin and Paulina Olowska, filmstill from the exhibition *Salty Water/What of Salty Water*, Portikus, Frankfurt, 2007

Building on Boty's insights into the interrelatedness of the canvas showing pictures and the body striking poses, Olowska has worked on choreographies that amalgamate the picture and the pose. Indeed, the manner in which she paints fashion choreographs the space of desire before and around the picture. Facing her paintings you may find yourself attracted by openly flagged colors. Enticed by coded innuendo. Or kept at bay by the type of cool that commands respect. All of this might remain implicit to the way a picture is painted. But it can also be actualized when a picture is performed and the vocabulary for new choreographies emerges in the act. With *Bauhaus Yoga* (2001), Olowska took the avant-gardist desire for art to give form to life at face value by devising a series of daily exercises for posing in a seriously abstract manner. She then further formalized this body language of applied abstractions by working out poses to perform the alphabet. This she did, letter by letter, in a red dress (double breasted, high collar, very Futurist women-engineers' brigade) with blue stockings and a scarf (2001). With your own alphabet ready, the point is to use it. The letter X entered into the painting *X* (2002), with the alphabet city engineer, all blue, raising crossed arms over her bent head to ward off looks and demands in the limelight of the canvas. Which is only one step away from the stage. So in 2005 Olowska worked with Daniel Yamada on a choreography for alphabet moves performed to poetry by Josef Strau, Frances Stark, and Paulus Mazur. Call it a form of multiple mediumship: moves relayed words guided by a voice, as the poems were read out by Josef Strau and the three dancers—Olowska, Yamada, and Joanna Zielinska—froze in letter shape or swiftly traversed the roof of the pavilion building, Galerie Meerettich, on which the nocturnal event was staged (and subsequently restaged in The Museum of Modern Art, New York, in 2012).

Looking at Olowska's work, you therefore get a first-hand idea of how serious commotion must have been spread in the *Sternstunden* (magic moments) of the avant-garde. Consider how close her way of working is to that of Natalya Goncharova, for instance. Opening Constructivism onto Fauvism and folklorism, Goncharova kept moving into the space of dance, designing costumes and settings for the Ballets Russes in long-lasting collaborations with Sergei Diaghilev, Bronislava Nijinska, and Igor

Stravinsky.[14] Moving sideways in her work has little to do with mere opportunity seeking, since problems must have occurred on all steps of the way during her collaborations. The production of *Les Noces* (1923) was 11 years in the making. The exceptional quality of the outcome must have been the result of a long struggle between the artist, the producer, the choreographer, and the composer. Goncharova changed her visual concept entirely during the process. So the arts and crafts of improvising—turning the day around and saving a whole ballet production—are part and parcel of what made Goncharova the extraordinary artist she became when, as the painter she was, she acted as the conduit for the realization of a choreographic, musical, and social vision.

But how to meet and face so prominent a mother of invention? Father figures are easy to meet. You will find them standing in your way, all the time, in front of doors that they claim only they can open for you. Who cares? In a house that you move through sideways, other doors open to all sides all the time anyhow. So you can let the fathers bore themselves sick on their doorstep. But the mothers … The power of their influence is directly proportional to the difficulty of clearly locating it. They are never to be found in one place only. Mothers are with you all the time. They are in your bones, the back of your mind, and on the phone wherever you pick it up. They talk to you from behind your ear, walking beside you, a lateral presence just outside your field of vision. Indeed you may only catch a glimpse of it when you turn sideways and have a good look around. Much art has been born out of struggles with father figures because it is so easy: you know where to find them. The superior challenge is to meet the mothers. Because to do so, you need to invent truly circumspective ways of relating to their lateral presence.

Keeping the side windows rolled down while driving, so that the air comes in is a way to smell what is around you. It is how Olowska drives painting into the landscape. The air, smell, and flavor of what surrounds her comes in, ventilates through, and emanates from it, on all sides. So the work is not *about* certain subjects. It is *among* them. Through painting Olowska lays out scenarios or situations in which she can literally be surrounded by her subjects. Many, many subjects. And also mothers. In *Virginia, Charlotte, Dolores, Jean, Mary, Nina, Djuna, Vanessa* portraits on wheels create a theater of the imagination in which, stepping onto the stage among the actors—the paintings—you may feel as though you are becoming one of them. It is exciting. But also quite eerie. For with spirits you never know who is controlling the show. You summoned them, so it could be you. But they might stay and haunt you and then you might come to be possessed by them, obsessed as you may become with making them come or go. You turn the tables on them, or they turn them on you. And whether it is going to go one way or the other is never too clear when you are in the middle of it all.

And into the middle of her subject Olowska indeed went, in *Collaged Stryjeńska* (2008). From black and white reproductions she repainted pictures by Zofia Stryjeńska (1891–1976) in large sizes that did not necessarily match the originals. She made her big. And then she brought her in, borrowing the originals for an installation at the Schinkel Pavillon during the 5th Berlin Biennale. In the octagonal space, paintings were hung from the ceiling in pairs, back to back, Olowska on Stryjeńska, Stryjeńska on Olowska, big on small, small on big, in a geometric pattern forming an architecture of suspended canvases, a small labyrinth of sorts. Stryjeńska is indeed a mother of modernism who knew how to move sideways, from Cubism into neo-pagan folklore, rigorous, constructive,

14 For my initiation to the world of Goncharova I am strongly indebted to the artist Silke Otto-Knapp who has been exploring the (multi-)lateral space of the Ballets Russes in her paintings in a painterly dialogue that is certainly also with Olowska.

seeking to tap into the collective imagination, but doing so in such an exuberant manner as to make her sit awkwardly in any canon one might want to try to construct around her. You might not find her in certain history books. But now she was there, all around, in an installation that resembled a dance of two painters, a ghost dance perhaps where it was not quite clear who was leading whom, but also a merry peasant dance, a wedding festivity, where it does not matter who takes the lead, because all somehow do. Black and gray, blue, white, red, green, and yellow, reeling around each other in a roundelay with an eerily merry, merrily eerie mother.

To summon a spirit is a way to engage its lateral presence in a circle dance. But sometimes to summon her may actually not even be necessary. Because she is, has been, and will be there, always, already, anyhow. The point is only that too many painters may have chosen just to turn their eyes the other way and, in painting monochrome, inserted frosted glass into their windows, to avoid seeing who has been looking in, watching over them while they worked. *Mother 200* (2012) defrosts the glass. She's there, with big hair, a cigarette between her lips, her eyes closed, inhaling the smoke; yellow black paint drips around her over light blue patches. Clifford Still, had he looked, could have seen her too, had he not preferred to keep things simple by putting sublime nothingness center stage. It's not like you had to look at her. You don't. She's enjoying a smoke and looks like she is all by herself, quite content in fact with herself, for she knows how to take pleasure, a *père* turned *mère jouissance*, if you will. How to engage her *and* let her be? Drawing smoke in with her in tar-colored strokes and letting the air out in blue fields. It is the terms of cohabitation in a painting negotiated by the painting, making a strong figurative presence and the flow of abstraction coexist, side by side, not peacefully necessarily, but *avowed* in their conflictual coexistence.

It is not a battle over space. And not a fight for time. It is a struggle in and with the medium of painting, in the course of which the modalities of being with and among subjects, spirits, historical and material dynamics are being worked out, by Olowska, here as in her other works. If there is a certain calm here, it is because one mode of struggle is indeed the circular dance of cycles of paintings in which the return to rhythmicality of the art and craft daily improvisation is possible. Part of the series for the exhibition *Mother 200* was *Untitled (For Ulrike Ottinger)* (2012), showing a female figure seen from behind, wearing a blue scarf and a long coat, with a broom and a dustpan in her hands—the broom like a big paintbrush really—looking into a monochrome patch. The work was hung by the gallery door. So the lady was looking outside, ready to *brush things up* and *dust them off*. A strong reminder that the question was never who finished modernism first, but—in the light of possible alternative futures and pasts—on any given day anywhere, on the main streets and big stages and side streets and adjacent spaces alike, the really tough question again and again is how, with style, to turn the day around.

Untitled (For Ulrike Ottinger), 2012
Oil on canvas, 110 × 78 cm
Private Collection

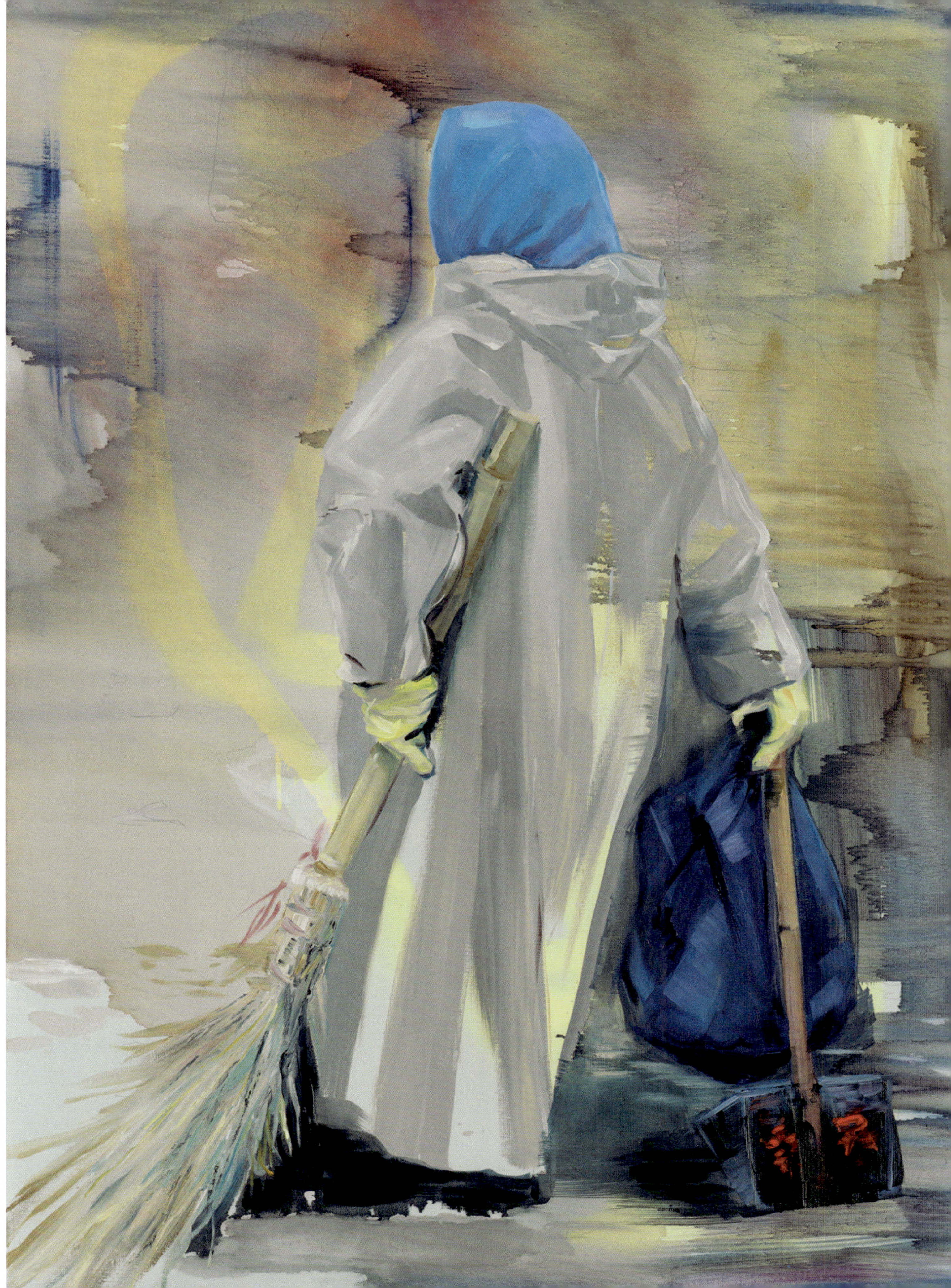

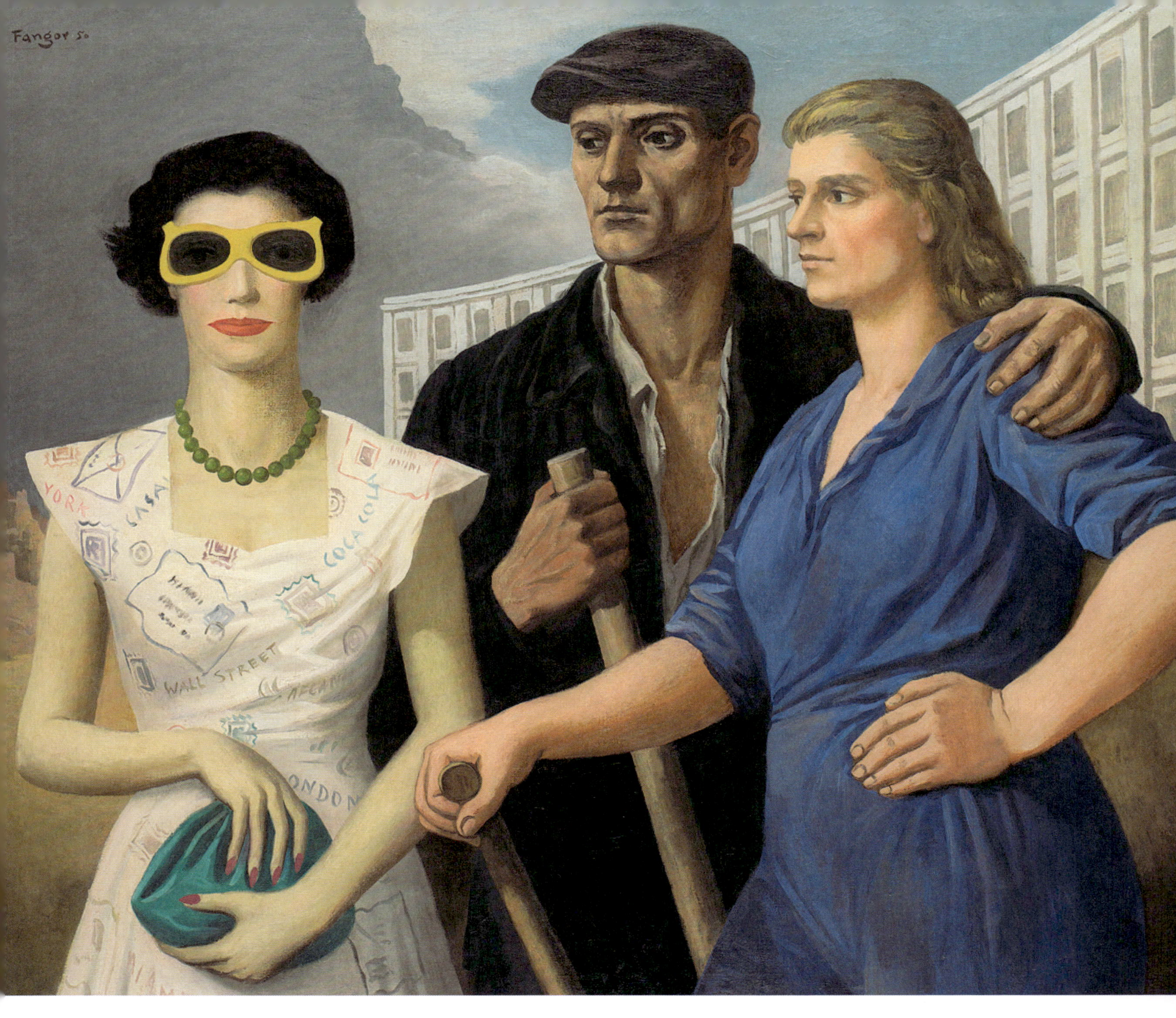

Wojciech Fangor, *Postaci*, 1950
Oil on canvas, 100 × 125 cm
Muzeum Sztuki in Łódź Collection

I lived Around the Corner from Modernism Paulina Olowska in Conversation with Adam Szymczyk

AS There are certain recurring locations, styles, or genres in your works that you treat as forms for your own individual stories: the history of exhibitions, "abandoned modernism," and the clash between applied arts—fashion, architecture, design—and high art.

PO Yes, I try to come up with the most suitable form for my statements, so as to narrow the gap between the theme and the way it is communicated. For instance, the method of speaking about the aesthetics of abandoned modernism would be to reactivate an actually abandoned, broken neon sign from the modernist era that I light up again in its original setting.

AS What is the source of your interest in the residues of aesthetics and techniques from the past that you meticulously collect in order to piece together a new whole in your works?

PO For a long time I have been interested in degraded things, in beauty of dubious origins. The loose ends that you mention interest me for a particular reason—because they were questioned. This opens up a field of work that is different to the official canon as recognized by different authorities. I have the impression that statements coming into dialogue with such oppressed objects stand a better chance of addressing a whole range of topics, and their form is more expressive.

AS You are not only interested in degraded objects, but also in languages that have fallen out of use, or never gained popularity. This is evident in the titles of your works.

PO I like using transformed, distorted, or abridged words. I create new phrases, make half-conscious spelling mistakes, and search for an alternative language of expression. The most important things take place between the official canon and all the jabbering … which, in fact, has a lot to do with my approach to objects. Esperanto, which I explored in one of my works, is also such an abandoned form of language—a failed and somewhat forgotten experiment.

AS In some of your works you created an elaborate setting that was, to a certain extent, functional—a kind of stage for the invited guests or random spectators to perform on.

PO The multi-layered perspective that I would like to achieve is close to such forms as reconstruction or *tableaux vivants*. My first works involving staging were quite spontaneous, straightforward, and playful. This was the case with the performance *Alphabet* (2005), the posters *Reconstucting Modernism* [sic] (2001), and the performance *Bauhaus Yoga* (2001). Then my settings became more and more elaborate, accommodating objects, painting, and textiles—things that are found and reworked. It seemed to me then that such reconstructions were a good tool for examining the specific forms of urban existence—for instance an artistic salon or a bohemian café, as in the Warsaw project *Nova Popularna* (2003).

In the second half of the 1990s, my reconstructions looked for inspiration to the tailor or the cobbler, and to textile shops, as well as travel agencies which, at that time, were going out of business at a record pace, having lost their economic raison d'être.[1]

AS Shops offering custom-made clothes and accessories, cafés, libraries ... All these are characteristic public spaces with their own patterns of human interaction that are now fading away. Much as with neon signs—a technique and a genre that you revive and put in working order.

PO Or out of order ... The *Volleyball Player* (2006), a neon in Warsaw's Constitution Square, quite often malfunctions and goes out, and I need to keep an eye on it constantly.

AS Let us stay for a moment with the stage, or the theatrical aspect, as I get the impression that it is the key to many of your installations. The concept for *Nova Popularna* shows references to the first Kraków cabaret Cricot, which in the 1930s was a political provocation, ridiculing the parochial mentality of the bourgeoisie.

PO I find cabaret as a form inspiring due to the inherent dynamism with which it transforms visual artistic forms, as well as its flippant approach to political content. Because of its ephemeral character that is immersed in a specific context, the cabaret as a form is also somewhat deficient. Conjuring it up from the past resembles a séance. Advertising is a little similar in this respect.

AS Speaking of which, do you remember that in Poland before 1989, advertisements did not have a direct relationship with the products, because the latter were not available? The advertisements actually replaced them. Instead of an item you had ... a representation of an item. Plus there was the personal aspect: moonlighting artists were covering the blind walls of bleak buildings with colorful painting-advertisements. Some of these murals survive to this day, but all of them will probably disappear under a layer of Styrofoam insulation sheets before long.

PO I find this issue particularly relevant: an art that is present in the everyday, accessible to everyone rather than just the connoisseur—this was what the Russian avant-garde had called for. What you have in the end is a mixture of different elements, the blurring of the boundary between art and craft, which I like very much. In addition I think that applied arts are captivating, due to the fact that while developing pieces connected with craft—such as textiles, silk prints, or ceramics—I have the chance to work with practical minds, people who are not busy pondering useless ideas. Which is great for a change.

AS While being critical of the commercialization of today's production, your works try to point out alternative models. In her 2005 book on Russian Constructivism, *Imagine No Possessions* (the title borrows from John Lennon), the art historian Christine Kiaer gives an account of the attempts to create a realm of utilitarian objects that would be free from the stigma of capitalism. Kiaer is not concerned with condemning the use of objects or tools, or the idea of decorating, or other aspects of object production *in toto*. Instead, she describes an attempt to reclaim the object and return it to the empowered users rather than marketing a fetish to manipulated consumers. This is a different kind of economy, and I think of it as a recurring motif in your practice.

1 These inspirations were noticeable in several installations exhibited by Paulina Olowska including *Dreams and Conflicts: The Viewer's Dictatorship. Clandestine*, 50th International Art Exhibition, Venice Biennale, curated by Francesco Bonami, Venice, Italy, 2003 (a travel agency); *Metaloplastyka*, Galerie Buchholz, Cologne, Germany 2005 (the Polish word "metaloplastyka" refers to small metal workshops in Poland in the 1970s and 1980s); and *Attention à la Peinture*, Galerie Buchholz, 2008 (a tailor's shop).

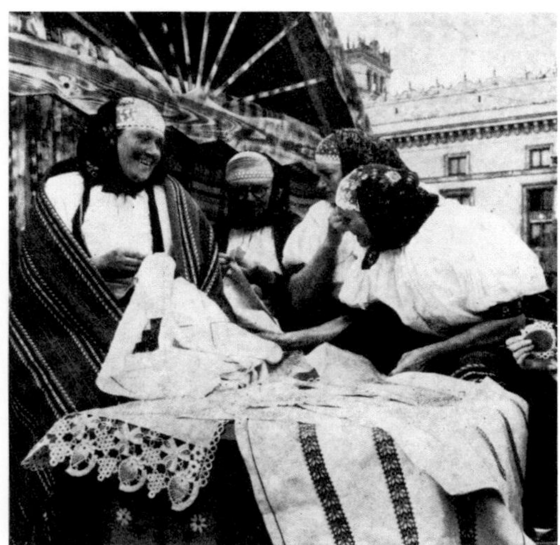

Talented embroiderers in Cepelia Festival in Warsaw, 1973, in *Piękno Użyteczne. Ćwierćwiecze Cepelii*, Warsaw 1975, p. 90

PO You are right. As in the sculpture to be sold for scrap, the forgotten technique of "metaloplastyka"—artistic metalwork—or the mosaic in the Azoty Plant. I am looking for situations where the object—be it a painting, an item, or a design for an interior—has been cast out to the margins of the mainstream and, in this way, deprived of its literally understood "value." Reduced to the role of useless junk, at best. Making it into a work, or a symbol, is what restores its value. I am fascinated by this process—this exceptional game in which the artist adopts an active role, while art becomes a field for retrieving lost meanings.

AS A solitary figure, facing or pointing at something, is another recurring element in your work. Quite as if it were calling to action. Such self-presentation—a form of basic performance—requires a great deal of courage, and holds the promise of activity.

PO You could say that it is a call in response to a call.

AS On the part of the degraded, crippled, and rejected forms that you attempt to reclaim and reinstate?

PO There is something of that. While speaking of modernism we said that I am not interested in its mainstream variant ... You could say that I am trying to modernize modernism in a modernist way ... After all, my works are not limited to revitalizing bygone forms. Essentially, they are an attempt at establishing a dialogue with the past. It is only natural that I should explore these fields that lost their voice to history or to the passing of time. It is enough to think of the massive political upheaval that swept through Poland and Europe in the 1990s—one of its side effects was the eager dismantling of all unwanted nostalgic forms that were seen as relics of the communist past. Metal work and ceramic mosaics, neon signs, and the characteristic design of folk-art-inspired goods marketed by the chain of Cepelia stores,[2] are all elements of that order.

AS Do you feel a particular connection with that fragment of history?

PO I prefer personal histories to History with a capital H. I'm also not a fan of any particular system or aesthetics. What is at stake here is a process that took place then: at the heart of that political transformation was its totalitarian character, its drive to supremacy in all possible fields, while leaving no trace of the past. I challenged this force and, as if to spite the mainstream, I retrieved objects and techniques that had been consigned to annihilation and oblivion.

AS This sounds like a political manifesto.

PO But manifestoes are typically preceded by action, whereas in my case it is the opposite. For me, art offers a way of facing reality in an intuitive way, which only becomes a theme once it is read by the audience. At the same time, I am happy to use such techniques as shorthand, as a contrast, and as modes of expression characteristic of political statements. In this sense, yes, my art happens to be a visual manifesto, a form of placard or poster. Anyway, I have already said that I try to make the form of my statements correspond to the content. And since the themes I address are slightly irritating in themselves—as they are repressed from the mainstream—so the way they are presented happens to be irritating as well: a bit haphazard, uneven, pieced together.

2 The Polish Art and Handicraft Foundation created in 1949 to promote and sell goods made or inspired by the work of Polish folk artists.

AS Is this the reason why you find the technique of collage so appealing? Collage as a structure seems to define many of your works, both two- and three-dimensional. Your paintings are quite often literally pieced together into a collage, and take actual collages as their point of reference.

PO Collage is an instantaneous and expressive technique, and I like its fanzine-like form that is based on associations. I am glad to use it in official contexts like, for instance, in the design for an invitation to an exhibition. Besides, I feel it somehow suits my temperament—I am an impatient person, so I try to deal with a subject quickly.

AS Collage is also a frequent feature of the punk aesthetic, which you evoked in the show *Neue Polnische Welle 1978–1986. Robert Jarosz Music Archive*, at MD 72 in Berlin (2008), where you exhibited a collection of DIY cassette covers with punk music.

PO What I wanted to show is an archive in which I see, perhaps naively, the world of creation, the making of things—the flipside of the rebellion and destruction that characterized the Polish alternative music of the 1980s. You could say that rebellion—as an approach—and utopia are the fundamental themes of my early works.

AS The collage as the language of rebellion, a symbol of creation that can be found in destruction ... Yet it seems to me that, in your case, there is more to using copies of photographs or paintings than simple cut-and-paste.

PO To begin with, tearing out and photocopying different photographs is the first stage of my work. Then, I put them together and observe how they influence and establish links with one another. I think that, for example, Pauline Boty worked in a similar manner.

AS So did Aby Warburg.

PO And of course there is Malevich, and his *Analytical Charts* from the 1920s—theoretical plates illustrating the relationship between the painterly perception of the artist and the surrounding environment. Malevich's theoretical plates awakened in me the need for my own set of categories. This was the intention behind *Accidental Collages* (2004). The work is exceptional in the sense of it being my own "autobiographical autopsy." It speaks about me, my surroundings, and the people around me, and the failure of a certain idea. I lived around the corner from modernism. I tried to breathe life into my surroundings, to create something vivid, using the best of modernist methods—most often, without success.

AS Objects, language, surroundings ... What else are you trying to breathe life into? Painting?

PO Absolutely. I am interested in the idea of the economy of painting—that is, conveying the maximum content as concisely as possible. To work on a painting is an intimate thing. My early canvases highlighted the dramatic aspect of female representations along with their attributes and references. When I was at the Academy [of Fine Arts in Gdańsk], I painted works based on movie stills from filmmakers such as Bergman, Fellini, and Hamilton. Then I became preoccupied with exploring the political aspect of human poses and the language of Socialist Realism. This was when I was looking for inspiration in

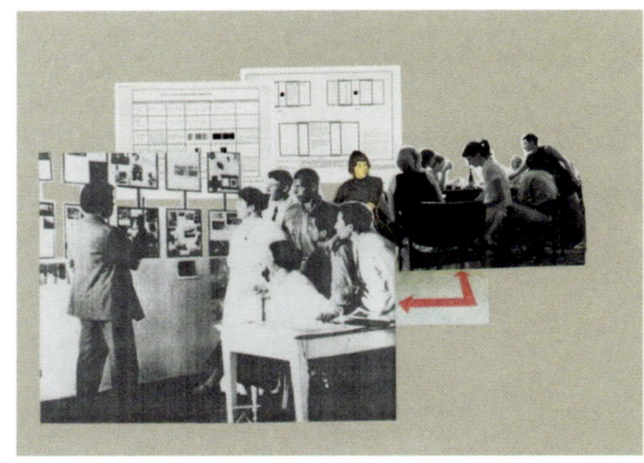

Malevich Class, 2004
Photo-collage, cardboard, 69.5 × 99 cm

illustrated magazines from the 1950s and 1960s, among them *Moda i Życie* and *Przyjaciółka*. A case in point here is the painting by Wojciech Fangor, *Figures* [*Postaci*] from 1950.

AS You were particularly interested in the magazine *Ty i Ja [You and I]*, which was addressed to intellectuals.

PO *Ty i Ja* was exceptional as it combined the spirit and style of the 1960s with a hands-off design—created by Roman Cieślewicz—and a provocative character. It went beyond the typical women's magazine format and toward an artistic hodgepodge.

AS What about other themes in your painting?

PO There was a period of loose reconstructions, one of the stages of my reflection on modernism that dates back to my stay at the CCA Kitakyushu in 2001. I transformed the lettering found in advertisements into small-scale abstract paintings, and applied constructivist forms onto the pages of the Japanese edition of *Vogue*. I made paintings that directly referenced the Bauhaus, the Russian avant-garde, abstract painting, and art theory—for example the book *Reconstructing Modernism*.[3]

AS Another figure that recurs in your work is the woman artist in her studio—either after or before making the work.

PO I am fascinated with stock representations of women artists at work. Here I mean such works as *Szapocznikow in Her Studio* (2001), *Bridget—1964* (2002), as well as *Untitled* (*Abakanowicz Working on a Tapestry*) (2001), and *Two by Empty Canvases* (2002). I was interested in how women artists position themselves in relation to their work, and how they are perceived by others. For instance, the painting *Bridget—1964* (2001) presents the British artist Bridget Riley posing in a black-and-white outfit next to her massive black-and-white canvases. You get the impression that she is being sucked in by the works. Or the Polish artist Alina Szapocznikow—frozen, before she gets down to work on her colossal bellies of marble.

AS In this particular photograph Szapocznikow props up her chin. It is a meaningful gesture. The motif of a head propped on hands returns in a number of your paintings.

PO Meditation, process, reflection ...

AS You might see it as a form of retrospective meditation in a rare moment of idleness—which has a special ring to it when talking of an artist as prolific as Szapocznikow. Skillful, efficiently working with a mallet, chisel, drill, or other tool in many other photographs, here we see Szapocznikow elegantly dressed, sitting on a chair, her gaze fixed upon the background of the composition—originally, the interior of her exhibition—which in your collage is the background of some other story.

PO Often, when I am working on an exhibition, there comes this decisive moment, a kind of intense focus that you can only find in weariness. I have a very emotional and physical approach to my work, which has to do with the exploration of limits—seeing how far I can go in becoming exhausted—and its results.

AS One of your works mentions the word "convalescence," fatigue ...

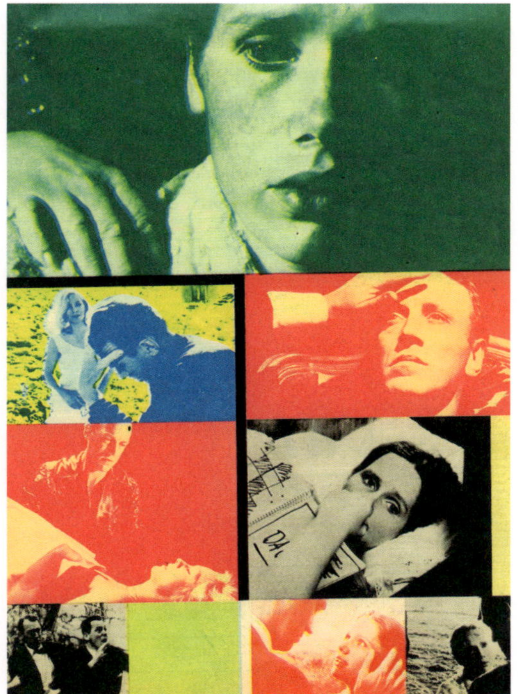

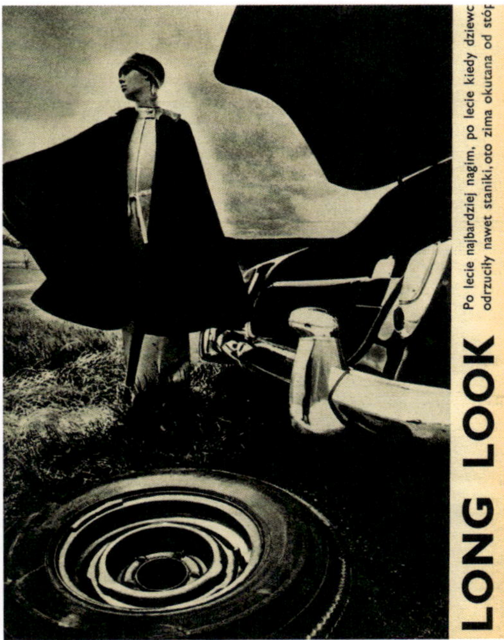

Ty i Ja, Polish magazine, 1969

3 Serge Guilbaut, *Reconstructing Modernism: Art in New York, Paris, and Montreal 1945–1964*, MIT Press, Cambridge, Massachusetts, and London 1990.

PO That would be the painting *Convalescent*, after James Tissot (1836–1902).

AS It seems to me that you are, in fact, interested in the dynamics of opposites—such as illness/convalescence. On the one hand, this condition is seen socially as abnormal, yet potentially valuable, capable of expanding the means of expression or the experience of a collective. On the other hand, you have convalescence—a process of return or of being caught in-between.

PO There is a stereotypical image of the restless, efficient artist. But what I consider more genuine and captivating is a situation in which the artist crosses the border and requires a convalescence—due to which, things do not seem so obvious. Despite being exhausted and in pain, with turpentine-itchy eyes, the artist can get no rest because of the haunting images that give rise to restless thoughts. Because the artist's thoughts are so obsessive.

AS This reminds me of the American artist Lee Lozano (1930–1990) and the *Wave Series*, her crowning achievement as a painter, after which she never returned to that genre again. Reading her notes and writings, you can learn that she tried to complete a painting in a single sitting, throughout which she was constantly on drugs. The number of waves grew with each consecutive painting, based on a mathematical formula she adopted. And as the paintings became more and more strenuous, the artist became weaker and weaker—and, in consequence, more and more stoned. She planned to paint a wave with 128 undulations on a canvas exactly the size of the one she used for the first panels, where the line undulated no more than twice. Then it became evident that this would be physically impossible, and the work did not go beyond a drawing. She was not able to make it into a painting not only because of technical complexities, but also her physical exhaustion, which is nothing like the theater of effort of a male artist painting an expressionist canvas.

Her exhaustion, just like the exhaustion of the women artists we have mentioned, has a neurotic character, it is inscribed into the creative process, or drive, as an inherent part of it.

PO Such a neurosis—a protest in the face of compulsion—I wanted to express this in the painting *X* (2002). It is pieced together from two images: Lady Pink in the subway, and the figure that in my alphabet stands for the letter X. The X-shaped person has lost its original red color—the character hides her face with her hands in a gesture that says "Enough!" You could say she looks rather as though she is up against the wall, as in a line-up. The background is rather vulgar.

AS Or would you say defensive?

PO Possibly … Anyhow, continuing my exploration of women artists at work, I came up with projects focusing on the manipulated female portrait. These include the paintings *Provocative* (2002), *Stripteaser* (2005), images and objects from the show *Salty Water/What of Salty Water?* (2007, Portikus, Frankfurt), as well as paintings from the exhibition *The Revenge of the Wise-Woman* (2011, Foksal Gallery Foundation, Warsaw).

AS The idea of revenge, or a symbolic vengeance for artists who were forgotten, degraded, rejected, etc., is not accidental in this case.

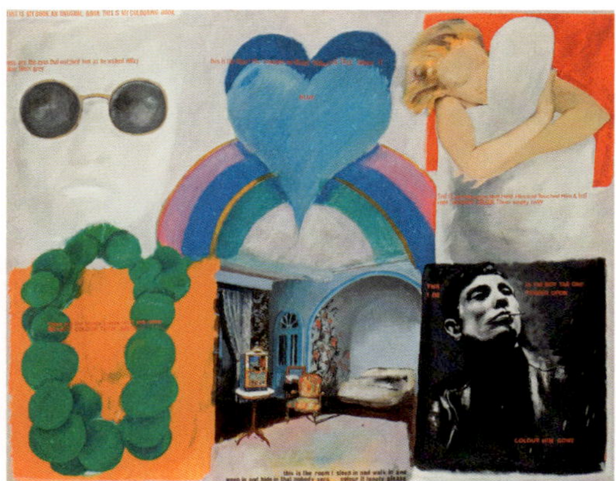

Pauline Boty, *My Colouring Book*, 1963
Oil on canvas,122 × 152 cm
Muzeum Sztuki in Łódź Collection

PO Taking revenge on the demon of history lies in recovering the suppressed themes ensnared by conventional interpretations that are out there to be discovered. In this way I stir things up—plotting, making a mess, shifting positions, trying to reexamine the existing models of thinking. My muses undergo a metamorphosis: women workers, crane operators, rebels of all sorts, avant-garde artists, suffragettes and prostitutes, eclectic minds and specters.

AS The list of liberated female characters you took an interest in is indeed diverse.

PO Mad women and women on the edge, women whose unusual expression was incomprehensible—which was precisely what made them fascinating. Zofia Stryjeńska, Alina Szapocznikow, Pauline Boty, Evelyne Axell, Eva Hesse. Their works seem to defy reason. At times, they are "awkward objects," as Szapocznikow referred to her works. The historical readings of these artists' output are often banal or fraught with fallacy.

AS What is your idea for correcting them?

PO In the case of Stryjeńska, it was a work of mapping—documenting the attempts at understanding her and learning the way she worked. By repeating her style, I tried to distill her method. The exhibition *Hello to You Too* (2006), on the other hand, was a tale revolving around Pauline Boty and some aspects of her practice that I find especially interesting—the motif of the awkward gesture or playing with codes. Imagine a neoclassicist room where like minds meet: Virginia Woof, Vanessa Bell, Charlotte Perriand, Nina Hamnett, Romaine Brooks, and a couple of anonymous women.[4] They meet to share their stories, or I should rather say "her story," that of Boty.[5] By inviting them I hoped to confront their autonomous identities, which rebelled against convention and created the avant-garde.

AS What prompted you to focus on Zofia Stryjeńska, one of the most clichéd figures of Polish modernism?

PO With Stryjeńska, I was surprised by how distorted the public perception of her art actually was. The popular idea about this artist was that Stryjeńska took commissions to produce applied art, and that her interest in folklore bordered on infatuation. Whereas what I saw in her works was a certain ambiguity, a complexity of visions and representations, an anticipation of future aesthetics, as well as a deeply feminine perspective on human relations, and an erotic, mythological metaphysics. Her biography, on the other hand, involved issues as fundamental as the artist facing the tension between her own art and its relationship to the society of the day.

AS Stryjeńska embodies the type of artist who is independent, tragic, and labeled as bordering on kitsch …

PO To a certain extent she is the victim of a stereotypical, simplified reading that I hope to change for good.

AS What else are you trying to avenge? The exhibition *The Revenge of the Wise-Woman* took its title from a painting by Francis Bacon—which was photographed by Norman Parkinson with a female model standing next to it. There is a certain malice in the way this poor twisted wretch of Bacon's on a stool contrasts with the charm, openness, and self-confidence of the woman in the foreground of Parkinson's photograph.

4 Paulina Olowska is referring to Hélène Cixous' seminal text from 1975, *The Laugh of the Medusa.*

5 Paulina Olowska organized this "meeting" in her exhibition *Sie musste die Idee eines Hauses als Metapher Verwerfen* (She Had to Discard the Idea of the House as a Metaphor), Kunstverein Braunschweig, Brunswick, Germany, 2004, bringing together images of the writer Virginia Woolf (1881–1941), her sister the painter Vanessa Bell (1879–1961), the architect and designer Charlotte Perriand (1903–1999), their fellow Bloomsbury bohemian Nina Hamnett (1890–1956), and the American painter Romaine Brooks (1874–1970).

PO Malice? I would rather say this photograph illustrates the triumph of fashion over art. This woman uses Bacon's painting as wallpaper. She is the contemporary witch. Besides, I prefer to see this painting in terms of a mise-en-scène …

Untitled, 2006

AS How about another starting point for your painting *Emmy Hennings* (2011)?

PO Being a poet and a prostitute out of choice, Emmy falls well within the tradition of border-crossing women. On the other hand, it is said that she brought an aura of mysticism and spirituality to the circles of the Cabaret Voltaire.

AS It is a rather extraordinary painting. An existential portrait with your own freaky alter ego that is, to a certain extent, under control, yet is still presented in a moment of ceasing, or consideration—a suspension of action. This is also where you deploy another of your typical devices. Tell me about the moments in your paintings that are left incomplete, as if they have been painted slapdash, where the background seems to be showing through, or certain elements seem unfinished. Why is this lack of finish important?

PO This is the effect of exhaustion, a fatigue that comes as a natural part of the painting process.

AS So exhaustion helps you either to extract or to highlight something from the original image or photograph. You only focus on what it is that you find interesting, rejecting things that are an unnecessary waste of energy.

PO Such deliberate fragmentariness in my canvases also questions the traditional thinking of a painting as something finished. For instance, *Cigarette Break* (2006) is an example of a deliberately unfinished painting, an actual break for a cigarette. While paintings from the exhibitions *Metal Work* (2005) and *Attention à la Peinture* (2008) were built from my old canvases that were cut and, at times, turned inside out or flipped to the other side.

AS Every now and then you collaborate with other artists.

PO Yes, in a number of ways. I believe that art is, above all, a sharing of experience. I collaborate with others because it inevitably brings a change of style and emotion, as well as a division of work—both physical and intellectual—which is a healthy thing. I think that collaboration belongs to the model of "emergence"—in my case, it is typically based on the very natural need to address a specific subject collectively. [6]

6 Paulina Olowska is referring to Bonnie Camplin's lecture at Foksal Gallery Foundation, Warsaw, entitled *Witches Brew—Subjective Emergence Where Theory Is Manifested In Practice*, 2011.

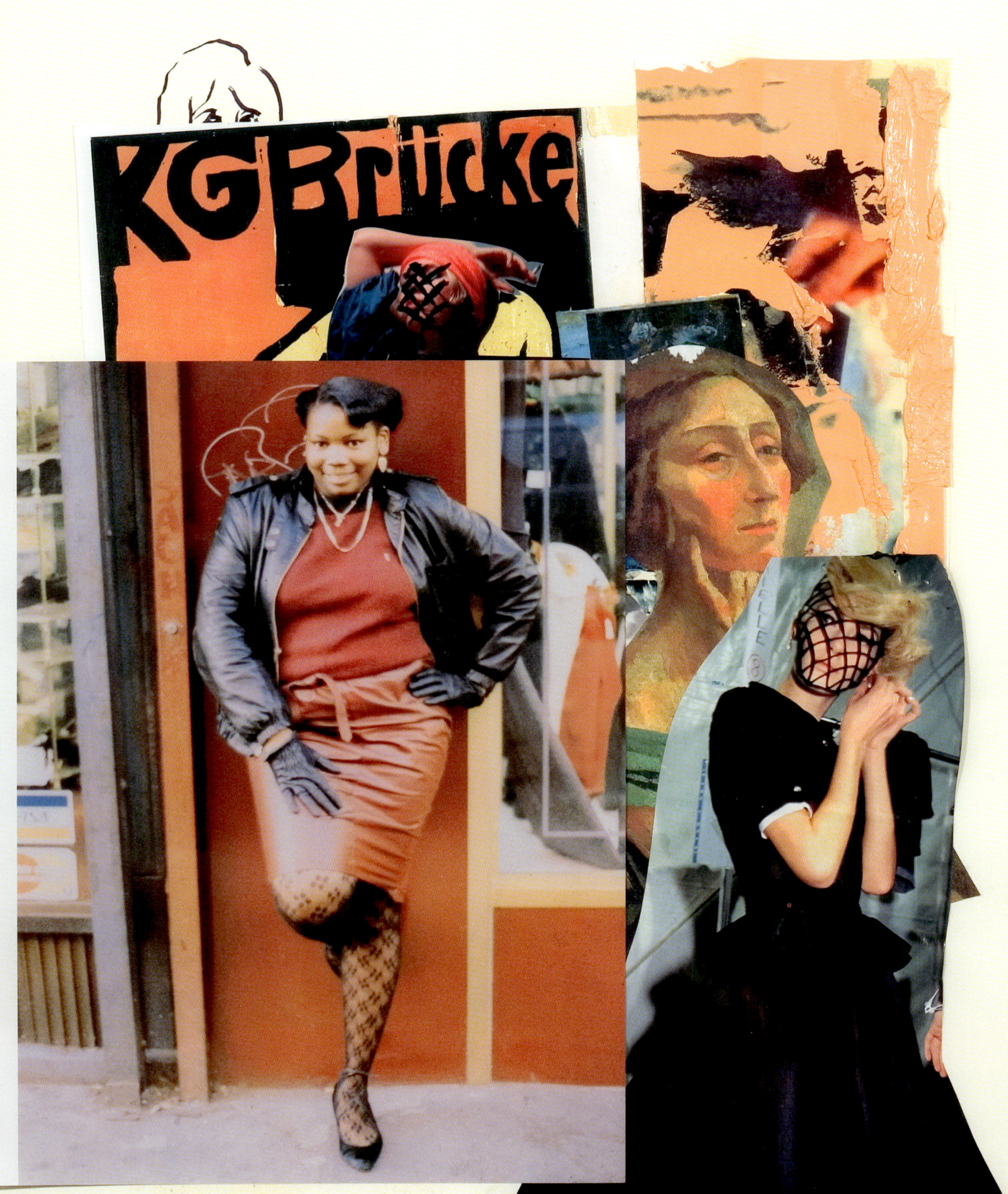
KGBrucke

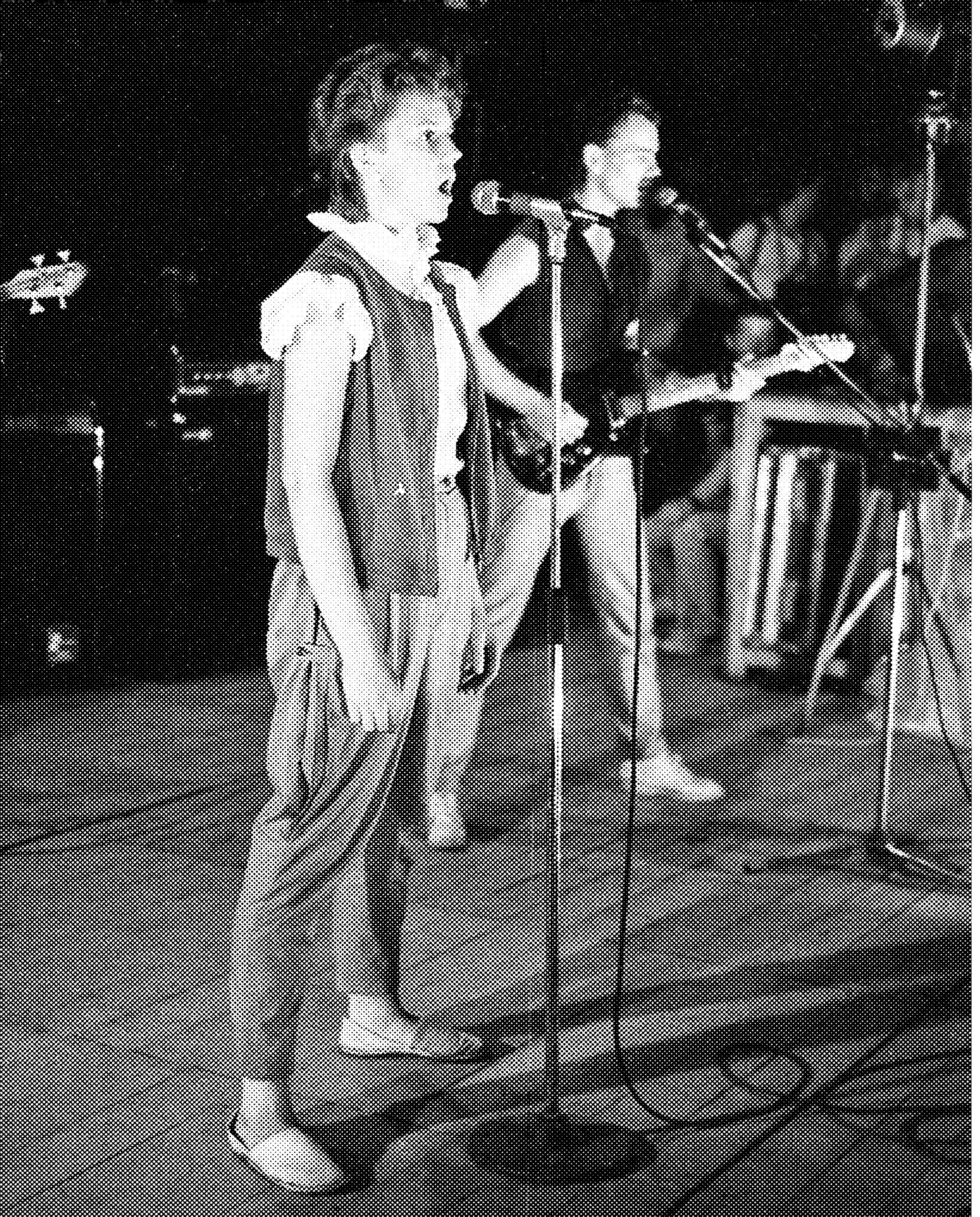

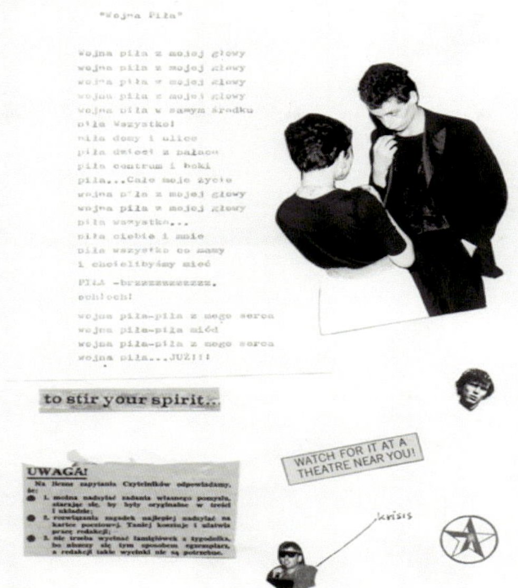

From left to right
Ryszard Gajewski, Kontrola W., Jarocin Rock Festival, 1983
Andrzej Amok Turczynowicz, *Untitled*, from *Kanal Revue*, a fanzine collage, 1981
Neue Polnische Welle 1978–1986. Robert Jarosz Music Archive, exhibition view, MD 72, Berlin, 2008

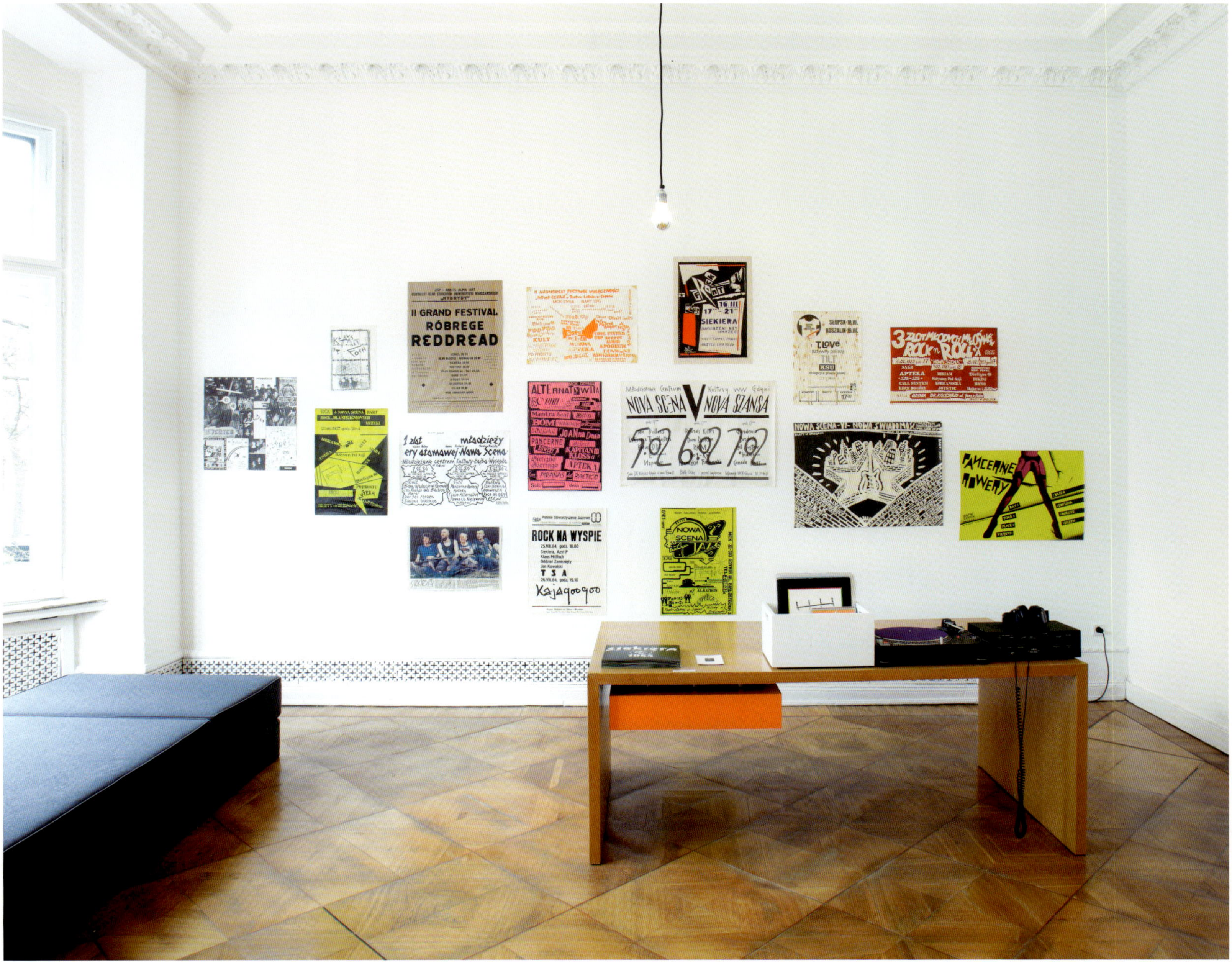

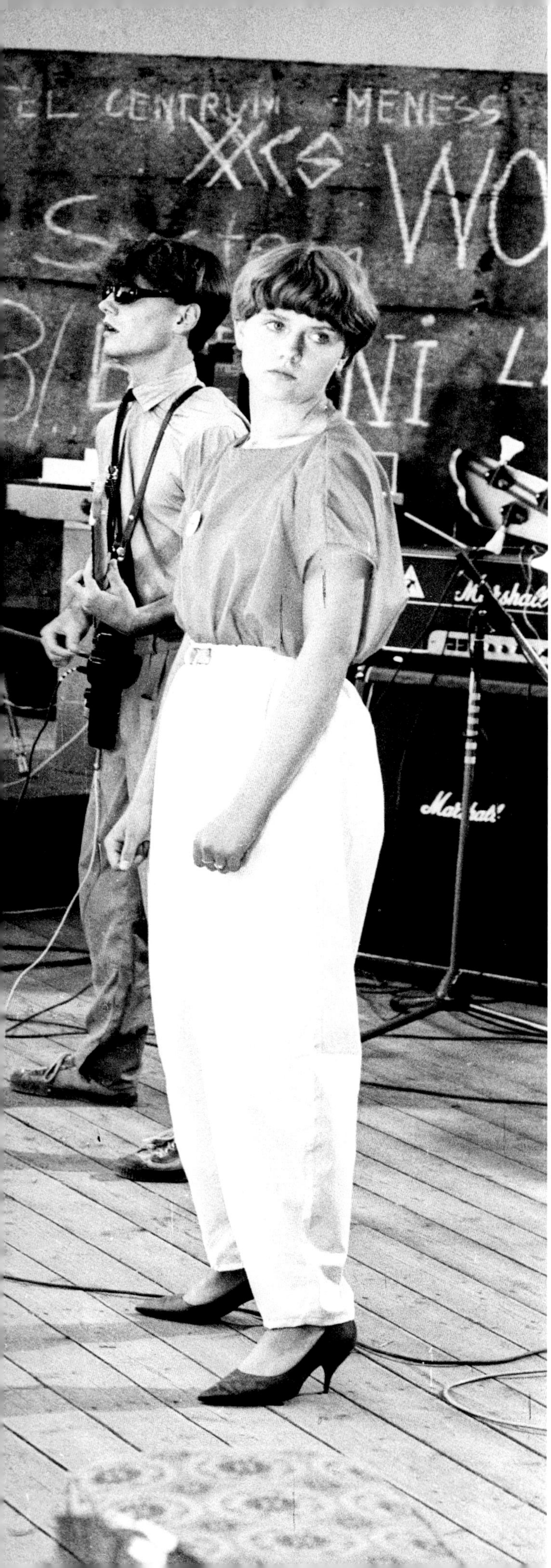

From left to right
Jacek Awakumowski, Kontrola W., Jarocin Rock Festival, 1982
Ryszard Gajewski, Kontrola W., Jarocin Rock Festival, 1983
Neue Polnische Welle 1978–1986. Robert Jarosz Music Archive (after M.R. Makowski), exhibition poster, 2008

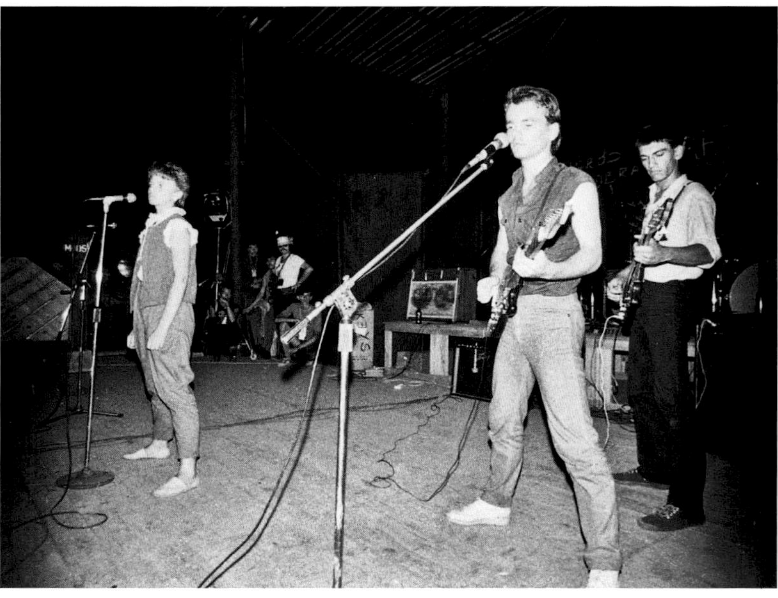

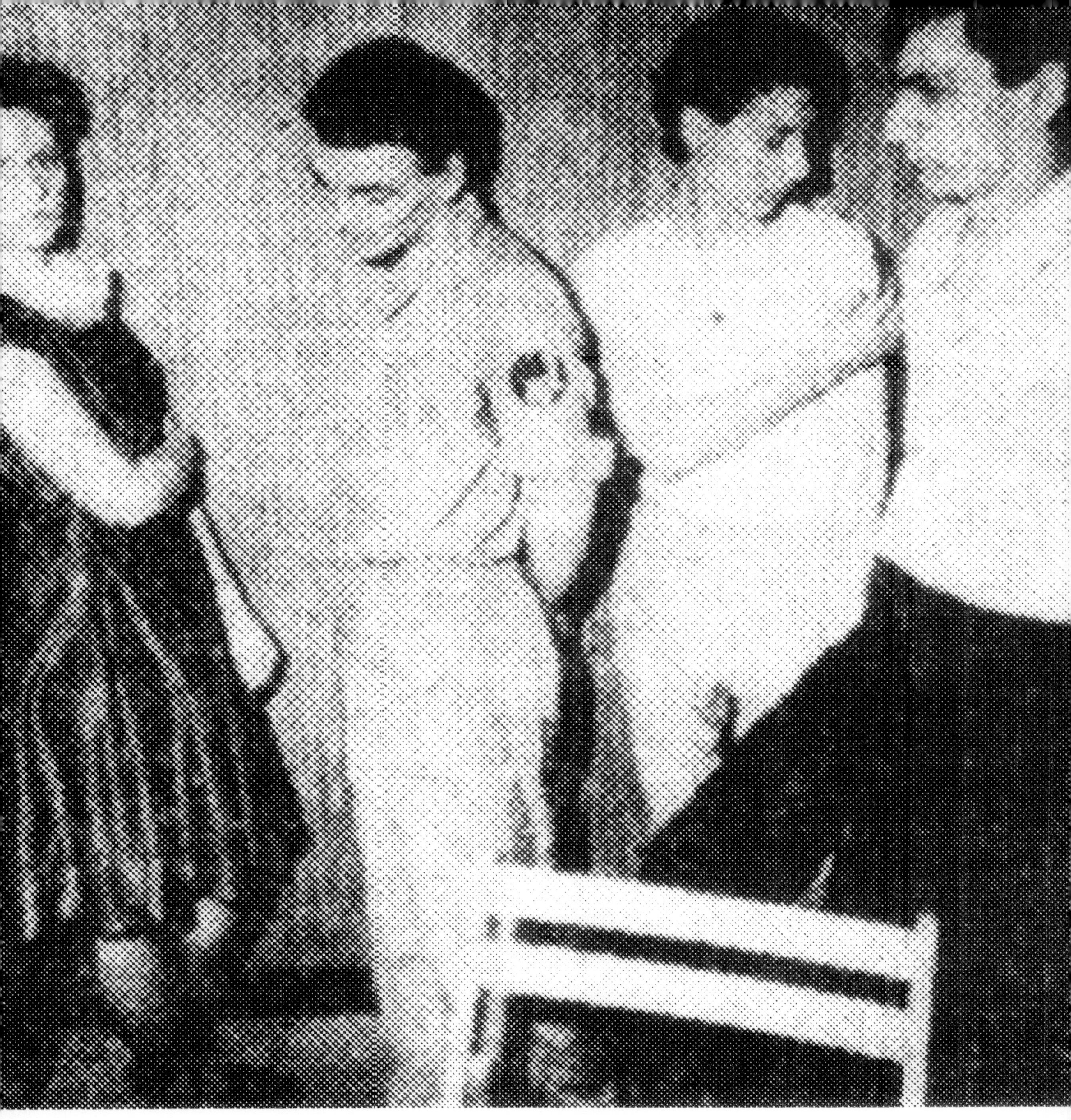

...tilt,siekiera,
madame,kosmetyki mrs.pinki,
armia,

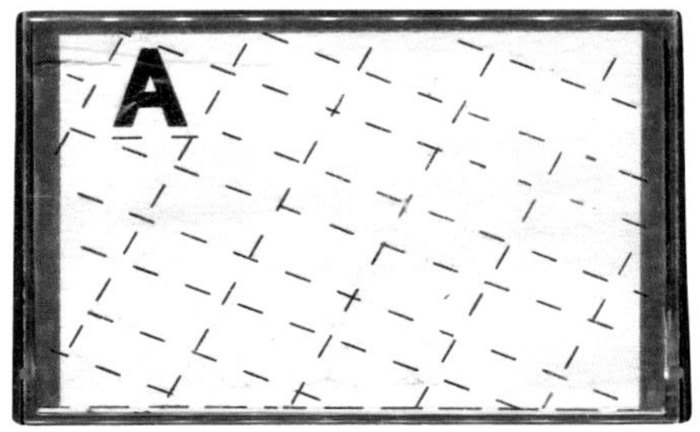

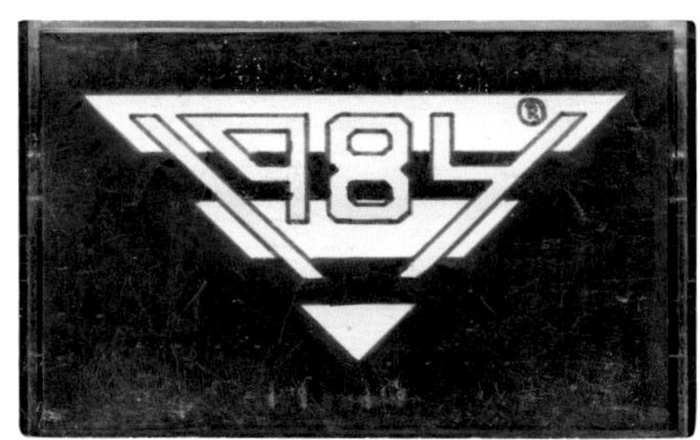

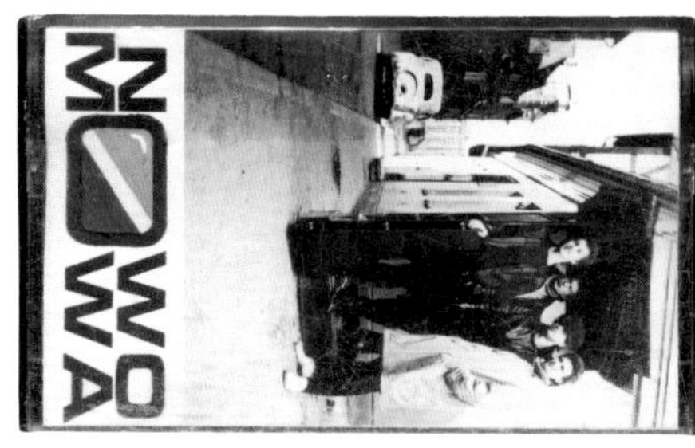

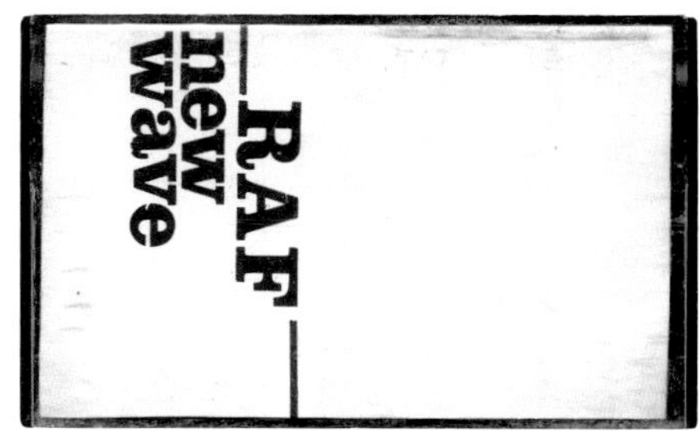

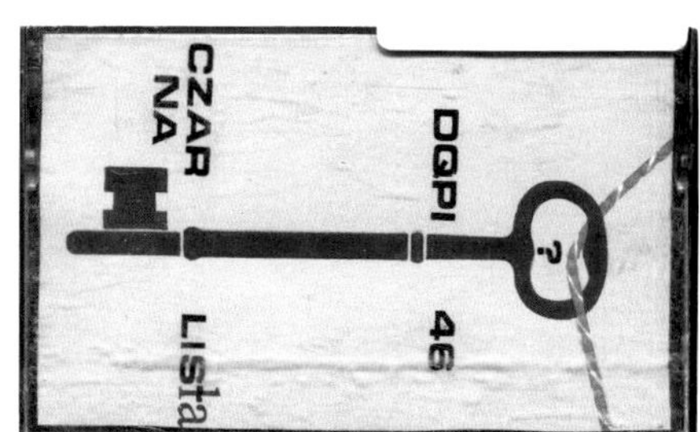

Handmade cassettes sent by bands to the Jarocin Rock Festival, 1980s
Neue Polnische Welle 1978–1986. Robert Jarosz Music Archive, exhibition view, MD 72, Berlin, 2008

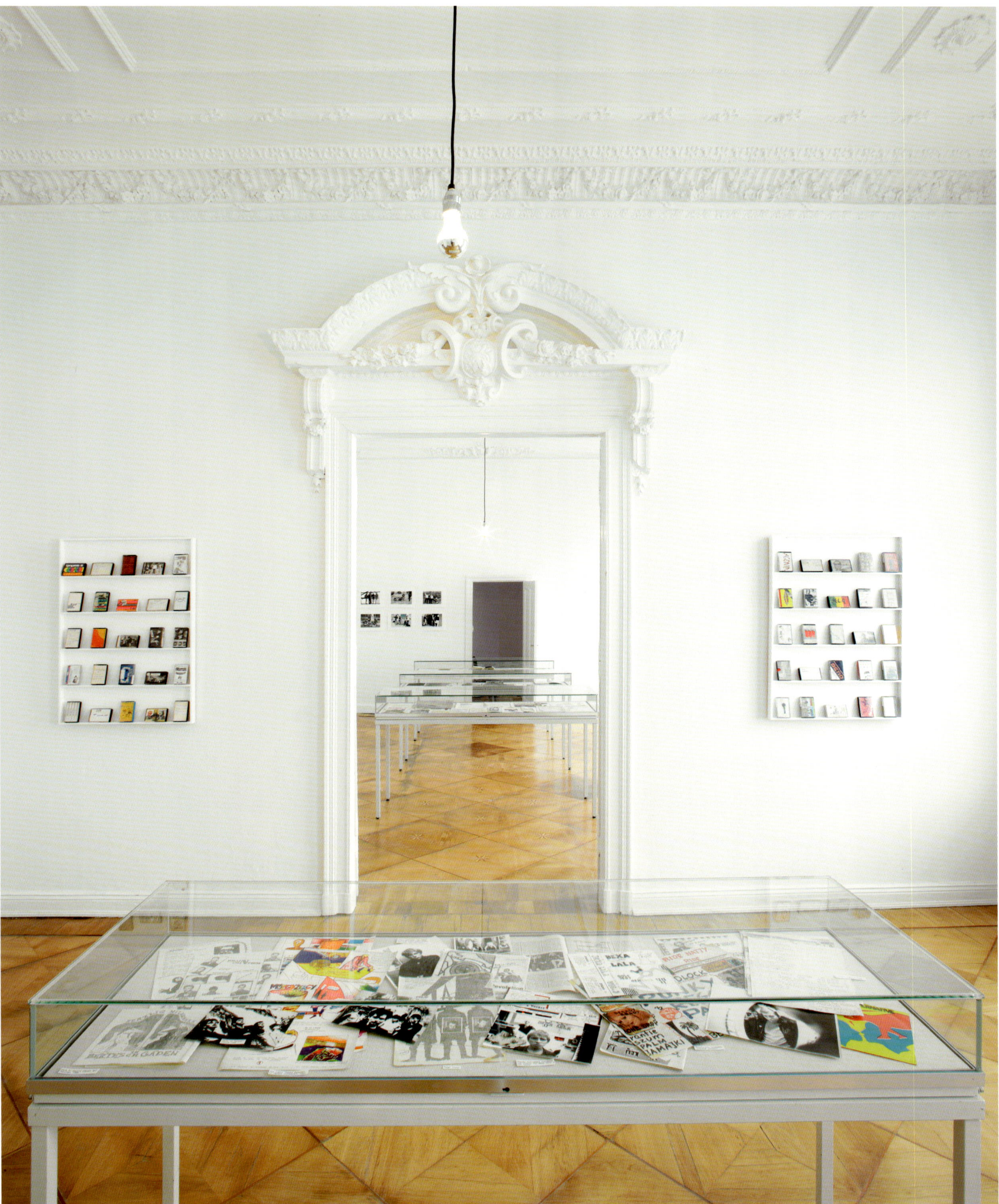

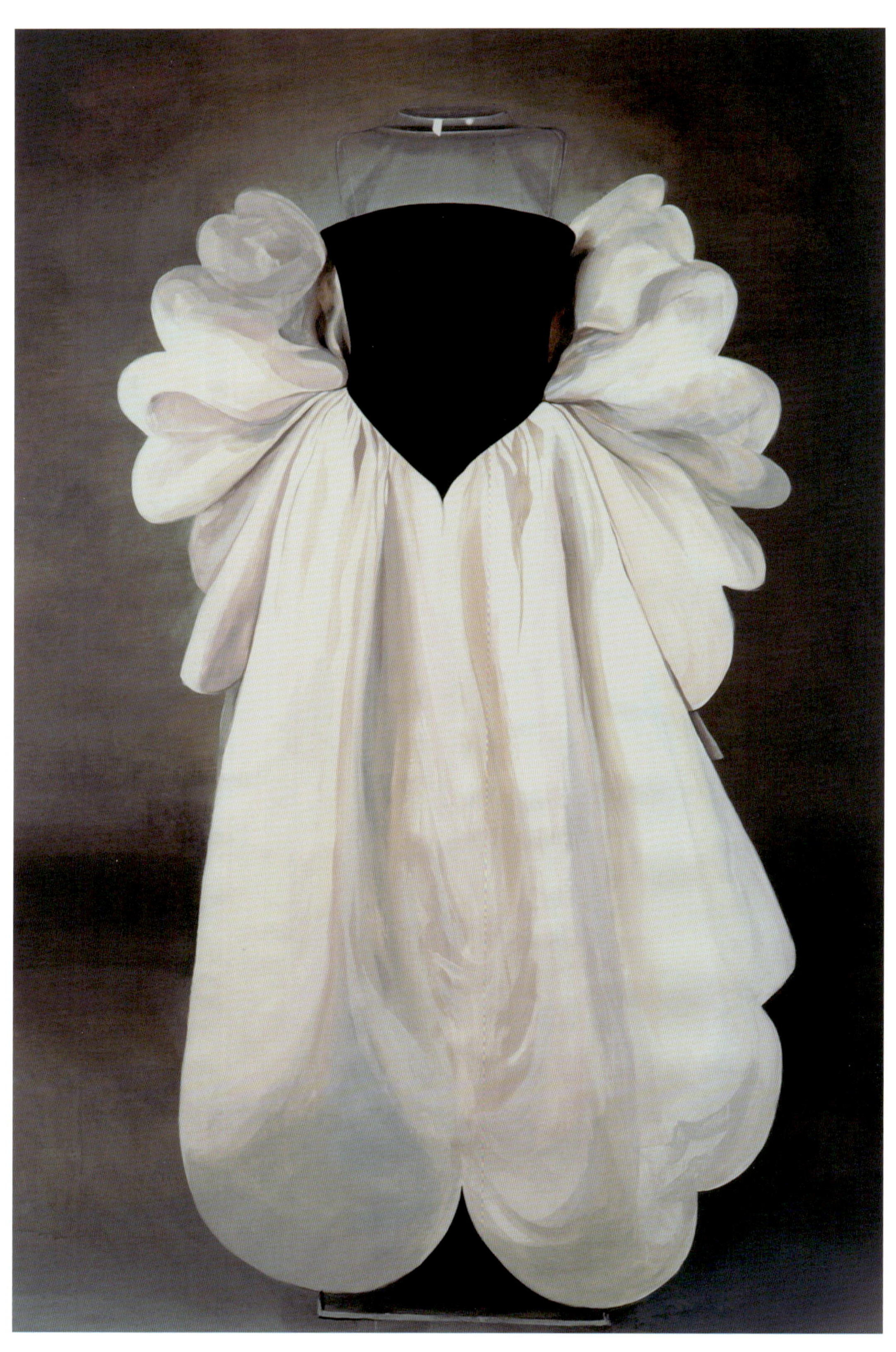

Abendkleid, 2008
Rock, Bluse und Hut, 2008

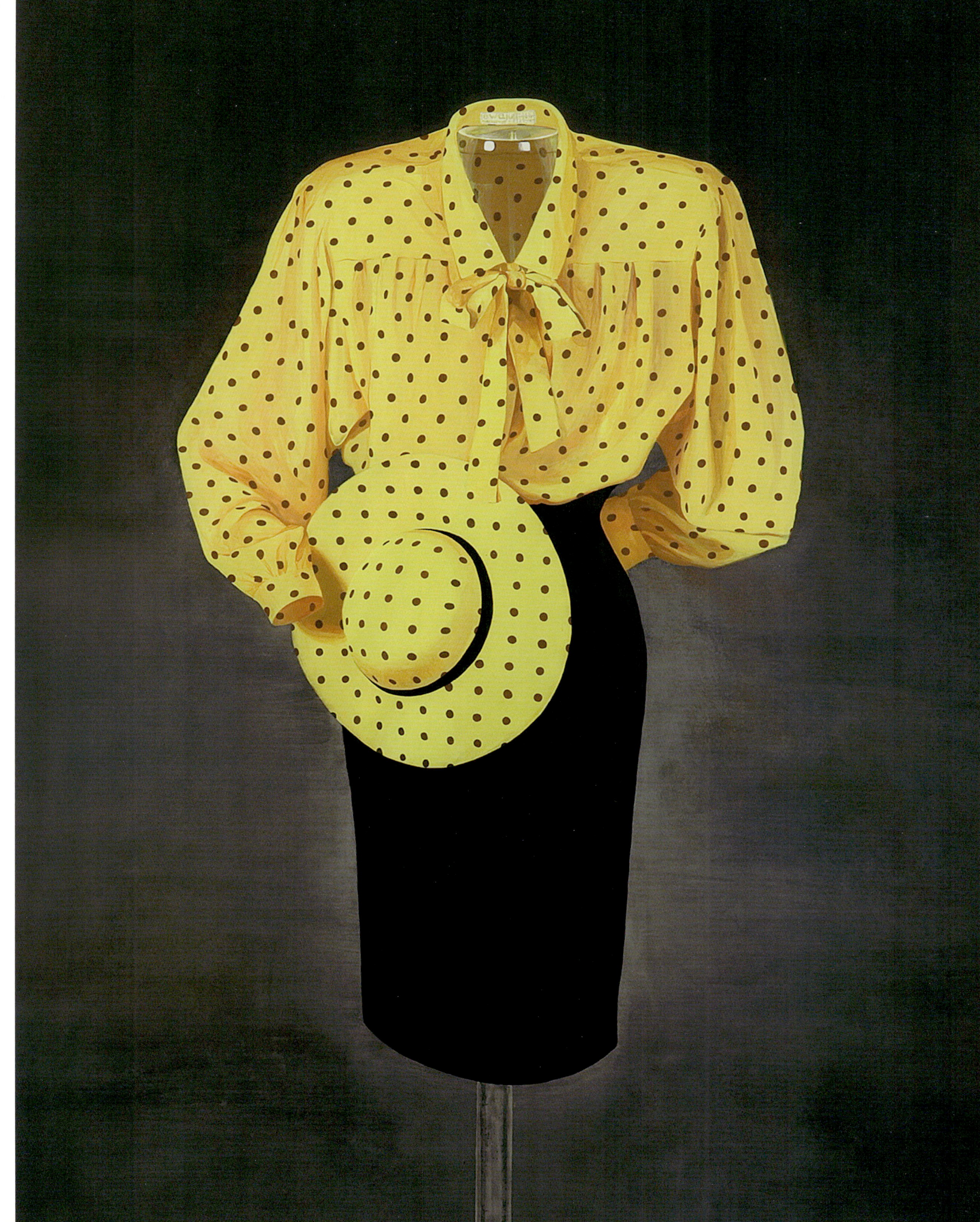

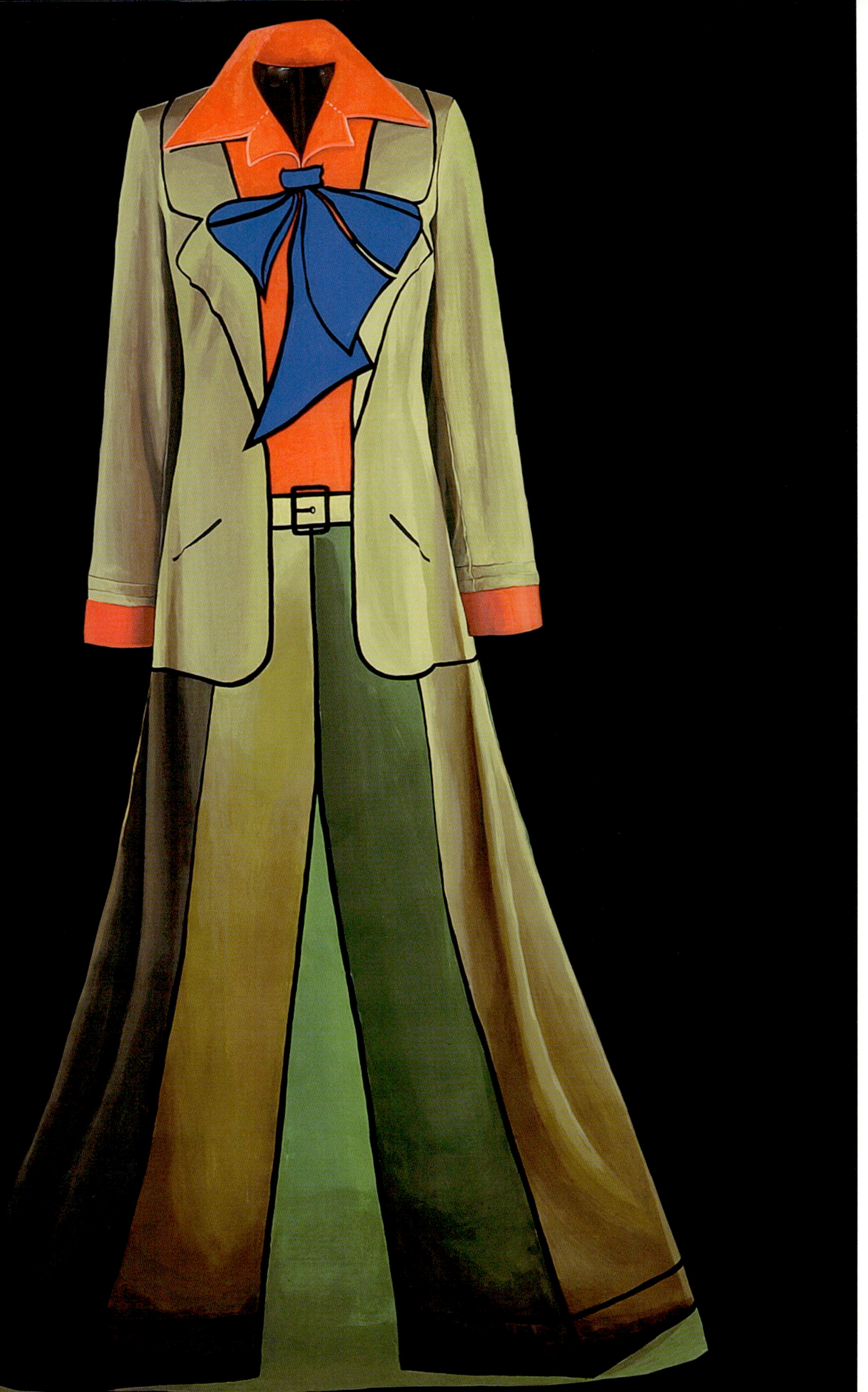

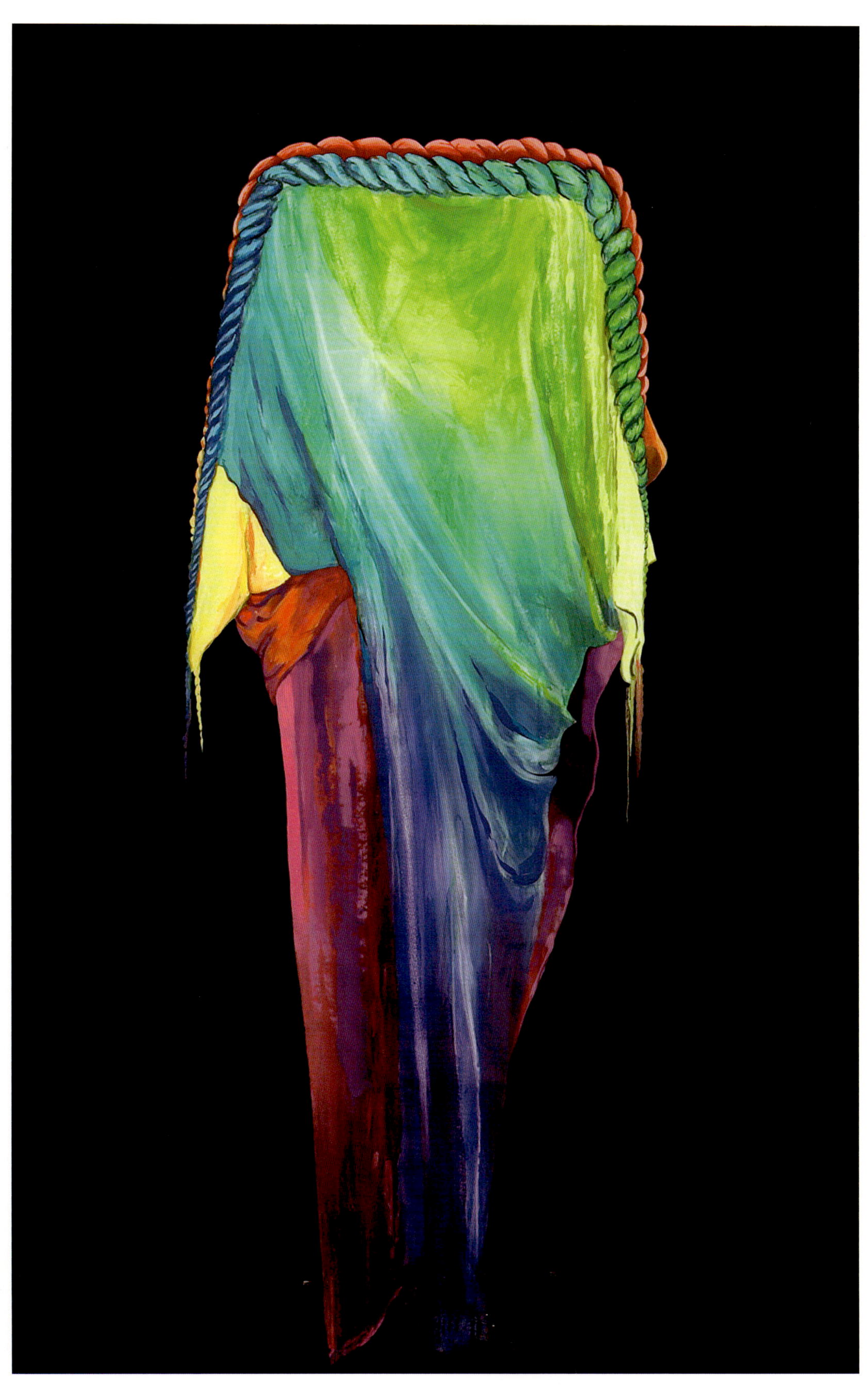

Party-Kleid, 2008
Festliches Gewand, 2008

Attention à la Peinture, exhibition views, Galerie Buchholz, Cologne, 2008

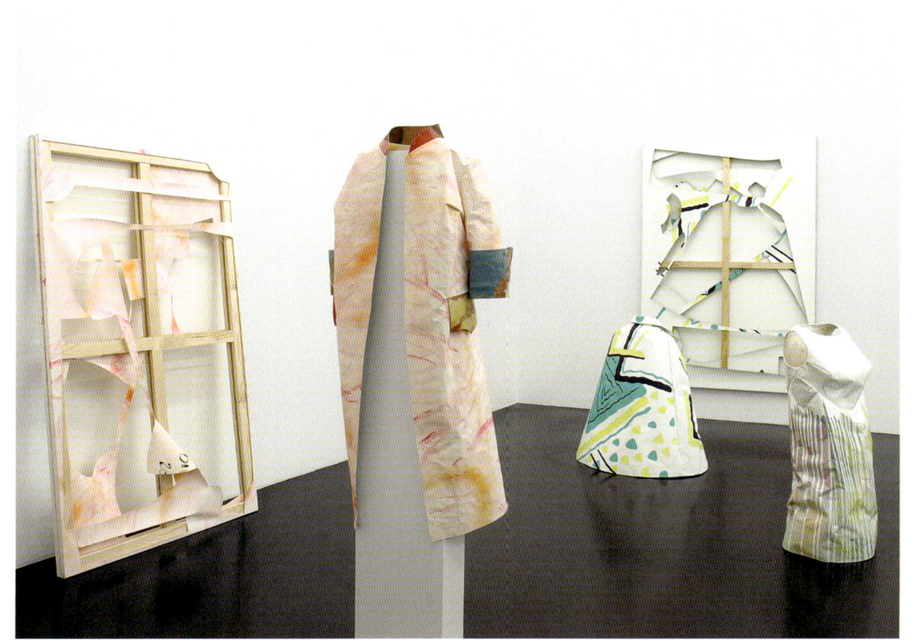

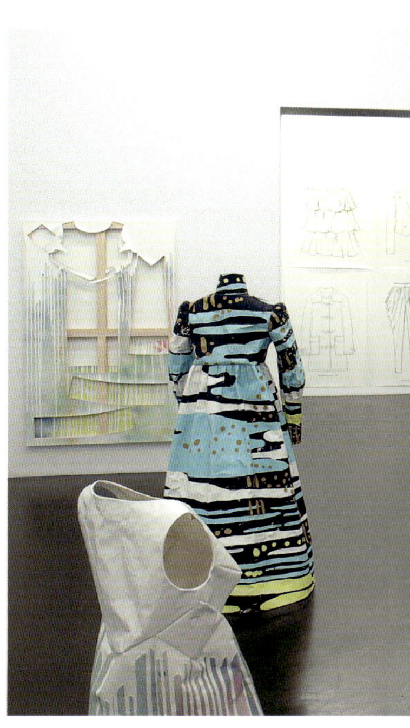

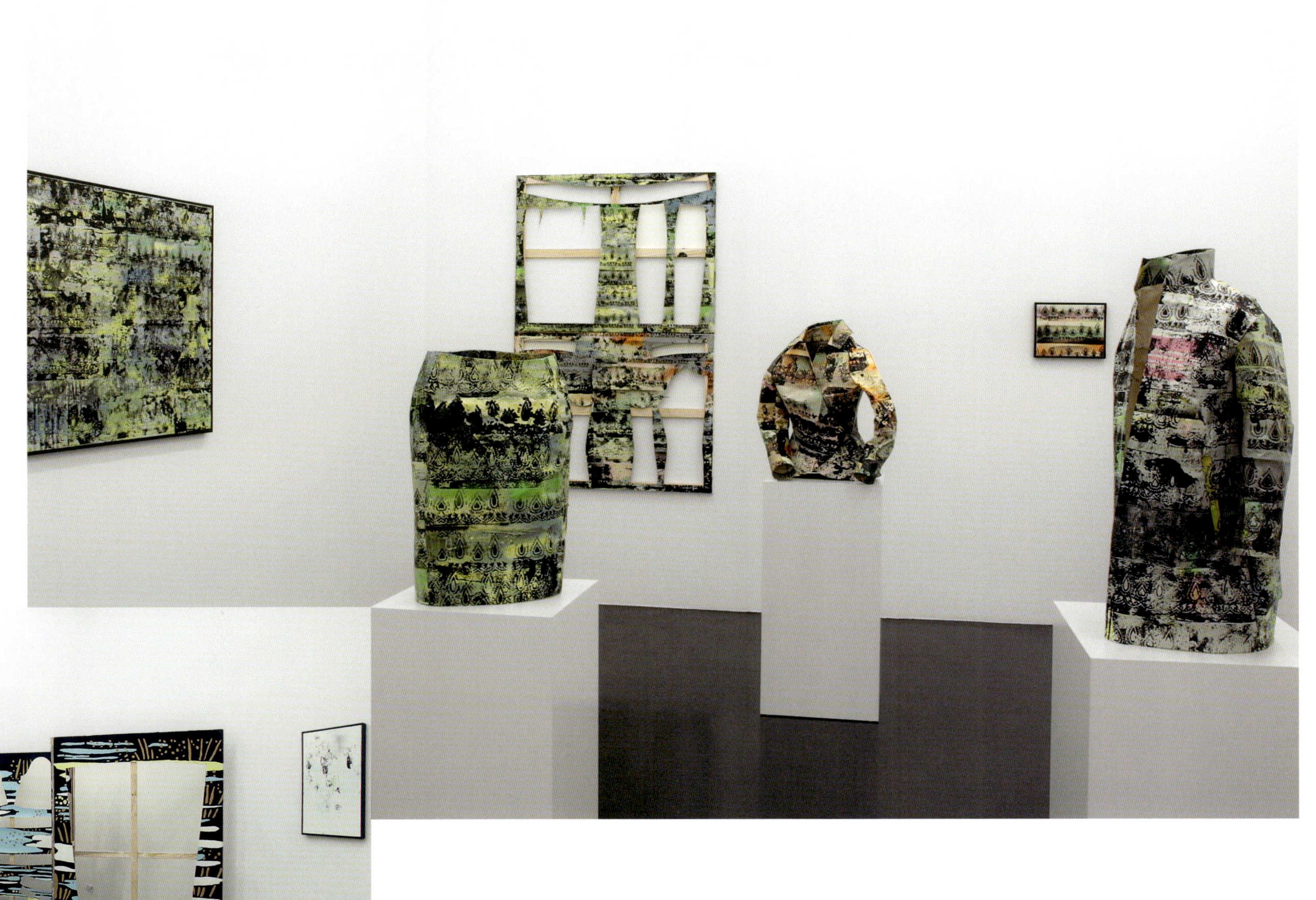

→
Zofia Stryjeńska, exhibition view, Neue Nationalgalerie, 5th Berlin Biennale for Contemporary Art, 2008

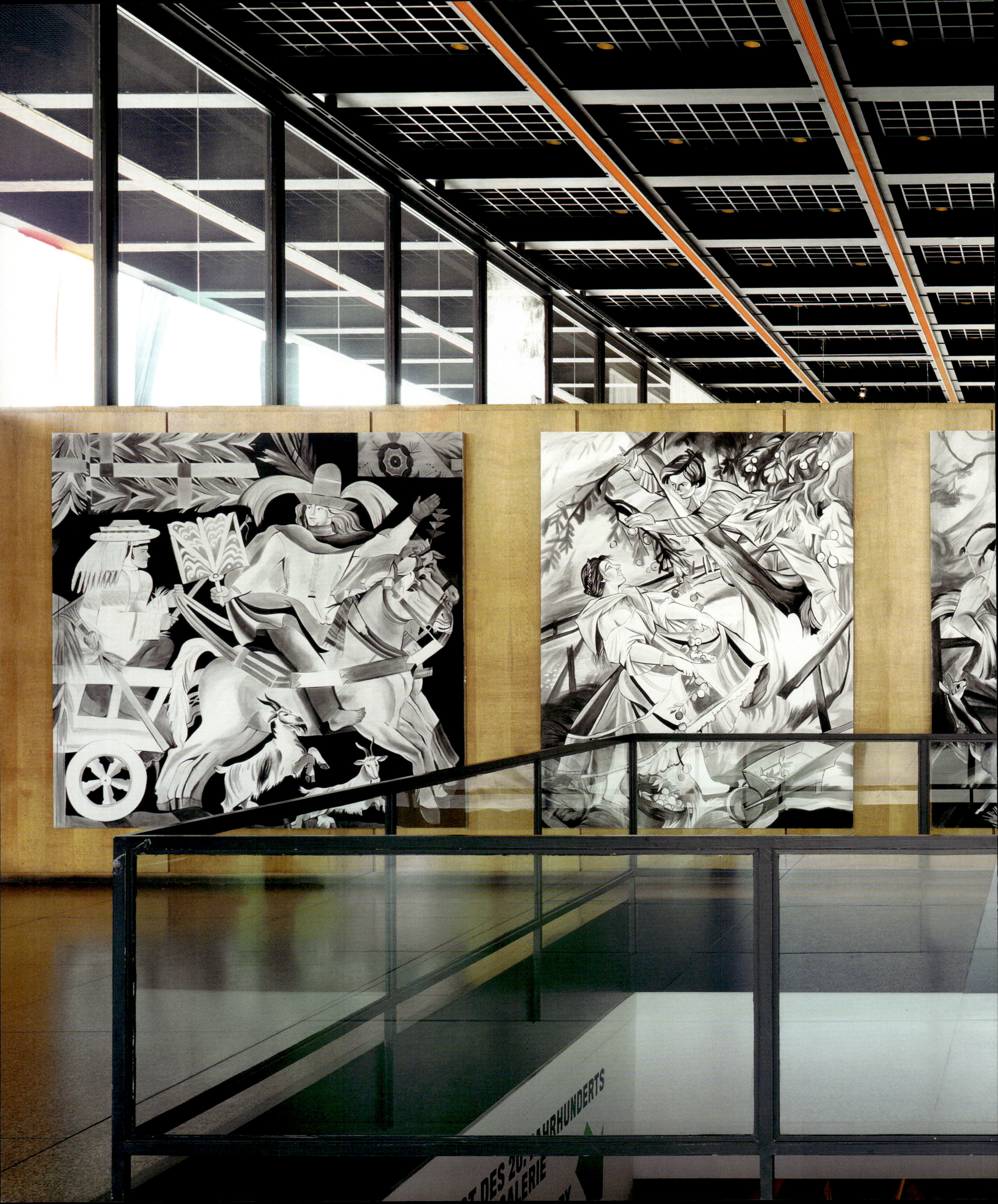
DES 20.

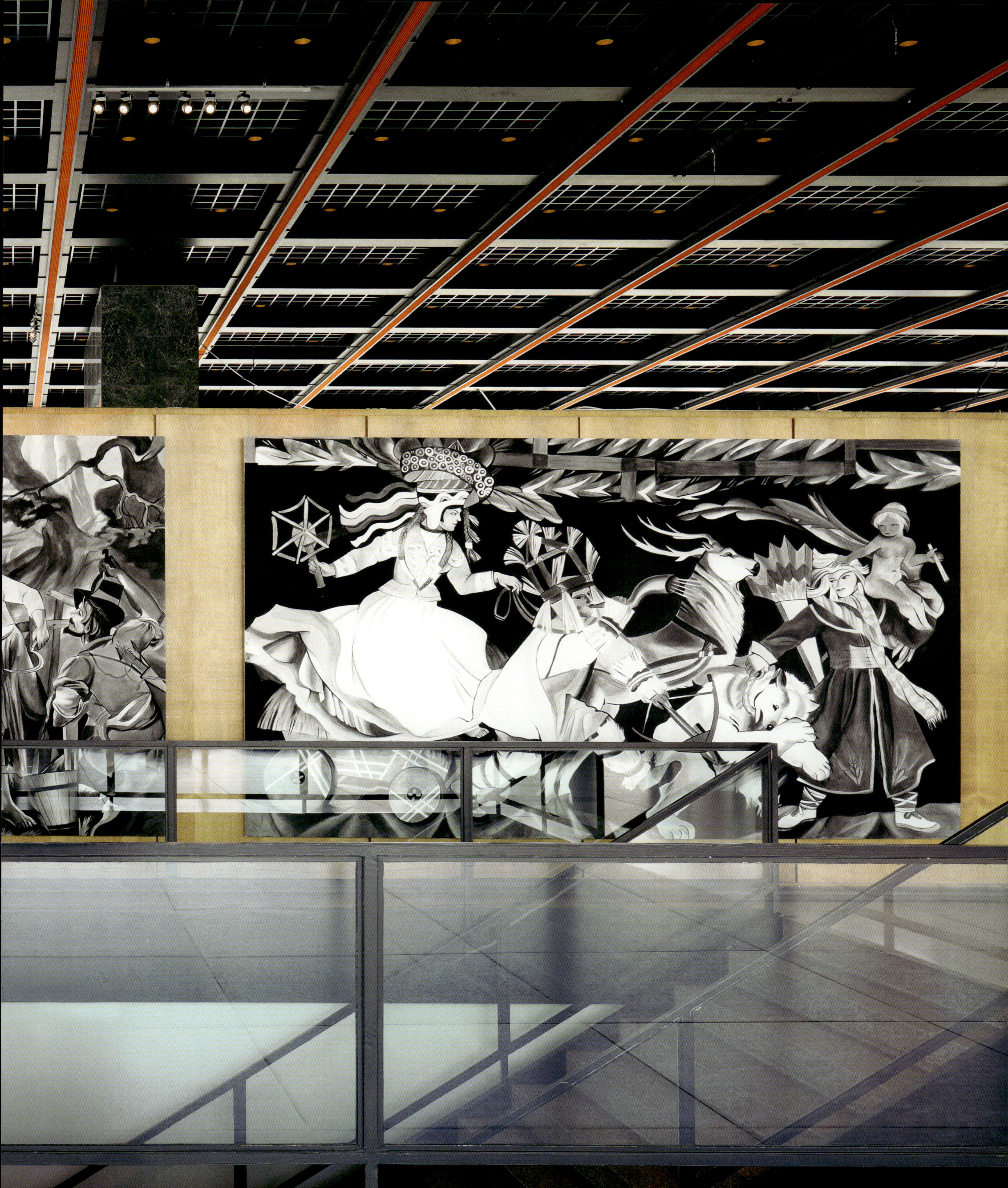

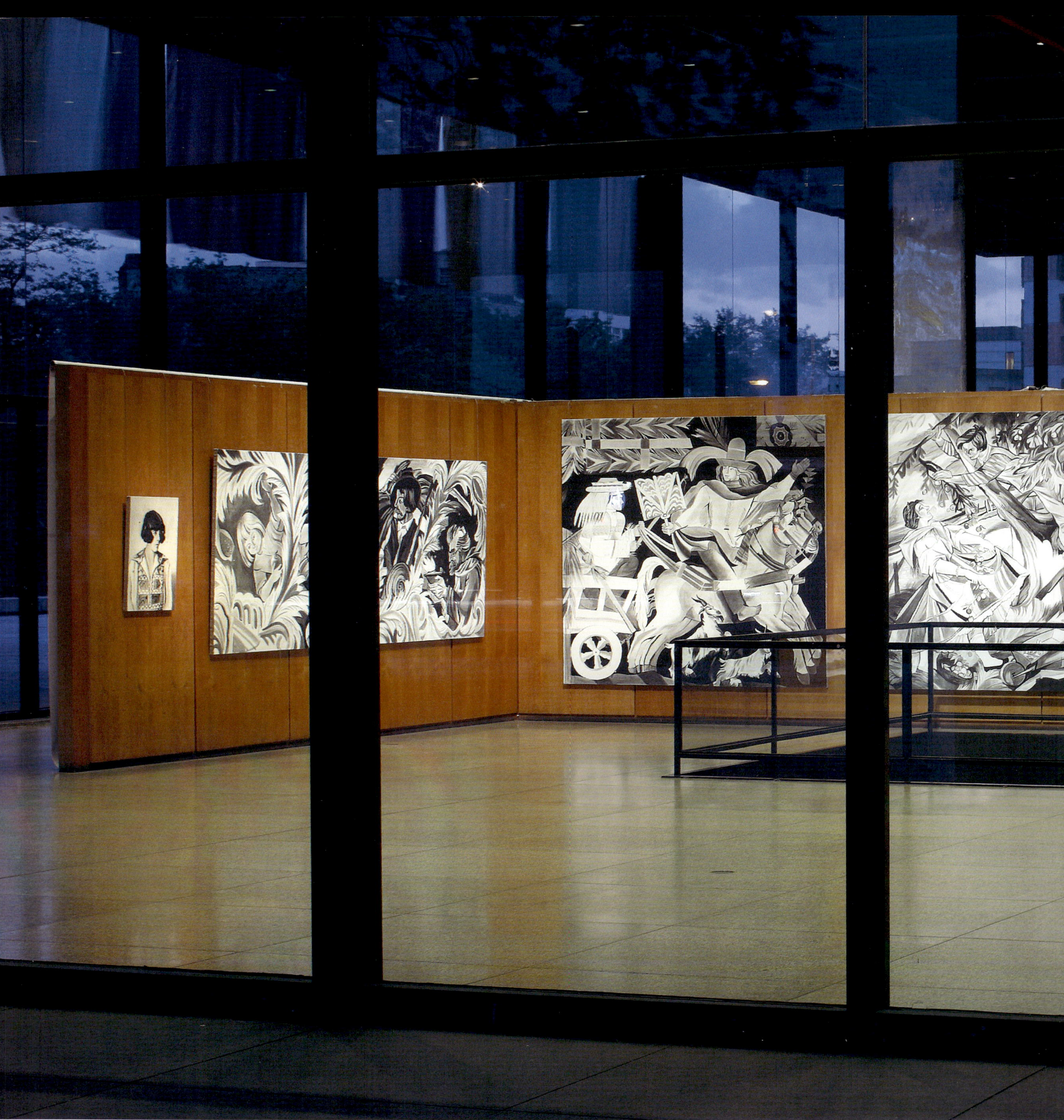

Zofia Stryjeńska, exhibition view, Neue Nationalgalerie, 5th Berlin Biennale for Contemporary Art, 2008

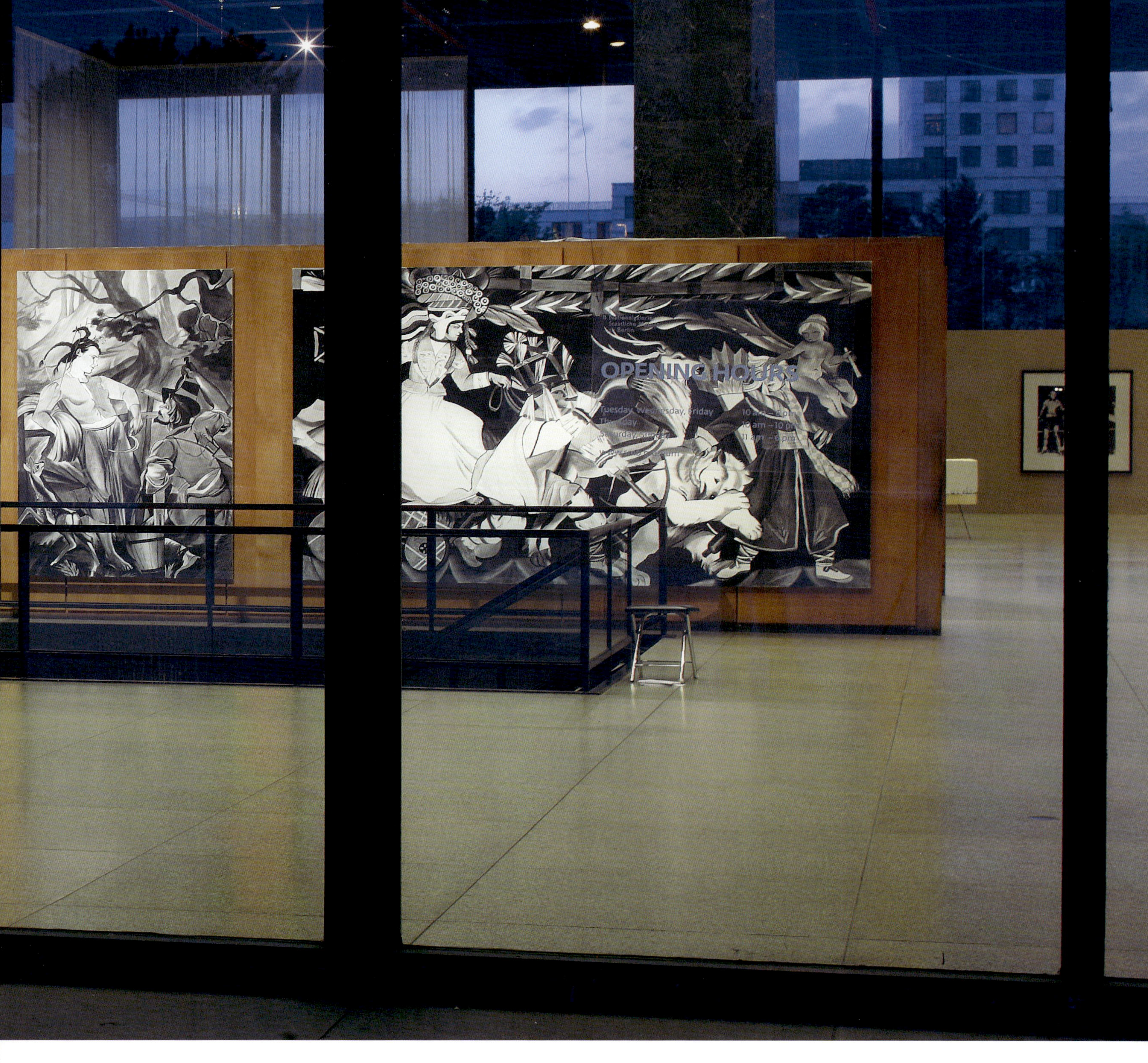

→
Zofia Stryjeńska, exhibition view, Schinkel Pavillon, 5th Berlin Biennale for Contemporary Art, 2008

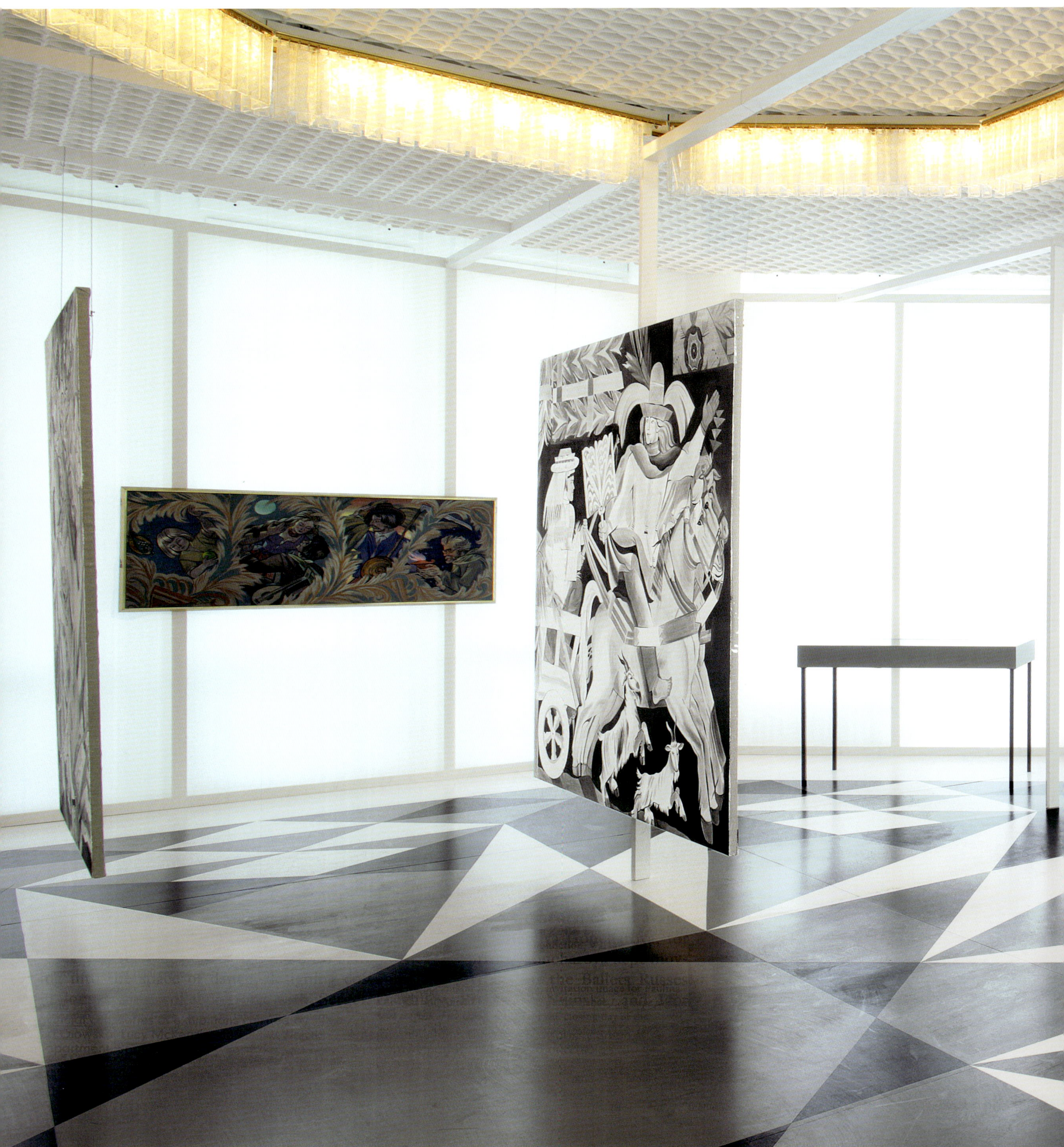

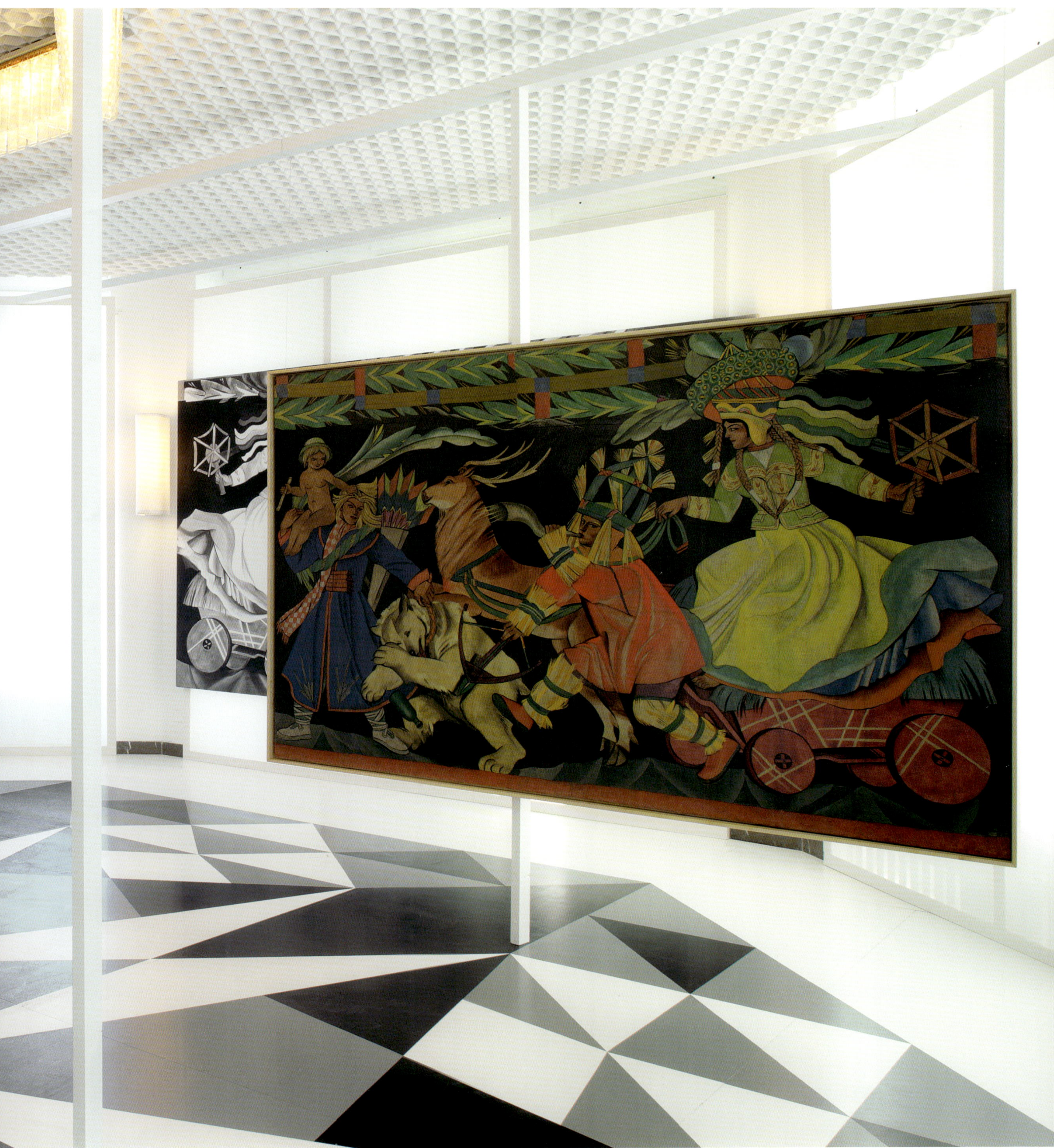

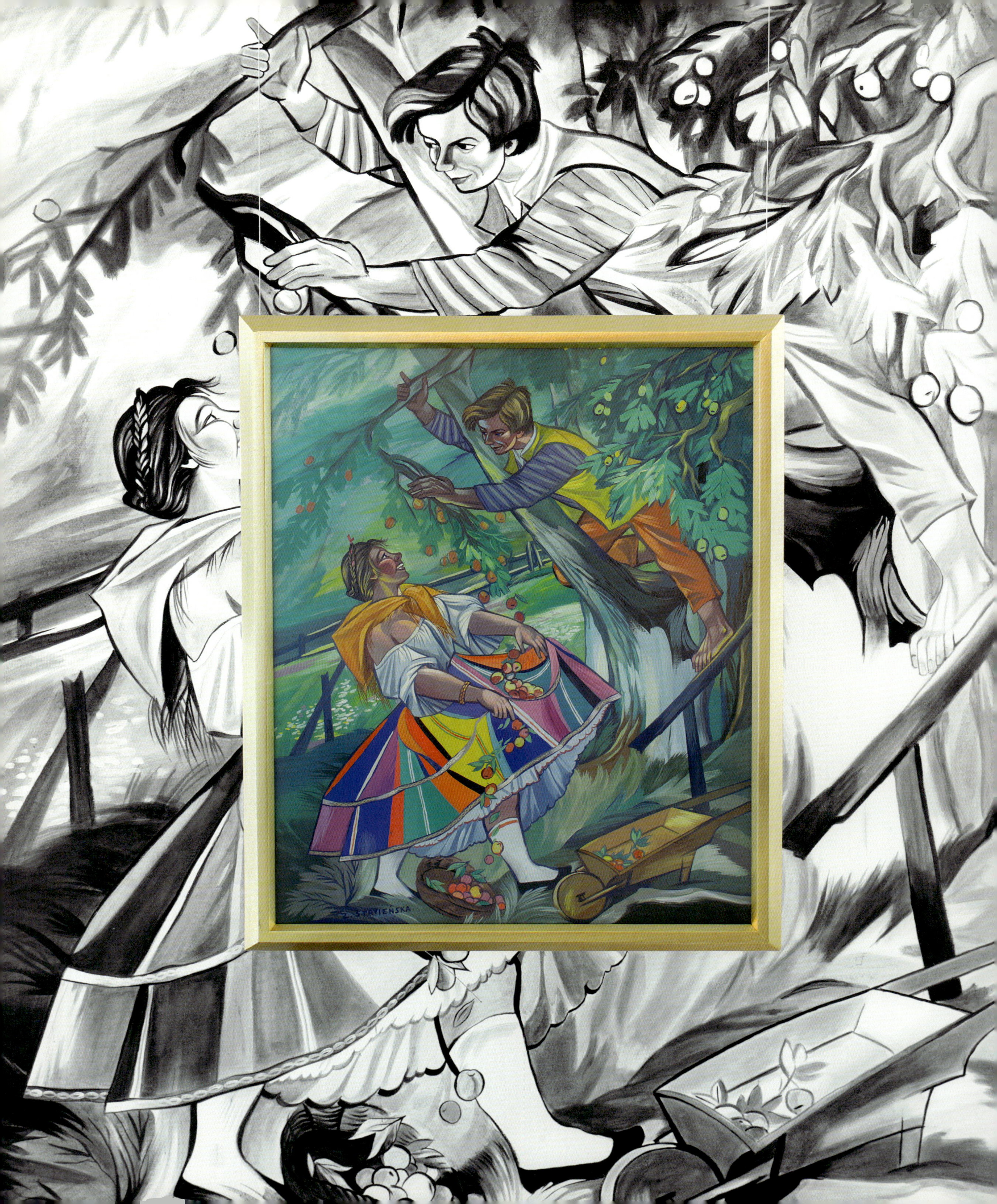
Z. STRYJEŃSKA

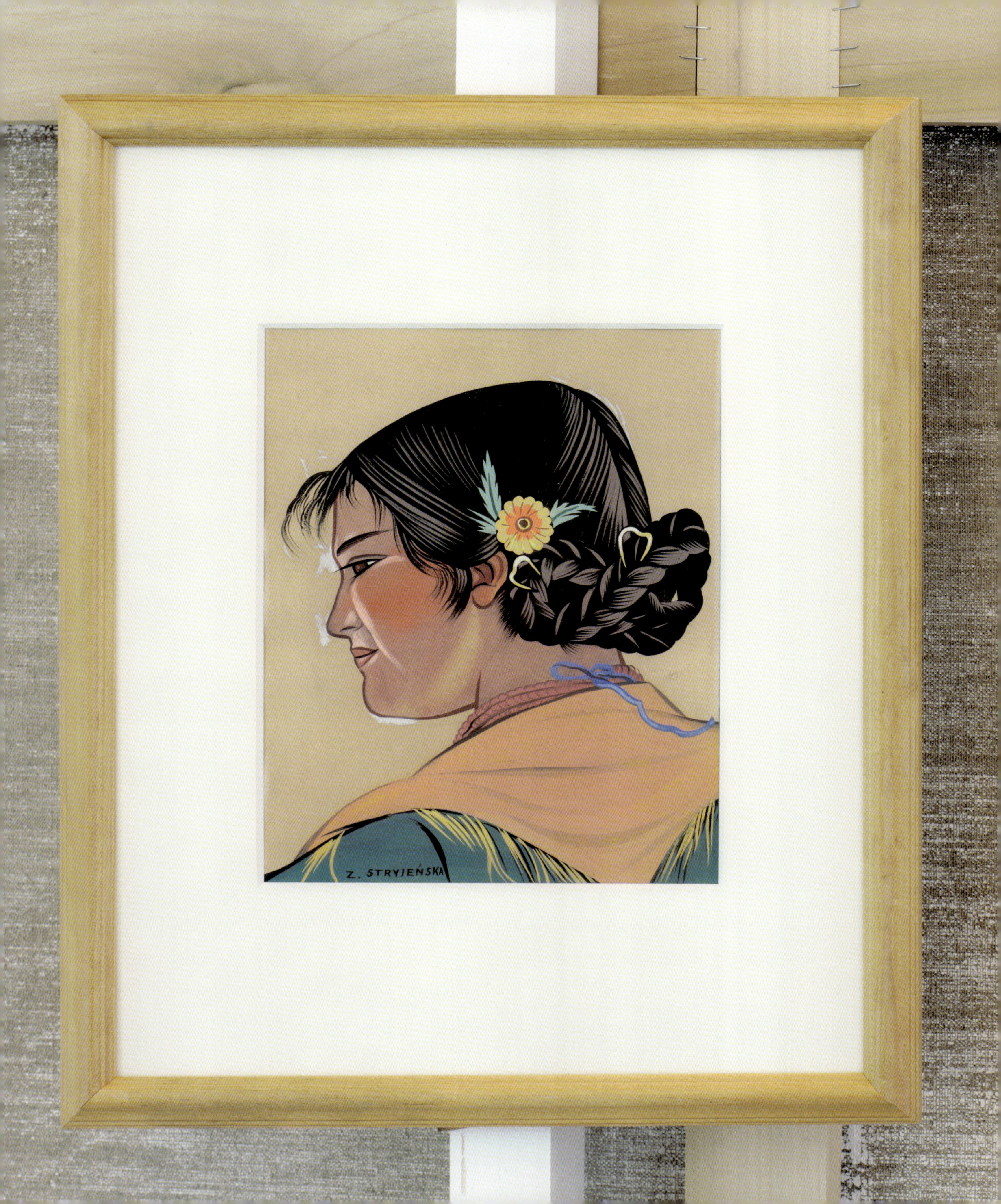
Z. STRYJEŃSKA

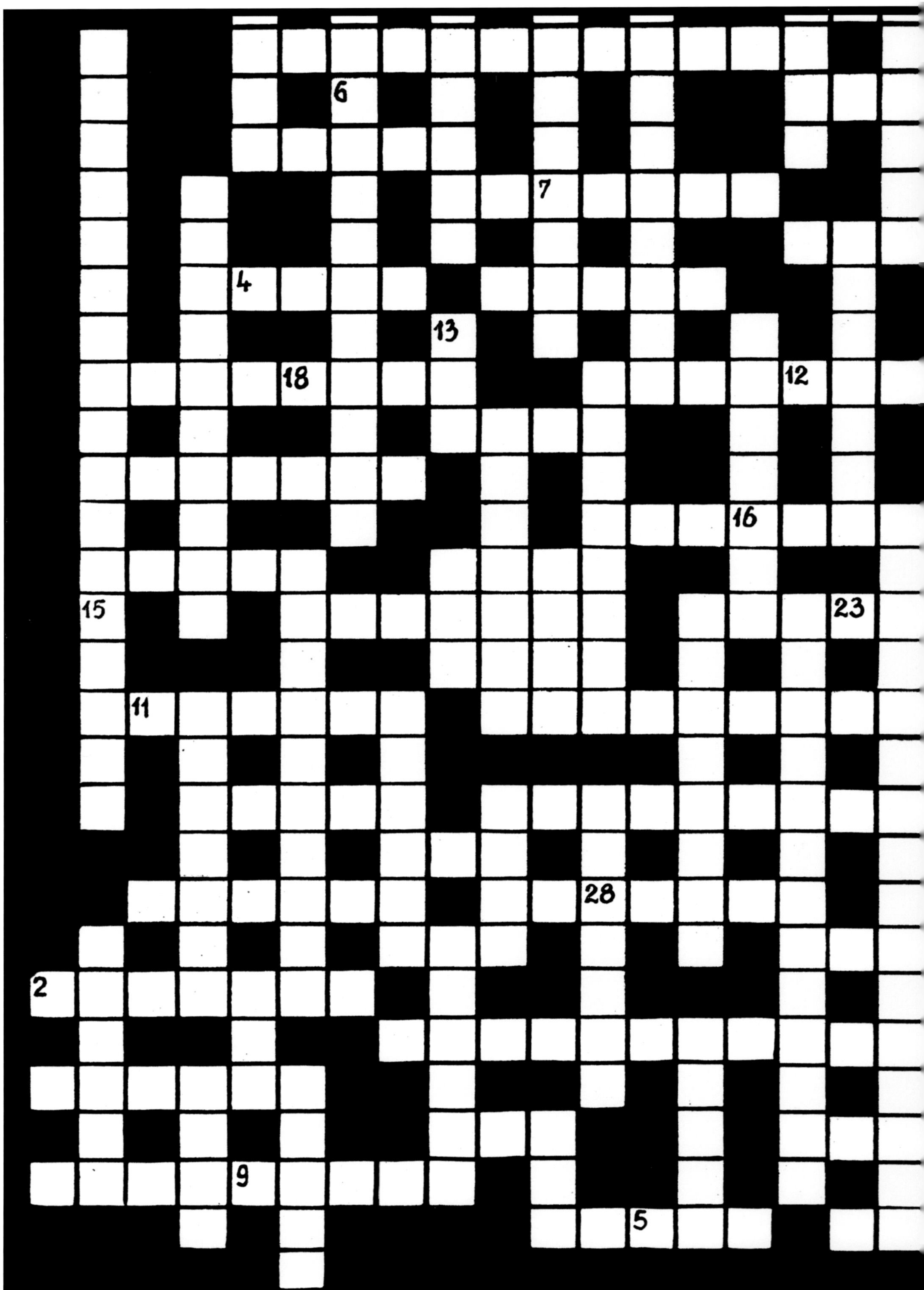

Crossword Puzzle with Lady in Black Coat, 2009

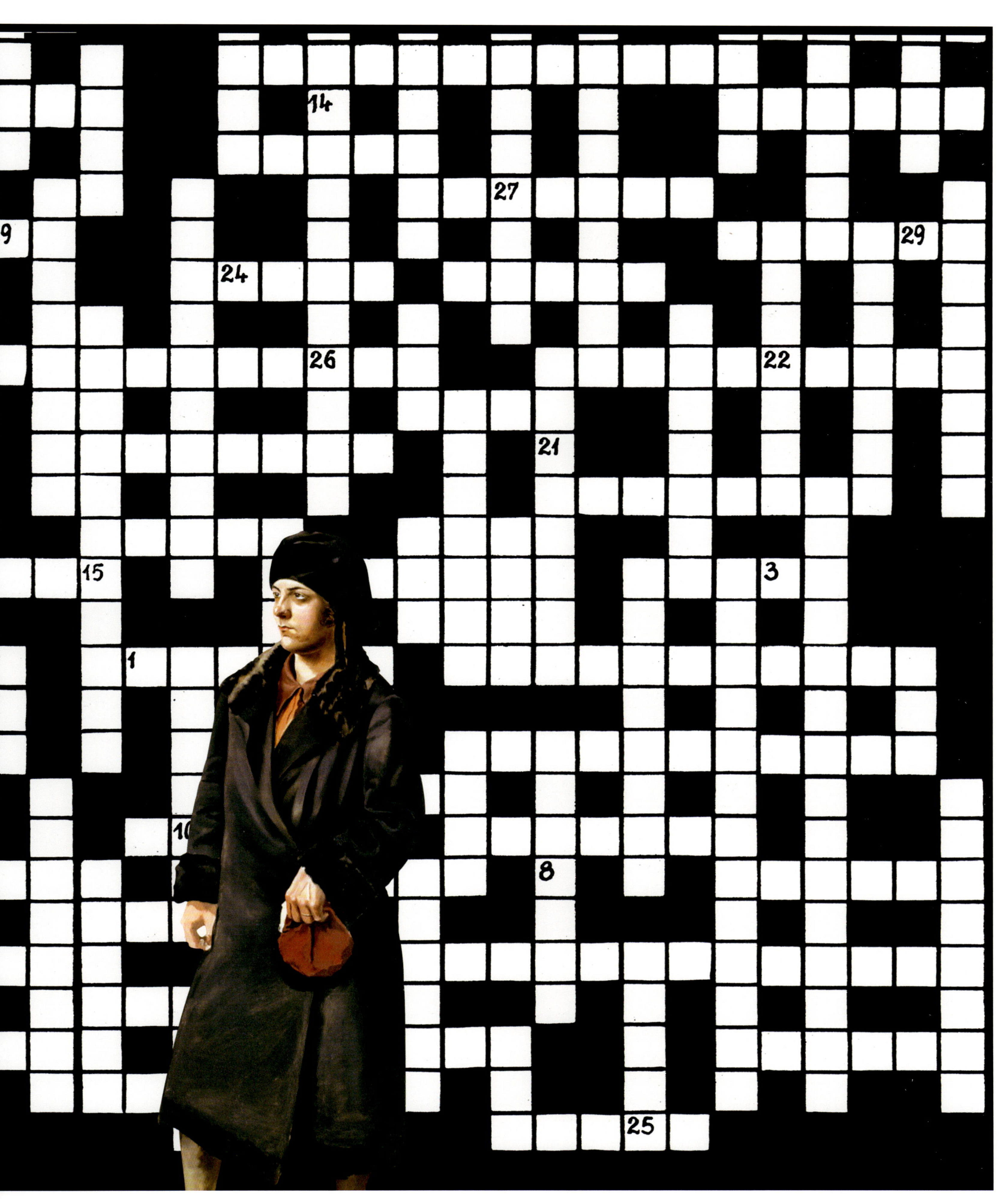

14
27
9
29
24
26
22
21
15
3
1
8
25

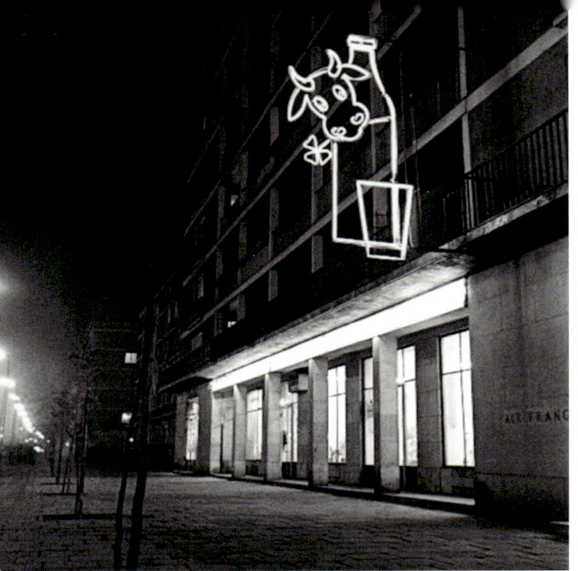

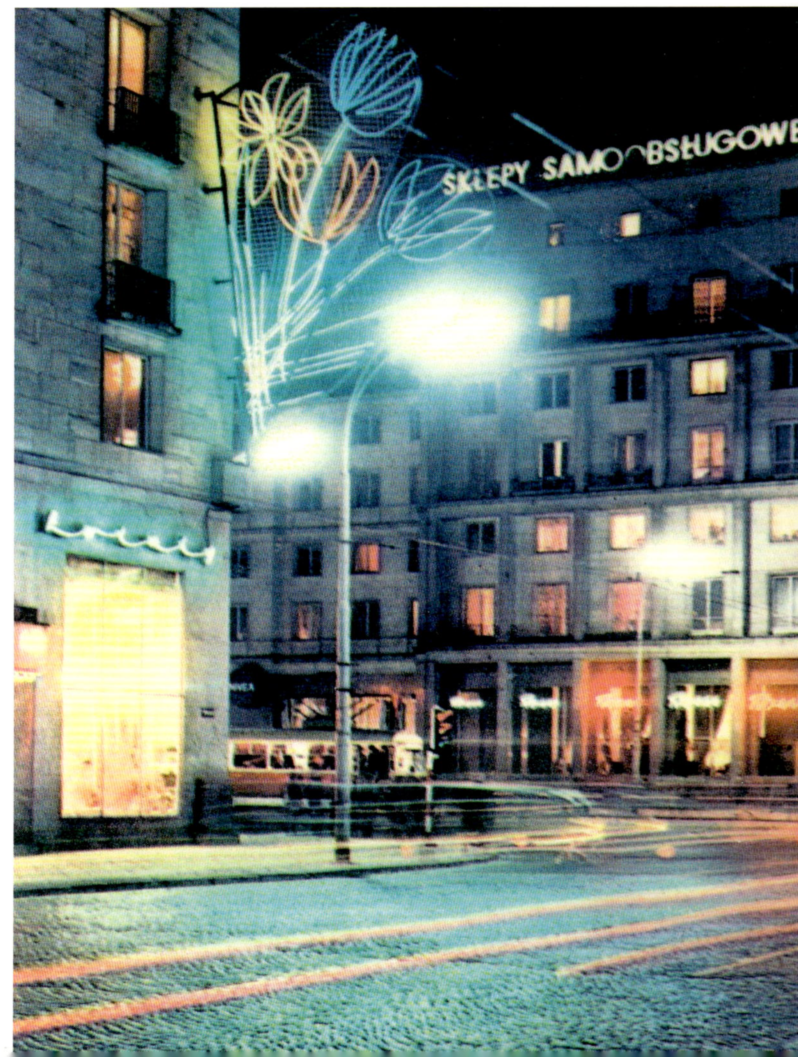

←←←←
Zofia Stryjeńska, exhibition view, Schinkel Pavillon, 5th Berlin Biennale for Contemporary Art, 2008
With Paulina Olowska, *Zofia Stryjeńska (Couple with Apples)*, 2008, and Zofia Styjeńska, *Zrywanie Jabłek/Apple Picking*, 1960

←←←
Zofia Stryjeńska, exhibition view, Schinkel Pavillon, 5th Berlin Biennale for Contemporary Art, 2008
With Zofia Styjeńska, *Popiersie góralki*, 1939

Warsaw neons from the 1960s

→
Natasza, Worker Canteen, Flowers, 2010

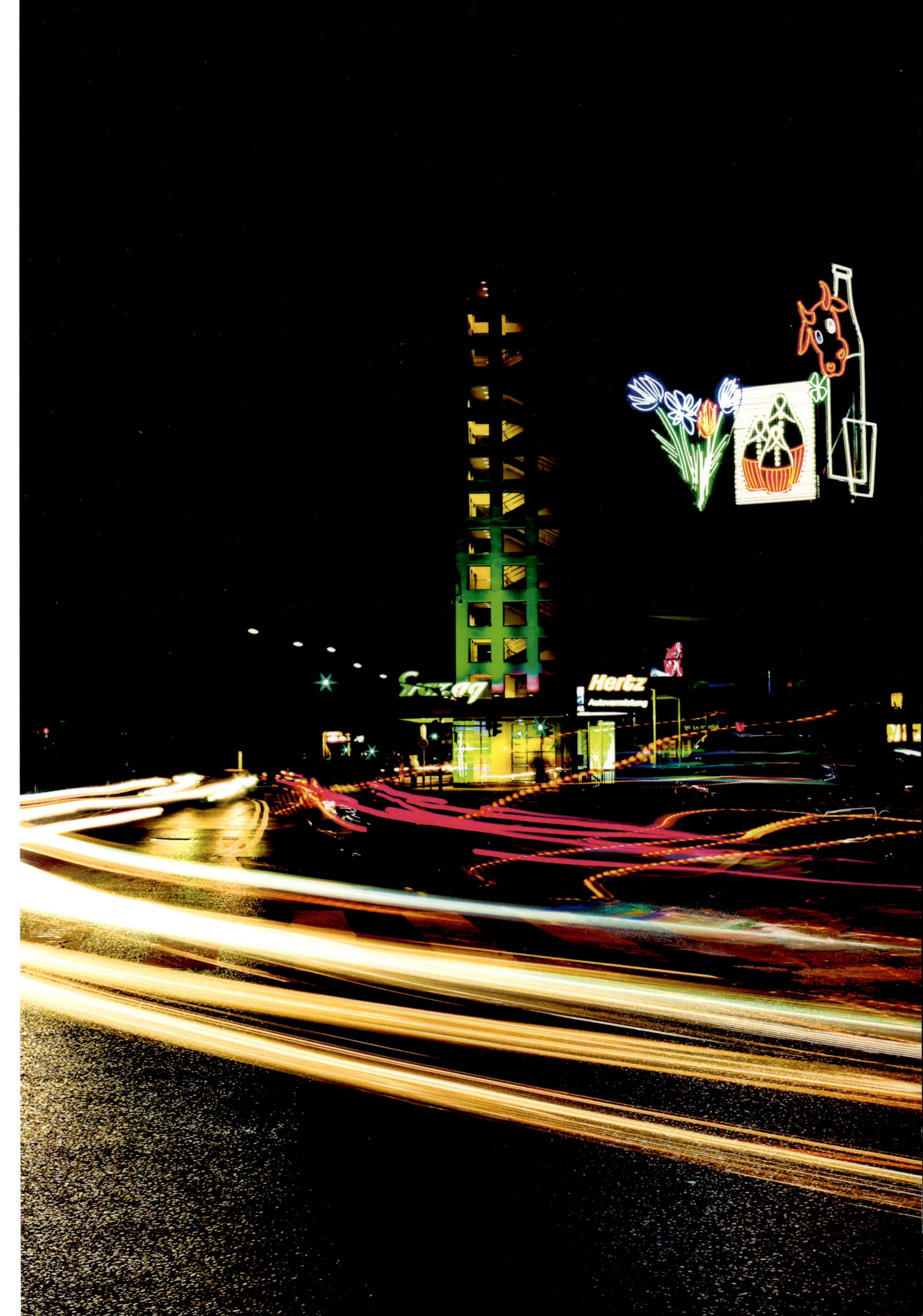
Hertz
Autovermietung

Applied Fantastic, exhibition view, Metro Pictures, New York, 2010
Applied Fantastic, Inspiration Wall, 2010

→→
Klaun/Clown, 2010

→→→
Szachista I/Chess Player 1, 2010

→→→→
Torcik/Cake, 2010

→→→→→
Pszczoła/Bee, 2010

→→→→→→
Ela, 2010

→→→→→→→
Polowanie/Hunting, 2010

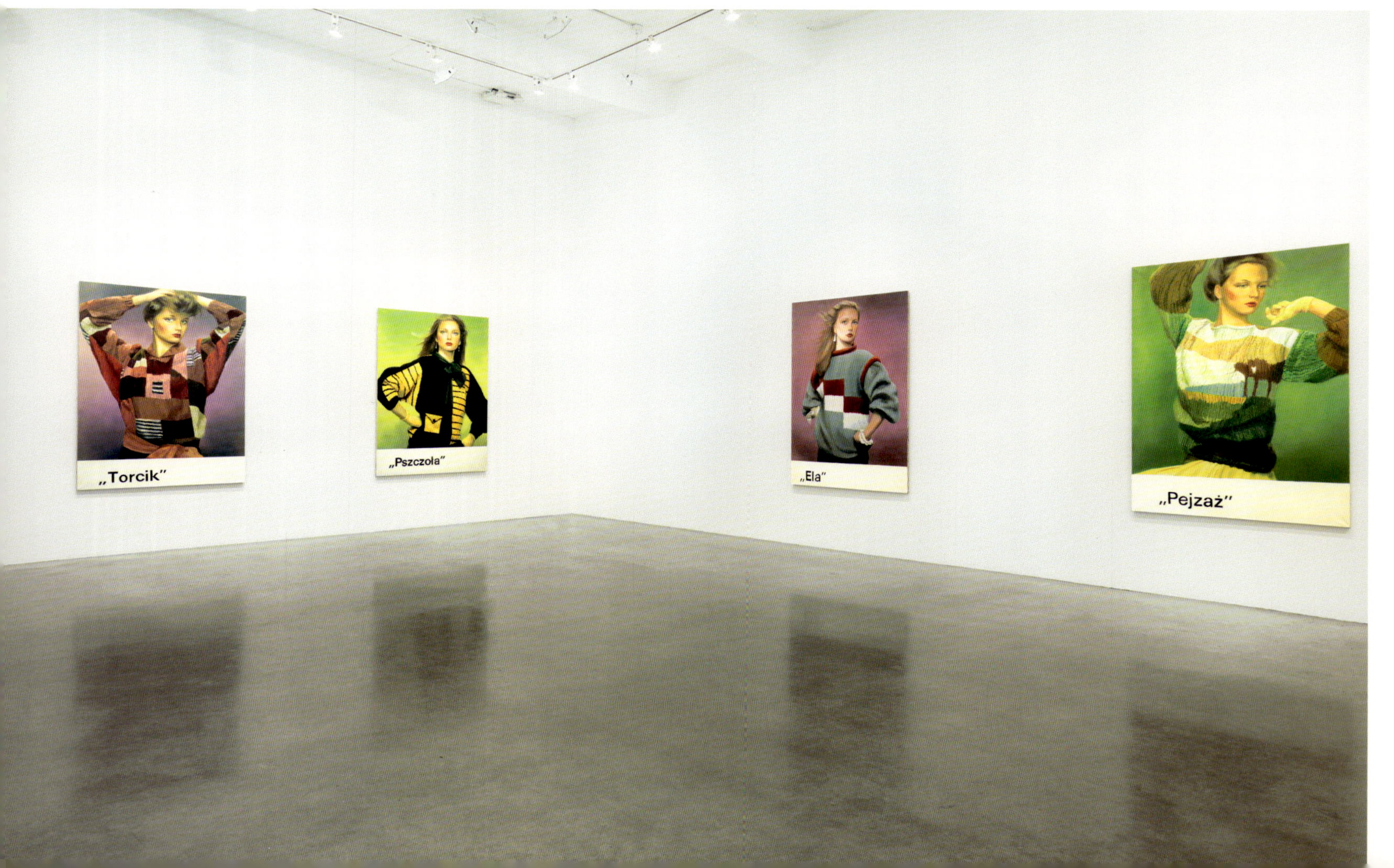

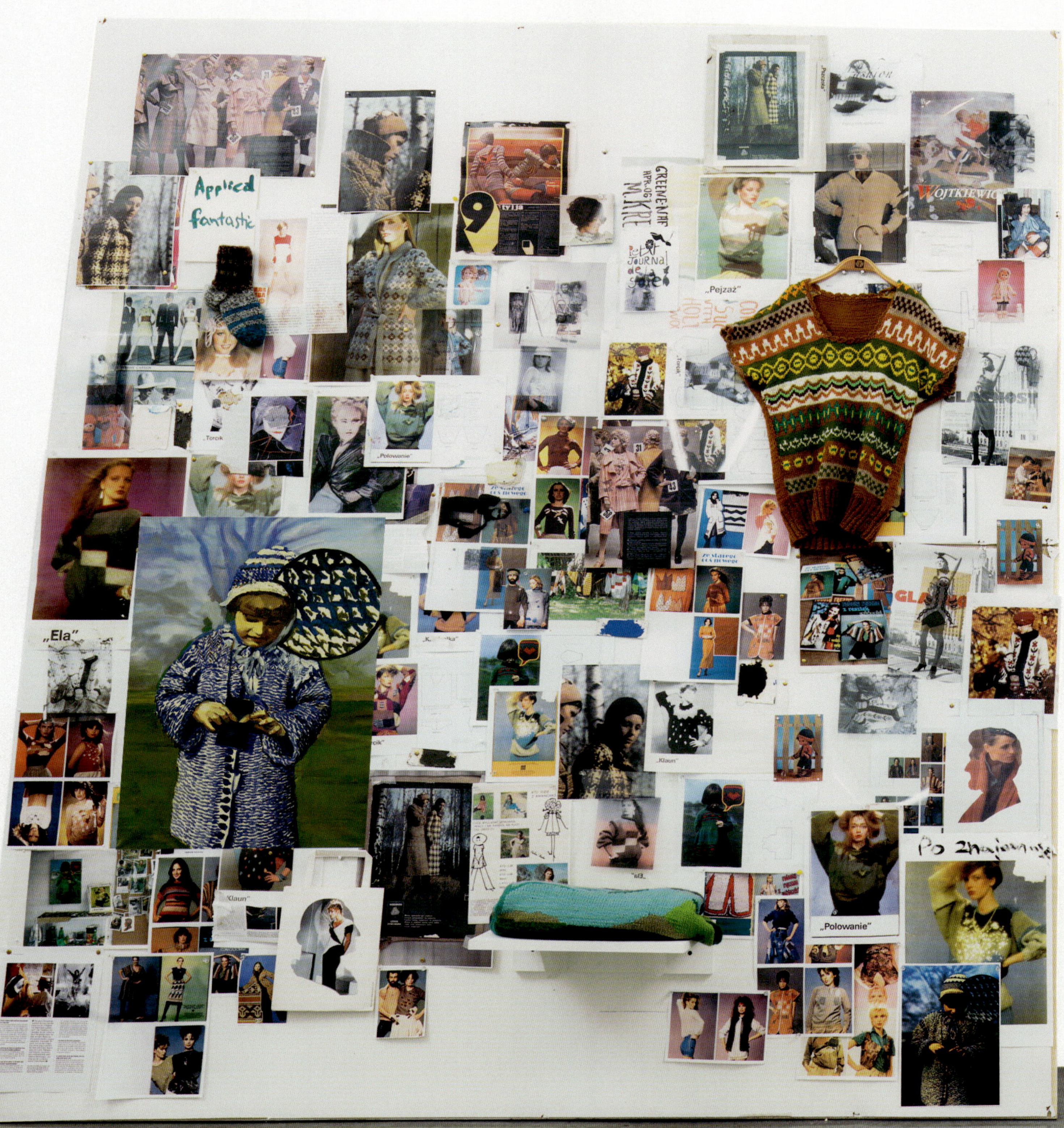

Applied
fantastic
„Ela"
„Pejzaż"
„Polowanie"
„Polowanie"

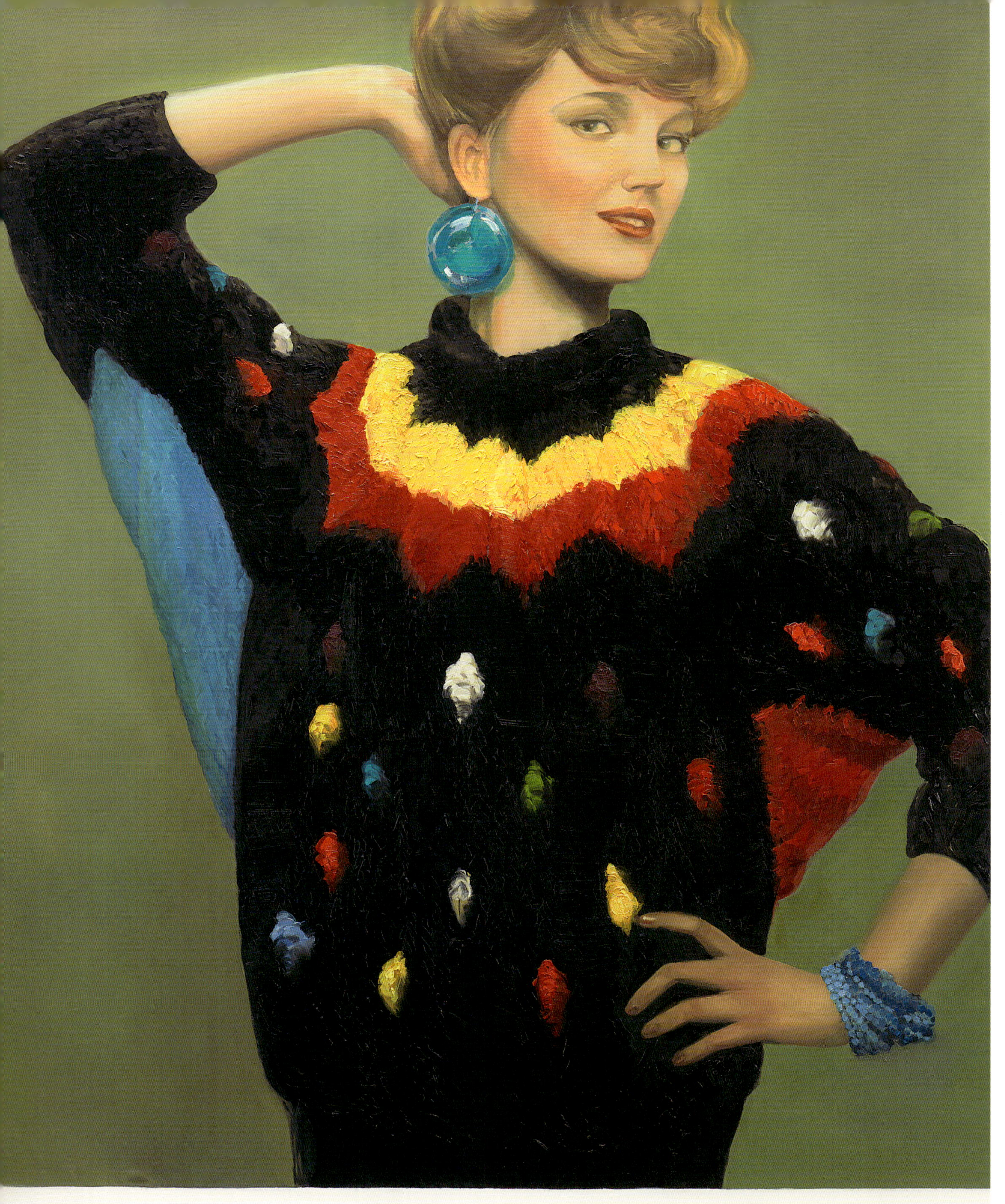

„Klaun”

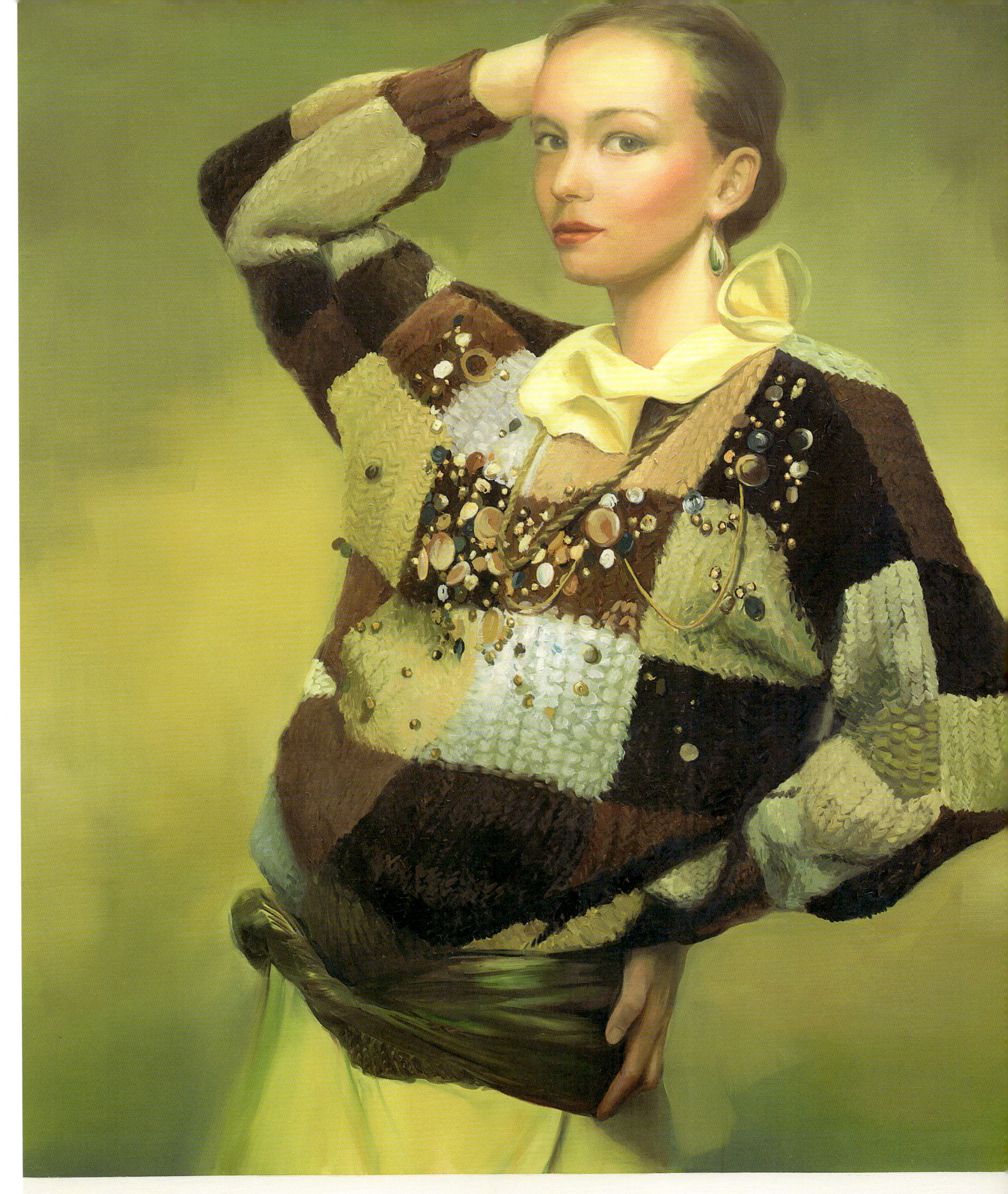

„Szachista I”

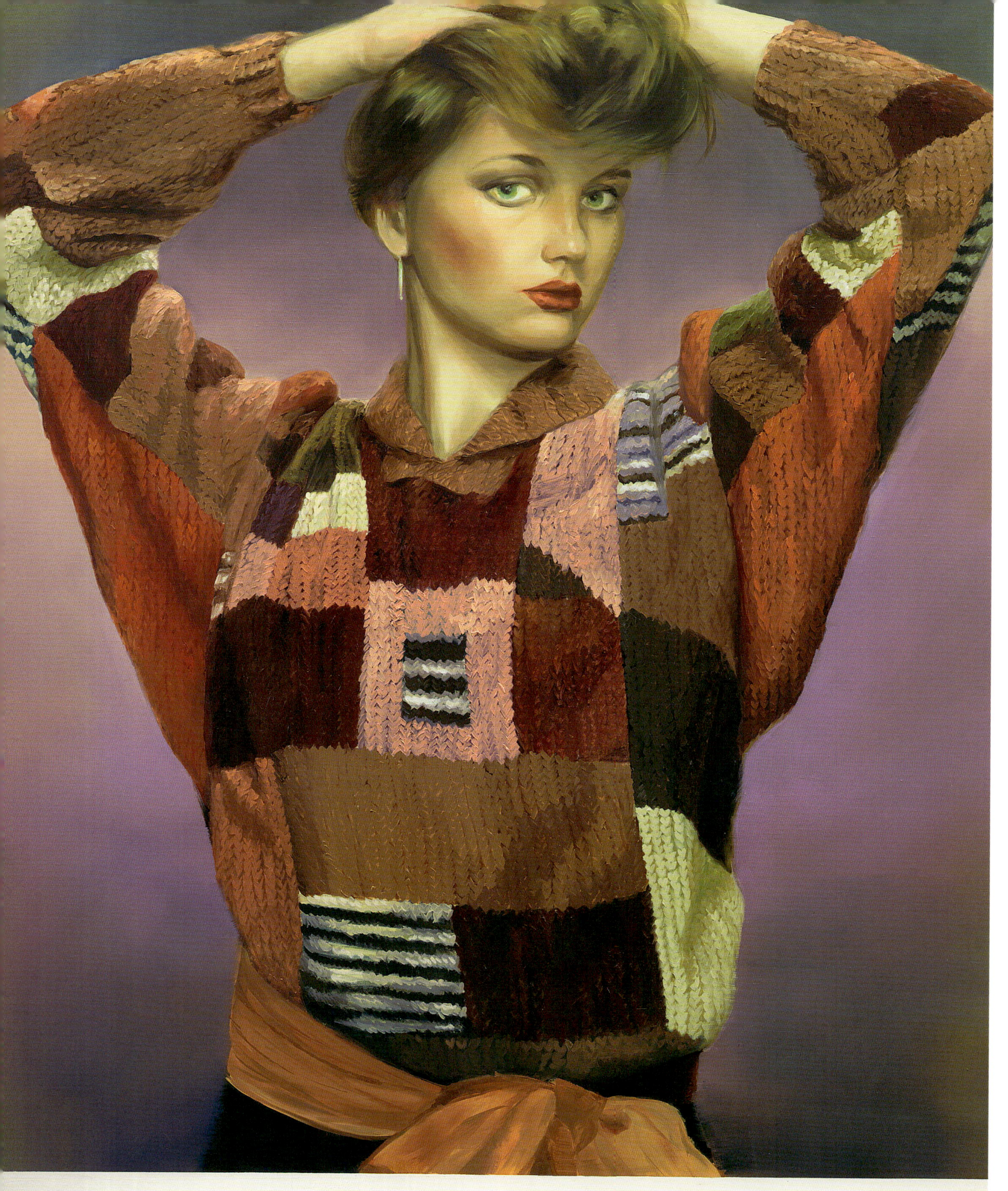

„Torcik"

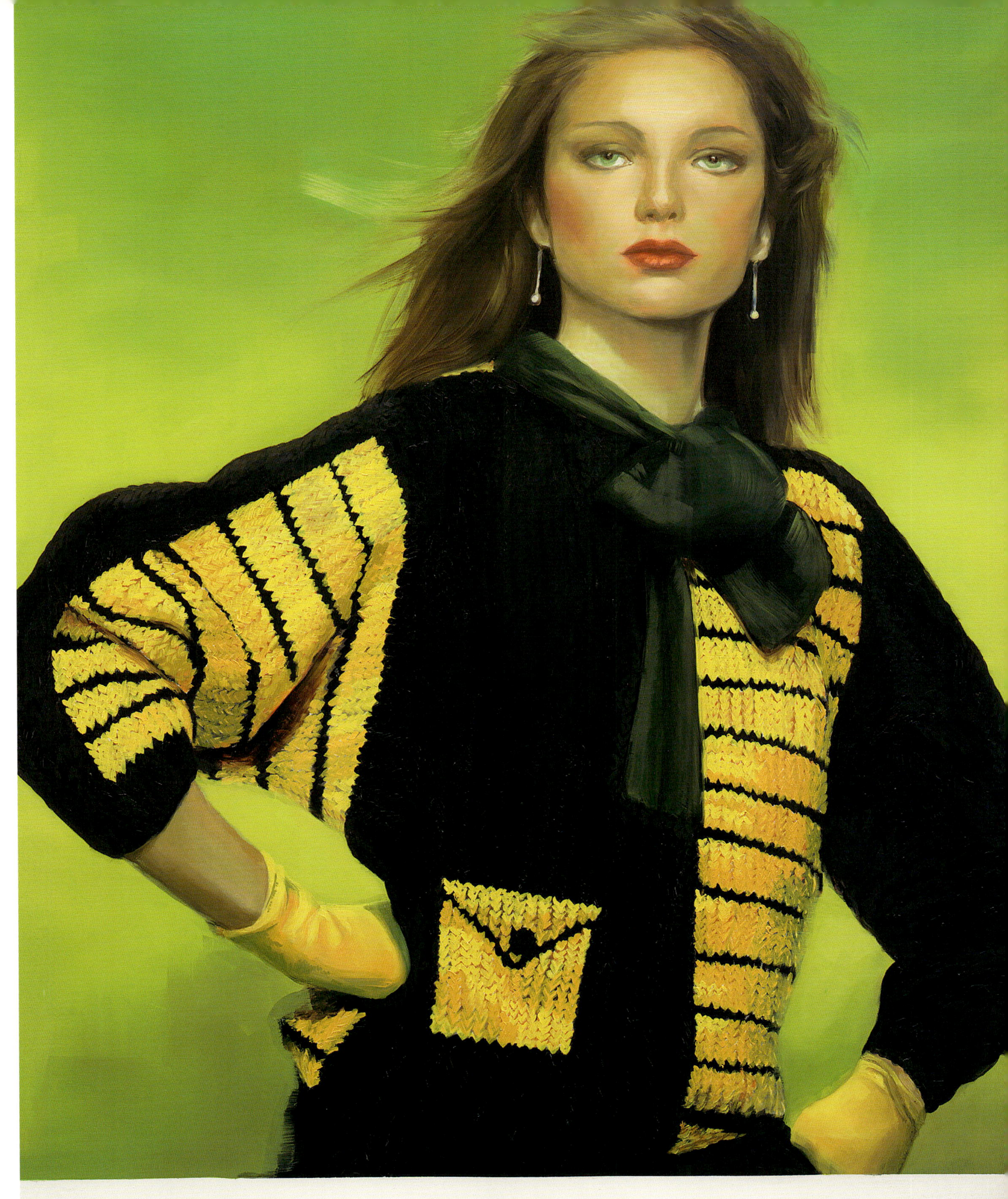

„Pszczoła"

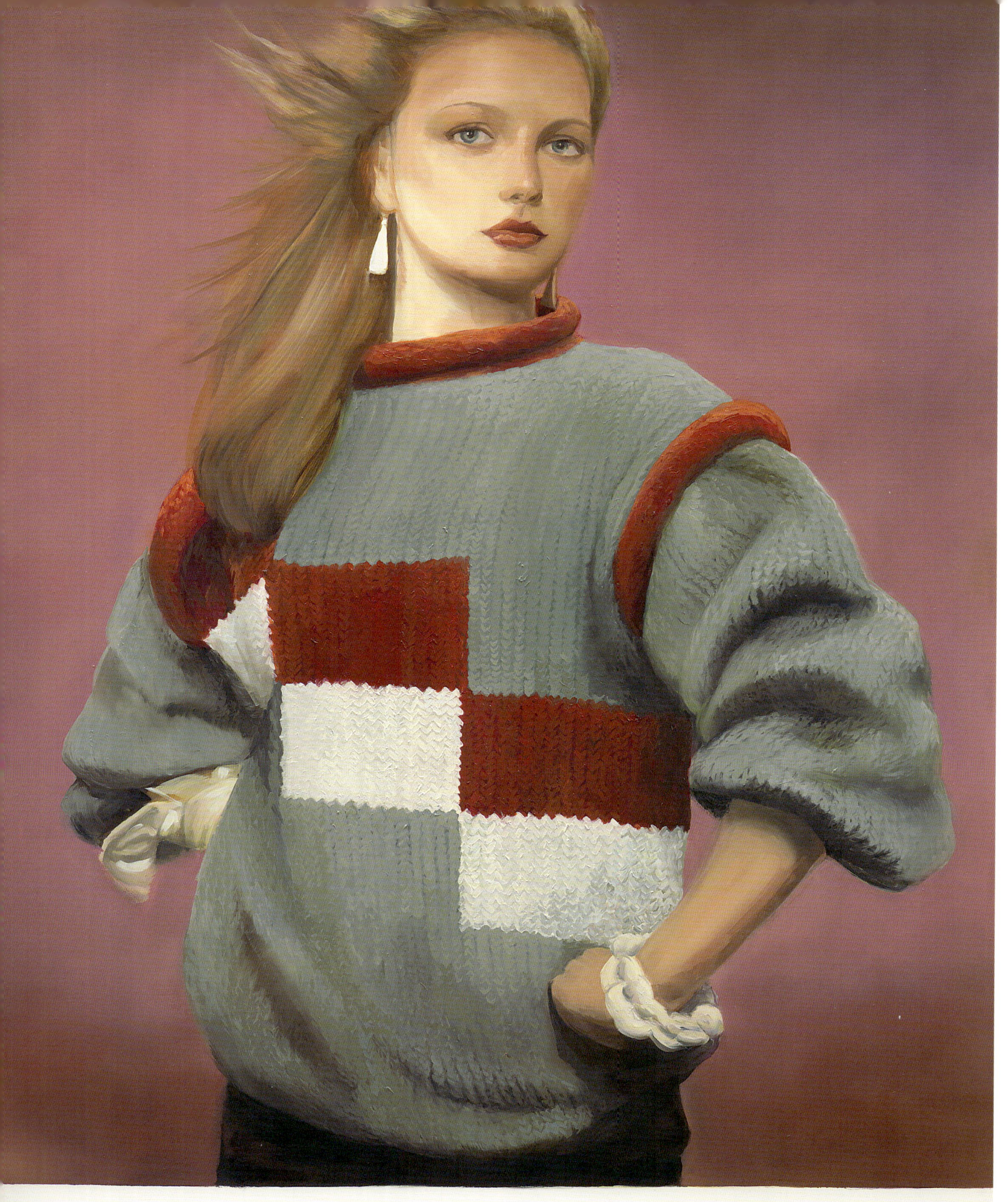

„Ela"

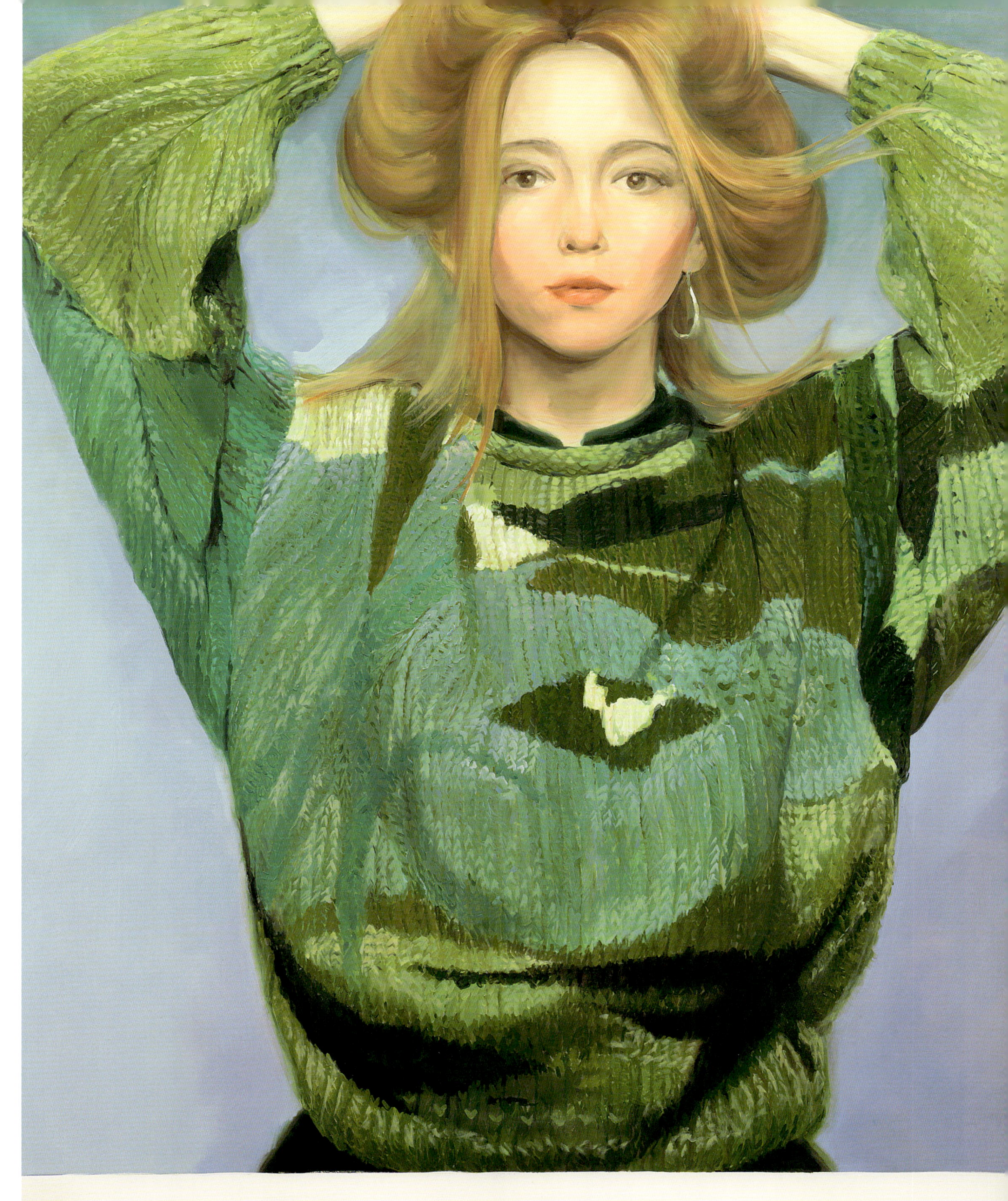

„Polowanie"

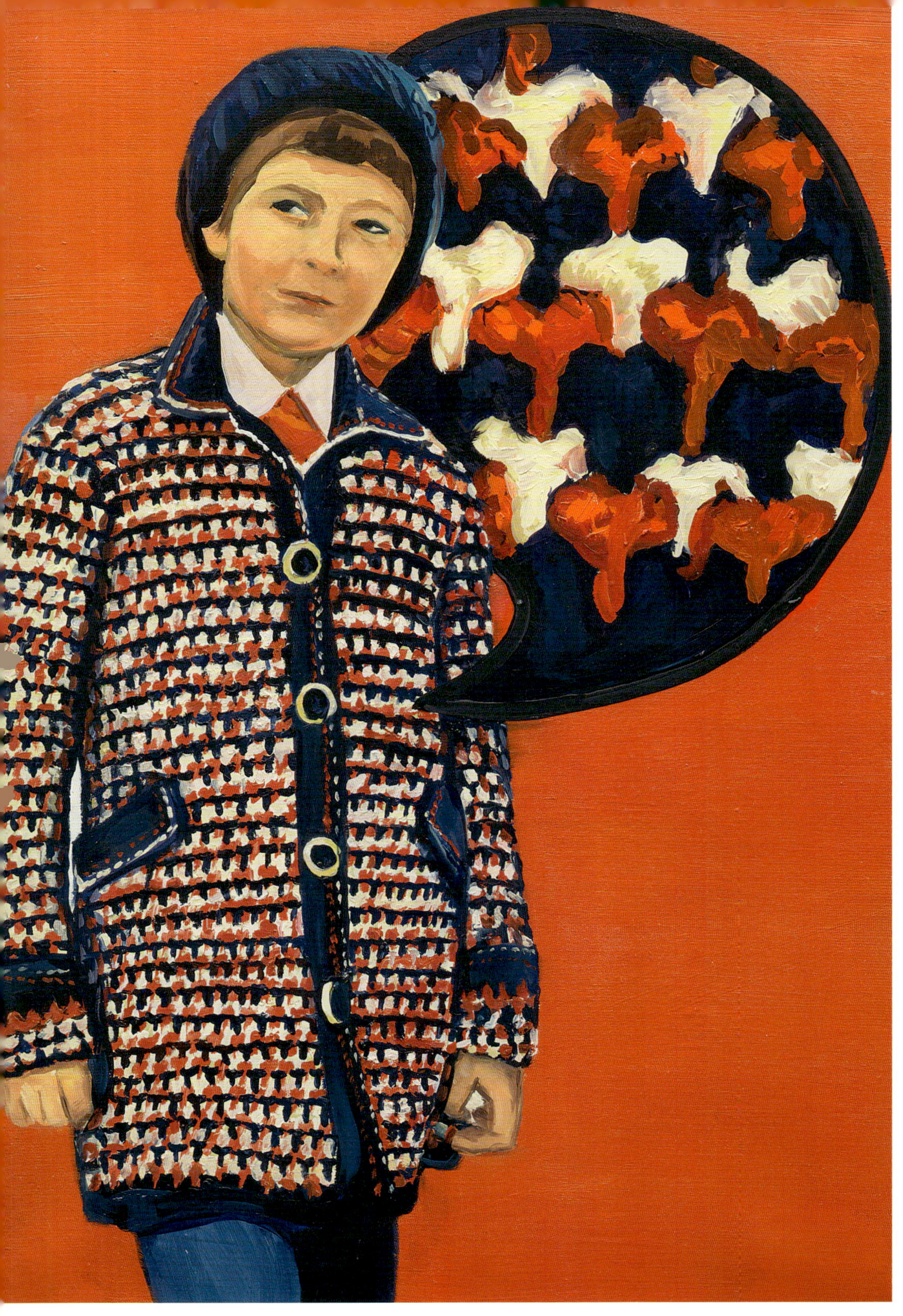

Crochet Coat, 2010
Coat with a Crochet Cap, 2010

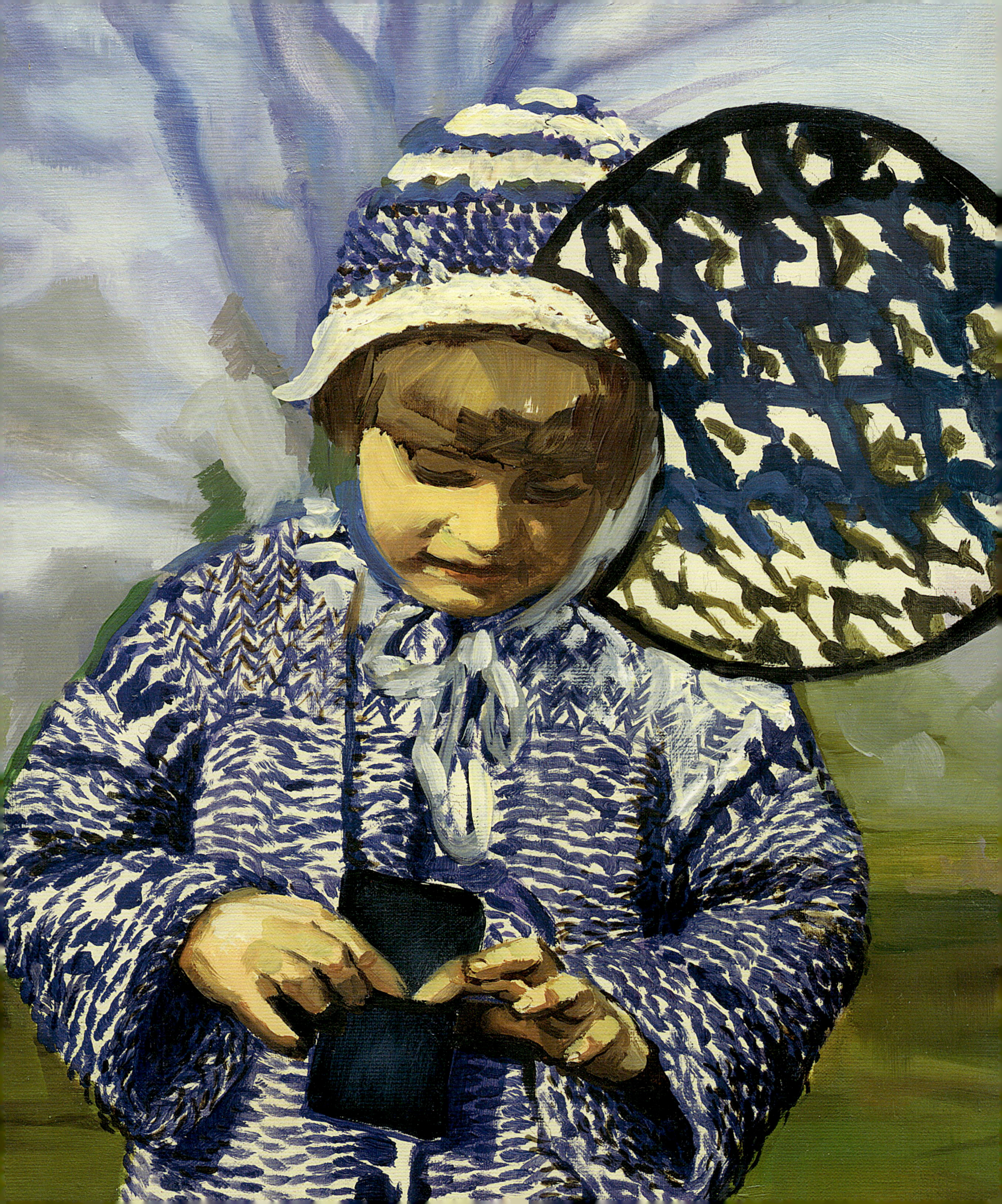

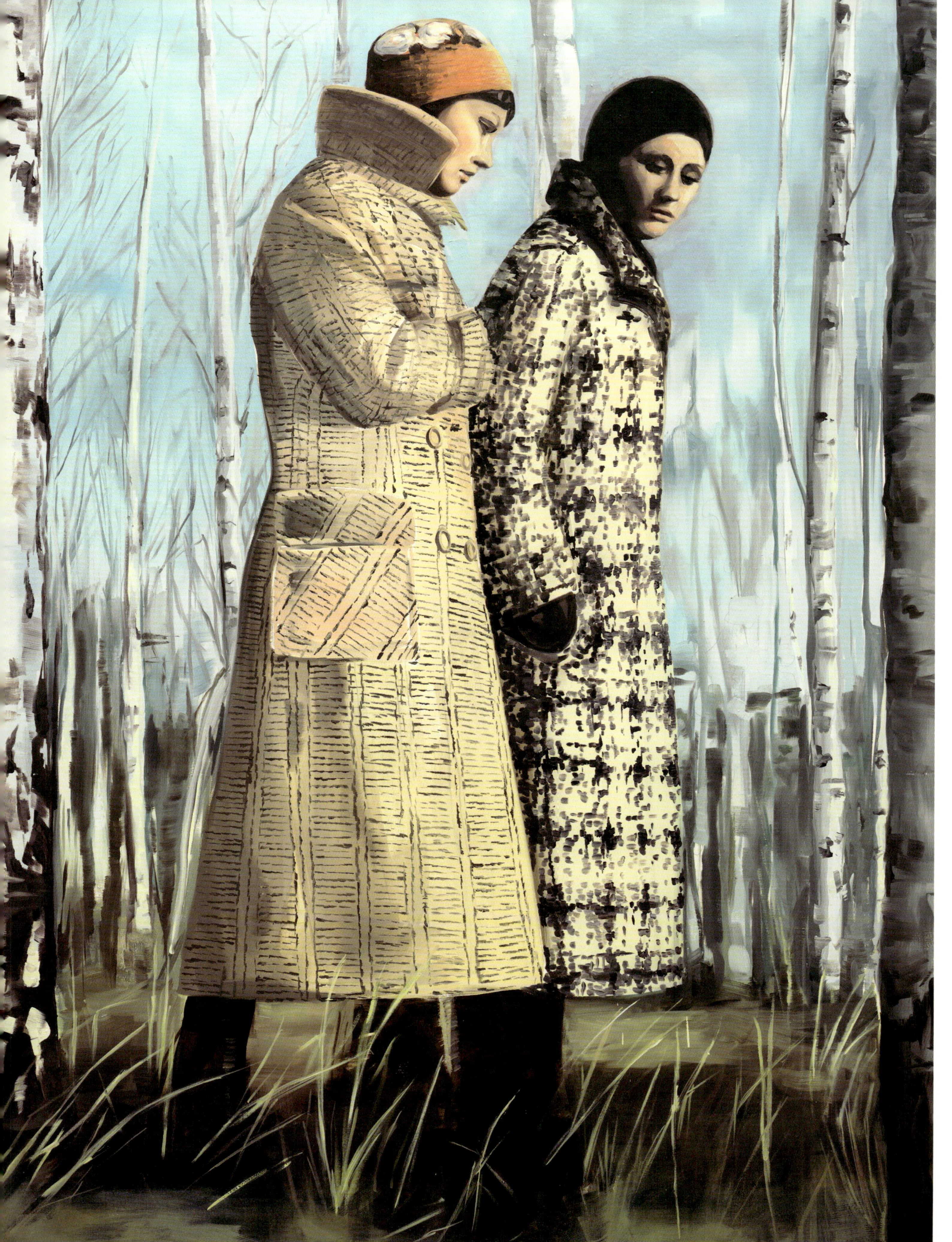

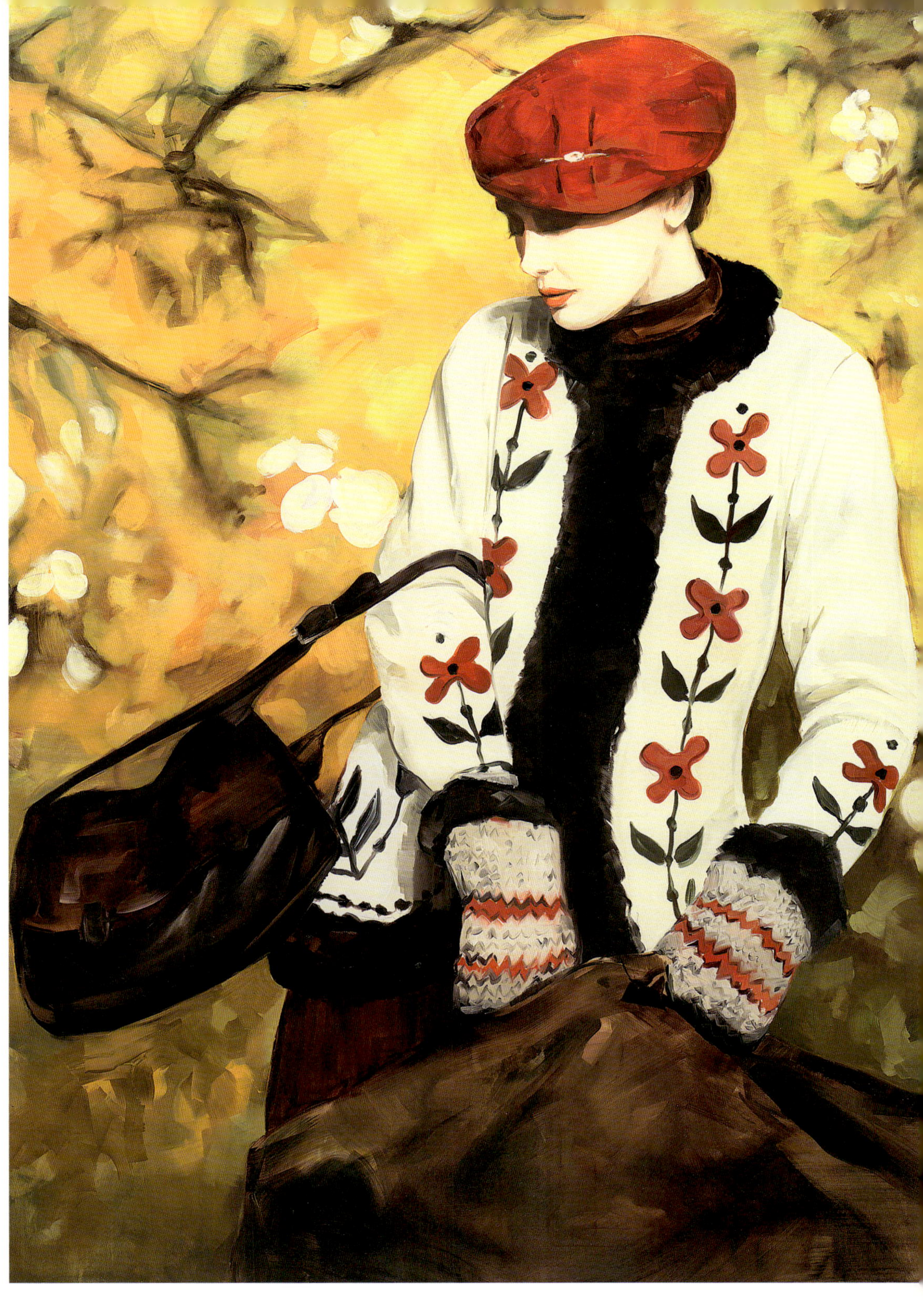

Woolmark, 2010
Cardigan Smrek, 2010

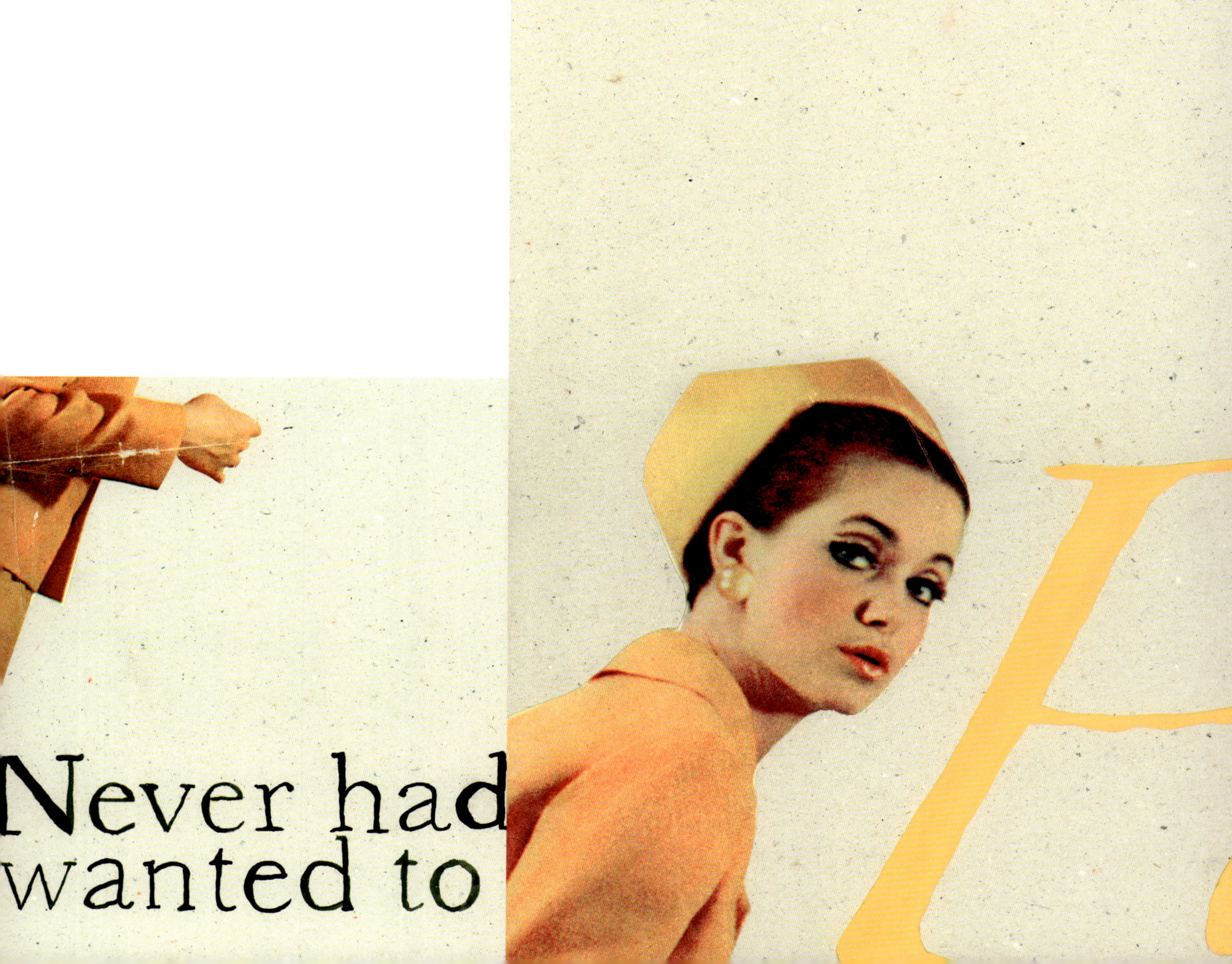
Never had
wanted to

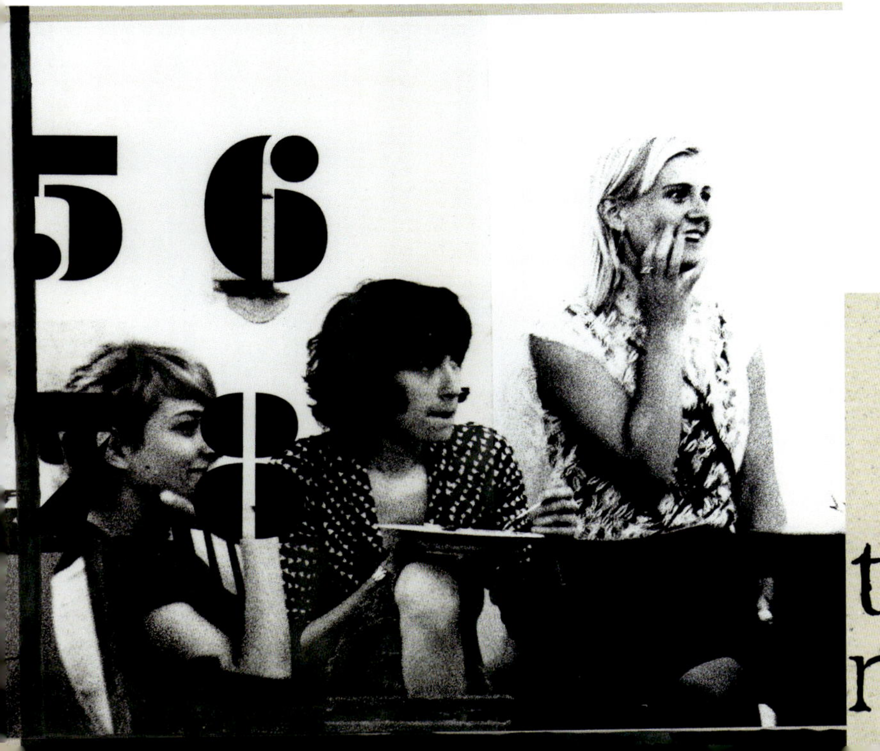

the courage, but
make.

Accidental Collages, 2004

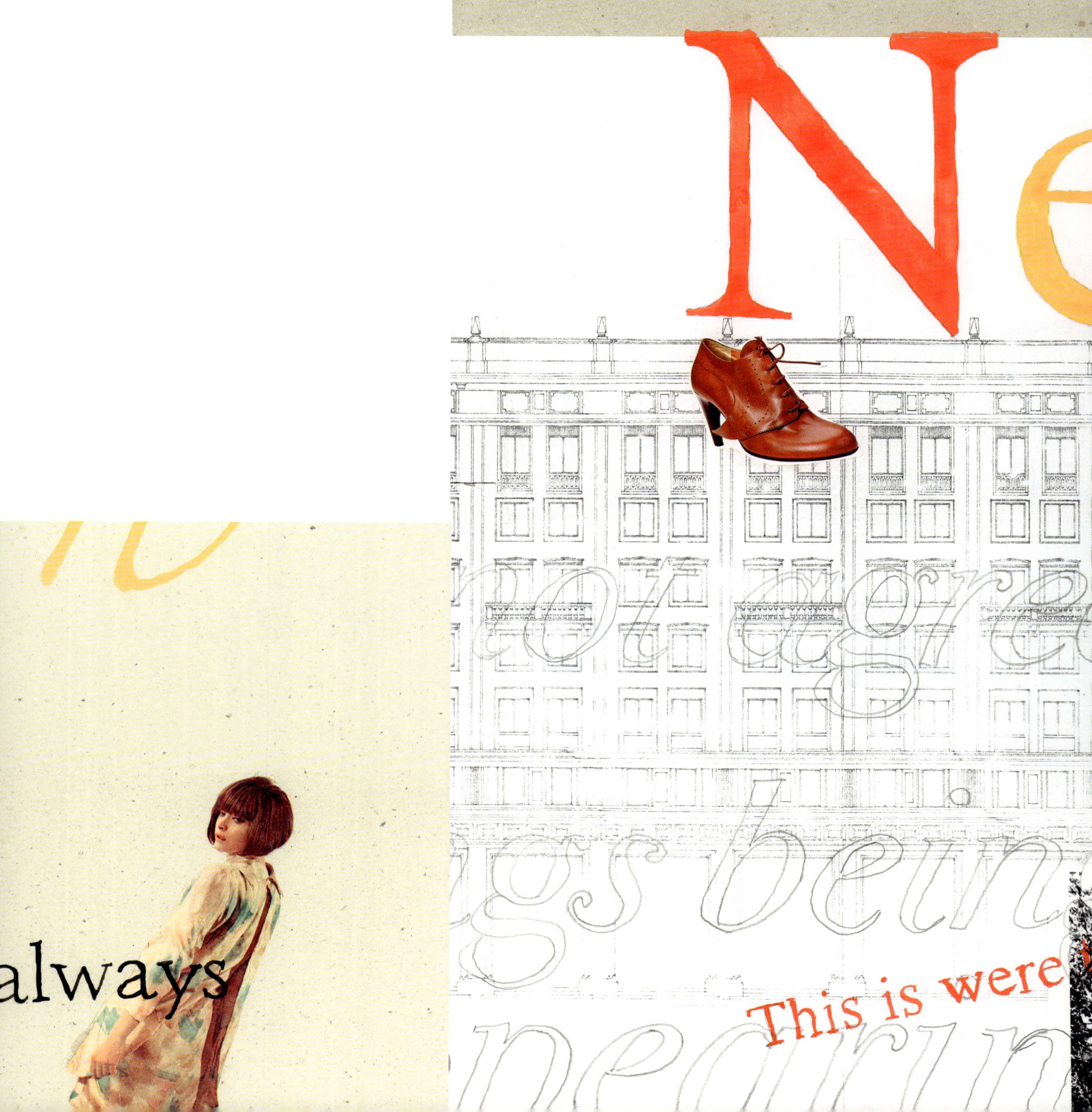

→ *Café Bar,* exhibition view, National Museum, Krakow, 2011

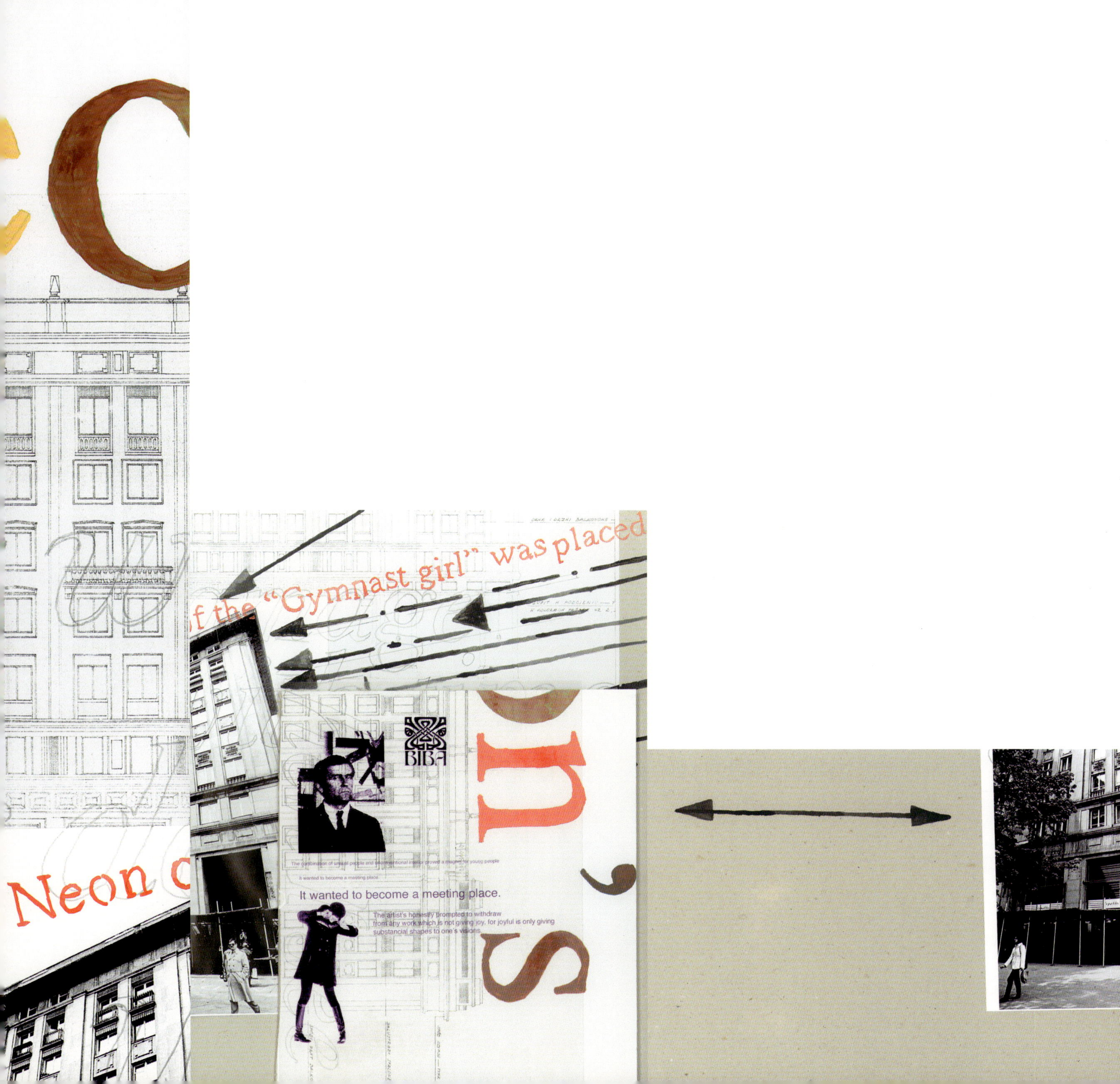

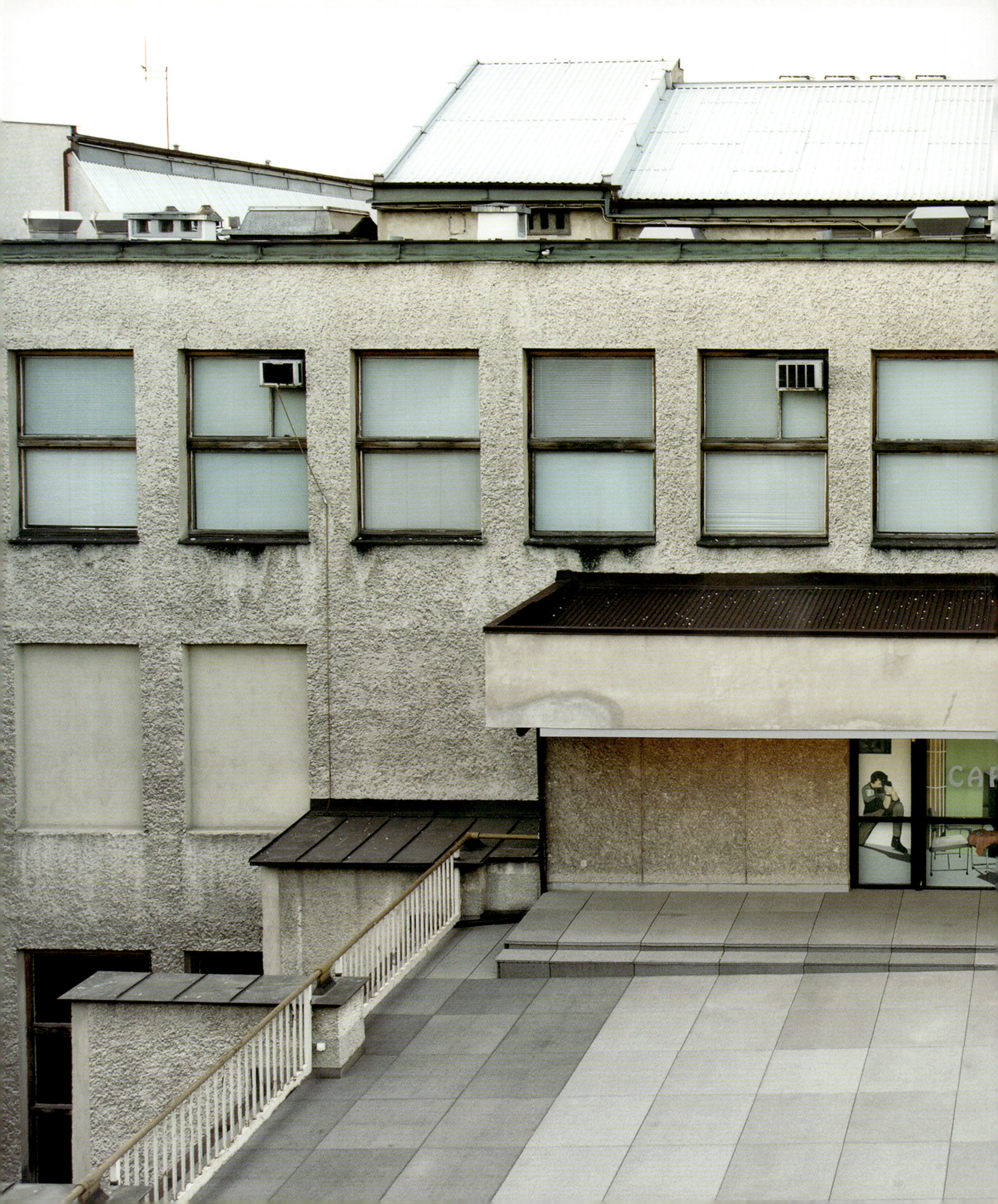

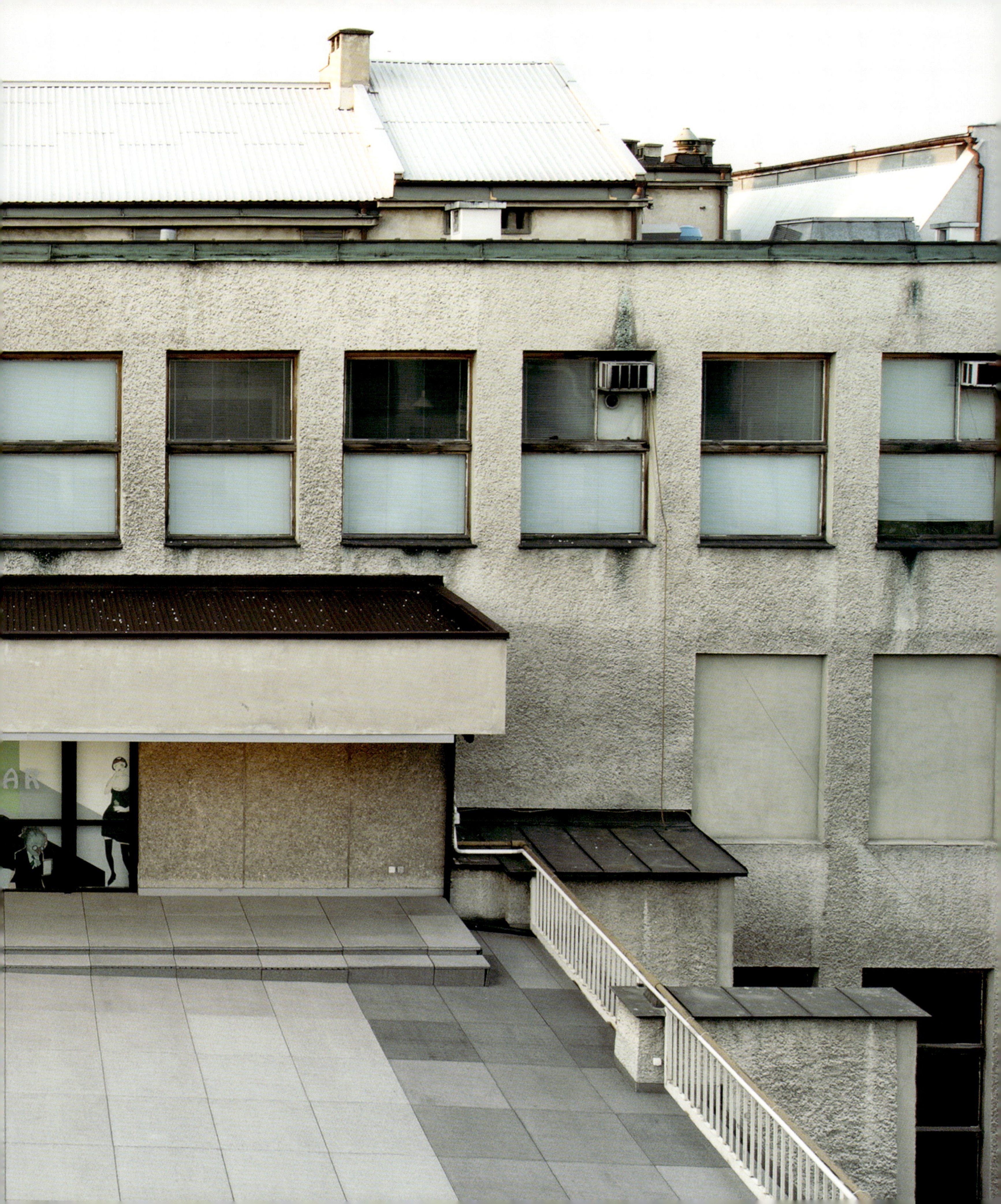

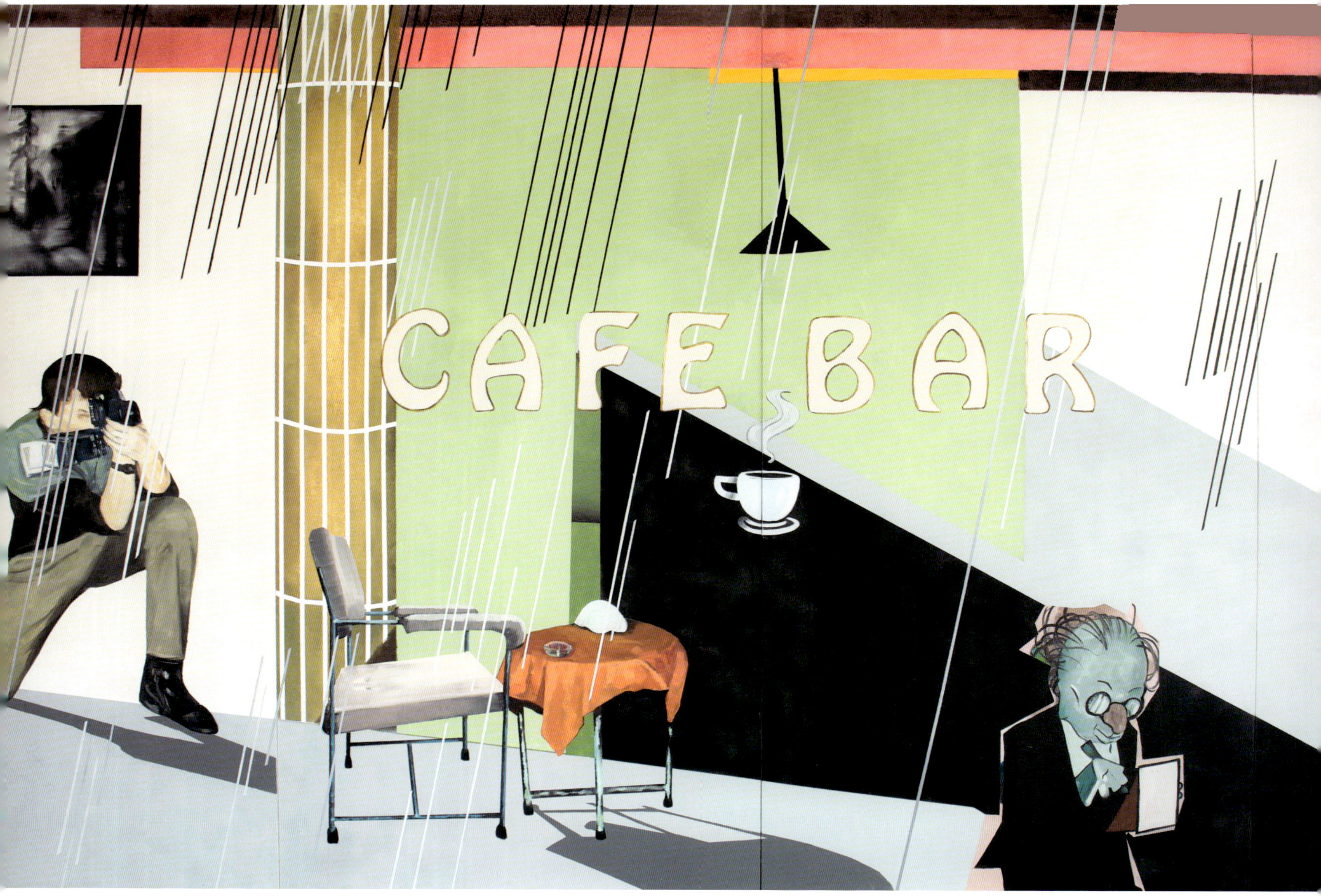

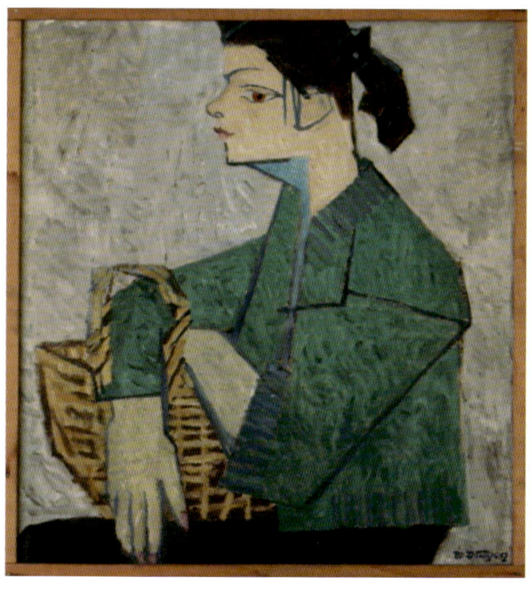

Café Bar MNK, 2011
Wojciech Długosz, *The Girl with a Basket*, 1956
Café Bar, exhibition view, National Museum, Krakow, 2011

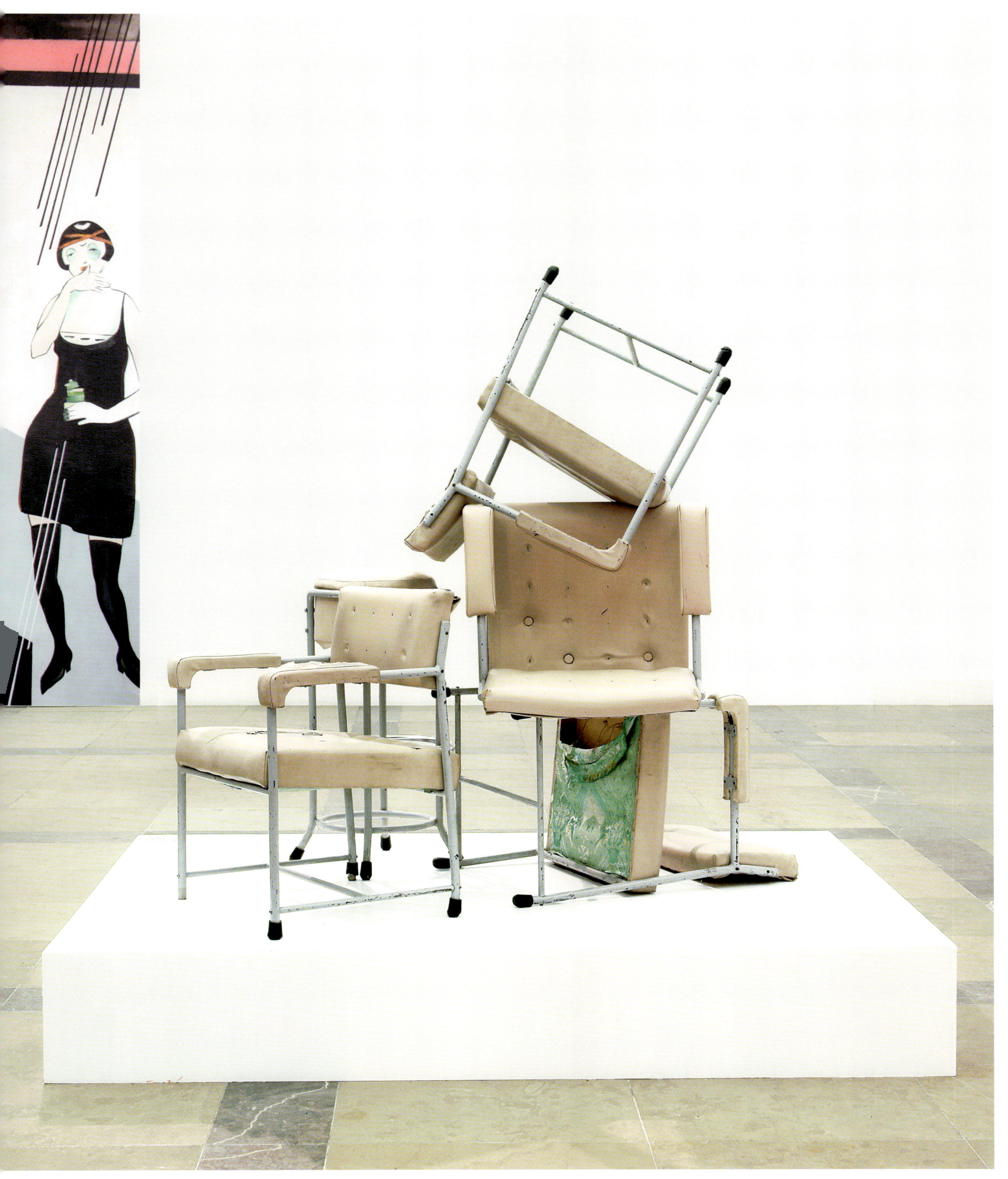

The Revenge of the Wise-Woman, exhibition views, Foksal Gallery Foundation, Warsaw, 2011

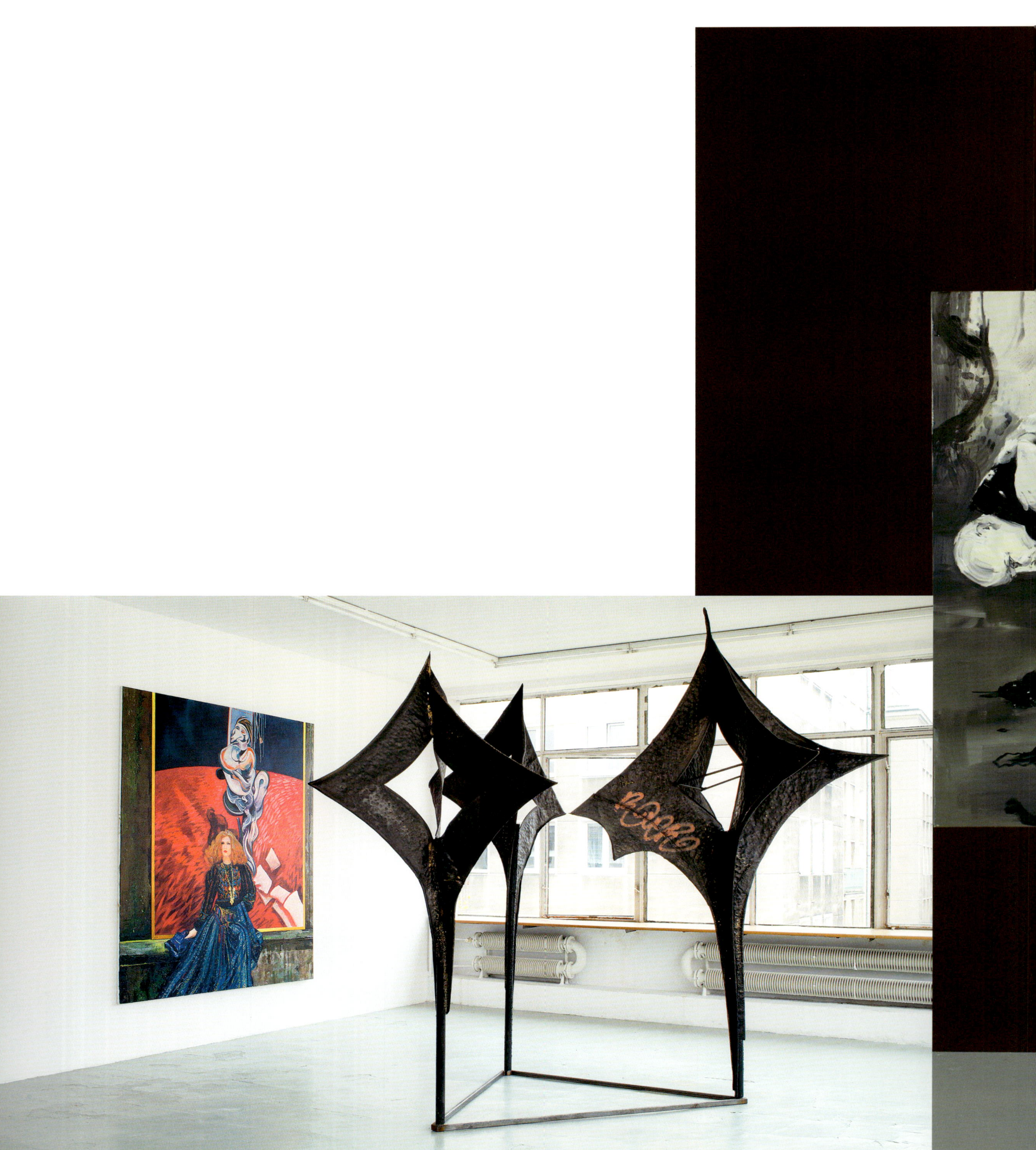

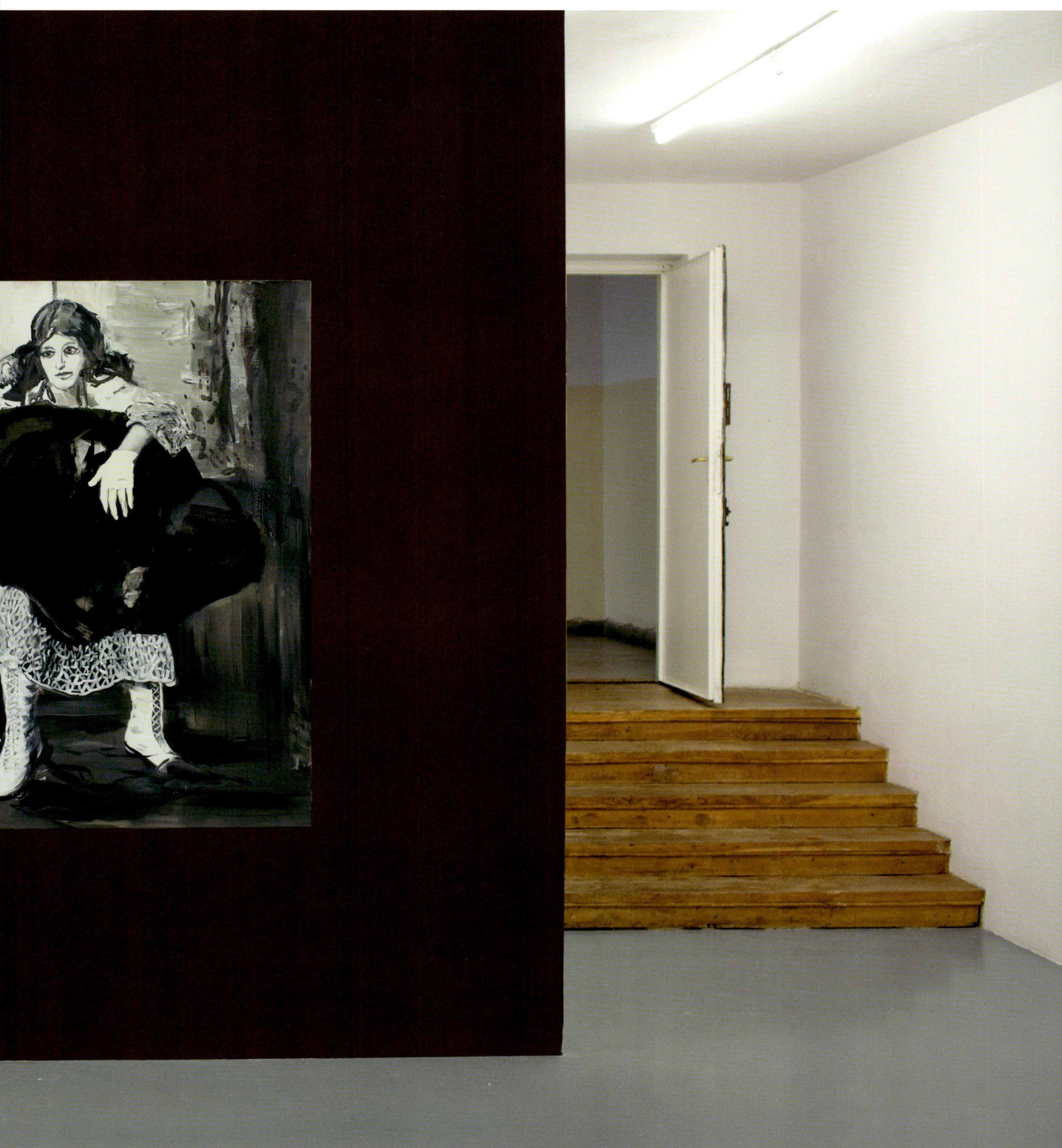

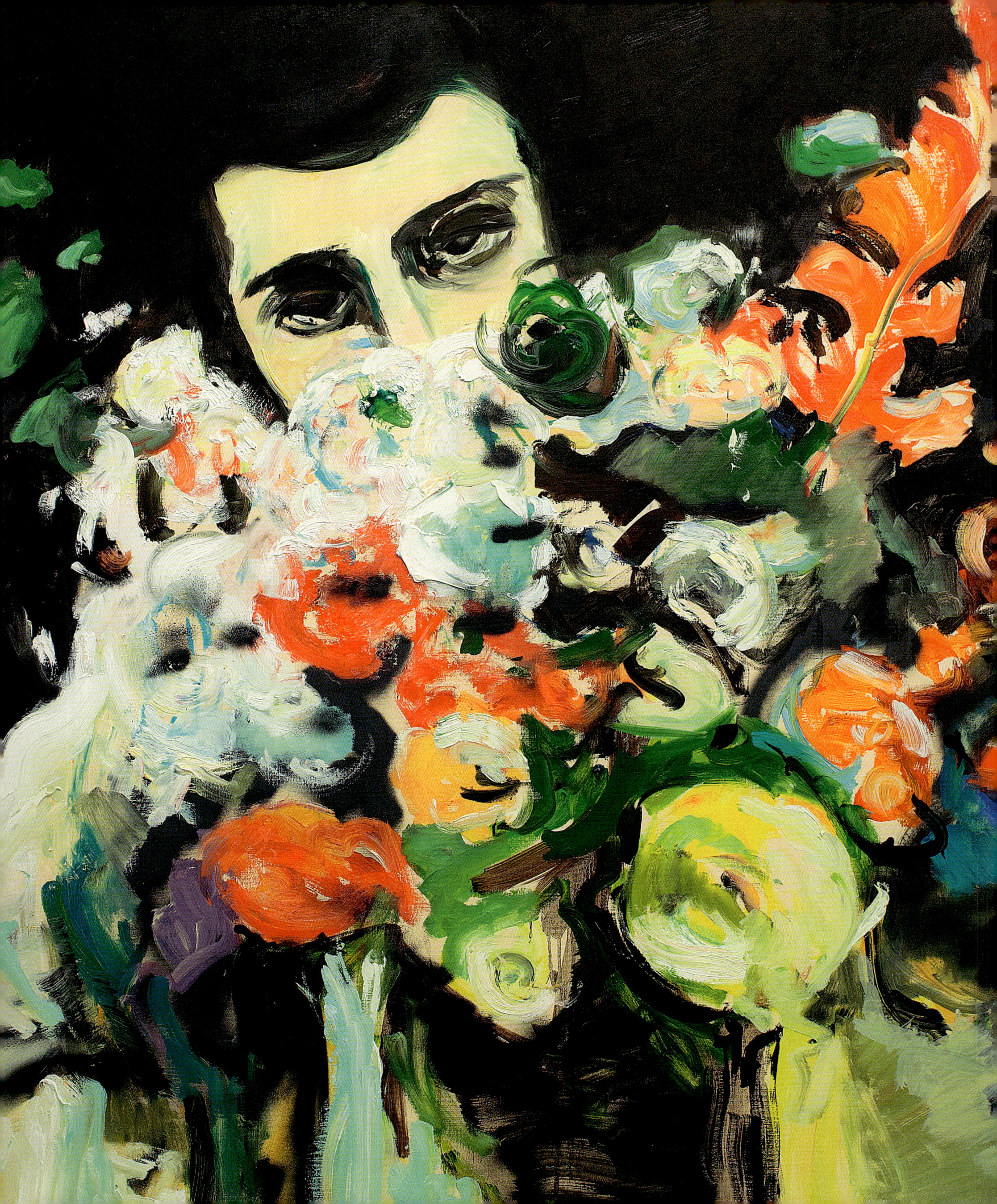

Portrait with Flowers (After M.), 2009
Emmy Hennings, 2011

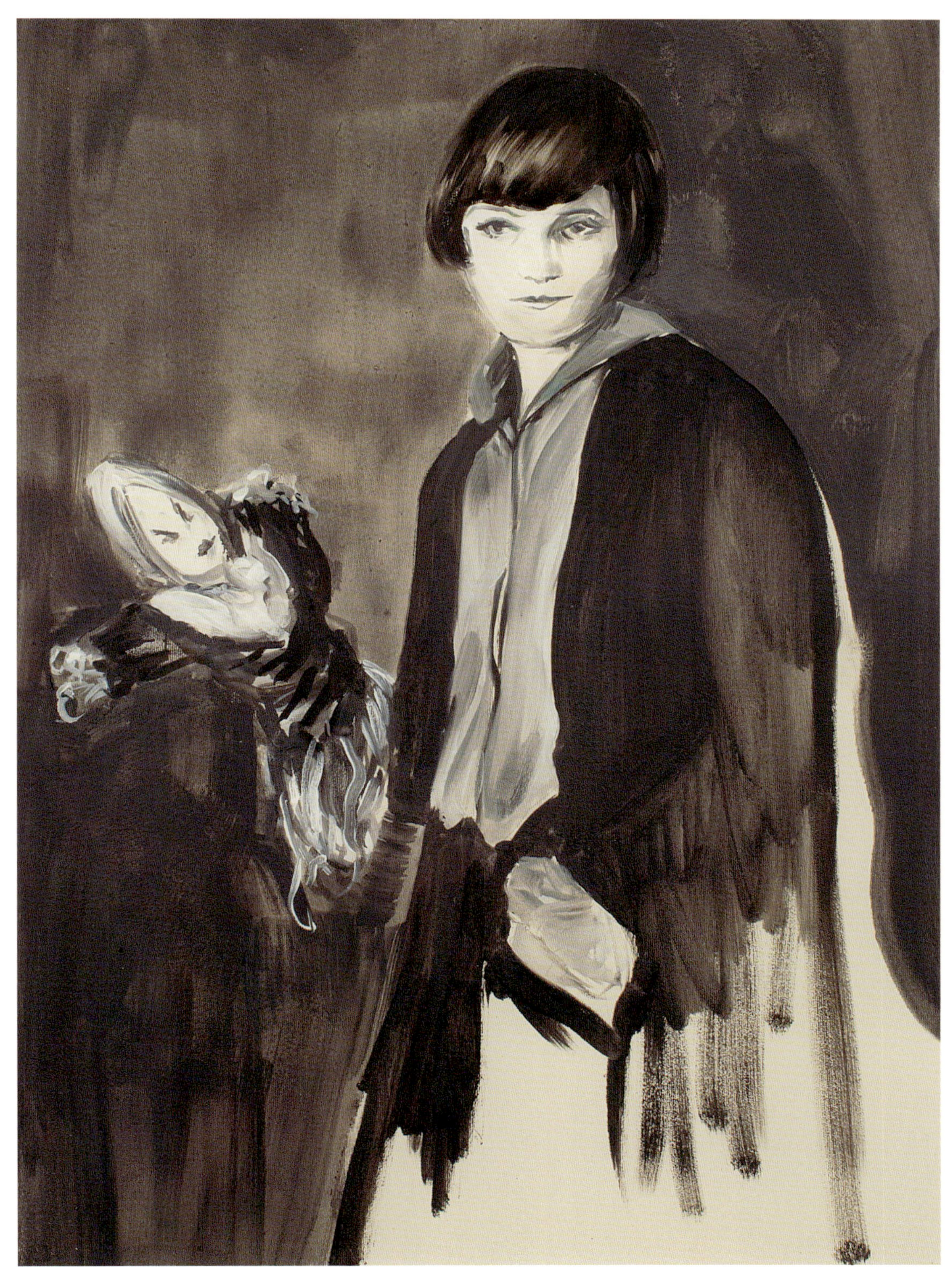

Granny, 2012

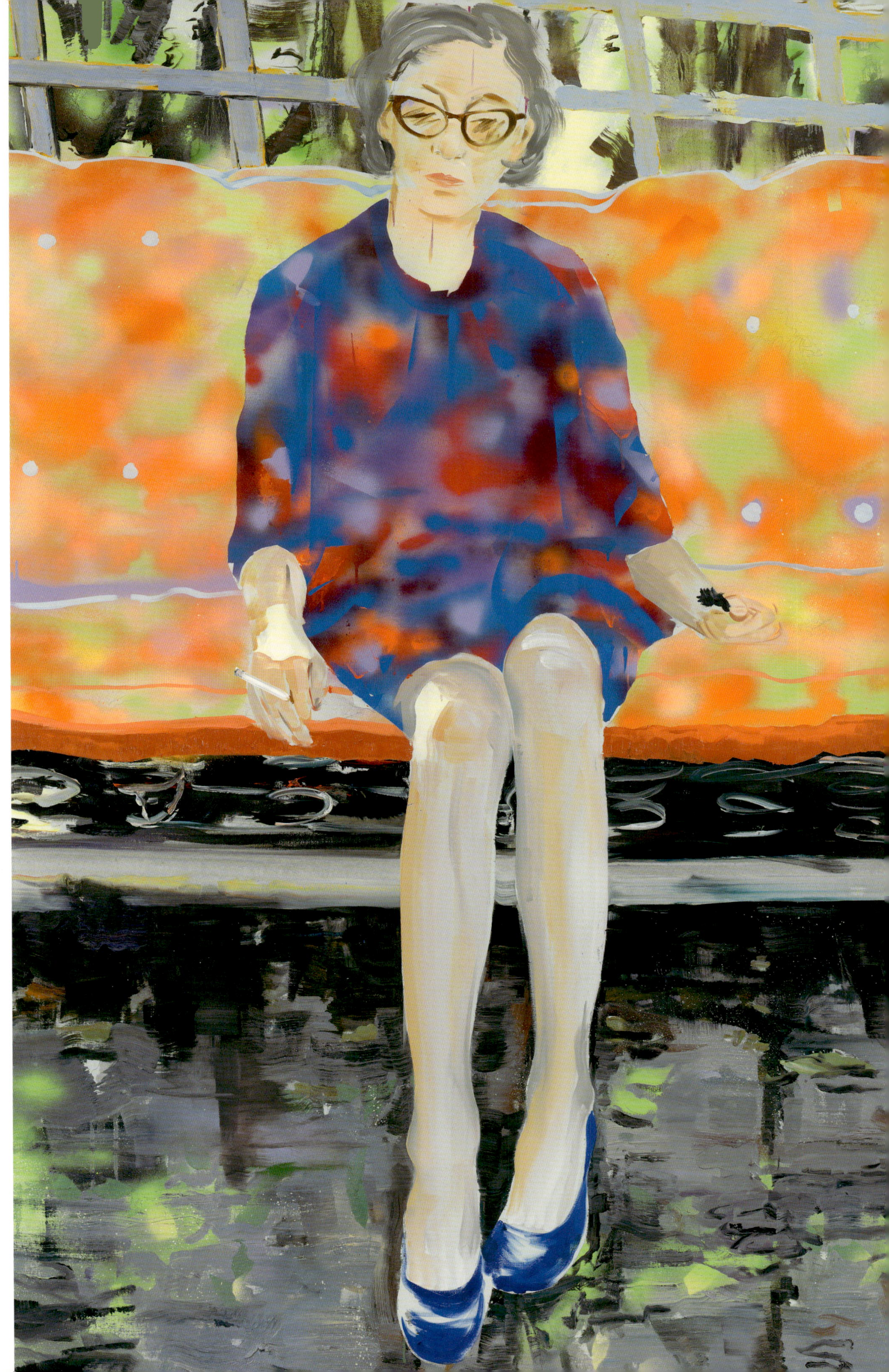

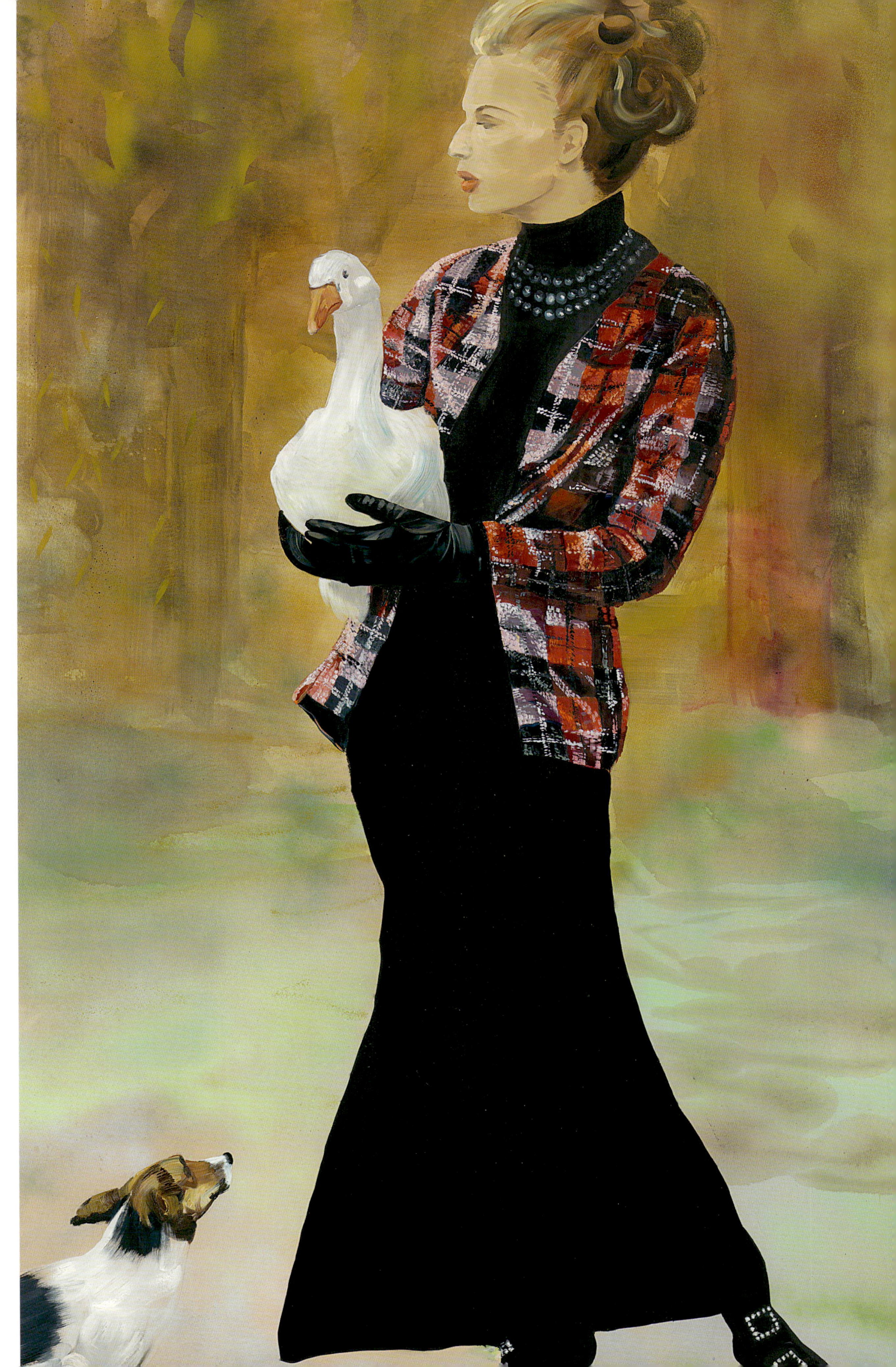

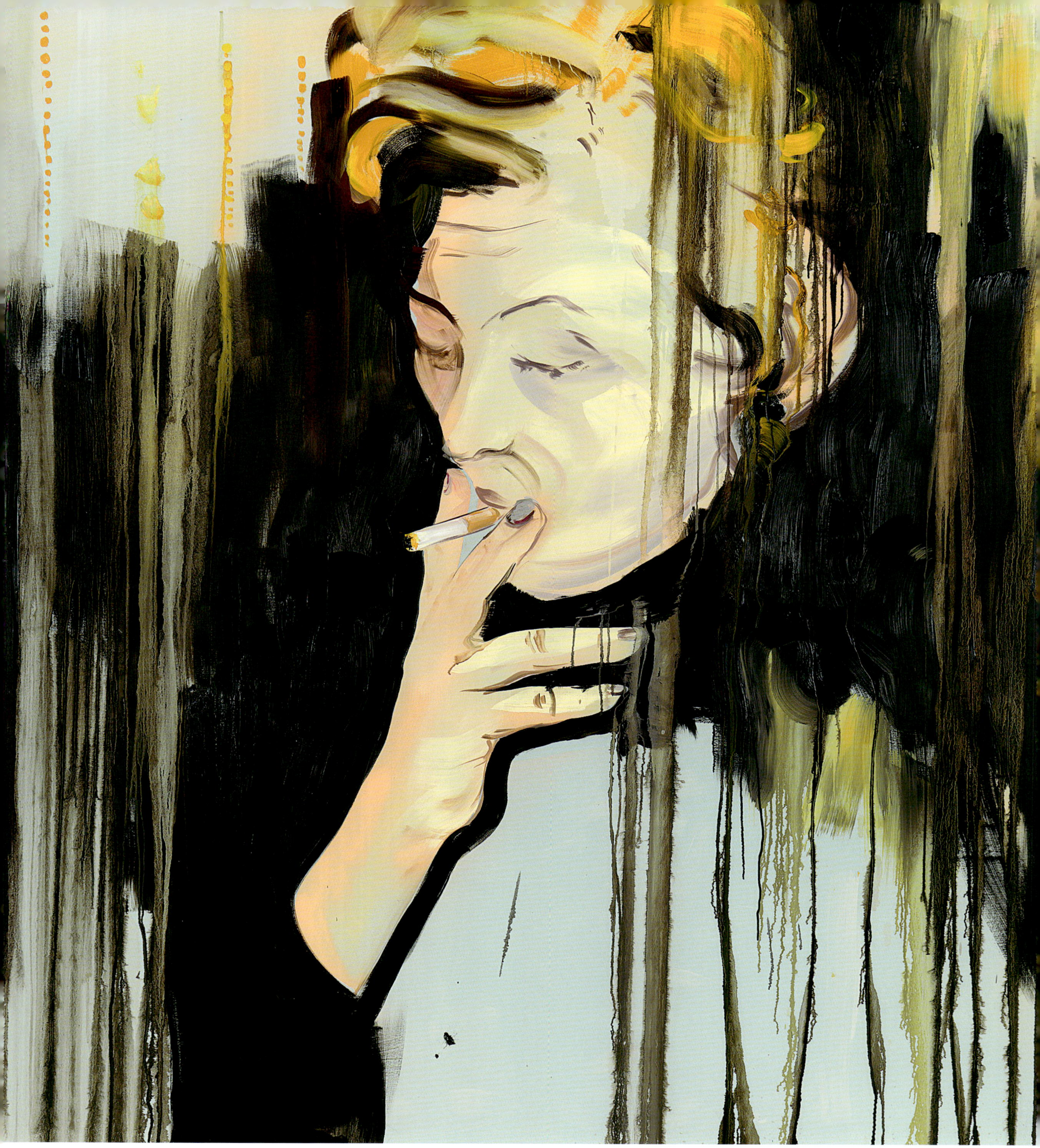

Mother 200, 2012
L'introvertie, 2012

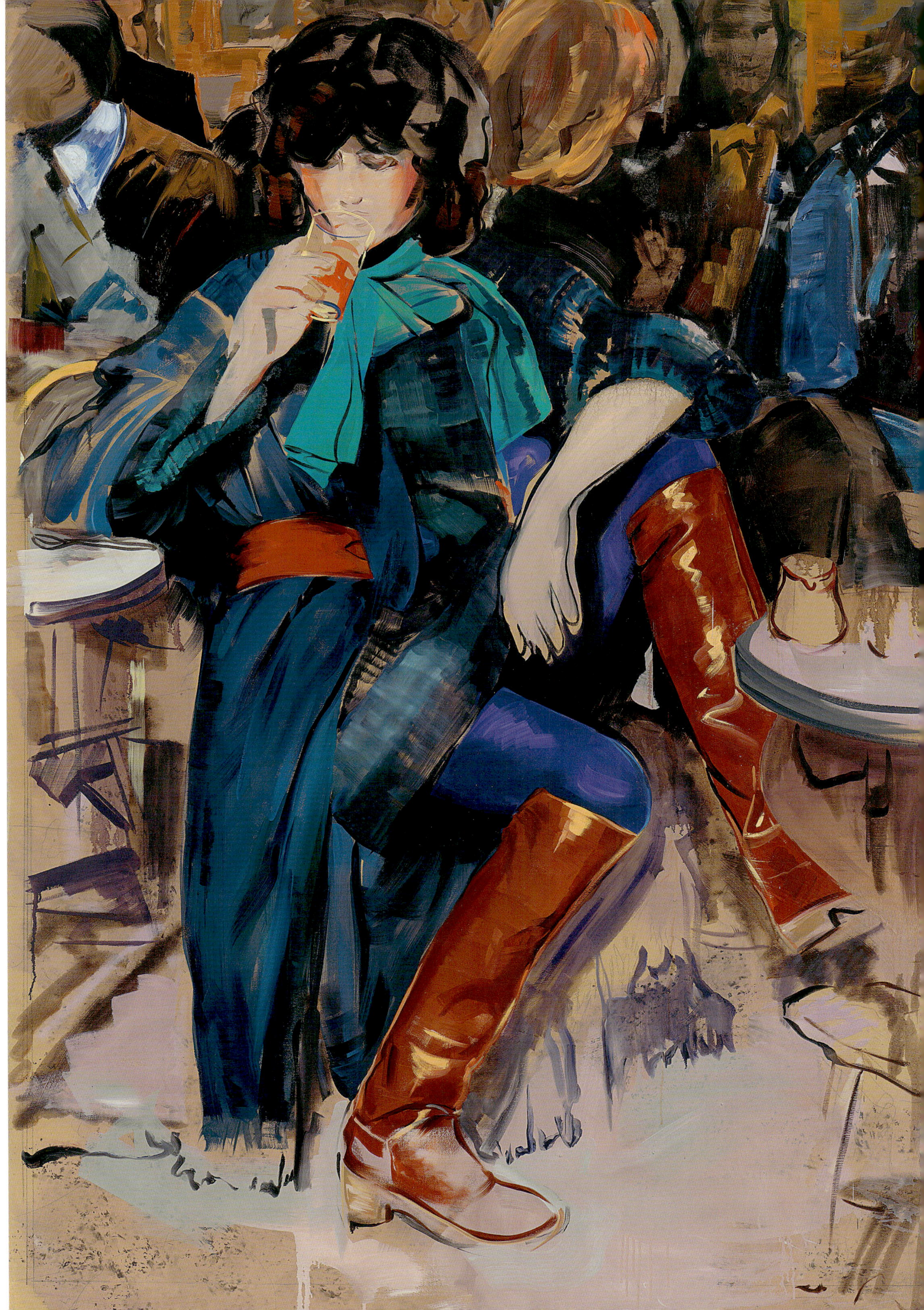

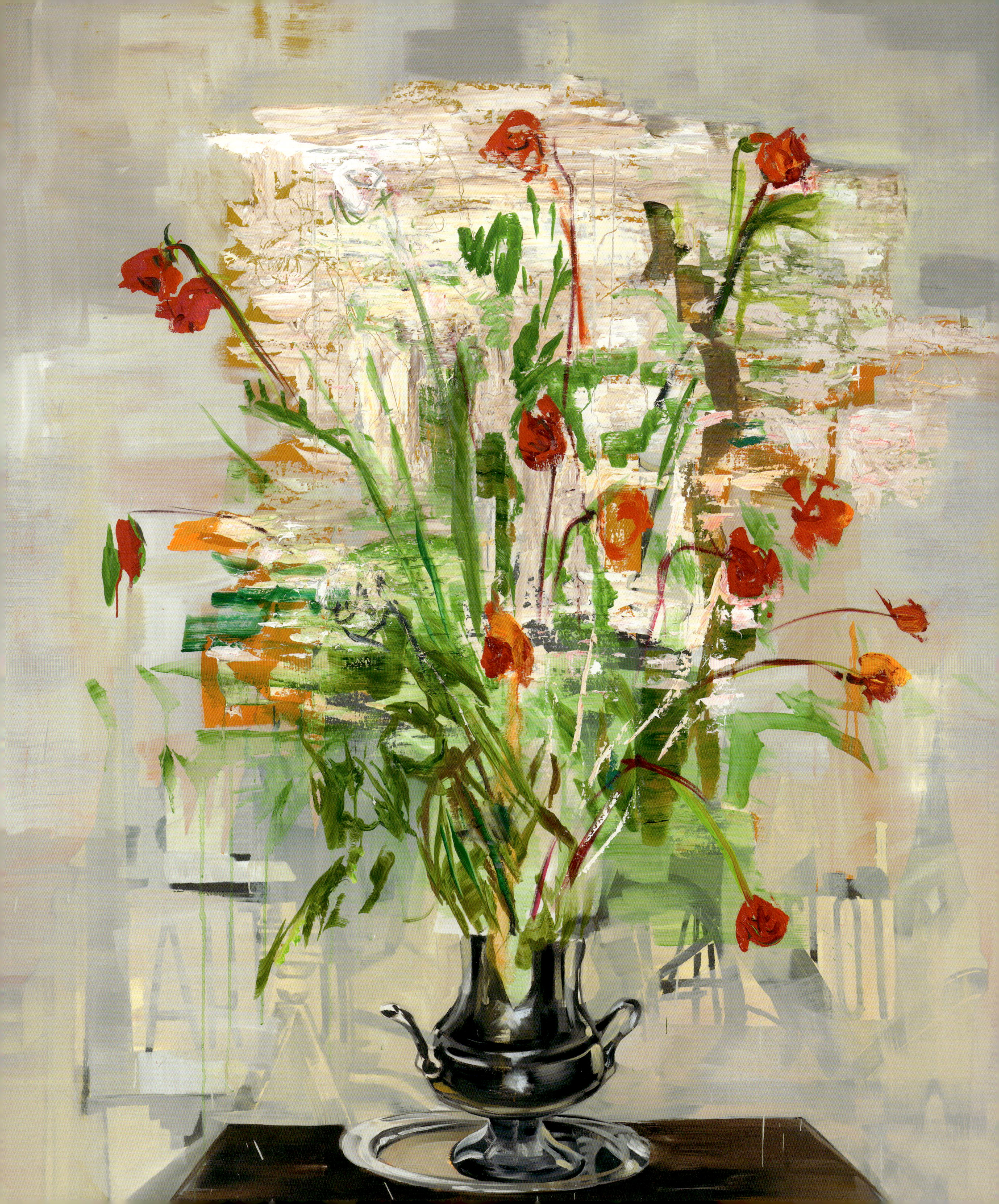

Chronology

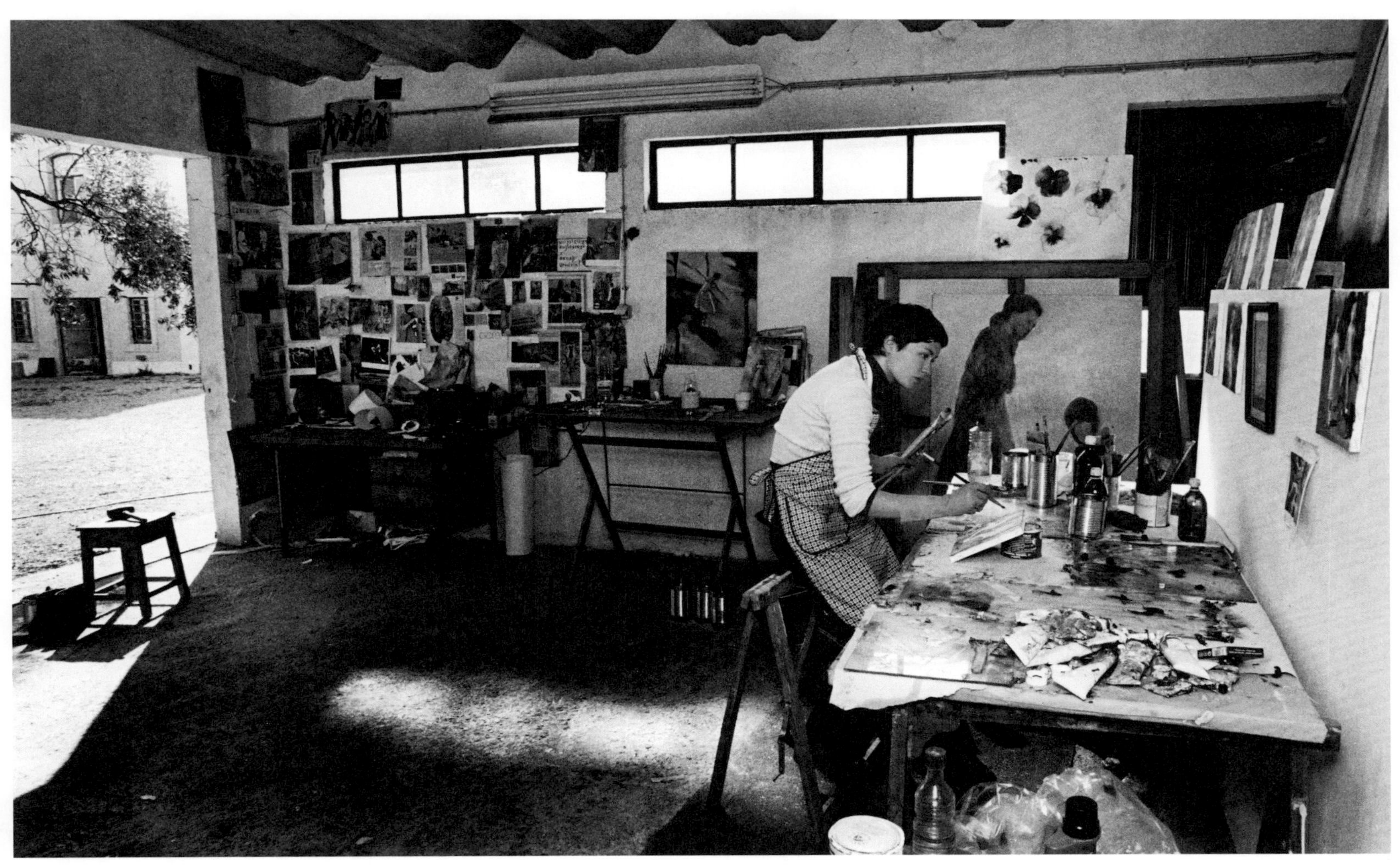

Silver Vase, 2012
Paulina Olowska in her studio, Lisbon, 1999

1993–1998

Born in 1976 in Gdańsk, Poland; attended the School of the Art Institute of Chicago, from 1993 to 1996, and received an MFA in Painting and Graphic Arts from the Academy of Fine Arts of Gdańsk in 2000. Participated in the Student Exchange Program of the Royal Academy of Art in The Hague in 1998. Was awarded a residency at the Arts and Visual Communication Center in Lisbon, Portugal from 1998 to 1999.

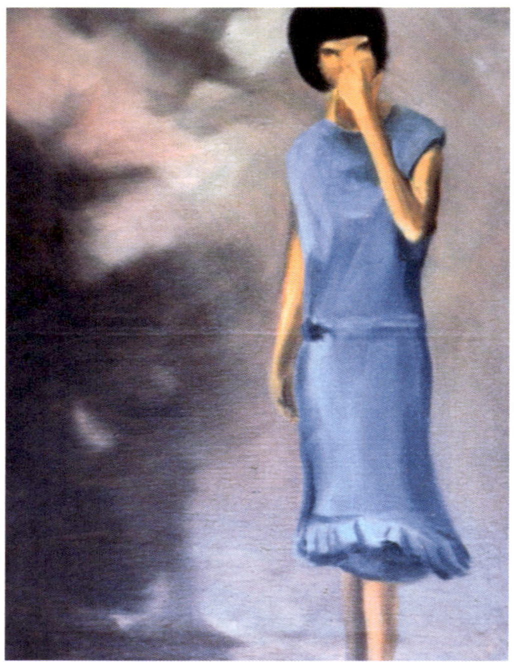

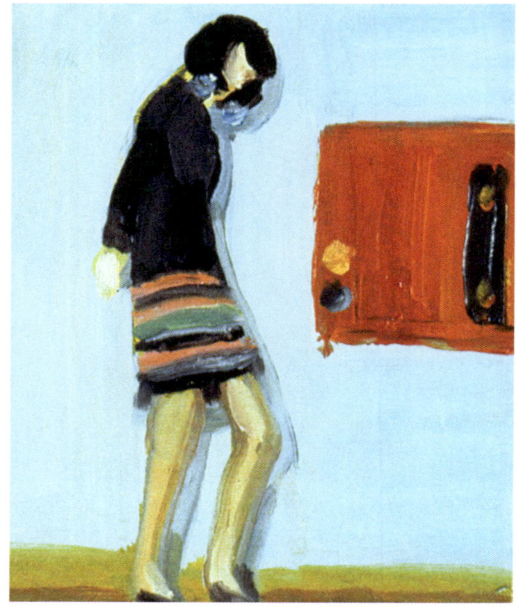

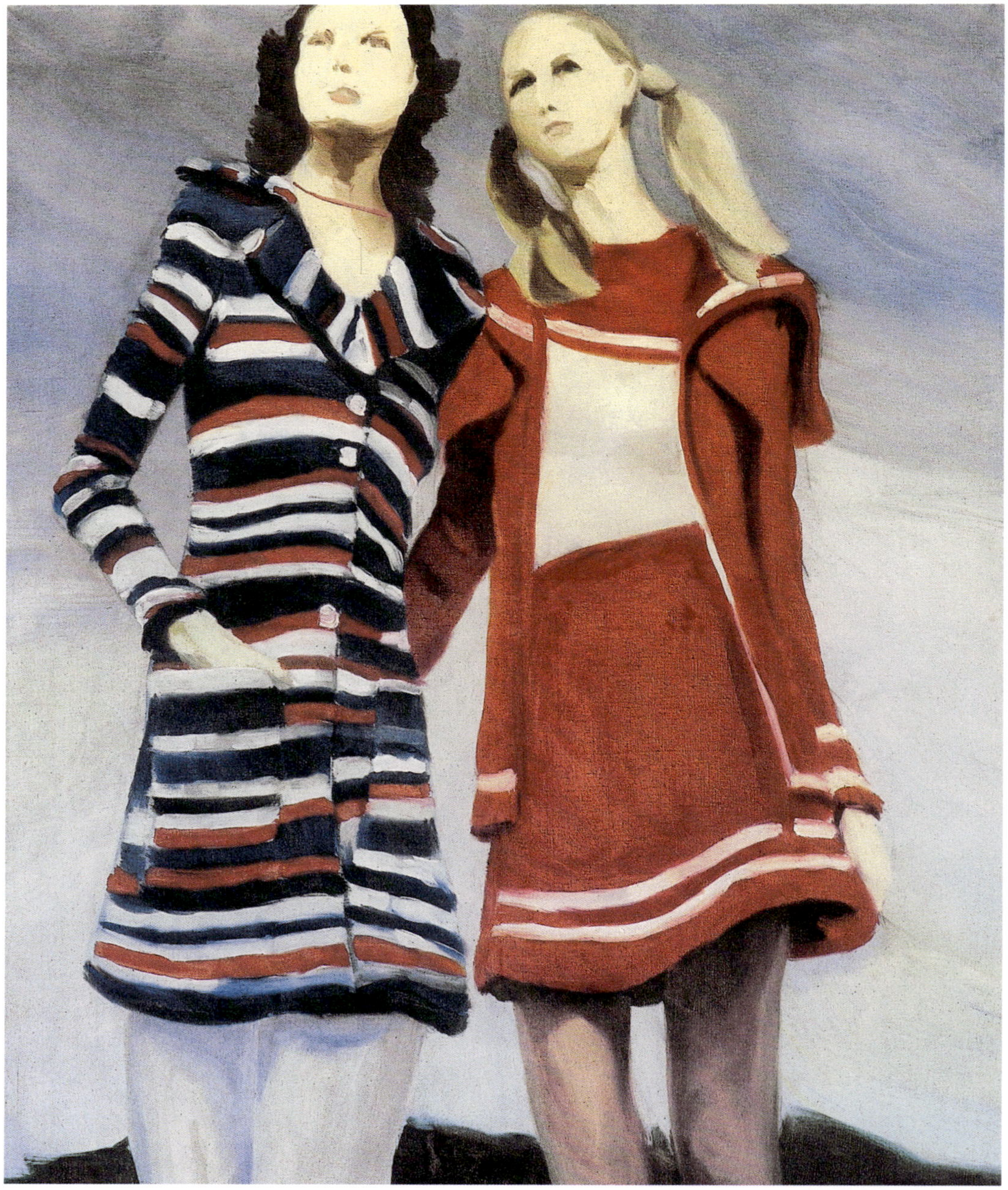

Slightly Disappointed; Do You Like Minimal Art?; Looking Up not Down, from the "Utopian Optimism" series, 1998–1999

While in Portugal, painted a series of paintings entitled Utopijny Optymizm/Utopian Optimism based on fashion photographs from Ty i Ja (You and Me), a 1960s cult magazine for young Polish intellectuals.

1999

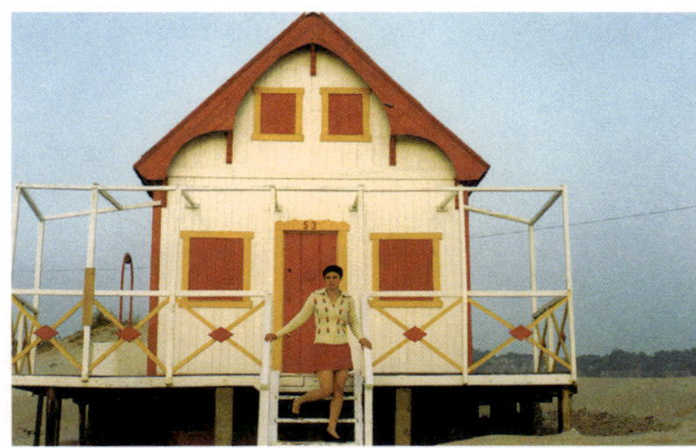

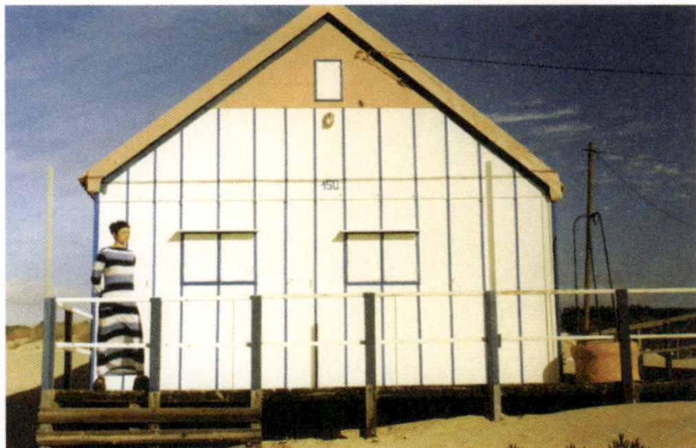

New Hobby–Summer Houses, 1999

Produced New Hobby—Summer Houses, a video projection and series of photographs
Posing against colorful beach bungalows on the outskirts of Lisbon, her outfits corresponding to the houses' decor. Inspired by 1960s advertisements for a real-estate agency. The film was an ironic comment on contemporary consumerism.

Shake the Disease, Lower Foyer Gallery, Duncan of Jordanstone College of Art & Design, Dundee, Scotland (group exhibition)
Curated by Lucy McKenzie, the exhibition included the works of Kai Althoff, Keith Farquhar, Ewan Imrie, Richard Kern, Lucy McKenzie, Alan Michael, Valerie Norrie, and Paulina Olowska.

Kto lubi styl sportowy?/Who Likes Sport Style?, Rua do Telhal 59, Lisbon (solo exhibition)
First solo exhibition held in an independent artists' space in Lisbon included paintings inspired by *Ty i Ja* magazine, a video, and performance entitled *Breezy, Light, and Colorful* inspired by Věra Chytilová's film *Sedmikrásky/Daisies* (1966), and "amateurish" fashion shoots.

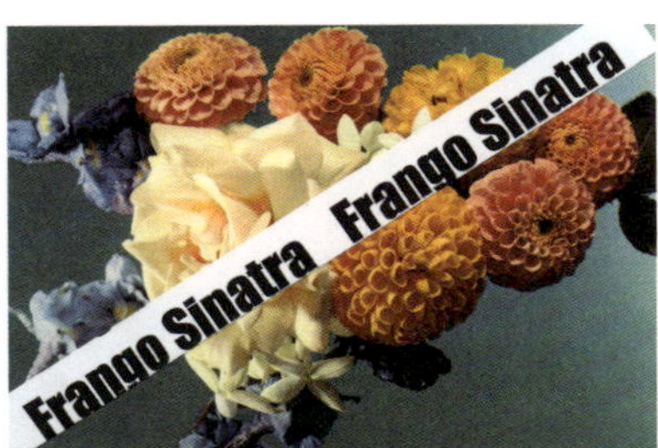

Invitation card for the exhibition *Frango Sinatra*, 1999

Frango Sinatra, Exposição No Moinho, Casalinho, Portugal (group exhibition)

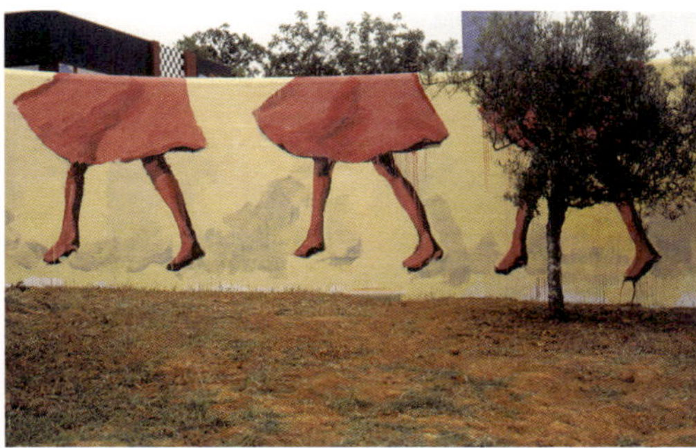

Mural painting, 1999

ZEFA Contemporary Art Centre, Almancil, Portugal (mural project)

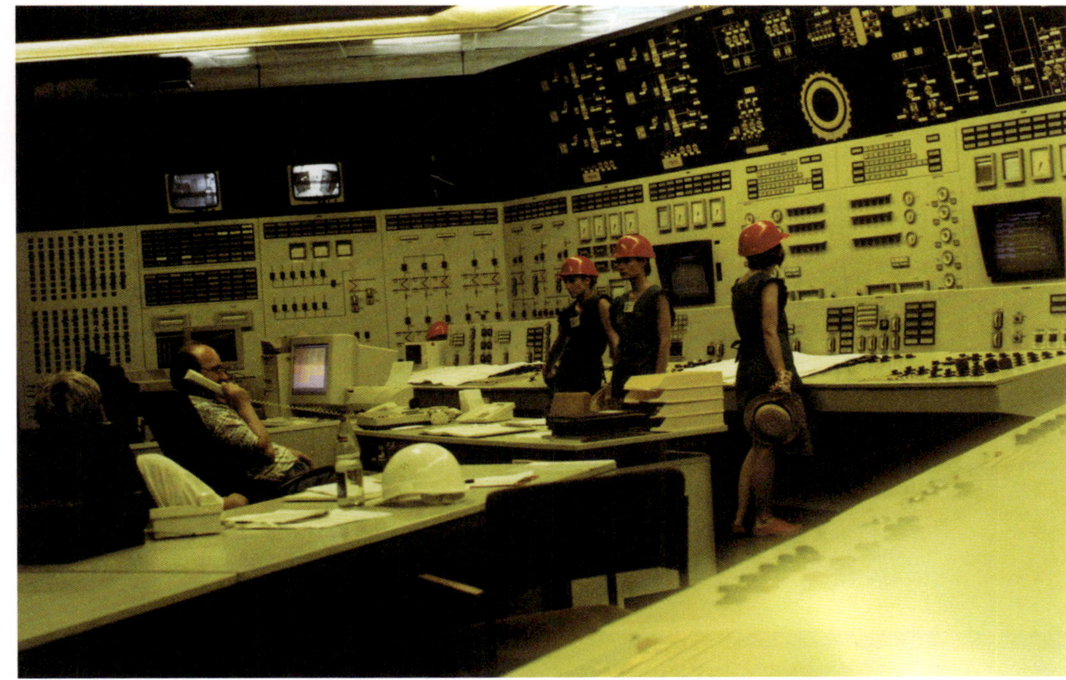

Gardeners of all Countries … , 1999

ARS NOVI-99 5 International Workshop, Greifswald, Germany (group exhibition)
Olowska presented *Gardeners of all Countries …* , a video shot in a former nuclear power station in Lubmin, Germany.

Center for Contemporary Art (CCA) Kitakyushu, Japan (residency 1999–2000)

2000

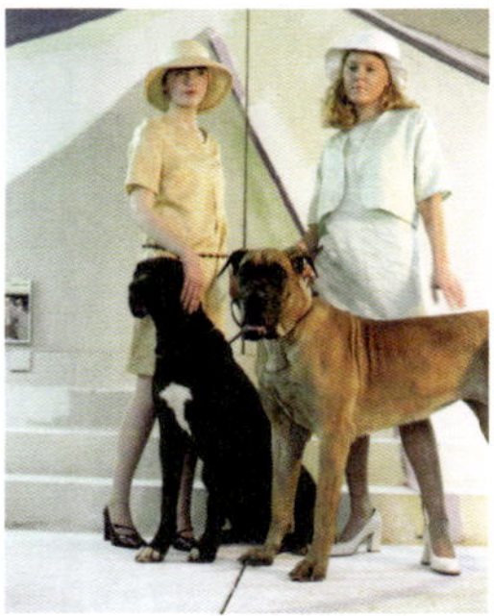

Documentation of the performance *Triumph of Youth*, 1999

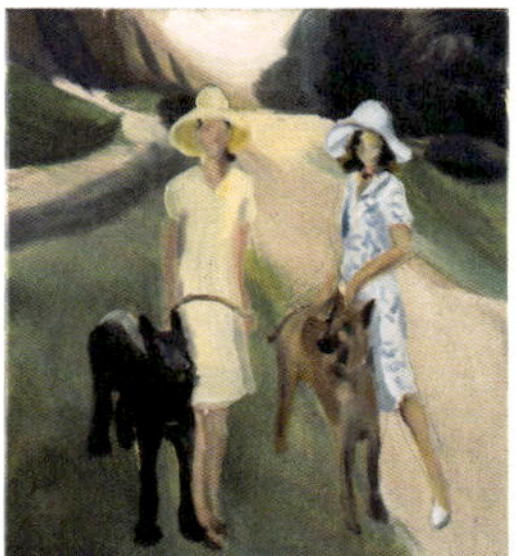

Triumph of Youth, 1999

Triumph of Youth, Academy of Fine Arts, Gdańsk, Poland (MFA thesis exhibition)

The exhibition comprised a group of paintings derived from awkward Eastern European fashion images, a Super-8 film entitled *Always Up*, and the performance *Społem* based on an advertisement for the 1960s monopoly shop named Społem. "I like the freedom I have for making decisions and not being connected to ideas that are too big. The choice of inspiration comes to me quite easily. Sometimes it is a tiny intrigue, an accident, the color of an image that starts working … I would like my pictures to be like fleeting memories … I want them to have no particular time, to be suspended in time … In my video works I am trying, maybe out of perversity, to extend the projection time."
(Excerpts from Olowska's MFA thesis essay)

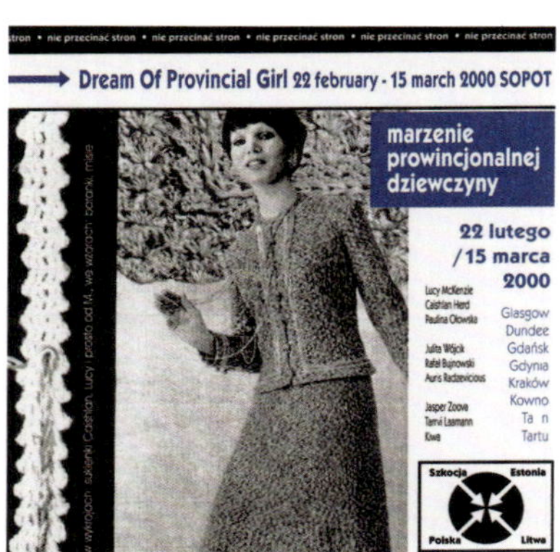

Catalogue *Marzenie Prowincjonalnej Dziewczyny*, 2000

Marzenie Prowincjonalnej Dziewczyny/The Dream of Provincial Girl, series of exhibitions curated by Paulina Olowska, Lucy McKenzie, and Julita Wojcik in an apartment, Sopot, Poland

"We wanted to create an alternative exhibition space, independent from any art institutions. A space in which, without big aspirations and without compromise, there will be young art displayed. This project totally depended on our own integration and motivation. We wanted to underline locality as a value. To focus on our closest neighborhood was a natural reaction to globalization in the arts."
(*Aktivist Magazine*, no. 30, November 2001)

"Our first performance together took place at the opening night of the *Dream of Provincial Girl* exhibition … The performance was a reaction to an image from one of Paulina's *Ty i Ja* fashion magazine shoots. While Paulina's younger brother DJ'ed house music, we stood in belted raincoats with very large aggressive dogs and shone torches into the faces of the audience in what was a very crowded room."
(Lucy McKenzie in: Lucy McKenzie/Paulina Olowska/Ken Okiishi/Nick Mauss, "K/L/M/N/O/P—A Conversation via email, January 2007," *Noël sur le balcon/HOLD THE COLOR*, exhibition catalogue, Sammlung Goetz, Munich 2007, p. 92)

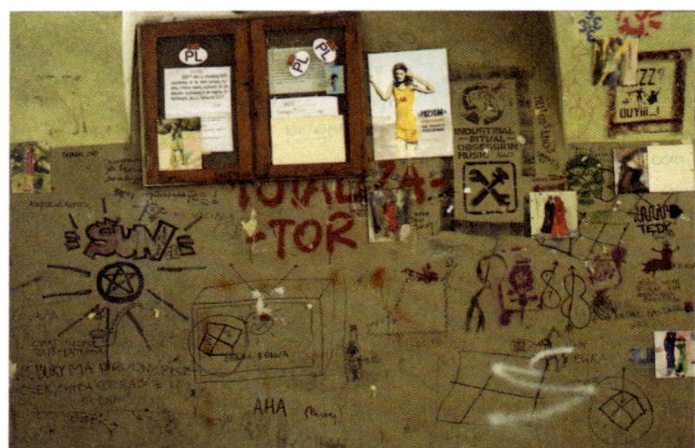

Na wiosnę, 2000

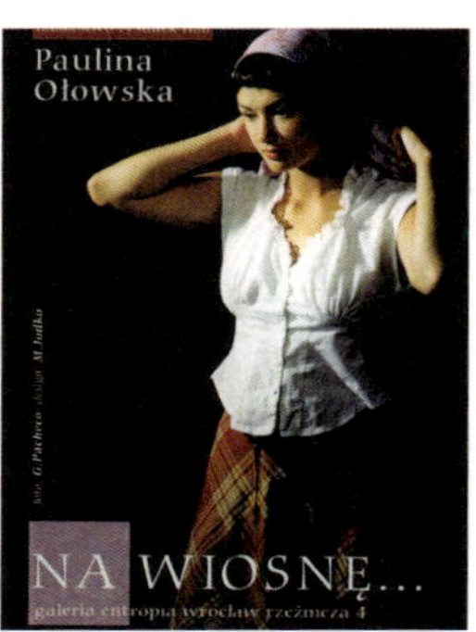

Invitation card for the exhibition *Na wiosnę*, 2000

Na wiosnę/For Spring, Entropia Gallery, Wrocław, Poland (solo exhibition)

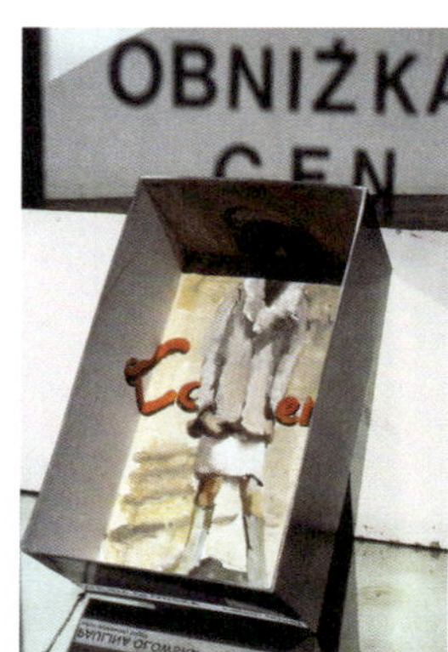

Latem Taniej, 2000

Latem Taniej/Summer Discount, Mobilny Salon Wystawowy Bagatt, Gdańsk, Poland (solo exhibition)

Mobilny Salon Wystawowy Bagatt was a non-commercial mobile gallery-in-a-shoebox, curated by Łukasz Gorczyca.

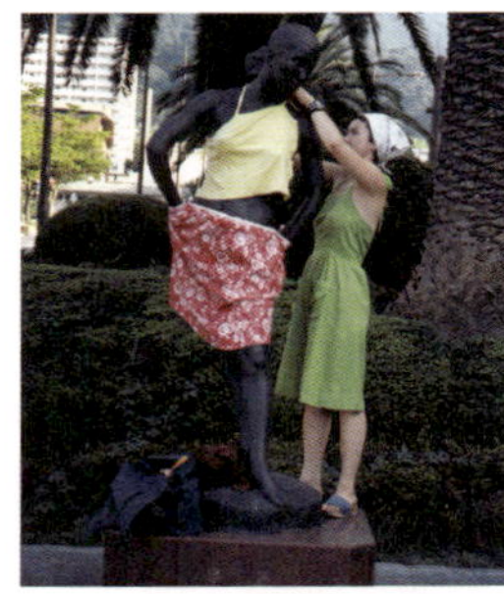

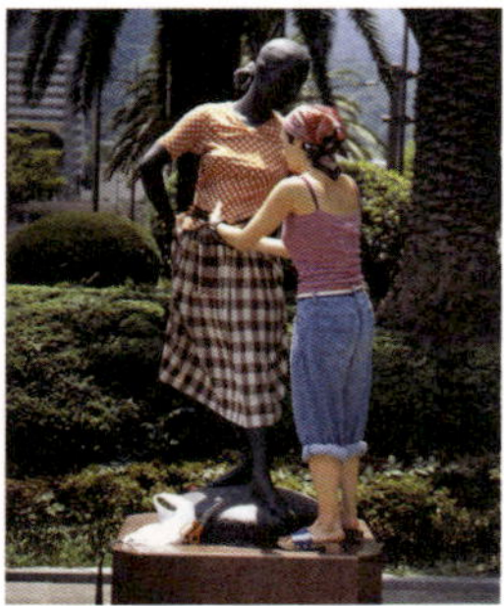

Documentation of the performance *I Like Traditionalism and Traditionalism Likes Me/For Sato Churyo*, 2000

I Like Traditionalism Traditionalism Likes Me/For Sato Churyo (performance made during a residency in Japan)

For one week in the city of Kitakyushu Olowska dressed and "cared for" a sculpture representing a nude woman made in the 1970s by a Japanese artist.

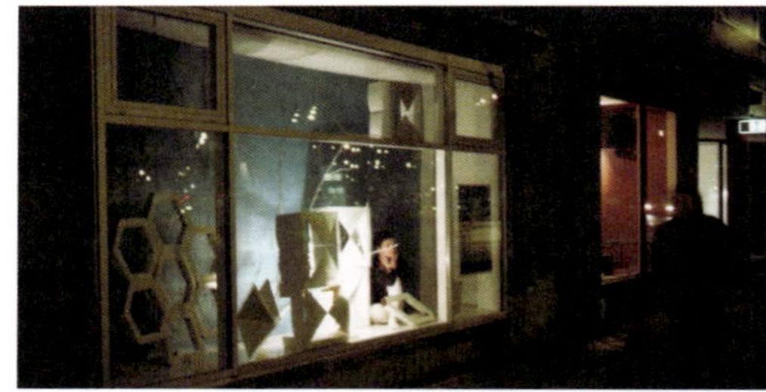

Documentation of the exhibition *Nurse with Wound*, 2000

Nurse with Wound, Art Hall Gallery, Tallinn, Estonia (group exhibition)

Olowska performed *Kiosk of Revolution*.

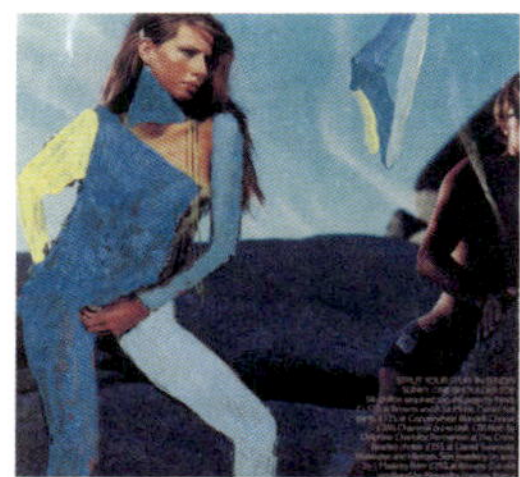

"Construction First–Collages from Japan" series, 2000

Abstraktsioon Töötluses/Abstraction in Process, Sebra Gallery, Tartu, Estonia (solo exhibition)

The exhibition referred to the myth of the avant-garde and included collages, paintings, paper installation, painted clothes, and a video of the performance *Kiosk of Revolution*.

Rijksakademie van Beeldende Kunsten, Amsterdam (residency program, 2000–2002)

2001

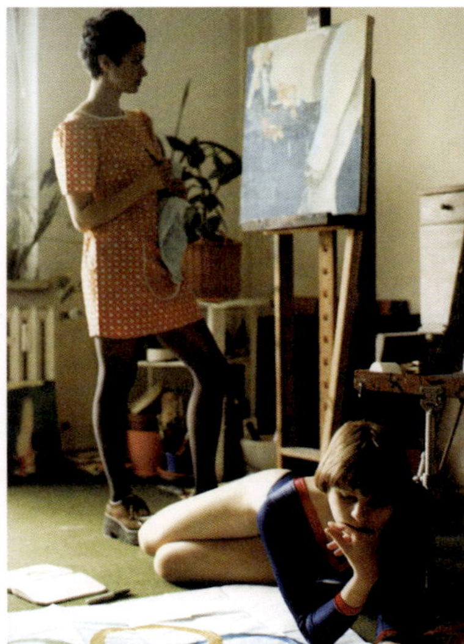

Heavy Duty, 2000

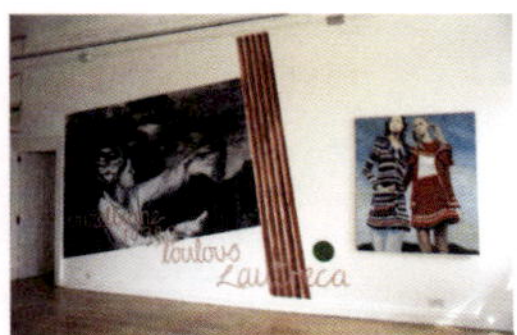

Lucy McKenzie and Paulina Olowska, *Heavy Duty*, 2001

Heavy Duty, with Lucy McKenzie, Inverleith House, Royal Botanic Garden, Edinburgh

"The first museum exhibition of works by Lucy McKenzie and Paulina Olowska embraces the ways in which the two artists work individually, and have interacted and collaborated since 1998 when they first met. The show includes new paintings, elements from their former projects, posters, sculptures, typography, two collaborative wall paintings, and a video travelogue to Moscow and St. Petersburg in Russia entitled *Full Moon*. The artists intentionally confuse the boundaries of categorization, creating a web of cross-references, influences, and jokes. The exhibition also includes paintings and sculptures brought by the artists that were either created or collected by their families—art they grew up with."
(From the exhibition press release)

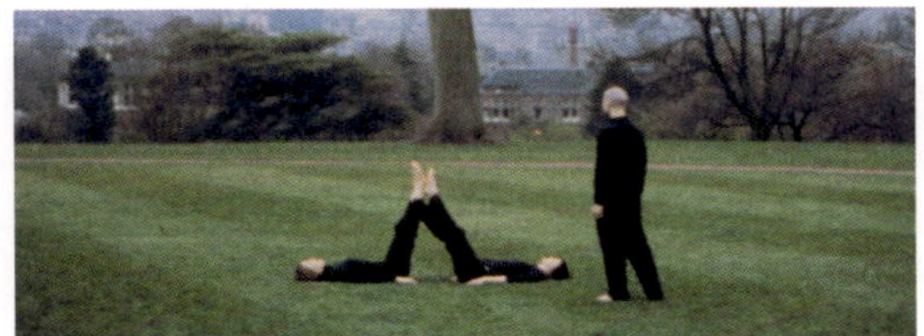

Bauhaus Yoga, 2001

Bauhaus Yoga, Inverleith House, Royal Botanic Garden, Edinburgh (performance)

"Bauhaus and yoga, both utopian, embody simplicity and practicality of progress. Their main goal is to reach perfection in a balance of body and mind ... *Bauhaus Yoga* wants to grasp the past and present utopias by reexamining them, romanticizing them, and thereby building a new future based on resemblance and mutual attraction."
(Paulina Olowska, "Bauhaus Yoga," *Dot Dot Dot*, no. 6, October 2003, p. 34)

Hotel Sub Rosa, Cabinet Gallery, London, UK (group exhibition)

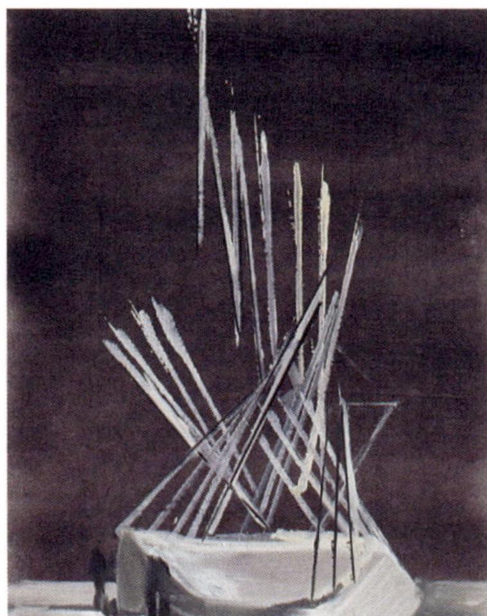

View of a Sculpture, 2001

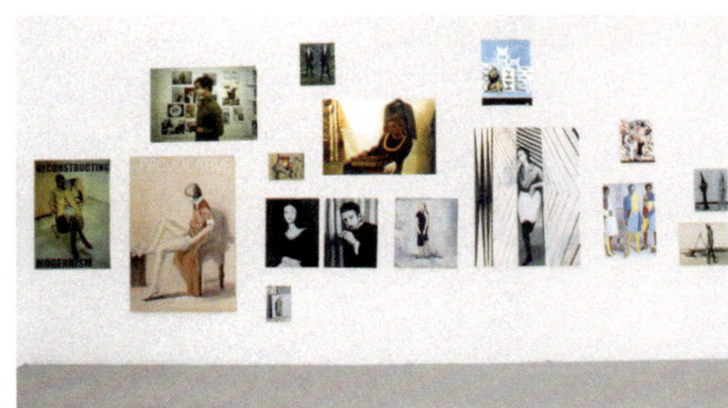

Salon de l'indépendent, 2001

Salon de l'indépendent, Project Room, Rijksakademie van Beeldende Kunsten, Amsterdam (installation and performance)

Installation of paintings—posters for non-existing exhibitions and a monumental wall painting based on a socialist design mural in Slupsk, Poland.
For the performance, five performers wearing scarves with hand-painted signs (*Avant-garde, Provocative, Subversive, Utopia, Fortunate Future*) posed in the space, mimicking the paintings, the posters, and each other.

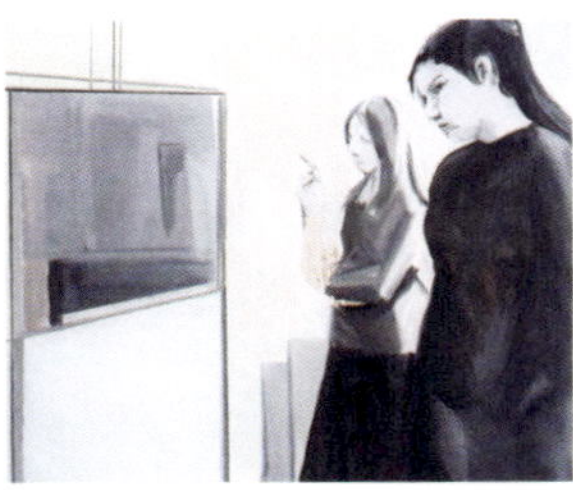

Untitled, 2001

Nailing a Few of the Taste Makers, presented at Open Studios, Rijksakademie van Beeldende Kunsten, Amsterdam (installation and performance)

An installation based on the idea of the studio as a singular but complex three-dimensional painting—*the painter's studio*. It was created with painters' objects such as an easel, chairs, a table, a mirror, music, and a series of paintings, sketches, drawings, and posters. The main inspiration was Piet Mondrian's studio in Paris—not a real working space, but an artificial replica with precisely selected and placed objects and paintings.
For the performance, along with three other women wearing wigs, outfits painted with geometric patterns, shoes, and makeup spontaneously sit and lie on the floor, "poisoned by the blue book" entitled *Performing Arts: The Economic Dilemma* (1966), with Bauhaus (the band) playing as a looped soundtrack.

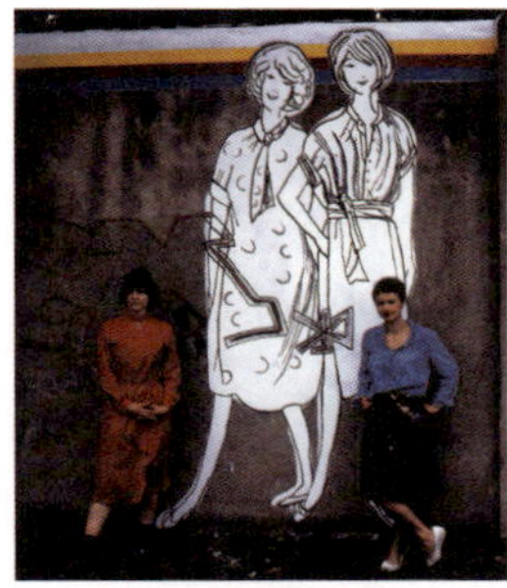

Lucy McKenzie and Paulina Olowska in front of their wall painting *Plastyczna integracja*, 2001

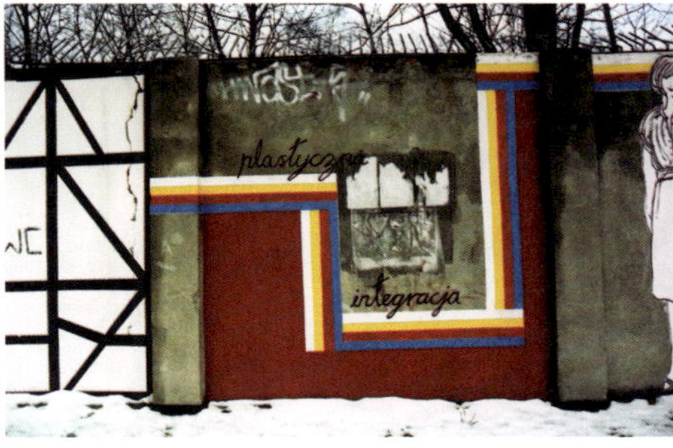

Lucy McKenzie and Paulina Olowska, *Plastyczna integracja*, 2001

Plastyczna integracja/Aesthetic Integration, with Lucy McKenzie, Festiwal Malarstwa, Sciennego, Kliniczna, Gdańsk, Poland (wall paintings)

"When we started the first wall painting ... in Gdańsk shipyards, Lucy and I basically layered some of our favorite readymade and typical mural images from both our backgrounds. For example, we used iconic graffiti lettering, Fachwerk, and Polish fashion advertising symbols from the 1960s. From then on, I started to approach art making like collage, pulling images from different places. I started collaborations with other artists quite spontaneously, to see where the work would lead."
(Paulina Olowska in: Lucy McKenzie/Paulina Olowska/Ken Okiishi/Nick Mauss, "K/L/M/N/O/P—A Conversation via email, January 2007," *Noël sur le balcon/HOLD THE COLOR*, exhibition catalogue, Sammlung Goetz, Munich 2007, p. 105–106)

2002

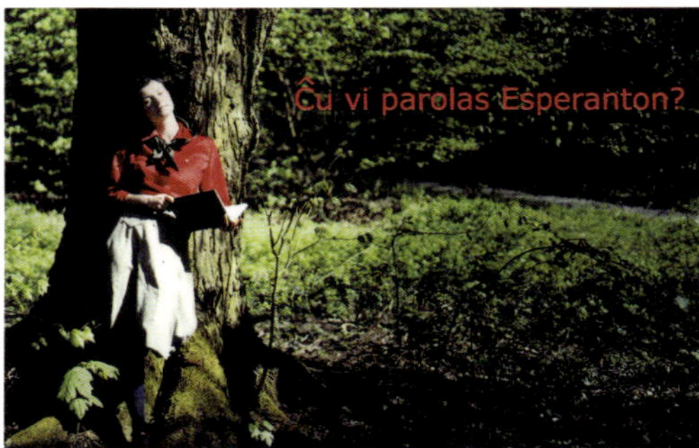

Cu Vi Parolas Esperanton?, 2002

Cu Vi Parolas Esperanton?, billboard project, AMS Outside Gallery, Center of Contemporary Art, Warsaw, and 400 locations in public spaces, Poland

"I often quote utopian movements like the Russian avant-garde and Bauhaus. I see them as significant examples of artistic engagement in a variety of fields—applied and fine arts, collaboration and team work, as well as social commitment. One such interesting and idealistic project was the use of the language of Esperanto. In order to examine what Esperanto means nowadays, I hosted an advertisement campaign on billboards, using this constructed language knowing that less than two percent of the population would be able to understand it ... For me Esperanto is about wanting to make a valuable change ... Esperanto was based on a concept in which everyone could choose to partake."
(Paulina Olowska in conversation with Maria Barnas, "Gentle Distortions," *Metropolis* M, no. 5, 2004, p. 120)

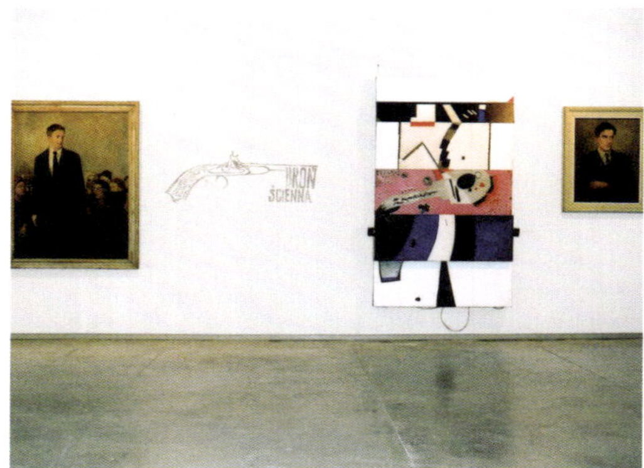

Romancing with Avant-Garde, 2002

Romansując z awangardą/Romancing with Avant-Garde, National Gallery of Art, Sopot, Poland (curated exhibition)

Selection and spatial arrangement of works from the collection of Sopot's National Gallery of Art.

"I decided to work with and engage the museum's permanent collection. The director asked me to speed up the process as the gallery would be soon shut down ... The beautiful pavilion was to be rebuilt and turned into a hotel and supermarket ... The gallery's collection contained works dating from 1950 to 1970 ... I decided to focus on tracing history rather than choosing works based on standards of aesthetics. The space of the gallery was divided by freestanding walls, which separated and organized individual groups by theme: 'Landscapes,' 'Women Only,' 'The Art of Pure Enjoyment,' and 'Freedom Seeker.' The work varied from a Socialist Realist sculpture of a tanker to strange abstractions made by amateur painters. I opted for an avant-garde approach for the presentation, and considered the installation as one big collage."
(Paulina Olowska in conversation with Maria Barnas, "Gentle Distortions," *Metropolis M*, no. 5, 2004, p. 114–119)

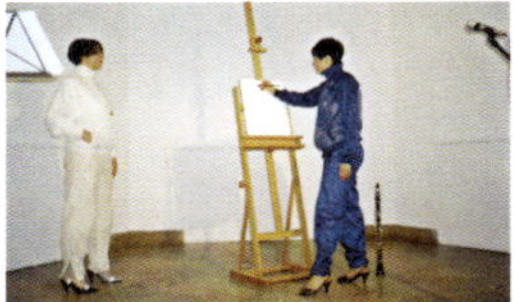

Lucy McKenzie and Paulina Olowska performing *Oblique Composition I*, 2002

Oblique Composition I, with Lucy McKenzie, Center for Contemporary Art Ujazdowski Castle, Warsaw (performance)

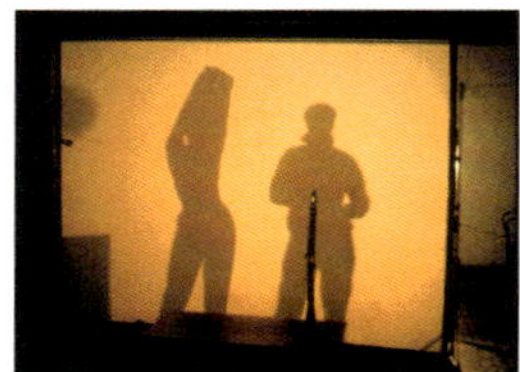

Lucy McKenzie and Paulina Olowska performing *Oblique Composition II*, 2002

Oblique Composition II, with Lucy McKenzie, Flourish Studios, Glasgow (performance)

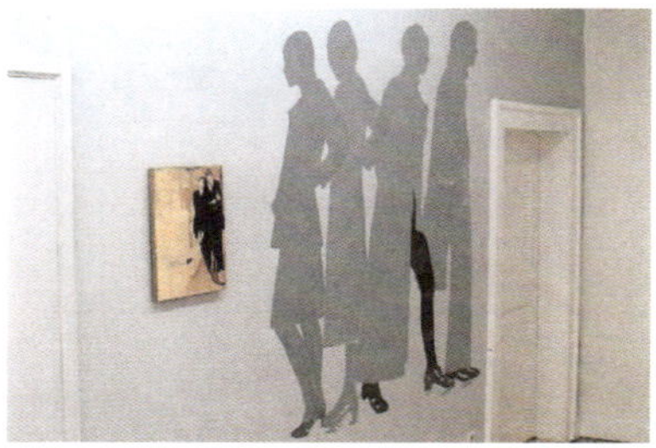

The Best Book About Pessimism I Ever Read, 2002

The Best Book About Pessimism I Ever Read, curated by Lucy McKenzie, Kunstverein Braunschweig, Brunswick, Germany (group exhibition)

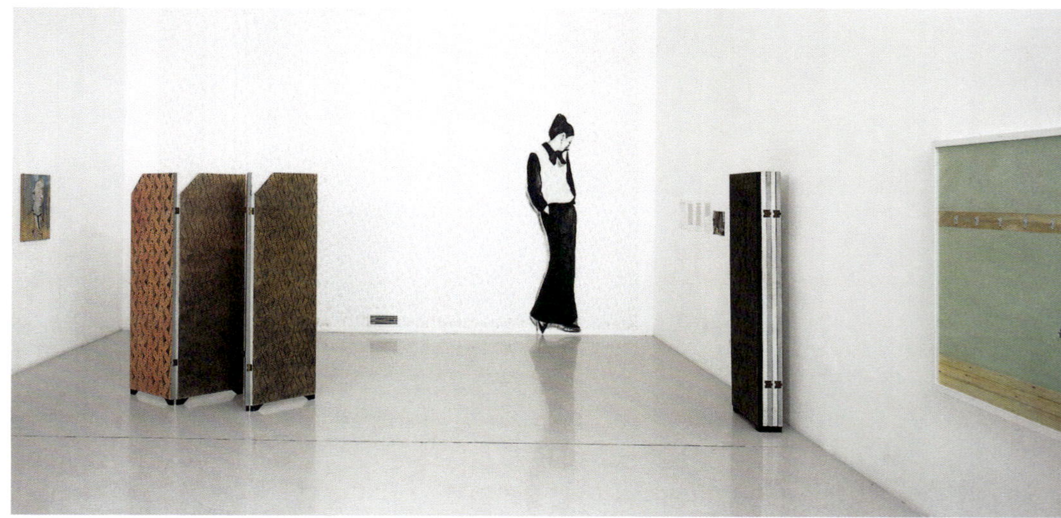

The Rule of Hospitality, 2002

The Rule of Hospitality, Galerie Neu, Berlin (group exhibition)

2003

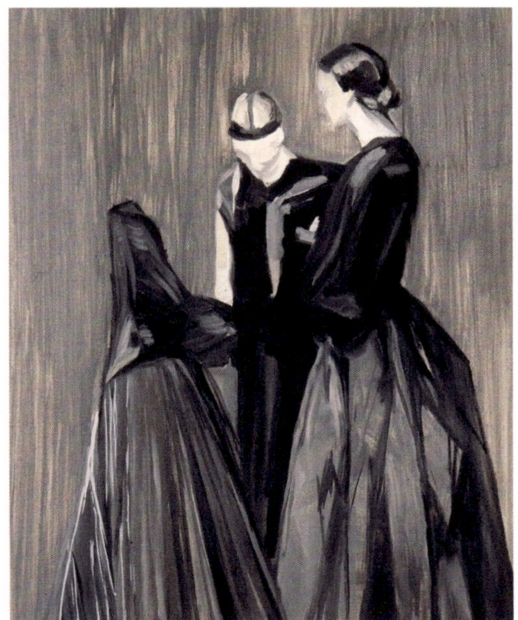

Three Greys, 2002

In Lubelian, Cabinet Gallery, London (solo exhibition)

"My exhibition at Cabinet Gallery was based on an utopian vision of an artistic community rather than a desire to establish that such a community actually existed. I'm showing what it could have been, unimpeded by historical facts."
(Paulina Olowska in: Dominic van den Boogerd, "Work in Progress. Interview with Paulina Olowska," *Stedelijk Museum Bulletin*, May 2004, p. 39)

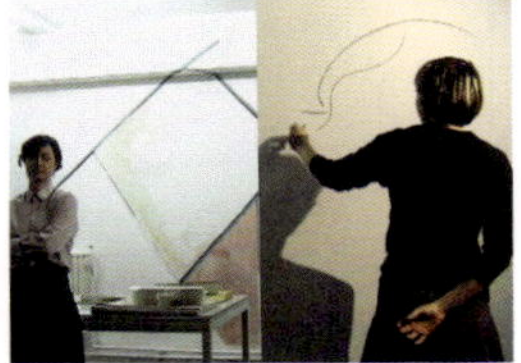

Paulina Olowska and Lucy McKenzie performing *Oblique Composition III*, 2003

Oblique Composition III, with Lucy McKenzie, Cabinet Gallery, London (performance)

"The video [documenting the performance *Oblique Composition III* at Cabinet Gallery] shows the two artists in an office. A painting by Olowska of the American actress Susan Strasberg (2001) hangs on the wall; opposite, McKenzie is seen drawing Olowska's portrait. With McKenzie's portrait of Olowska related to the painting of Strasberg in this way, the office becomes a studio and the artists become actors, the Strasberg picture also functioning as a self-portrait by Olowska."
(Stephan Urbaschek, "East Meets West," *Noël sur le balcon/ HOLD THE COLOR*, exhibition catalogue, Sammlung Goetz, 2007, p. 52)

"The three performance manifestations of *Oblique Composition* took on different shapes but had things in common, such as a female protagonist, the act of mimicry, and a celebration of abstraction. The final video of *Oblique Composition III* had a loose moody feeling like one of the Chantal Akerman films. One can watch it in a loop. For me it was a celebration of female friendship and contemplating work together."
(Paulina Olowska in: Lucy McKenzie/Paulina Olowska/Ken Okiishi/Nick Mauss, "K/L/M/N/O/P—A Conversation via email, January 2007," *Noël sur le balcon/HOLD THE COLOR*, exhibition catalogue, Sammlung Goetz, Munich 2007, p. 106)

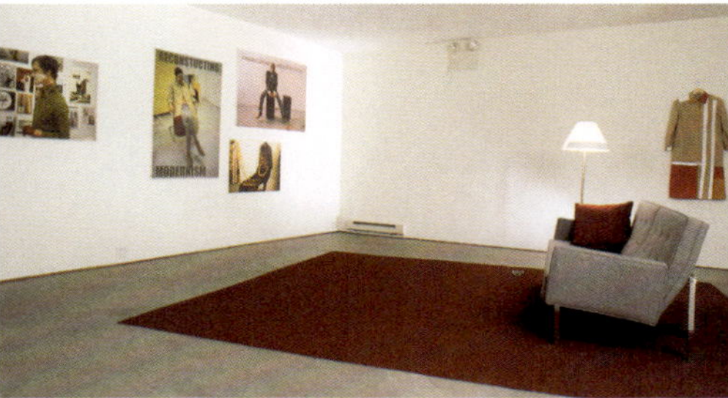

Architectures of Gender. Contemporary Women's Art in Poland, 2003

Architectures of Gender: Contemporary Women's Art in Poland, Sculpture Center, New York (group exhibition)

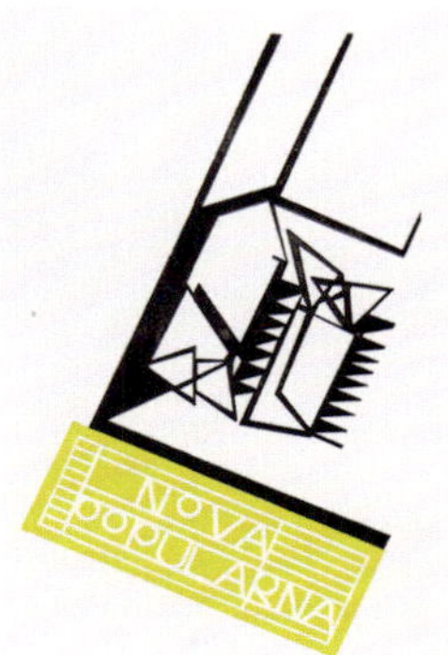

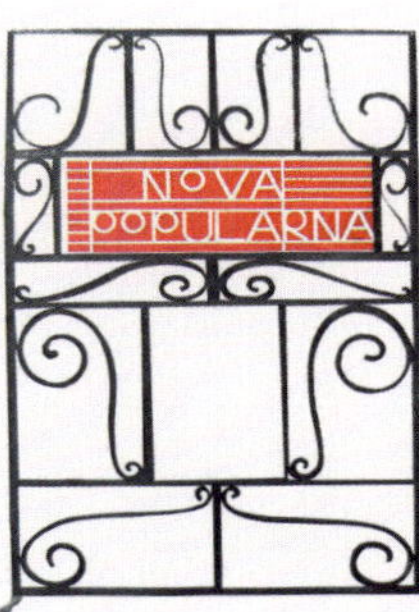

Lucy McKenzie and Paulina Olowska, posters for *Nova Popularna*, 2003

Nova Popularna in collaboration with Lucy McKenzie and Foksal Gallery Foundation, National Artist Club Gallery, Warsaw (event)

"*Nova Popularna* was an experiment [one month long] in revitalizing and investigating [not only] the idea of an art salon, but also three-dimensional painting—where we could express our love for and interest in arts and crafts, and the aesthetics of movements such as Polish folk design and Art Nouveau. Our bar/salon was located in the old National Artist Club Gallery, which permitted us to hide the fact we were running an illegal bar with hard liquor and loud concerts. As little as it was advertised in the media, it started to attract an audience by word of mouth ... We had a range of music styles and concerts from classical piano to electronic music ... I guess in the end it was quite an ambiguous place to hang out: was it an artist-run space? A bar? An exhibition of some kind? After it was closed down many people very quickly became nostalgic about it and wanted to start it up again. It became a bit of a legend. The *Nova Popularna* catalogue and record now function as fragments of a history, alluding to what the bar was like."
(Paulina Olowska in: Lucy McKenzie/Paulina Olowska/Ken Okiishi/Nick Mauss, "K/L/M/N/O/P—A Conversation via email, January 2007," *Noël sur le balcon/HOLD THE COLOR*, exhibition catalogue, Sammlung Goetz, Munich 2007, p. 96)

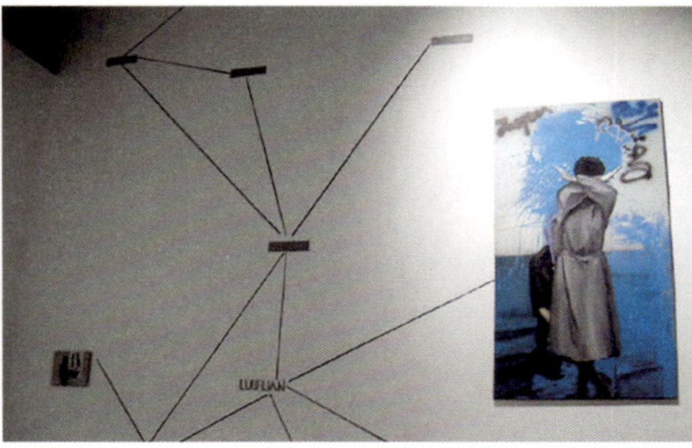

Clandestine, 2003

Dreams and Conflicts: The Viewer's Dictatorship. Clandestine, Venice Biennale, 50th International Art Exhibition, curated by Francesco Bonami, Venice (group exhibition)

Hidden in a Daylight, with Mathilde Rosier, exhibition curated by Foksal Gallery Foundation, in collaboration with the 3rd Era New Horizons Film Festival in Cieszyn, Poland (group exhibition)
Paulina Olowska and Mathilde Rosier presented *Entracte*, a site-specific video and sound installation at Hotel Pod Jeleniem, Cieszyn.

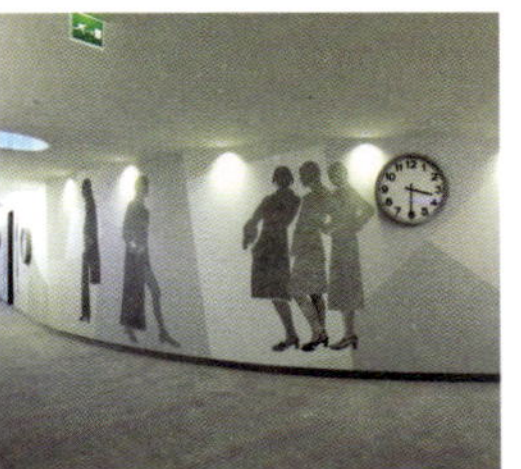

Gestützt von Poesie, wallpainting, 2003

Gestützt von Poesie, DekaBank Collection, Frankfurt am Main, Germany (wall painting)

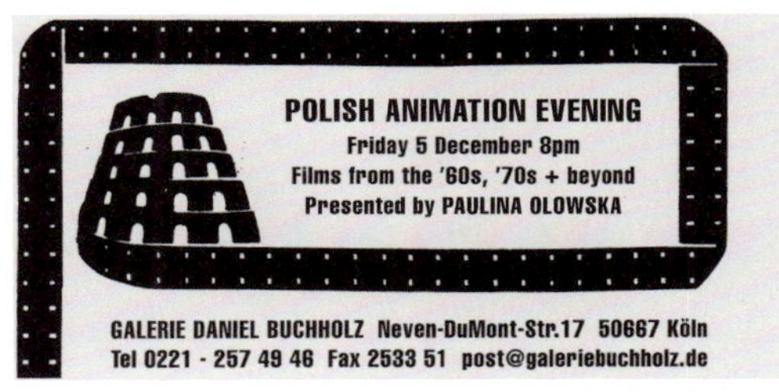

Invitation card for *Polish Animation Evening. Films from the '60s, '70s, & Beyond*, 2003

Polish Animation Evening: Films from the 1960s, 1970s & Beyond. Presented by Paulina Olowska, Galerie Buchholz, Cologne, Germany (curated event)

2004

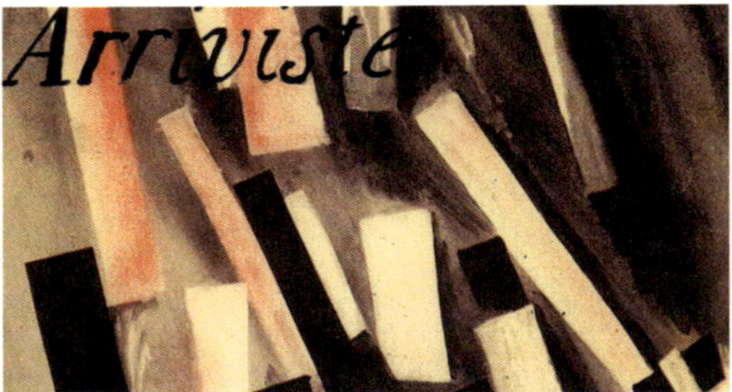

Invitation card for the exhibition *Arriviste (XZ)*, 2004

Arriviste (XZ), Galerie AKINCI, Amsterdam (solo exhibition)

"In her exhibition, Olowska presents paintings, furniture, and wallpaper … X and Z are furniture designed by the artist: X is two tables to display drawings, Z is three Z-shaped stools inspired by Rietveld chairs in order to sit down and contemplate. Contrasts like action and leisure, order and disorder, heaviness and lightness rule this show … The painting *Calder* is a hint at modernism as well as *Painting*, whereas the painting *Fall*, a portrait of an androgynous young man, contrasts with this theme in the show and gives it a dandy-like and decadent twist. There is wallpaper made from an archive of tapes in boxes—a 'Library of Spoken Books'—and there is a poem with the title *L'Arriviste* that Olowska found and declared to be the leading reference within the multi-layered show."
(Galerie AKINCI, press release)

Sans Soleil, Galerie NEU, Berlin (group exhibition)

Prym, BWA Gallery, Zielona Góra, Poland (group exhibition)

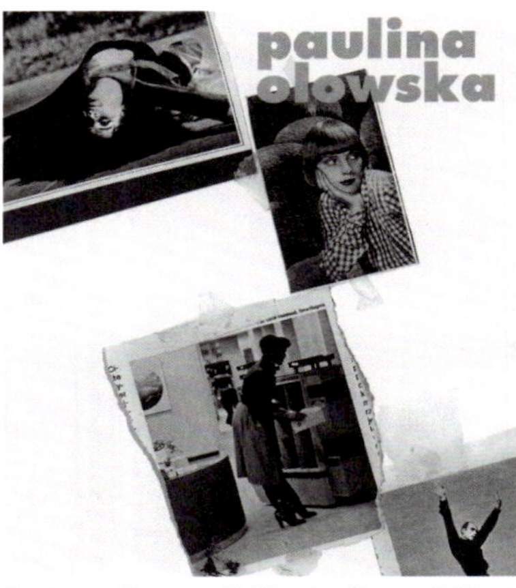

Catalogue *Sie musste die Idee eines Hauses als Metapher verwerfen*, 2004

Sie musste die Idee eines Hauses als Metapher verwerfen, Kunstverein Braunschweig, Brunswick, Germany (solo exhibition)

"Soaking up the atmosphere in the semi-darkness, Olowska produced a new series of portraits of formidable figures like Virginia Woolf, Vanessa Bell, Charlotte Perriand, and Nina Hamnett, rendered on larger than life-sized panels mounted on wheels and based on paintings used as illustrations in *Women Artists and Writers: Modernist (Im)positionings.* Confident and cultured women—some real, some imagined—who are either making, looking at, standing in the shadow of, engaged with, wearing, or performing modern-looking art are to be found throughout Olowska's work … The exhibition was structured around a radio play-like recording of the short story *Desky Maidens* (2002) by Lucy McKenzie."
(Dominic Eichler, "Gathering Like Minds, Paulina Olowska," in: *Sie musste die Idee eines Hauses als Metapher verwerfen*, exhibition catalogue, Kunstverein Braunschweig, Brunswick 2004, p. 21–22)

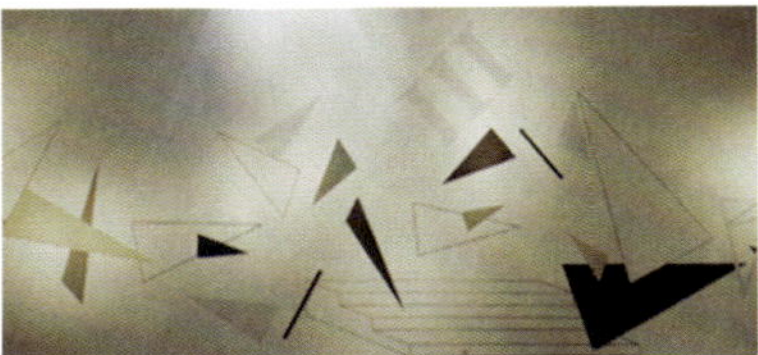

Etiuda Plastyczna, 2004

Etiuda Plastyczna, in collaboration with Kacper Kasprzyk, Nakkna Modeshow, Konstfack, Stockholm (wall painting)

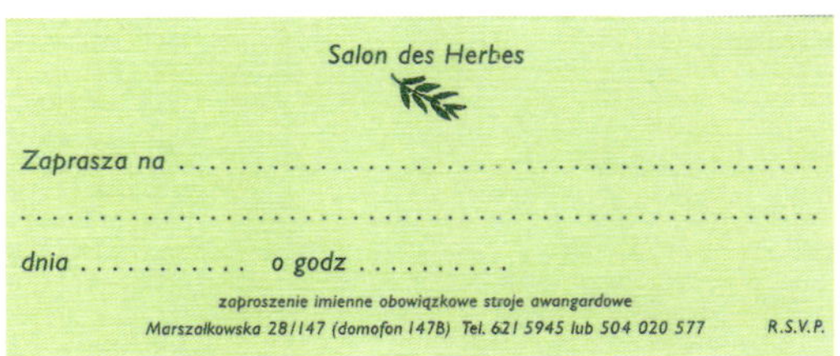

Salon des Herbes

Zaprasza na ....

....

dnia .... o godz ....

zaproszenie imienne obowiązkowe stroje awangardowe

Marszałkowska 28/147 (domofon 147B) Tel. 621 5945 lub 504 020 577 R.S.V.P.

Invitation card for *Salon des Herbes*, 2004

Salon des Herbes, Marszalkowska str. 28/147, Warsaw (curated event)

Casual, stylized "salon," a place for meetings and one-day exhibitions hosted in her Warsaw studio. Some of the invited artists who presented their work there were: Katrin Wosnitzka, Bonnie Camplin, Matthias Schaufler, and Susanne M. Winterling.

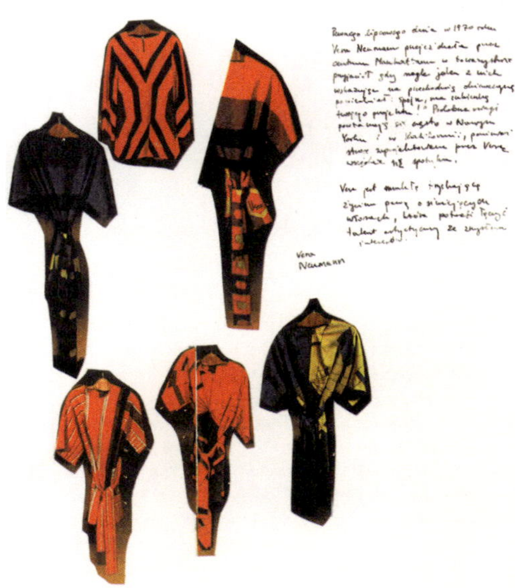

Invitation card for the exhibition *Asymmetric Display*, 2004

Asymmetric Display, Galerie Buchholz, presentation at Cologne Art Fair 2004 (solo exhibition)

"*Asymmetric Display* is an installation—a tableau vivant—that mediates reflections on the history of artistic window-dressing and the status of display/decoration in three-dimensional terms. It also refers to the problems inherent in making an artistic presentation for a trade fair in the form of an installation that is viewable only from the outside."
(Galerie Buchholz, press release)

Time and Again, part of Who if not we should at least try to imagine the future of all this?, Stedelijk Museum, Amsterdam (group exhibition)

"[Olowska presented] *Accidental Collages* … a series of works on paper that comprise personal and historical references. The 16 wall-mounted collage boards are loosely based around the 'analytical charts' of Russian artist Kazimir Malevich—diagrams from 1925 that illustrate Malevich's thoughts on the formal development of art history. Tracing the line between the romantic and the abstract, the pastoral and the industrial, Malevich's charts complemented a series of lectures he delivered in Warsaw and Berlin in 1927. Although the written content of the lectures has since been lost, Malevich's charts remain as visual springboards and prompters to other forms of action. These elements are central to *Accidental Collages*. Olowska takes on Malevich's personalization and customization of time, form, and image, and combines his diagrammatic format with a selection of photographs that include elements of the following: cut-outs of 1960s fashion models, found slogans and phrases, architectural plans of Warsaw buildings, blown-up pictures of Malevich and his students, as well as images of Olowska alongside Warsaw artists with whom she formed a local art salon [*Salon des Herbes*]."
(Isla Leaver-Yap, "Paulina Olowska's *Accidental Collages*," Exhibition Guide, Tramway 5, Glasgow 2010)

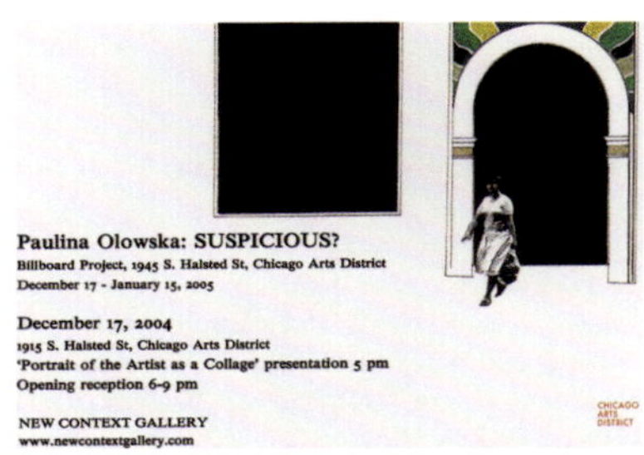

Invitation card for the billboard project *Suspicious?*, 2004

Suspicious?, Chicago Arts District, New Context Gallery, Chicago, USA (billboard project)

"The collages that make up the billboard were prepared by artists, graphic designers, and architects in Poland as proposals for a 1980 competition to modify the look of Sopot, a resort town on the Baltic Sea. None of the ideas, which ranged from new city signs to the development of a highway, ever was executed. Olowska found the collage boards in a bohemian artists' meeting place in Sopot. She now presents them in a new context as symbols of pure ideas that exist only as fiction, transplanted today to a new city and a different time. She entitled the billboard *Suspicious?* as a contradiction to its original title, *Functional Collages*. The two polar titles refer to the fragility of such visions and the general skepticism towards optimistic, functional modernism today."
(New Context Gallery, press release)

2005

Dialectics of Hope, 1st Moscow Biennale of Contemporary Art, curated by Joseph Backstein, Daniel Birnbaum, Nicolas Bourriaud, Iara Boubnova, Rosa Martinez, and Hans Ulrich Obrist, State Historical Museum, Moscow (group exhibition)

California Institute of the Arts (CalArts), Pasadena, California (lecture)

Otis College of Art and Design, Los Angeles (lecture)

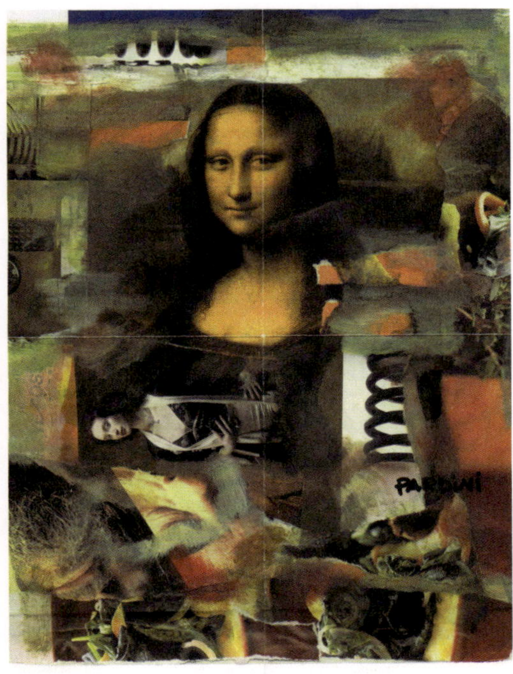

Invitation card for the exhibition *Metaloplastyka*, 2005

Metaloplastyka, Galerie Buchholz, Cologne, Germany (solo exhibition)
"In this exhibition it was important for Olowska to make transparent the process of the creation of an artwork. The word 'metaloplastyka' denotes items of decorative art made in Poland in the 1950s and 1960s not serially—by machine—but individually, in small workshops. Objects of this kind that survived the communist era were soon ditched in the 1990s to make way for supposedly better, more modern furnishings mass-produced in fashionable Western styles. In the *Metaloplastyka* works, as in many other areas of her oeuvre, Olowska invokes Polish achievements in fine art, decorative art, prints, society, and politics in the period from the end of the Second World War to the fall of the Berlin Wall."
(Stephan Urbaschek, "East Meets West," *Noël sur le balcon/ HOLD THE COLOR*, exhibition catalogue, Sammlung Goetz, Munich 2007, p. 56)

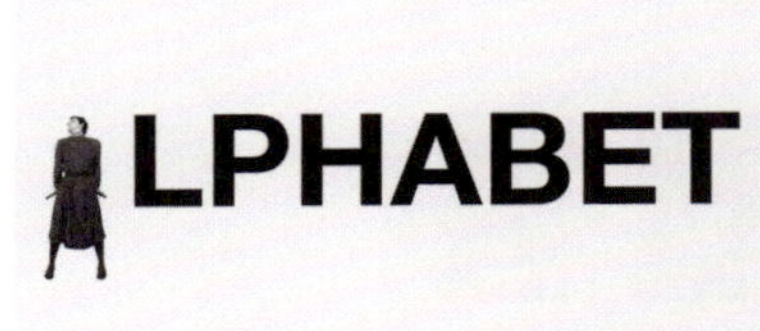

Invitation card for the book presentation and performance *Alphabet*, 2005

Alphabet, Galerie Meerrettich, Berlin, Germany (performance)
Presentation of the *Alphabet* edition published by Galerie Buchholz and performance by Paulina Olowska; choreography: Daniel Yamada; performing artists: Joanna Zielinska, Daniel Yamada, and Josef Strau.
"The performance *Alphabet* is inspired by Czech designer Karel Teige's typographic book *ABECEDA* (which was published in Prague in 1926 and recently reprinted). Referring to the poetics of typography and Eastern European avant-garde tradition, the work involves collaboration with other performers, who curve and stretch their bodies into 26 letters, from A to Z, to construct a new system for conveying meaning. The performance also includes the presentation of short poems by Josef Strau, Frances Stark, and Paulus Mazur. The physicality of text, writing, and the contexts in which words appear are all parts of Olowska's poetics."
(*Words in the World*, MoMA Performance Program, Museum of Modern Art, New York 2012)

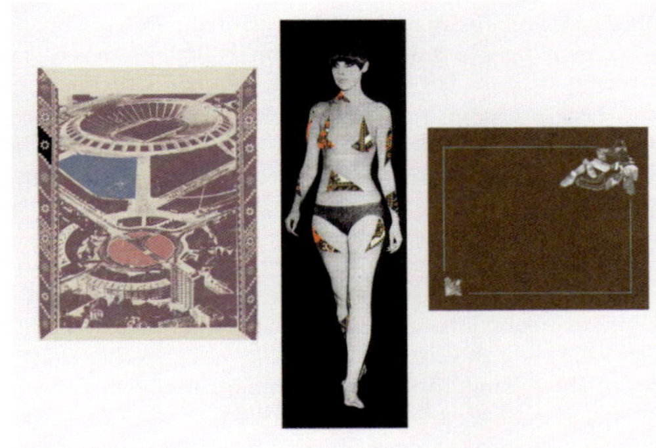

Warsaw Rug, *Peggy Rug*, and *Le Shoe*, 2005

9th International Istanbul Biennial, curated by Charles Esche and Vasif Kortun, various locations, Istanbul, Turkey (group exhibition)
"The walls of Olowska's chosen apartment are layered with the remains of pink striped wallpaper, graffiti, and a painted island view. These traces of time have been left untouched, becoming part of the presentation and backdrop for three carpets—*Peggy Rug*, *Warsaw Rug*, and *Le Shoe*—specifically created by Olowska for each of the three main rooms. Composed as if paintings, then crafted as traditional Turkish carpets, these striking compositions shift attention from eye to floor level, changing our normal perspective of an apartment space."
(November Paynter, "Paulina Olowska" in: *9th International Istanbul Biennial*, exhibition catalogue, Istanbul Kültür Sanat Vakfi, Istanbul Foundation for Culture and Arts, Istanbul 2005, p. 28)

Ukryty Skarb/Hidden Treasure, Novotel Hotel, Warsaw (group exhibition)

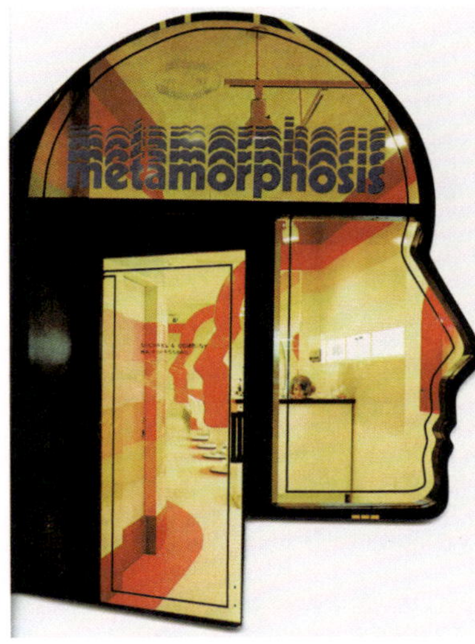

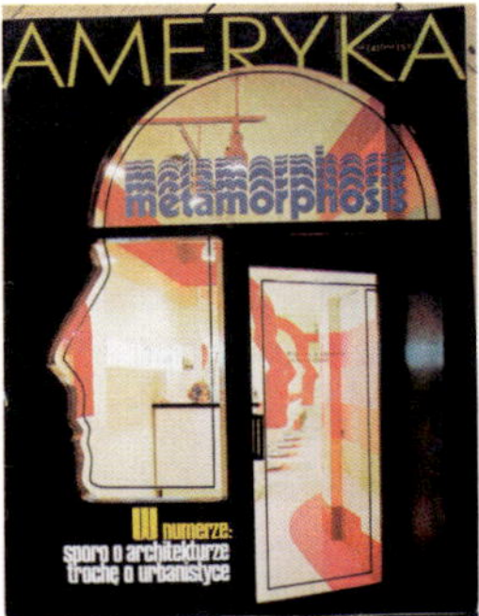

Polish magazine cover, *Ameryka*, no. 141, October 1970

Metamorphosis, Museum Abteiberg Mönchengladbach, Sammlung Provinzial Versicherung, Mönchengladbach, Germany (permanent installation)
"In 1972 the photograph of a futurist hairdresser's salon made it onto the cover of *Ameryka*, the Polish illustrated magazine of American popular culture ... As a characteristic example of 1970s avant-gardism the hairdresser's salon epitomizes a style of pop architecture pioneered by Hans Hollein among others. Coincidentally, Hollein is also the architect of the Abteiberg Museum in Mönchengladbach ... for which Paulina Olowska was recently invited to create a permanent installation. To rebuild the salon from *Ameryka* in Hollein's museum therefore seemed like a natural thing to do. Olowska closed off a room behind a glass wall that she designed to be like the hairdresser's shop front. In this space she constructed a replica of the salon interior with simple plywood elements in the original's strange but beautiful colors. Now, as the door to the room is locked, all you can do is look. The space behind the glass resembles a three-dimensional picture—a magnified mirror-image of the magazine cover, of which a hand-painted copy is displayed in the entrance hall."
(Jan Verwoert, "Paulina Olowska's *Metamorphosis* in the Abteiberg Museum," *Piktogram* 01, Summer 2005, p. 24)

2006

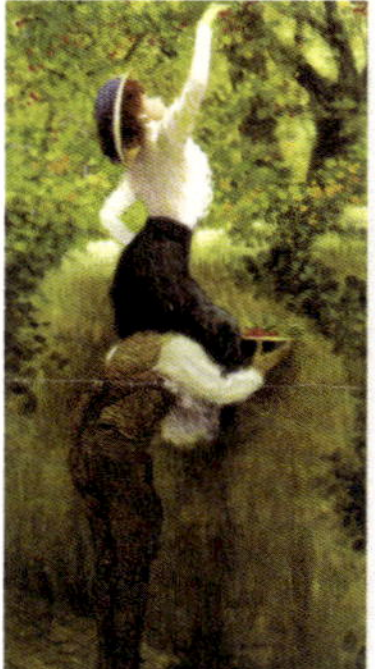

Invitation card for the exhibition *Hello to You Too*, 2006

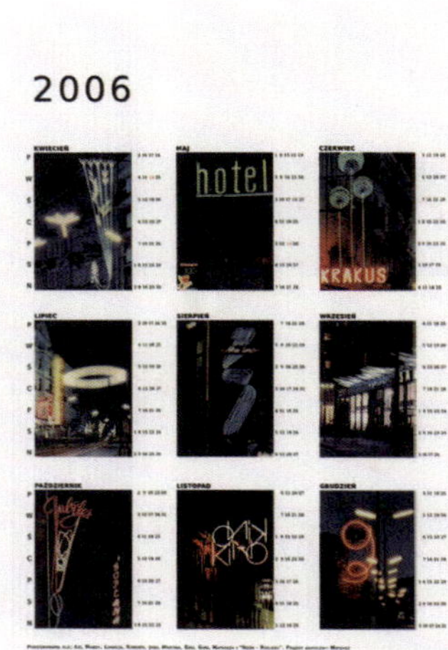

Invitation for the exhibition *Painting–Exchange–Neon*, 2006

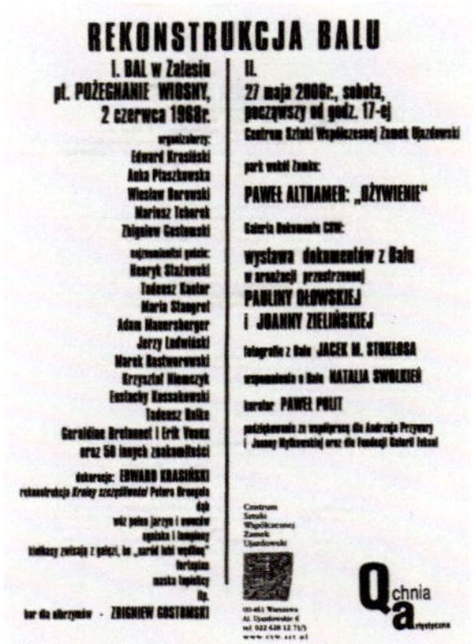

Invitation card for the exhibition *Reconstruction of the Ball "Farewell to Spring,"* 2006

Hello to You Too, Cabinet Gallery, London (solo exhibition)

On nine monumental, poster-like canvases with photographically enlarged details, using anti-painterly skills, *affichiste* methods, and bold statements, focused on the figure of the British Pop artist Pauline Boty, and in general on the idea of the muse and the artist in one.

"*Pauline Boty Acts Out One of Her Paintings for a Popular Newspaper* is literally and figuratively a palimpsest. It is made from reproductions of a British tabloid article on Boty, showing her in a state of undress in front of one of her canvases; photographic color views of the Manhattan skyline; and a (painted) female artist, sporting a cropped haircut, zebra-print dress, and leopard-skin shoes, holding a paintbrush and palette. The work 'reexposes' Boty as an artist and a sex symbol, a performative initiative that Boty took on board to challenge her legibility as a female artist. Olowska complicates this historical narrative with the 1980s-style, 'ironic' figure of the New York postmodern artist, quoted from an image in an old copy of *Art in America*, who 20 years later is more enabled by society to perform those roles; and finally there's Olowska herself, who, from our vantage point in history, has the ability to invent her own potential worlds and roles."

(David Bussel, "Final Girl. On Paulina Olowska at Cabinet Gallery, London," *Texte zur Kunst*, no. 62, 2006, p. 238)

Optik Schröder: Work from the Alexander Schröder Collection, Kunstverein Braunschweig, Brunswick, Germany (group exhibition)

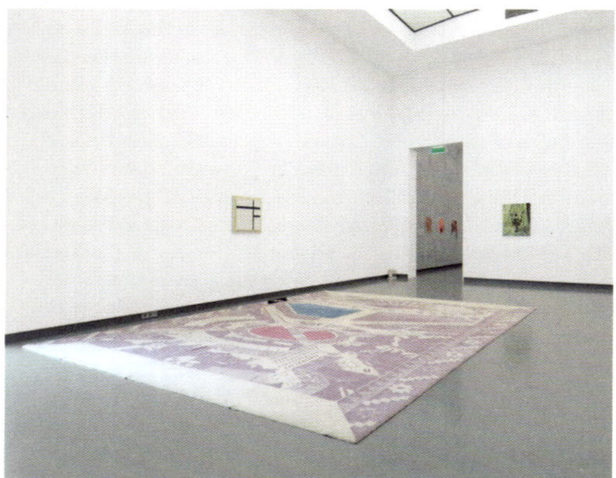

The Subversive Charm of the Bourgeoisie, 2006

The Subversive Charm of the Bourgeoisie, Van Abbemuseum, Eindhoven, Netherlands (group exhibition)

Obraz–wymiana–neon/Painting–Exchange–Neon, Foksal Gallery Foundation, Warsaw (solo exhibition)

The exhibition at the Foksal Gallery Foundation was accompanied by an illuminated neon installed at Plac Konstytucji 5 in Warsaw.

"The work *Painting–Exchange–Neon* was inspired by the gradual extinction of Warsaw's historic neon signs. From the late 1950s to the mid-1980s, they were an important feature of the cityscape. Installed in large numbers by the Communist authorities, they were a way to give Warsaw that big-city feel without spending too much money … For the exhibition at the Foksal Gallery Foundation [Olowska] prepared a collage of various neon signs, mixing the best from the 1960s with very contemporary ones. The exhibition also featured paintings referring to the history of the signs. One of these, painted with thick black paint, provided a surface against which the light of a neon hanging in the window could be reflected. Another was an alphabetical list of all textual neon signs in the city. By being presented in the contemporary artistic context, the old neon signs gained both a documentary and a market value. Olowska decided that the proceeds from the sale of the paintings would be used to renovate one of Warsaw's best-known neon signs, the so-called 'Volleyball Player' near the Konstytucji Square. The *Painting–Neon–Exhibition* show reversed the direction of the flow of money in the contemporary art market and raised funds for the revitalization of a modernist neon sign that had once been an important part of the city's image but which, ownerless for a couple of years, had been slowly dilapidating."

(Joanna Mytkowska, "Paulina Olowska. Neon for Neon: The Revitalization of Aesthetic Codes," in. *Le Nuage Magellan*, exhibition catalogue, Centre Pompidou, Paris 2007, p. 55)

Le Gai Savoir: Moving Pictures & Living Money, Cabinet Gallery, London (group exhibition)

Reconstruction of the Ball "Farewell to Spring," Center for Contemporary Art Ujazdowski Castle, Warsaw, Poland (group exhibition)

The "Farewell to Spring" Ball was an unofficial initiative of critics and artists working with the Foksal Gallery. It took place on June 2, 1968, in Anka Ptaszkowska and Edward Krasinski's house and garden in Zalesie near Warsaw.

The reconstruction of the ball was arranged by Paulina Olowska, Joanna Zielinska, Paweł Althamer and Paweł Powit in Ujazdowski Castle. To recreate its atmosphere the artists used music, the recordings of voices of participants of the original ball who were still alive, objects, photographs, and documents.

Poster for the exhibition *At the Very Center of Attention*, 2006

At the Very Center of Attention, Center for Contemporary Art Ujazdowski Castle, Warsaw (project)

2007

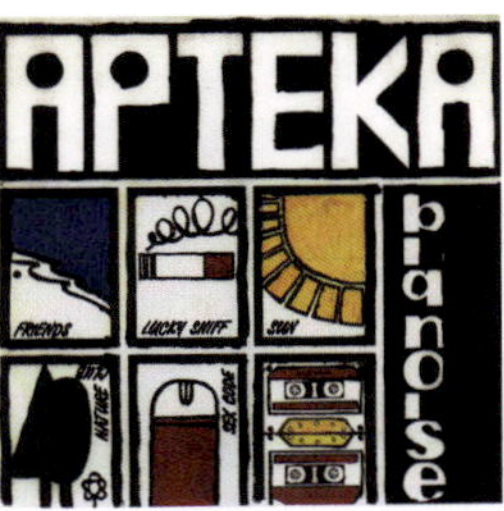

Invitation card for the exhibition *Nowa Scena*, 2007

Nowa Scena, Metro Pictures, New York (solo exhibition)

"Olowska exploits the style and esthetics of the 1960s propaganda war between the US and the Soviet bloc as well as the underground flow of popular culture as evidenced in the Polish punk movement of the 1980s. Olowska's paintings, drawings, and collages borrow imagery from *USSR/Soviet Life* (a Soviet publication intended for distribution in the US) and *Amerika* (a US Information Agency periodical distributed in Soviet countries), as well as Polish punk band imagery. The amalgam of cross-cultural influence has been evident in Olowska's earlier projects that reference manifestations of Eastern European modernist design and political feminism."
(Metro Pictures, press release)

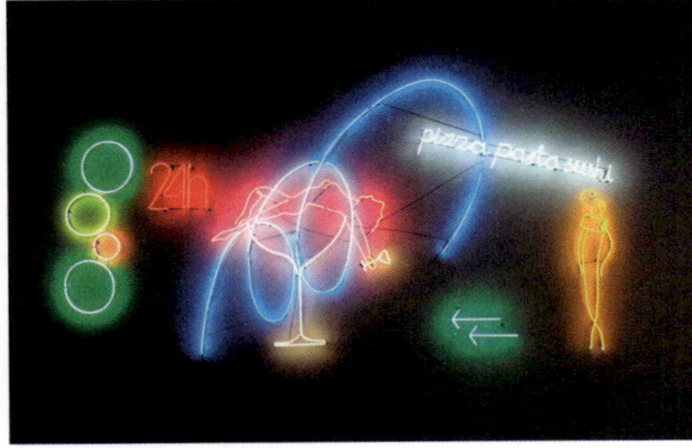
Le Nuage Magellan, 2007

Le Nuage Magellan, Centre Pompidou, Paris (group exhibition)

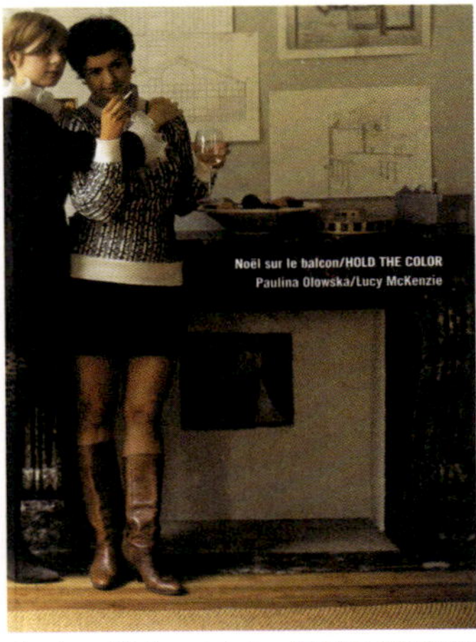

Catalogue Noël sur le balcon/HOLD THE COLOR, 2007

Noël sur le balcon/HOLD THE COLOR, with Lucy McKenzie, Sammlung Goetz, Munich, Germany (joint exhibition)

"In the Goetz Collection we present work from a variety of projects produced both separately and as a two-person team … It was a challenge to juxtapose works which are separated by time, distance, and theme, to identify their unifying features and discrepancies, and to reposition their meanings in relation to each other. In both our works we exploit painting's relationship to photography. Our inclusion of large photographic images collaged onto canvas and our attempts to replicate in paint the expression of someone having their photograph taken are examples of this. We examine scale and monumentality. Oversized mobiles and architectural drawings blown up to overbearing proportions, and the uncanny effect of trompe l'oeil's 1:1 produce a spatial effect on the viewer which encourages an awareness of corporeality."
("Statement. Lucy McKenzie and Paulina Olowska on their exhibition," in. *Noël sur le balcon/HOLD THE COLOR*, exhibition catalogue, Sammlung Goetz, Munich 2007, p. 22)

Anachronism, Argos Center for Art and Media, Brussels (group exhibition)

Conditions of Display, The Moore Space, Miami, Florida (group exhibition)

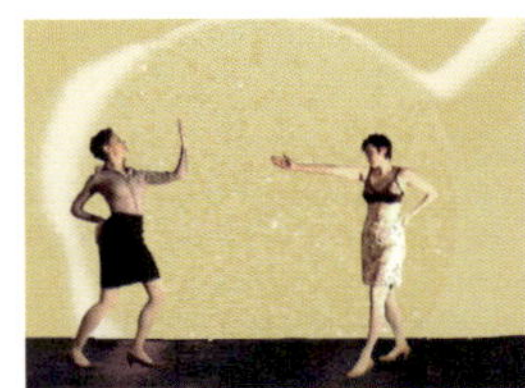
Bonnie Camplin and Paulina Olowska, *A Like Akarova*, 2007

A Like Akarova, with Bonnie Camplin, Wiels Contemporary Art Center, Brussels, Belgium (film screening)

"The film is dedicated to the work and persona of Marguerite Acarin (Akarova), the celebrated dancer, choreographer, stage and costume designer, based in Brussels, who realized her avant-gardist vision of an integrated total dance project in the 1920s. In a series of short improvised scenes and evocative images the video seeks to revive the spirit of visionary creation inherent in the modernist approach of Akarova's work by translating it into the contemporary language of the video montage."
(Paulina Olowska and Bonnie Camplin, artists' statement, London 2007)

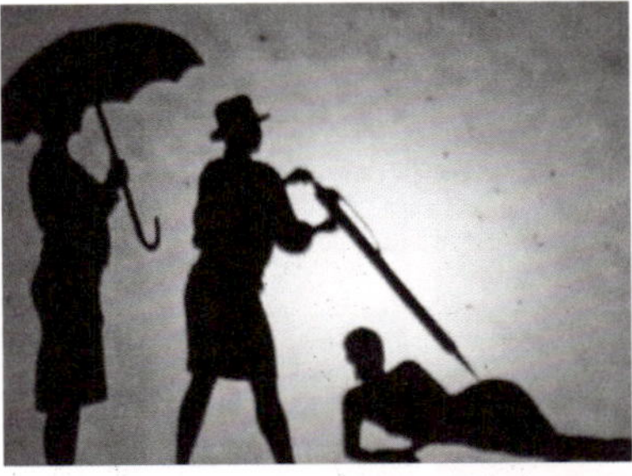

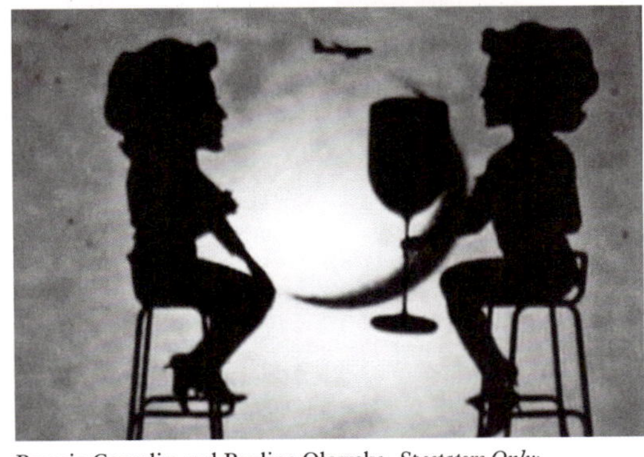
Bonnie Camplin and Paulina Olowska, *Spectators Only: A Shadow Play*, 2007

Spectators Only: A Shadow Play, with Bonnie Camplin, Wiels Contemporary Art Centre, Brussels, Belgium (performance)

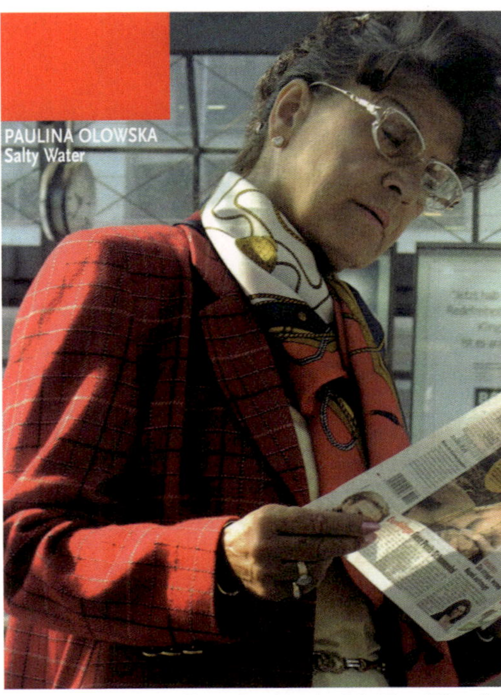

Catalogue *Bonnie Camplin, Paulina Olowska. Salty Water/What of Salty Water*, 2007

Salty Water/What of Salty Water, with Bonnie Camplin, Portikus, Frankfurt am Main, Germany (joint exhibition)

"[The exhibition is] an intricate configuration of made and gathered objects and images, a product of collaboration, and a shared extemporaneous (free fall) voyage, a way into comprehending the modern world and coming to terms with the consequences and manifestations of industrialization and free market economy. Also it is an intense meditation on the nature of trade, exchange, and trust. This includes the sex trade and the ways in which it incorporates versions of solidarity and collaboration between women. As both artists view themselves as women workers, they consider how this relates to their position as professional artists."
(Portikus, press release)

2008

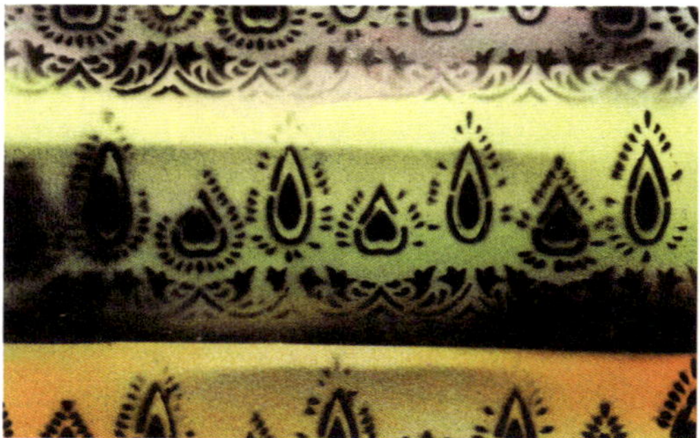

Invitation card for the exhibition *Attention à la Peinture*, 2008

Attention à la Peinture, Galerie Buchholz, Cologne, Germany (solo exhibition)

"In her exhibition, Paulina Olowska refers to Elsa Schiaparelli and in particular to her collection 'Attention à la Peinture' from the 1930s. Here, Schiaparelli's clothing designs took a decidedly painterly gesture, while for the accessories she drew on distinctive forms of everyday objects, creating hats in the shape of ice cream cones and handbags reminiscent of balloons. A central focus of the exhibition … are freestanding sculptures of gowns that Olowska developed in collaboration with Min Stiller out of canvases she had previously painted … The artist's main concern seems to be the visible process of the transformation of the material of painting into objects, along with the presentation of painting as material. While up until now Paulina Olowska's paintings have been almost exclusively figural, focusing on the representation of the female figure, her recent works are primarily abstract. The process of abstraction that can be seen in the ornamental designs of her canvases/pictures, and above all in the artist's cutout pictures—canvases on stretchers out of which sewing pattern forms have been carefully excised—is reversed here, with the pictures presented as sample patterns or as remnants left over from dressmaking that are then arranged into picture objects."
(Galerie Buchholz, press release)

Estratos, curated by Nicolas Bourriaud, Contemporary Art Project, Murcia, Spain (group exhibition)

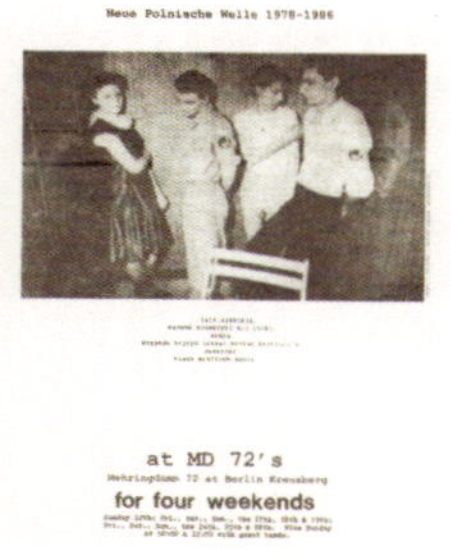

Poster for the exhibition *Neue Polnische Welle 1978–1986, Robert Jarosz Music Archive*, 2008

Neue Polnische Welle 1978–1986, Robert Jarosz Music Archive, MD 72, Berlin, Germany (curated project)

"Dedicated to Polish Punk and the New Wave movement, the exhibition contained the materials from the personal archive of Robert Jarosz who, as a producer, collector, archivist, and most importantly, fan, has collected thousands of cassette tapes from the underground, hand-to-hand trade, published LPs, and their original artworks, concert posters and flyers, countless photographs, and other memorabilia. Polish New Wave represented a creative, cultural landscape whose trajectory differs quite drastically from those of other countries, partly due to the cultural and economic situation in Poland at that time, but also shaped by the enormous—and quite touching—enthusiasm of a generation of youth."
(MD 72, press release)

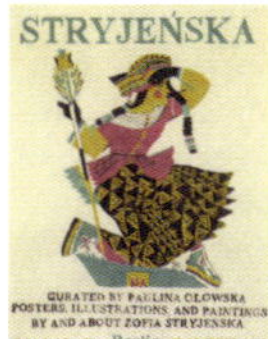

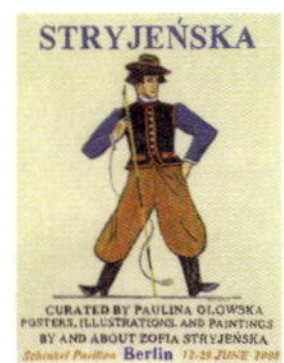

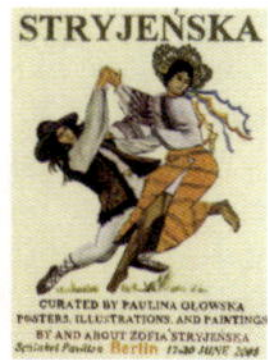

Posters for *Zofia Stryjeńska*, 2008

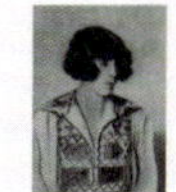

Cover for the set of postcards for *Zofia Stryjeńska*, 2008

When Things Cast No Shadow, 5th Berlin Biennale for Contemporary Art, curated by Adam Szymczyk and Elena Filipovic, KW Institute for Contemporary Art, Neue Nationalgalerie, Skulpturenpark Berlin Zentrum and Schinkel Pavillon, Berlin (group exhibition)

"Paulina Olowska's series of large-format tableaux entitled *Zofia Stryjeńska* is a painterly dialogue with the extensive oeuvre of Polish artist Zofia Stryjeńska (1891–1974). Stryjeńska's paintings, which draw on Art Deco, Slavic mythology, and folk art from the Tatra mountains, are joyful celebrations of idealist, bizarre worlds from the past. The unique imagination and sense of optimism that radiate from her paintings have fascinated Olowska since her initial encounter with the late artist's work. As a result, Olowska has created a series of monumental grayscale replicas based on a choice of exemplary gouaches and paintings by Stryjeńska found in the collections of Poland's national museums in Warsaw and Krakow … In the exhibition curated by Paulina Olowska at the Schinkel Pavillon for the 5th Berlin Biennale, she creates a frame in which her own paintings from the series *Zofia Stryjeńska* provide a background for original works by Polish painter Zofia Stryjeńska. Olowska lines the Schinkel Pavillon with a painted floor piece, based on the design of the Polish Pavilion at the 1925 International Exhibition of Decorative Arts in Paris, for which Stryjeńska conceived and displayed her paintings."
(Silke Baumann, "Paulina Olowska," in *Modernologies: Contemporary Artists Researching Modernity and Modernism*, exhibition catalogue, Museu d'Art Contemporani de Barcelona, 2009, p.168)

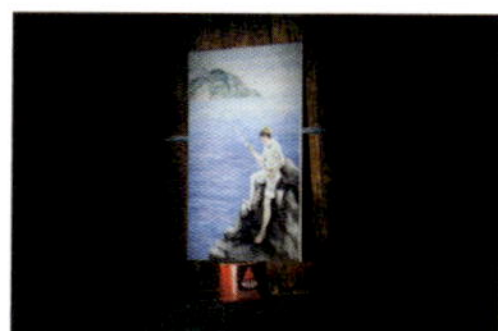

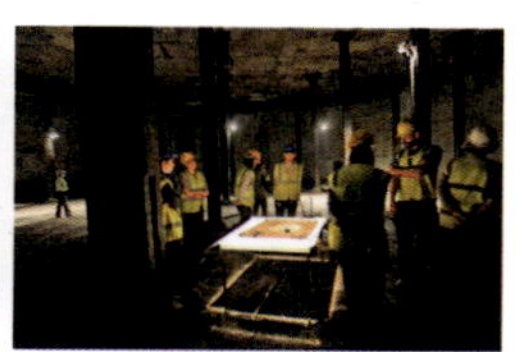

Documentation of Bonnie Camplin and Paulina Olowska performance *Usher We (Down There)*, 2008

Usher We (Down There), with Bonnie Camplin, Tate Modern, Oil Tanks, London (performance)

"[The performance took] the form of a guided tour, led by the artists, in which the participants become intricately involved in the strange ritual and drama of the event. *Usher We (Down There)* consists of a multifaceted installation featuring independent and collaboratively produced works by Camplin and Olowska as well as found objects. The artists themselves feature in the piece through their thematic exploration of the recovered space, evoking a spirit of adventure and ceremony."
("UBS Openings: Saturday Live: Bonnie Camplin and Paulina Olowska: *Usher We (Down There)*," leaflet, Tate Modern, London 2008)

Dark Continents, Museum of Contemporary Art, Miami, Florida (group exhibition)

50 Moons of Saturn, collaboration with Bonnie Camplin, T2, Turin Triennale, curated by Daniel Birnbaum, Castello di Rivoli Museum of Contemporary Art, Fondazione Sandretto Re Rebaudengo and the Promotrice delle Belle Arti, Turin, Italy (group exhibition)

Doing Things with Sculpture, with Achim Hochdörfer, Museum Moderner Kunst Stiftung Ludwig (MUMOK), Vienna, Austria (public talk)

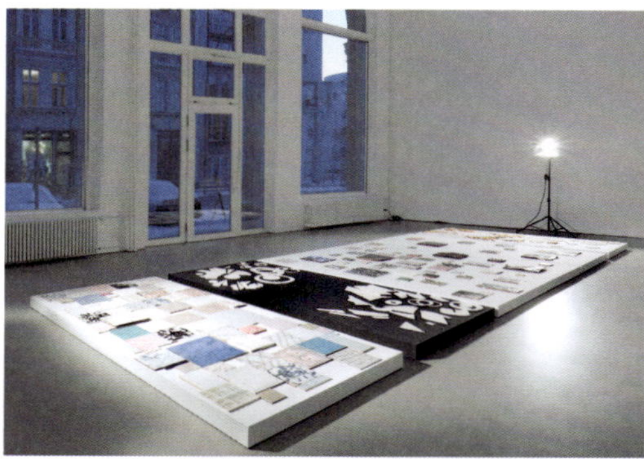

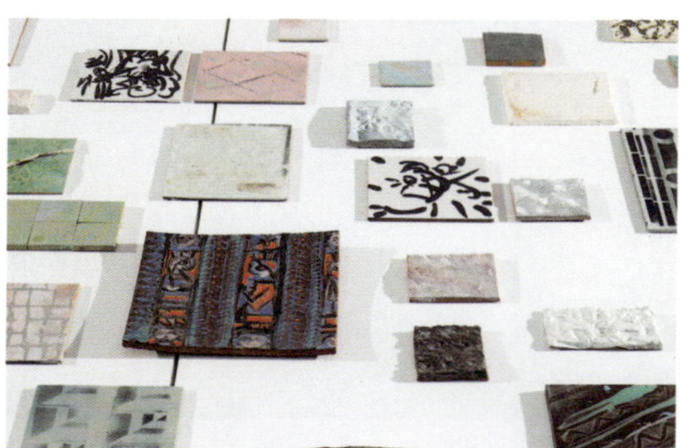

Sarah Crowner and Paulina Olowska, *Ceramics and Other Things*, 2008

Ceramics and Other Things, with Sarah Crowner, daadgalerie, Berlin (joint exhibition)

"Artists investigate the medium of ceramics. In the process, each artist develops her own approach toward an idea of ceramics, both working predominantly with one of its most basic forms, the tile … Paulina Olowska has previously referred to crafts in her work, such as the Polish metalwork of the 1950s and 1960s and its particular position outside of the command economy, combining this with elements of modernism. For *Ceramics and Other Things* she uses found and newly produced objects as compositional elements, creating minimalist, collage-like installations arranged throughout the exhibition space. She focuses on the flatness of the tiles, their surface textures, and various types of glaze."
(daadgalerie, press release)

2009

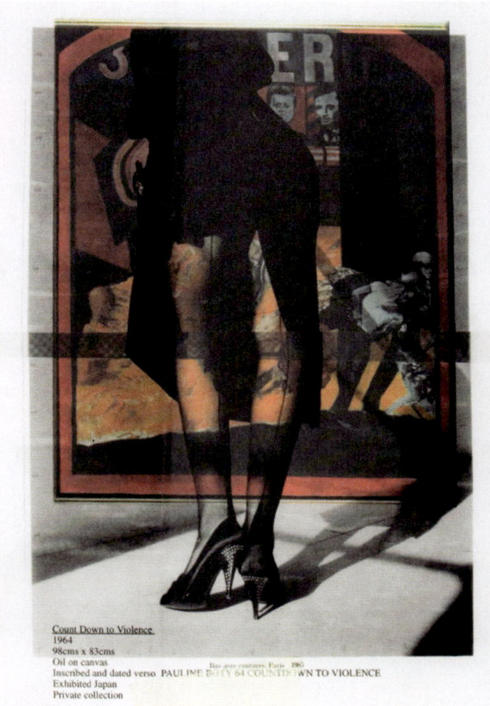

Countdown to Violence, 2009

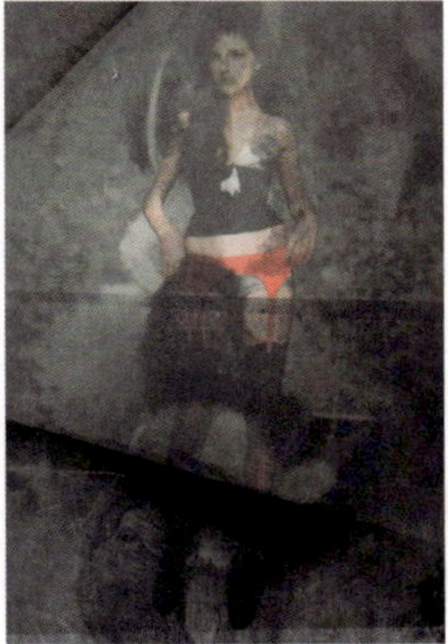

Cherry Picking, 2009

Niezgrabne przedmioty/Awkward Objects, Museum of Modern Art, Warsaw, Poland (group exhibition)
"Both the exhibition *Awkward Objects: Alina Szapocznikow and Maria Bartuszova, Pauline Boty, Louise Bourgeois, Eva Hesse, and Paulina Olowska* and the accompanying conference devoted to Szapocznikow and her work are a response to the clear change in the perception of this artist's oeuvre, and to a general revision of the way the art of female artists of her generation is viewed."
(Museum of Modern Art, press release)

Modern Modern, Chelsea Art Museum, New York (group exhibition)

Compass in Hand: Selections from The Judith Rothschild Foundation Contemporary Drawings Collection, The Museum of Modern Art, New York, USA; traveling to IVAM Instituto Valenciano de Arte Moderno, Valencia, Spain, 2010, and Martin Gropius Bau, Berlin, 2011 (group exhibition)

Quodlibet II, Galerie Buchholz, Cologne, Germany (group exhibition)

Paulina Olowska, Stephen G. Rhodes, and Catherine Sullivan, Metro Pictures, New York (group exhibition)

Moby Dick, CCA Wattis Institute for Contemporary Art, San Francisco (group exhibition)

Modernologies: Contemporary Artists Researching Modernity and Modernism, Museu d'Art Contemporani de Barcelona (MACBA), Spain; traveling to Museum of Modern Art, Warsaw (group exhibition)

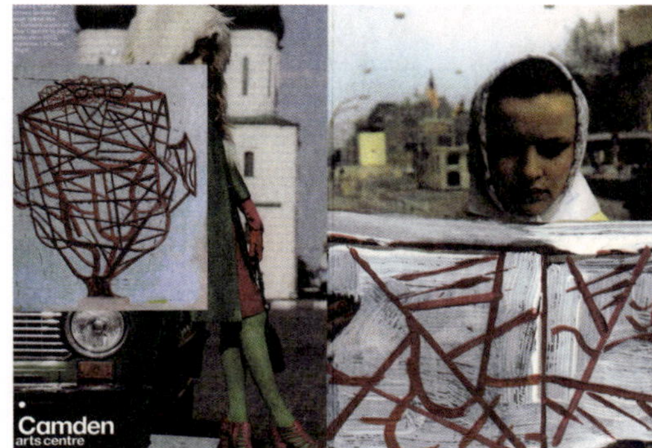

Invitation card for the exhibition *Head–Wig (Portrait of an Exhibition)*, 2009

Head–Wig (Portrait of an Exhibition): Selected by Paulina Olowska, Camden Arts Centre, London, UK (curated exhibition)
Head–Wig included works by Jarosław Bauc, Simon Ling, Nina Köennemann, Elka Krajewska, Ken Okiishi, Paulina Olowska, Mathilde Rosier, Cindy Sherman, Catherine Sullivan, Cathy Wilkes, Katharina Wulff, and Jakub Julian Ziolkowski.
"*Head–Wig (Portrait of an Exhibition)* is about looking and being looked at. It is subjective, less culturally knowledgeable and therefore more speculative. Constructing a portrait, constructing a portrait of a show, is not only about selecting likable works; the assembly confronts classic genre portraits with 'imposed portraits.' What I mean by 'imposed portraits' or 'covert portraits' are portraits that hide, reverse, or mystify the idea that something or someone is being portrayed. A split between mechanical versus intellectual life. A painting that turns the face into its own medium. The entire painting is a face."
(Paulina Olowska, "Gestures of Friendship. Please Don't Leave That Painting!" in *Head–Wig (Portrait of an Exhibition)*, exhibition catalogue, Camden Arts Centre, London 2009)

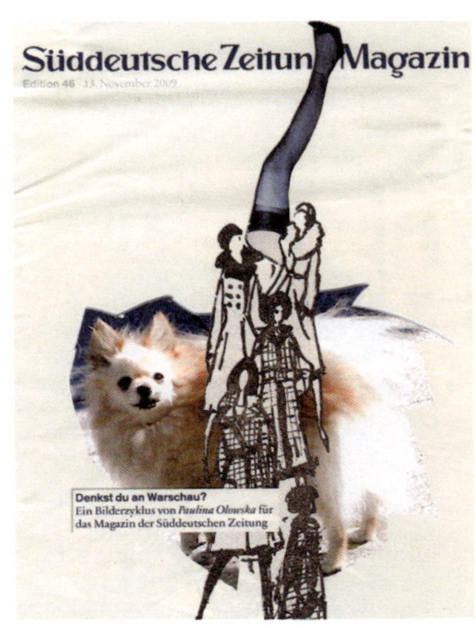

Cover for *Süddeutsche Zeitung Magazin*, 2009

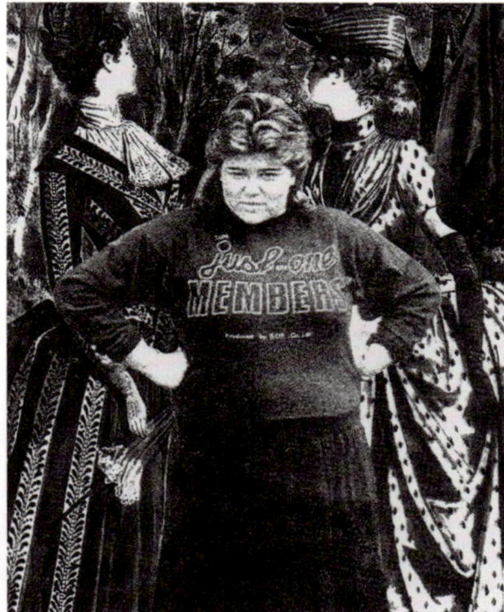

Shadow with A Sneak, 2009

Shadow with a Sneak, Pinakothek der Moderne, Munich, Germany (solo exhibition)
The exhibition was accompanied by "Denkst du an Warschau?" *Süddeutsche Zeitung Magazin*, special artist's edition no. 46.
"Paulina Olowska's project for the Pinakothek der Moderne is a reorchestration of history using curatorial means. A particular focus of her work is on female role patterns and the way these are shown in paintings and graphic works, especially in those from the first half of the 20th century. Historical correlations are illustrated using a variety of different presentation techniques and new facets are brought to light.
Olowska establishes points of reference between her own works and those in the collection at the Pinakothek der Moderne by incorporating pictures from the permanent exhibition and from the depository in her installations. Unconventional combinations conjure up an atmosphere of their own not typically found in a museum. Parameters traditionally associated with exhibitions and documentation are challenged and redefined."
(Pinakothek der Moderne, press release)

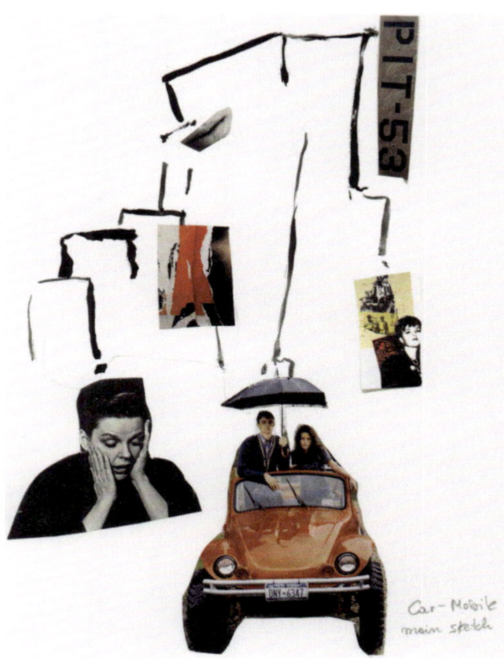

Car Mobile, 2009

Car Mobile, De la Cruz Collection Contemporary Art Space, Miami, Florida (installation)

2010

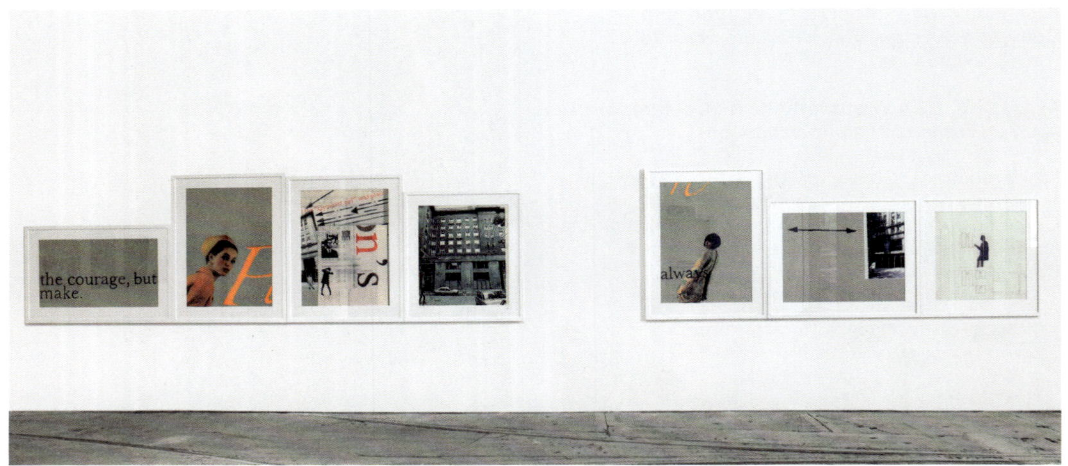

Accidental Collages, 2010

Accidental Collages, Tramway, Glasgow (solo exhibition)

Early Years, KW Institute for Contemporary Art, Berlin (group exhibition)
Olowska presented *Museum*, a permanent neon installation for the Museum of Modern Art in Warsaw.
"Paulina Olowska's neon sign (created in collaboration with Mateusz Romaszkan) is an institutional 'relict,' a testimony of the early and conflict-ridden times of the Museum of Modern Art in Warsaw. Olowska has emphasized the harsh and 'heroic' times of the museum by applying simple typography and cheap light bulbs. For the neon presentation in the *Early Years* exhibition, the contemporary composer and artist Anna Zaradny created a sound recording of Olowska's voice pronouncing the word 'museum' with different intonations."
(Museum of Modern Art, press release)

While Bodies Get Mirrored: An Exhibition About Movement, Formalism, and Space, Migros Museum für Gegenwartskunst, Zurich (group exhibition)

The Falmouth Convention, Cornwall, UK (lecture)

Utopia and Monument II: On Virtuosity and the Public Sphere, Steirischer Herbst Festival, Andreas-Hofer-Platz, roof of the gas station/car park, Graz, Austria (group exhibition)
Olowska contributed the works *Natasza*, *Workers Canteen*, and *Flowers*—reconstructions of three neon signs from 1950s and 1960s Warsaw.
"Graz has acquired a rather *unmonumental* monument. Paulina Olowska has installed a new, temporary public sculpture above a gas station and café in the city's center. An assemblage of neon signs, this monument has been fixed on the towering street light ... One architectural icon of automotive modernity, a 1965 gas station, has been overwritten with one of the chief scripts of the 20th-century city: neon advertising. Olowska's work not only uses the *language* of advertising; these neon monuments are actual advertisements, albeit coming from an unlikely setting. These signs were once fixed on the walls of buildings in Warsaw. Testimony to the material and symbolic economy of Eastern European socialism, *Natasza* once announced the chain of Soviet gift shops that operated across the Eastern Bloc, while the bouquet of flowers was the marker of socialist achievement, awarded on high days in the ritual calendar of socialist symbolism."
(David Crowley, "Reanimating the Future," *Utopia and Monument*, exhibition catalogue, Steirischer Herbst Festival, Graz 2010, p. 194)

Onethousandsixhundredandseventeen Neons in Warsaw, Andreas-Hofer-Platz, roof of the gas station/car park, Steirischer Herbst Festival, Graz, Austria (performance)

Reference vs Reverence, Frieze Talks 2010, Frieze Art Fair, London (lecture)

Graduate and Postgraduate Program in Fine Arts, California College of the Arts, Capp Street Project, (CCA) Wattis Institute for Contemporary Arts, San Francisco, USA (residency in The Magnificent Seven program)

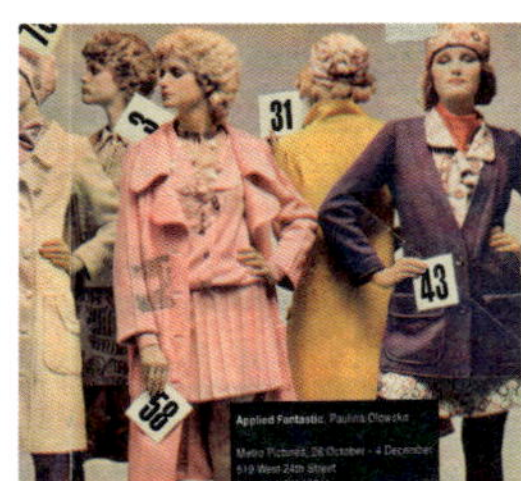

Invitation card for the exhibition *Applied Fantastic*, 2010

Applied Fantastic, Metro Pictures, New York (solo exhibition)
"The show presents paintings and knitted sweaters adapted from postcards of home knitting patterns from late communist-era Poland. With these works Olowska continues her engagement with communist Poland's fascination with Western consumerism and celebrates the spirit and stylish improvisations of the 'Applied Fantastic.' Polish writer Leopold Tyrmand, describing the localized recreations of Western styles, coined the term 'Applied Fantastic' in 1954. Olowska incorporates text and graphics from the illustrations including the Polish names for the pattern styles. The paintings are done in a realist style that achieves the same disjointed effects of the postcards. The illustrations used by Olowska depict high-fashion looks to be fabricated at home and, however glamorous, the images have a decidedly 'behind the Iron Curtain' look. These works also pay tribute to American Pattern and Decoration art of the 1970s and its use of nontraditional contemporary art mediums such as tiles and textiles."
(Metro Pictures, press release)

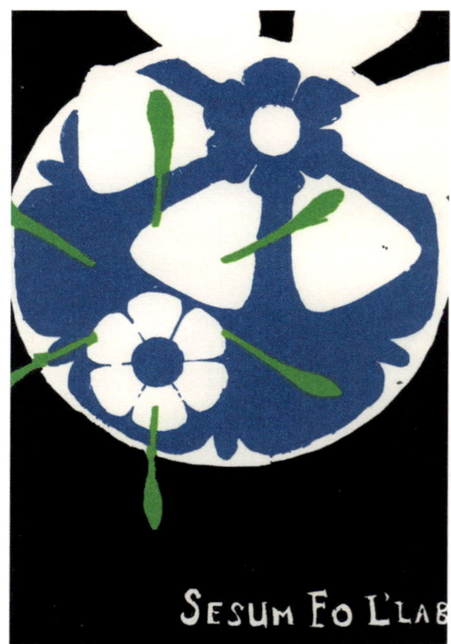

Invitation card for *Sesum fo L'lab*, 2010

Sesum fo L'lab, a result of The Magnificent Seven Residency, Capp Street Project, (CCA) Wattis Institute for Contemporary Arts, San Francisco (costume ball)

2011

De Ateliers, Amsterdam (studio visits and lecture)

Is It About Man and Woman?, with Jan Verwoert, as part of the seminar Who if Not She Gender Performance, the Feminist Concern: Towards a Different Artistic Repertoire, a project organized by Jan Verwoert, Piet Zwart Institute, Rotterdam (lecture/performance)

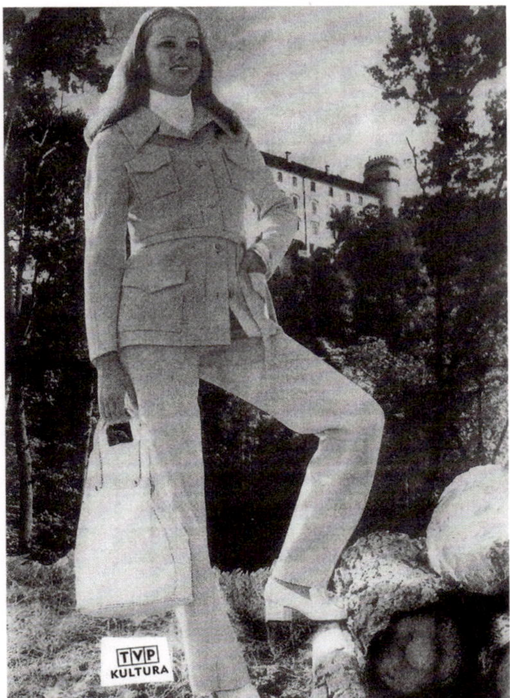

Catalogue *Brudna woda*, 2011

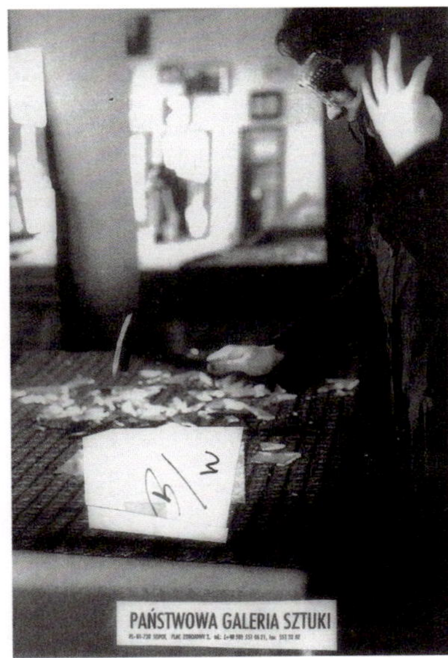

Catalogue *Brudna woda*, 2011

Brudna woda, curated with Ewa Juszkiewicz, PGS Sopot, Poland (group exhibition)

Passion of an Ornithologist. On Myth Making, BWA Sokoł Gallery of Contemporary Art, Nowy Sącz, Poland (group exhibition)

The Power of Fantasy. Modern and Contemporary Art from Poland, Palais des Beaux-Arts (BOZAR), Brussels (group exhibition)

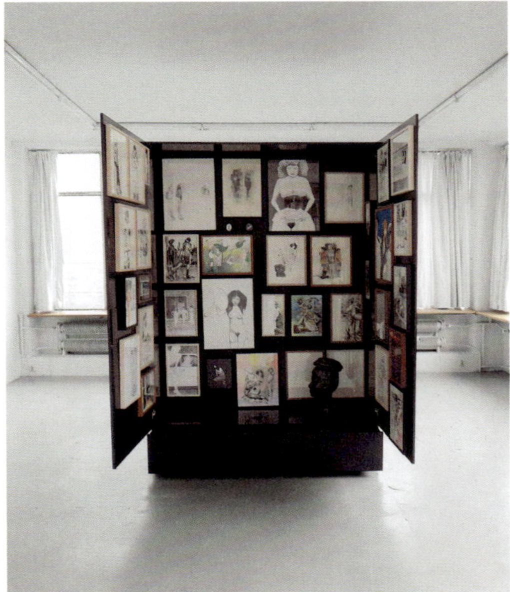

Piekna pogoda, 2011

Piękna pogoda, Foksal Gallery Foundation, Warsaw (group exhibition)

Ostalgia, New Museum of Contemporary Art, New York (group exhibition)

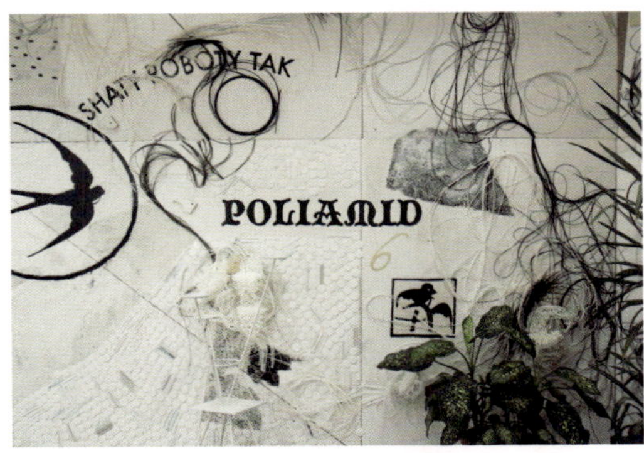

Detail of the mural, *Tarnów. 1000 Years of Modernity*, 2011

Tarnów. 1000 Years of Modernity, BWA Galeria Miejska w Tarnowie, Tarnów, Poland (group exhibition)

"Paulina Olowska's work has been created in collaboration with current and former students from the California College of the Arts in San Francisco. Together, during their two weeks' stay in Moscice near Tarnów, they have made a mural installation using paint, graphite, and plastic industrial waste from the nitrogen factory. The mural decorates the control room of the K-25 section of the factory. Due to the security concerns of this place, the result was photographed and displayed in a showcase in the city of Moscice.

The project references one of the utopian ideas of the artistic avant-garde: a collective creating work for the benefit of society. Historically, the failure of these plans was a result of the opposing aspirations of the artists and those for whom the artists designed and created the art."

(Tarnów. 1000 Years of Modernity, exhibition guide, Galeria Miejska w Tarnowie, Tarnów 2011, p. 10)

Bellevue: Contemporary Painting from the Collection, Stedelijk Museum, Amsterdam (group exhibition)

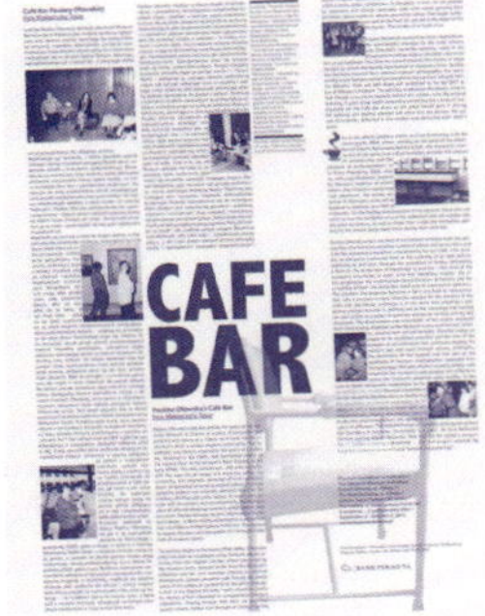

Poster for the exhibition *Café Bar*, 2011

Café Bar, National Museum in Krakow, Poland (solo exhibition)

"The installation was directly inspired by the space of a coffee bar, designed in the 1960s, that functioned briefly on the second floor of the Museum's main building in the early 1990s ... Paulina Olowska became interested in the defunct space—a blank window separated by a plaster wall from the gallery of 20th-Century Polish Art. She decided to reopen the place and lead guests to it through a labyrinth of museum rooms ... A quasi-theatrical situation has been created here, the scenography provided by the main window with Olowska's mural-like painting, made in the characteristic collage style of the artist who works like an art historian. This time she turned toward the climate of stage designs by artists like Natalia Goncharova or Alexandra Exter. Besides bar elements sourced from archival museum photographs, the represented scene features motifs borrowed from cartoons ... published in the 16/1927 issue of Moscow's *Krokodil* [magazine]."

(Ewa Malgorzata Tatar, Paulina Olowska's Café Bar, poster accompanying the exhibition, National Museum in Krakow, 2011)

Quodlibet III. Alphabets and Instruments, Galerie Buchholz, Berlin (group exhibition)

Onethousandsixhundredandseventeen Neons in Warsaw, in the Warsaw Under Construction Festival, Culture and Science Palace, Museum of Modern Art, Warsaw (performance)

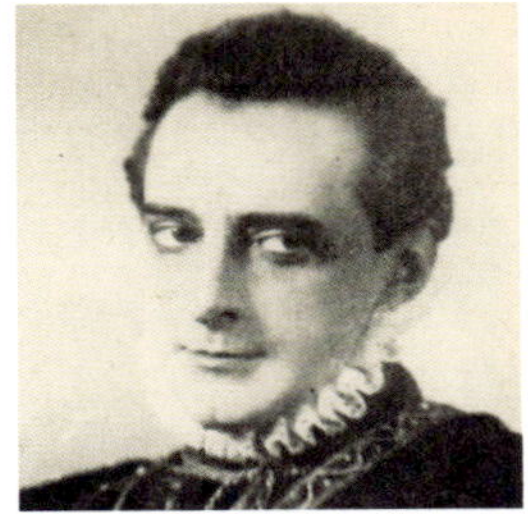

Józef Węgrzyn as Don Juan Zorilli, 1925

Zemsta wróżki/Revenge of the Wise-Woman, Foksal Gallery Foundation, Warsaw (solo exhibition)

"*Revenge of the Wise-Woman* is about: mysticism, misunderstanding, perfidiousness, perversity, disharmony, unity in multitude, suffering, and death that join together while pirituality, complex masculinity, the delusion of professionalism, expressing emotions in an exaggerated manner, theatricality as a rudimentary expression, pain, restaurant, bohemia, mumble, the closeness of life and death, anarchy, expression, darkness, silence, new forms in painting, naivety, wisdom, direct experience, not calculating, melancholy, meditation, sentimentalism without being sentimental, sadness, tragedy which can be represented in painting, melancholy, doubleness, the illusion of the stage, and the truth of life."

(Artist's statement)

2012

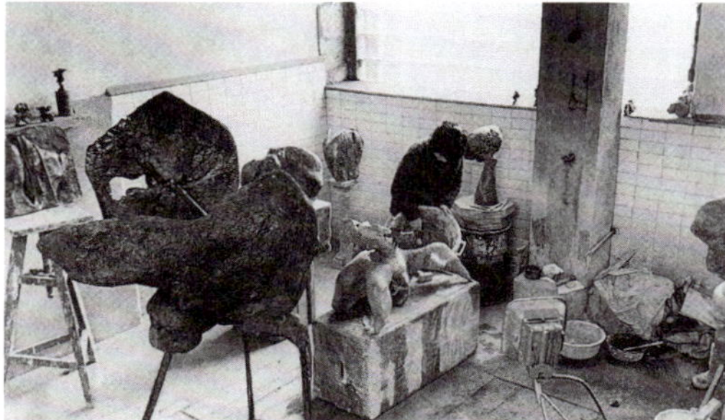

Invitation image for Paulina Olowska and Anna Zaradny sound performance *Le groupe panique with the flesh of the world*, 2012

<u>Le groupe panique with the flesh of the world</u>, with Anna Zaradny, WIELS Contemporary Arts Centre, Brussels (sound performance conceived for the finissage of the exhibition "Alina Szapocznikow: Sculpture Undone, 1955–1972")

<u>Dla Was/For You</u>, Muzeum Sztuki in Łódz, Poland (group exhibition)

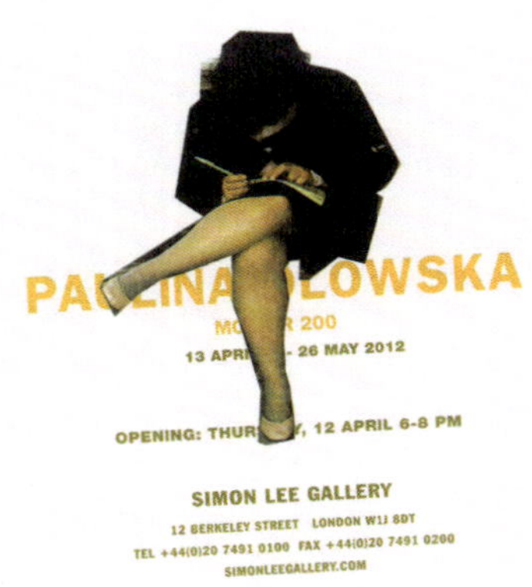

Invitation card for the exhibition *Mother 200*, 2012

<u>Mother 200</u>, Simon Lee Gallery, London (solo exhibition)

A group of new paintings that continue Olowska's exploration of feminist and socially engaged themes, of shifts in cultural perspective between East and West, and of the female figure as an archetype.

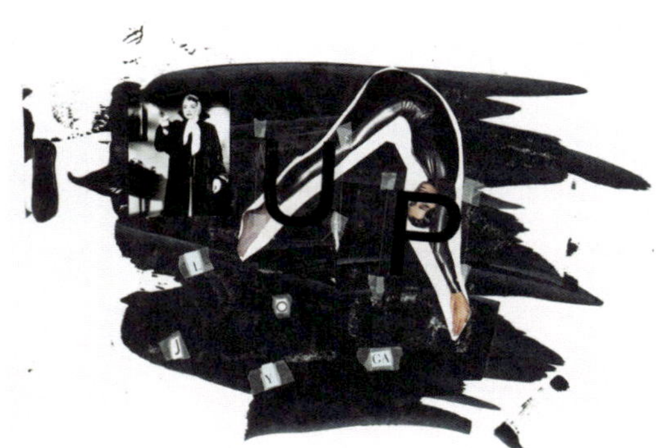

Body Movement. Alphabet Studies, 2007

<u>Ecstatic Alphabets/Heaps of Language</u>, The Museum of Modern Art, New York (group exhibition)

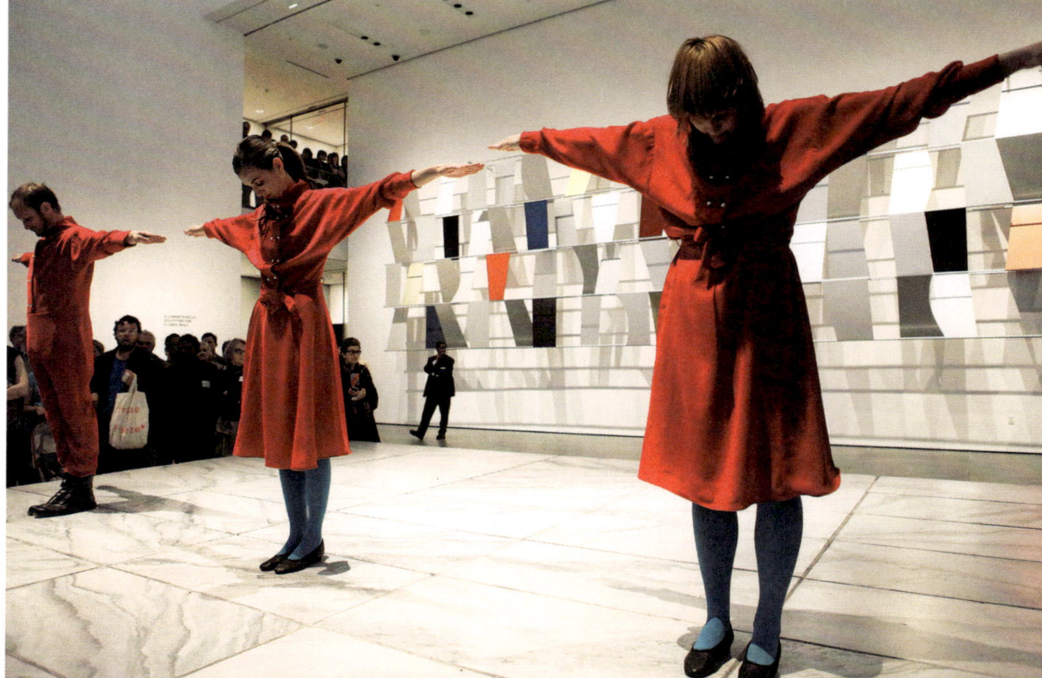

Choreographed performance *Alphabet*, 2012

<u>Alphabet</u>, Abby Aldrich Rockefeller Sculpture Garden, The Museum of Modern Art, New York (choreographed performance)

Performing artists: Katy Pile, Jessie Gold, Daniel Squire, and Kevin Hurley.

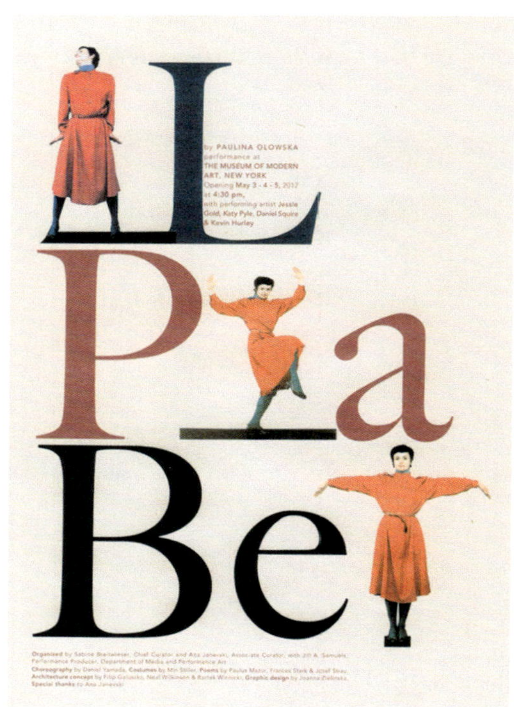

Poster for the performance *Alphabet*, 2012

List of Illustrations

p. 3
Reconstucting Modernism [sic], 2001–2013
1 photograph of a set of 4, 29 × 19.5 cm

p. 4
"Construction First–Collages from Japan" series, 2000
Gouache paint on glossy magazine, 22 × 30 cm

Modernist Rockabilly Shoes, 2000
Shoes, 21 × 30 × 9 cm
Museum of Modern Art Collection, Warsaw

p. 5
Painted Dress, 2000
Oil on fabric, 88 × 56 cm

"Asymmetric Women" series, 2000
Gouache on printed pages, 36.8 × 48.9 cm

p. 6
Bridget–1964, 2001
Oil on canvas, 180 × 120 cm
Private Collection

Big Pollock, 2001
Oil on canvas, 50 × 60 cm
Private Collection

p. 7
X, 2002
Oil on canvas, 180 × 100 cm
Rosette Delug Collecttion

p. 8
The Observer, 2000
Oil and crayon on canvas, 51 × 41 cm
Goetz Collection, Munich

p. 10–11
Lucy McKenzie and Paulina Olowska
Nova Popularna, installation views, Warsaw, 2003

p. 10, right, top: Various Artists, *Nova Popularna*, 2004
LP, color gatefold sleeve, front, 31.5 × 31.5 cm
Label: Decemberism
Graphic design: Lucy McKenzie and Paulina Olowska

p. 11, top: Lucy McKenzie and Paulina Olowska
Poster for *Nova Popularna*, 2003
Silkscreen, 56 × 42 cm

p. 12–13
Paulina Olowska and Mathilde Rosier
Entr'acte, 2003
Stills, PAL video, sound, 6' loop

p. 14–15
Paulina Olowska and Mathilde Rosier
Entr'acte, site-specific video installation in the former Hotel Pod Jeleniem in Cieszyn, staged for the exhibition *Hidden in a Daylight*, 3rd Era New Horizons Film Festival, 2003

p. 16
Calder, 2003
Oil on canvas, 120 × 120 cm
Private collection, Heteren (Netherlands)

p. 17
Arriviste (XZ), exhibition view, AKINCI Gallery, Amsterdam, 2004

Library of Spoken Books/Spoken Library, 2003
Wallpaper, approx. 3 × 3.5 m
Thomas Borgmann, Berlin

p. 18
America, 2003
Oil on canvas, 41 × 27 cm
Thomas Borgmann, Berlin

p. 19
Diesel, 2003
Oil on canvas, 140 × 100 cm
Thomas Borgmann, Berlin

Fall 1984–85, 2003
Oil on canvas, 93 × 74 cm
Chadha Art Collection, Voorschoten (Netherlands)

p. 20–23
Sie musste die Idee eines Hauses als Metapher verwerfen (She Had to Discard the Idea of the House as a Metaphore), exhibition views, Kunstverein Braunschweig, Brunswick, 2004

p. 20, bottom: *Automatic Bar*, 2004
Bar, paint, foil, metal, mirror, dimensions variable

p. 21: *Charlotte*, 2004, acrylic on wood, wheels, 250 × 150 cm

p. 24–25
Asymmetric Display, installation view and detail, Galerie Buchholz, Art Cologne, 2004
Thomas Borgmann, Berlin

p. 26
Etiuda Plastyczna, poster design for fashion show in Stockholm, 2004
Collage on paper, 45.5 × 36 cm (framed)
Thea Westreich Wagner and Ethan Wagner Collection, New York

p. 27
A Study with Oscar Wilde, 2004
Collage, ink, drawing on paper, 45.5 × 36 cm (framed)
Thomas Borgmann, Berlin

p. 28–29
Suspicious?, 2004
Site-specific billboard, located at 1915 S. Halsted St., Chicago Arts District, New Context Gallery, Chicago

p. 30
Alphabet, 2005
26 coloured cards, 4 black & white cards in box, 21 × 15 × 2 cm
With poems by Frances Stark, Josef Strau, and Paulus Mazur
Edition of 100 signed and numbered

p. 31
Alphabet, 2012
Choreographed performance, Abby Aldrich Rockefeller Sculpture Garden, The Museum of Modern Art, New York
Performing artists: Jessie Gold, Katy Pile, Daniel Squire, and Kevin Hurley

p. 32
Metaloplastyka III, 2005
Mixed media on canvas, 65 × 55 cm
Thea Westreich Wagner and Ethan Wagner Collection, New York

p. 33
Metaloplastyka, exhibition views, Galerie Buchholz, Cologne, 2005

p. 35
Metaloplastyka IV, 2005
Acrylic and oil on canvas, 180 × 120 cm
Private Collection

p. 36
Metaloplastyka VI, 2005
Acrylic and oil on canvas, 40 × 50 cm
Private Collection

p. 37
Verena, 2004
Acrylic on canvas, 50 × 40 cm
Goetz Collection, Munich

p. 38–39
Metamorphosis, permanent installation, Museum Abteiberg Mönchengladbach, Sammlung Provinzial Versicherung, Mönchengladbach, 2005

p. 40
Warsaw Belongs to Bourgeoisies, 2006
Oil, collage on canvas, 220 × 150 cm
The Craig Robins Art Collection, Miami

p. 41
Painting–Exchange–Neon, exhibition view, Foksal Gallery Foundation, Warsaw, 2006

p. 42–43
Lighting up of the renovated neon sign *Siatkarka (Volleyball Player)* [1962] in Warsaw, a final part of the project and exhibition *Painting–Exchange–Neon*, Foksal Gallery Foundation, Warsaw, 2006

p. 45
Stripteaser [Nashville], 2005
Oil, pencil, paper on canvas, 220 × 150 cm
Goetz Collection, Munich

p. 46
From Idea to Szapocznikow, 2006
Collage on linen, 220 × 150 cm
Private Collection

p. 47
Achievement (Black Cheerleader), 2005
Oil, pencil, paper on canvas, 200 × 100 cm
The Craig Robins Art Collection, Miami

p. 48
Olivia Newton-John, 2005
Oil, pencil, paper on canvas, 200 × 100 cm
Private collection, New York

About Her, 2005
Oil, pencil, paper on canvas, 200 × 100 cm
Private Collection

p. 49
Pauline Boty Acts Out One of Her Paintings for a Popular Newspaper, 2005
Oil, acrylic, paper on canvas, 220 × 150 cm
Thea Westreich Wagner and Ethan Wagner Collection, New York

p. 50–51
Hello to You Too/Impressionist–Cherry Picking, 2006
Oil, acrylic, paper on canvas, 200 × 100 cm

p. 52
Cigarette Break, 2005
Oil, acrylic, paper on canvas, 200 × 100 cm

p. 53
Announcement Yet, 2005
Acrylic paint, oil, paper on canvas, 220 × 150 cm
Goetz Collection, Munich

Mieszkanie 626-83-36, 2005–2006
Oil, paper on canvas, 200 × 101 cm
Goetz Collection, Munich

p. 54–55
Bonnie Camplin and Paulina Olowska
A Like Akarova, 2007
Stills, film commissioned by Wiels Contemporary Art Centre, Brussels

p. 56
Ship Modern Girl, 2006
Acrylic, oil and collage on canvas, 50.8 × 40.6 cm
Private collection, Miami

Nowa Scena, exhibition view, Metro Pictures, New York, 2007

p. 57
Rock and Rolla, 2006
Acrylic and collage on canvas, 248.9 × 139.7 cm
The Craig Robins Art Collection, Miami

p. 58
Tree, 2006
Acrylic and collage on canvas, 40.6 × 50.8 cm
Private collection, Pennsylvania

p. 59
Pantomime, 2006
Acrylic and collage on canvas, 50.8 × 40.6 cm
Private collection, Italy

p. 60
Soviet Life, 2006
Acrylic and collage on canvas, 30.5 × 40.6 cm
Private collection, Belgium

p. 61
Ameryka–California, 2006
Acrylic, oil and collage on canvas, 50.8 × 40.6 cm
Private collection, New Jersey

p. 62
Musicians, 2006
Acrylic, oil, and collage on canvas, 39.4 × 30.5 cm
Eric Diefenbach Collection, New York

p. 63
Gestures as Art, 2006
Acrylic, oil, and collage on canvas, 39.4 × 30.5 cm

p. 64
Few Days, 2006
Acrylic and collage on canvas, 39.4 × 30.5 cm
Private collection, New York

p. 89
Untitled, 2006
Collage on paper, 43.2 × 35.6 cm

p. 90
Ryszard Gajewski, Kontrola W., Jarocin Rock Festival, 1983

p. 91
Andrzej Amok Turczynowicz, *Untitled*, from *Kanal Revue*, a fanzine collage, 1981
21 × 29.5 cm

Neue Polnische Welle 1978–1986. Robert Jarosz Music Archive, exhibition view, MD 72, Berlin, 2008

p. 92
Jacek Awakumowski, Kontrola W., Jarocin Rock Festival, 1982

Ryszard Gajewski, Kontrola W., Jarocin Rock Festival, 1983

p. 93
Neue Polnische Welle 1978–1986. Robert Jarosz Music Archive (after M.R. Makowski), exhibition poster (detail) for the exhibition held at MD 72, Berlin, 2008
Silkscreen on paper, 85.5 × 61 cm

p. 94
Handmade cassettes sent by bands to the Jarocin Rock Festival, 1980s
Top to bottom: A, 1984, Nowomowa (Newspeak), RAF, Czarna Lista (Black List)

p. 95
Neue Polnische Welle 1978–1986. Robert Jarosz Music Archive, exhibition view, MD 72, Berlin, 2008

p. 96
Abendkleid, 2008
Gouache on paper, 219 × 141 cm
Private collection, Cologne

p. 97
Rock, Bluse und Hut, 2008
Gouache on paper, 186 × 141 cm

p. 98
Party-Kleid, 2008
Gouache on paper, 197 × 139 cm
Thomas Borgmann, Berlin

p. 99
Festliches Gewand, 2008
Gouache on paper, 218 × 134 cm
Private collection, Cologne

p. 100–101
Attention à la Peinture, exhibition views, Galerie Buchholz, Cologne, 2008

p. 102–103, 104–105
Zofia Stryjeńska, exhibition views, Neue Nationalgalerie, 5th Berlin Biennale for Contemporary Art, 2008

p. 106–107
Zofia Stryjeńska, exhibition view, Schinkel Pavillon, 5th Berlin Biennale for Contemporary Art, 2008

p. 108
Zofia Stryjeńska, exhibition view, Schinkel Pavillon, 5th Berlin Biennale for Contemporary Art, 2008
With Paulina Olowska, *Zofia Stryjeńska (Couple with Apples)*, 2008
Gouache on canvas, 230 × 180 cm
Zofia Styjeńska, *Zrywanie Jabłek/Apple Picking*, 1960
Oil on canvas, 90 × 71.5 cm
National Museum in Warsaw

p. 109
Zofia Stryjeńska, exhibition view, Schinkel Pavillon, 5th Berlin Biennale for Contemporary Art, 2008
With Zofia Styjeńska, *Popiersie góralki*, 1939
Watercolor, gouache on cardboard, 31 × 22.5 cm
National Museum in Krakow

p. 110–111
Crossword Puzzle with Lady in Black Coat, 2009
Gouache on canvas, 230 × 360 cm

p. 112
Warsaw neons from the 1960s

p. 113
Natasza, *Worker Canteen*, *Flowers*, 2010
Installation view with three reconstructed neon signs from Warsaw, Andreas-Hofer-Plaz, roof of the gas station, Graz, in the context of the exhibition *Utopia and Monument II: On Virtuosity and the Public Sphere*, Steirischer Herbst Festival

p. 114
Applied Fantastic, exhibition view, Metro Pictures, New York, 2010

p. 115
Applied Fantastic, Inspiration Wall, 2010
Plywood, cork, mixed media collages, painting, knitted sock and two sweaters, 246.4 × 221 × 33 cm

p. 116
Klaun/Clown, from the "Applied Fantastic" series, 2010
Oil on canvas, 175 × 125 cm
Private collection, Puerto Rico

p. 117
Szachista I/Chess Player 1, from the "Applied Fantastic" series, 2010
Oil on canvas, 175 × 125 cm
Sender Collection, New York

p. 118
Torcik/Cake, from the series "Applied Fantastic" series, 2010
Oil on canvas, 175 × 125 cm
Private collection, New York

p. 119
Pszczoła/Bee, from the "Applied Fantastic" series, 2010
Oil on canvas, 175 × 125 cm
Private collection, London

p. 120
Ela, from the "Applied Fantastic" series, 2010
Oil on canvas, 175 × 125 cm
Private collection, New York

p. 121
Polowanie/Hunting, from the "Applied Fantastic" series, 2010
Oil on canvas, 175 × 125 cm
Collection of Stedelijk Museum, Amsterdam

p. 122
Crochet Coat, from the "Applied Fantastic" series, 2010
Oil on canvas, 72 × 50 cm

p. 123
Coat with a Crochet Cap, from the "Applied Fantastic" series, 2010
Oil on canvas, 72 × 50 cm

p. 124
Woolmark, from the "Applied Fantastic" series, 2010
Oil on canvas, 195 × 140 cm
Goetz Collection, Munich

p. 125
Cardigan Smrek, from the "Applied Fantastic" series, 2010
Oil on canvas, 195 × 140 cm
Private Collection

p. 126–129
Accidental Collages, 2004
16 parts, digital print, edition of 5 + 1 AP
(About Fashion), 93.2 × 78.5 cm; *(About Jackie Kennedy)*, 106 × 78.5 cm; *(About Woman Only Salon)*, 78.5 × 88.5 cm; *(About Courage)*, 64.5 × 108.5; *(About a Woman)*, 105 × 78.5 cm; *(About a New Neon)*, 101 × 78.5; *(About Malevich)*, 103.5 × 78.5 cm; *(About Lack of a Neon)*, 78.5 × 103 cm
Stedelijk Museum, Amsterdam; Museum of Modern Art, Warsaw; Thea Westreich Wagner and Ethan Wagner Collection, New York; Galerie Buchholz, Berlin/Cologne

p. 130–131
Café Bar, exhibition view, National Museum in Krakow, 2011

p. 132
Café Bar MNK, 2011
Oil on MDF board, 440 × 250 cm

Wojciech Długosz, *The Girl with a Basket*, 1956
Oil on canvas, 69 × 58 cm
National Museum in Krakow

p. 133
Café Bar, exhibition view, National Museum in Krakow, 2011

p. 134
Zemsta wróżki/The Revenge of the Wise-Woman, exhibition view, Foksal Gallery Foundation, Warsaw, 2011
With Three Roses, 2011, former fountain sculpture from Rabka Zdroj, Poland, ca 1970, rearranged by the artist, painted metal, 200 × 200 × 280 cm

p. 135
Zemsta wróżki/The Revenge of the Wise-Woman, exhibition view, Foksal Gallery Foundation, Warsaw, 2011
With Teatr, 2011
Oil on canvas, 160 × 135 cm

p. 136
Portrait with Flowers (After M.), 2009
Oil on canvas, 160 × 135 cm

p. 137
Emmy Hennings, 2011
Oil on canvas, 70 × 50 cm
Ursula Hauser Collection, Switzerland

p. 139
Granny, 2012
Oil on canvas, 200 × 135 cm
Private Collection

p. 141
She–The Collector, 2012
Oil on canvas, 200 × 135 cm
Private collection, New York

p. 142
Mother 200, 2012
Oil on canvas, 220 × 200 cm
Private Collection

p. 143
L'introvertie, 2012
Oil on canvas, 200 × 134 cm
Private Collection

p. 144
Silver Vase, 2012
Oil on canvas, 160 × 135 cm
Private Collection

p. 145
Paulina Olowska in her studio, Lisbon, 1999

p. 146
Slightly Disappointed, from the "Utopian Optimism" series, 1998–1999
Oil on canvas, 70 × 50 cm
Private Collection

Do You Like Minimal Art?, from the "Utopian Optimism" series, 1998–1999
Oil on canvas, 24 × 20 cm

Looking Up not Down, from the "Utopian Optimism" series, 1998–1999
Oil on canvas, 160 × 140 cm
Private collection, Naples

p. 147
New Hobby–Summer Houses, 1999
Stills

Invitation card for the exhibition *Frango Sinatra*, Exposição No Moinho, Casalinho, Portugal, 1999, 10.3 × 15 cm

Mural painting, ZEFA Contemporary Art Centre, Almancil, Portugal, 1999

Gardeners of all Countries… , 1999
Still

p. 148
Documentation of the performance *Triumph of Youth*, MFA Thesis Exhibition, Academy of Fine Arts, Gdańsk, 1999

Triumph of Youth, 1999
Oil in canvas, 60 × 50 cm
Private collection, Gdańsk

Cover of the exhibition catalogue *Marzenie Prowincjonalnej Dziewczyny/The Dream of Provincial Girl*, Sopot, 2000

Na wiosnę, exhibition view, Entropia Gallery, Wrocław, 2000

Invitation card for the exhibition *Na wiosnę*, Entropia Gallery, Wrocław, 2000, 14 × 9.5 cm

Latem Taniej, Shoe-box Gallery–Mobilny Salon Wystawowy Bagatt, Gdańsk, 2000

Documentation of the performance *I Like Traditionalism and Traditionalism Likes Me/For Sato Churyo*, Centre for Contemporary Art, Kitakyushu, 2000

Documentation of the performance *Abstraktsioon Töötluses/Abstraction in Process*, staged for the exhibition *Nurse with Wound*, Art Hall Gallery, Tallinn, 2000

From the series "Construction First–Collages from Japan," 2000
Gouache paint on glossy magazine, 22 × 30 cm

p. 149
Heavy Duty, 2000
Color photograph, 25.5 × 20 cm

Lucy McKenzie and Paulina Olowska
Heavy Duty, exhibition view, Inverleith House, Royal Botanic Garden, Edinburgh, 2001

Bauhaus Yoga, 2001
Performance, Royal Botanic Garden, Edinburgh

View of a Sculpture, 2001
Oil on canvas, 24 × 30 cm
Private Collection

Salon de l'indépendent, exhibition view, Project Room, Rijksakademie van beeldende kunsten, Amsterdam, 2001

Untitled, 2001
Oil on canvas, 100 × 70 cm

Lucy McKenzie and Paulina Olowska in front of their wall painting *Plastyczna integracja*, II Annual Polish Wall Painting Festival, Gdansk, 2001

Lucy McKenzie and Paulina Olowska
Plastyczna integracja, 2001

p. 150
Cu Vi Parolas Esperanton?, 2002
Billboard campaign image and invitation card for the project, AMS Outside Gallery, Centre of Contemporary Art, Warsaw, and 400 locations in public spaces in Poland

Romansując z awangardą/Romancing with Avant-Garde, exhibition view, National Gallery, Sopot, 2002

Lucy McKenzie and Paulina Olowska performing *Oblique Composition I*, Centre for Contemporary Art, Ujazdowski Castle, Warsaw, 2002

Lucy McKenzie and Paulina Olowska performing *Oblique Composition II*, Flourish Studios, Glasgow, Scotland, 2002

The Best Book About Pessimism I Ever Read, exhibition view, Kunstverein Braunschweig, Brunswick, 2002

The Rule of Hospitality, exhibition view, Galerie Neu, Berlin, 2002

p. 151
Three Greys, 2002
Oil on canvas, 40 × 50 cm
Private Collection

Paulina Olowska and Lucy McKenzie performing *Oblique Composition III*, Cabinet, London, 2003

Architectures of Gender. Contemporary Women's Art in Poland, exhibition view, SculptureCenter, New York, 2003

Lucy McKenzie and Paulina Olowska
Posters for Nova Popularna, 2003
Silkscreen, 56 × 42 cm

Clandestine, exhibition view, *Dreams and Conflicts: The Viewer's Dictatorship*, 50th Venice Biennale, Venice, 2003

Gestützt von Poesie, wall painting, Dekabank Collection, Frankfurt am Main, 2003

Invitation card for the *Polish Animation Evening. Films from the '60s, '70s, & Beyond*. Presented by Paulina Olowska, Galerie Daniel Buchholz, Cologne, 2003, 7 × 15 cm

p. 152
Invitation card for the exhibition *Arriviste (XZ)*, AKINCI Gallery, Amsterdam, 2004, 10.5 × 15 cm

Cover of the exhibition catalogue *Sie musste die Idee eines Hauses als Metapher verwerfen*, Kunstverein Braunschweig, Verlag der Buchhandlung Walther König, Cologne 2004

Etiuda Plastyczna, wall painting, *Nakkna Modeshow*, Konstfack, Stockholm, 2004

Invitation card for Paulina Olowska's private *Salon des Herbes*, Warsaw, 2004, 5.5 × 13 cm

Invitation card for the exhibition *Asymmetric Display*, Galerie Buchholz, Art Cologne, 2004, 21 × 14.7 cm, with *Vera*, 2004, collage, ink on paper, 45.4 × 36 cm, Judith Rotschild Foundation

Invitation card for the billboard project *Suspicious?*, Chicago Arts District, New Context Gallery, Chicago, 2004, 11 × 15.4 cm

p. 153
Invitation card for the exhibition *Metaloplastyka*, Galerie Daniel Buchholz, Cologne, 2005, 27.6 × 21 cm

Invitation card for the book presentation and performance *Alphabet*, Galerie Meerrettich, Berlin, 2005, 10.5 × 14.8 cm

Warsaw Rug, *Peggy Rug*, and *Le Shoe*, 2005
Projects for three dyed wool rugs, 370 × 285 cm, 526 × 183 cm, and 245 × 287 cm, for the 9th International Istanbul Biennale, 2005

Cover of the exhibition catalogue *Metamorphosis*, Städtisches Museum Abteiberg, Mönchengladbach, Revolver, Berlin 2005

Polish magazine cover, *Ameryka*, no. 141, October 1970

p. 154
Invitation card for the exhibition *Hello to You Too*, Cabinet, London, 2006, 14.9 × 21 cm

The Subversive Charm of the Bourgeoisie, exhibition view, Van Abbemuseum, Eindhoven, 2006
With *Warsaw Rug*, dyed wool rug, 370 × 285 cm

Invitation for the exhibition *Painting–Exchange–Neon*, Foksal Gallery Foundation, Warsaw, 2006, 29.5 × 42 cm, featuring a calendar with Warsaw neons from the 1960s and 1970s

Invitation card for the exhibition *Reconstruction of the Ball "Farewell to Spring,"* Centre for Contemporary Art, Ujazdowski Castle, Warsaw, 2006, 14.9 × 20.9 cm

Poster for the exhibition *At the Very Center of Attention*, Centre for Contemporary Art, Ujazdowski Castle, Warsaw, 2006, 96 × 67 cm

p. 155
Invitation card for the exhibition *Nowa Scena*, Metro Pictures, New York, 2007, 30.5 × 28.8 cm

Le Nuage Magellan, exhibition view, Centre Pompidou, Paris, 2007

Cover of the exhibition catalogue *Noël sur le balcon/HOLD THE COLOR. Paulina Olowska/Lucy McKenzie*, Sammlung Goetz, Kunstverlag Ingvild Goetz, Munich 2007

Bonnie Camplin and Paulina Olowska
A Like Akarova, 2007
Still, Wiels Contemporary Art Centre, Brussels, 2007

Bonnie Camplin and Paulina Olowska
Spectators Only: A Shadow Play, 2007
Still, Wiels Contemporary Art Centre, Brussels, 2007

Cover of the exhibition catalogue *Bonnie Camplin, Paulina Olowska. Salty Water/What of Salty Water*, Portikus, Frankfurt, 2007

p. 156
Invitation card for the exhibition *Attention à la peinture*, Galerie Daniel Buchholz, Cologne, 2008, 8.5 × 10.3 cm

Poster for the exhibition *Neue Polnische Welle 1978–1986, Robert Jarosz Music Archive*, Gallery MD 72, Berlin, 2008, 85.5 × 61 cm

Posters for *Zofia Stryjeńska*, exhibition view, Schinkel Pavillon, 5th Berlin Biennale for Contemporary Art, 2008
Gouache on paper, 61 × 83.5 cm each
Goetz Collection, Munich; Collection S.A. Weis & Kompanie; Collection Storch, Cologne

Cover for the set of 8 postcards *Zofia Stryjeńska* by Paulina Olowska, published by *A Prior Magazine*, in collaboration with the 5th Berlin Biennale for Contemporary Art, 2008, as part of the project *On Paper*.
Graphic design: Michaël Bussaer, Brussels
Limited edition of 1000 copies.

Documentation of Bonnie Camplin and Paulina Olowska's performance *Usher We (Down There)*, Oil Tanks, Tate Modern, London, 2008

Sarah Crowner and Paulina Olowska's *Ceramics and Other Things*, exhibition view, daadgalerie, Berlin, 2008

p. 157
Countdown to Violence, 2009
Collage on paper, 152.4 × 80 cm
Private collection, New York

Cherry Picking, 2009
Collage on paper, 152.4 × 80 cm
Private collection, London

Invitation card for the exhibition *Head–Wig (Portrait of an Exhibition): Selected by Paulina Olowska*, Camden Arts Centre, London, 2009, 10.4 × 14.8 cm

Cover for *Süddeutsche Zeitung Magazin*, special artist edition 46, November 13, 2009

Shadow with A Sneak, 2009
Etching, 35.3 × 30 cm
Edition of 25

Car Mobile, 2009
Collage on paper, 29.5 × 20.1 cm
De la Cruz Collection, Miami

p. 158
Accidental Collages, exhibition view, Tramway, Glasgow, 2010

Invitation card for the exhibition *Applied Fantastic*, Metro Pictures, New York, 2010, 21.5 × 20.9 cm

Invitation card for *Sesum fo L'lab*, CAAP Street Project, in the frame of the exhibition *The Magnificent Seven*, CCA Wattis Institute for Contemporary Arts, San Francisco, 2010, 20.3 × 13.3 cm

p. 159
Page from the catalogue/zine to the exhibition *Brudna woda*, PGS Sopot, 2011

Cover of the catalogue/zine to the exhibition *Brudna woda*, PGS Sopot, 2011

Piekna pogoda, exhibition view with Bonnie Camplin and Paulina Olowska, *Captain's Dream*, 2011, Foksal Gallery Foundation, Warsaw, 2011
Courtesy Foksal Gallery Foundation, Warsaw

Detail of the mural by Paulina Olowska and California College of the Arts students (Fredericko Alvarado, Matt Endler, Melissa Dickenson, Bean Gilsdorf, Kevin Krueger, and Blaz Pirnat) in the control room of the nitrogen factory Azoty-Tarnów S.A. in Mościce, in the frame of the exhibition *Tarnów. 1000 Years of Modernity*, BWA–Galeria Miejska w Tarnowie, 2011

Poster for the exhibition *Café Bar*, National Museum in Krakow, 2011, 68 × 49 cm
Graphic design: Joanna Zielinska

Józef Węgrzyn as Don Juan Zorilli, 1925
Invitation image for the exhibition *Zemsta wróżki/The Revenge of the Wise-Woman*, Foksal Gallery Foundation, Warsaw, 2011

p. 160
Alina Szapocznikow in her studio, invitation image for Paulina Olowska and Anna Zaradny sound performance *Le groupe panique with the flesh of the world*, staged for the closing day of the exhibition *Alina Szapocznikow: Sculpture Undone, 1955–1972*, WIELS Contemporary Arts Centre, Brussels, 2012

Invitation card for the exhibition *Mother 200*, Simon Lee Gallery, London, 2012, 21 × 14.7 cm

Body Movement. Alphabet Studies, 2007
Collage on paper, 42 × 58 cm

Documentation of the choreographed performance *Alphabet*, in conjunction with the exhibition *Ecstatic Alphabets/Heaps of Language*, The Museum of Modern Art, New York, 2012
Performing artists: Jessie Gold, Katy Pile, Daniel Squire, and Kevin Hurley

Poster for the performance *Alphabet*, The Museum of Modern Art, New York, 2012
Graphic design by Paulina Olowska and Joanna Zielinska, 102 × 66 cm

Imprint

This monograph is published in conjunction with the exhibition *Paulina Olowska: Pavilionesque* at the Kunsthalle Basel, June 13–September 1, 2013.

Kunsthalle Basel
Steinenberg 7
CH–4051 Basel
www.kunsthallebasel.ch

KUNSTHALLE BASEL

The exhibition was made possible by the generous support of LUMA Foundation, Fundación Almine y Bernard Ruiz-Picasso, and Adam Mickiewicz Institute

Publication

Edited by Lionel Bovier

Editorial Coordination
Anna Bujnowska and Clément Dirié

Texts
Anna Bujnowska (Chronology), Adam Szymczyk (Interview), Jan Verwoert (Essay)

Translations
Krzysztof Kosciuczuk (Interview)

Editing and Proofreading
Clare Manchester

Design
Gavillet & Rust / Piguet, Geneva

Typeface
Genath (www.optimo.ch)

Cover
Paulina Olowska's private *Salon des Herbes*, Warsaw, 2004
Photo: Mateusz Romaszkan

Dust Jacket
Book, with letter "O" from *Alphabet*, 2005, performed by Paulina Olowska; *Constructivistisch drieluik*, 2001, collage, spray on paper, 24 × 28 cm

Artist's Acknowledgments
Paulina Olowska would like to dedicate this book to Danuta Idzikowska.

Special thanks to Anna Bujnowska, Alicja Wysocka, Jacek Awakumowski, Stuart Bailey, Marcin Barski, Jarek Bauć, Claire Bishop, Bartek Borek, Thomas Borgmann, Sabine Breitwieser, Bonnie Camplin, Nikki Columbus, Sarah Crowner, Magda Drągowska-Romaszkan, Ryszard Gajewski, Robert Jarosz, Ewa Juszkiewicz, Werner Kaligofsky, Karolina & Kacper Kasprzyk, Kasia & Gregg Kay, Agata Kuś & Katarzyna Kukuła, Natalia & Sławek Lipiński, Mirosław Ryszard Makowski & Pracownia 52, Thomas Manneke, Katharina Marszewski, Marta Potaczek, Halina Przybył, Bartuś Przybył-Olowski, Jan Olowski, Caroline Paulick-Thiel, Razem Pamoja Foundation, Stephane Rebillard, Paul Roberts, Jerzy Sierosławski, Wolfgang Silveri, Michał Szymański, Adam Szymczyk, Wiesław Śliwiński & Sopockie Korzenie Foundation, Trasa W-Z Archive, Aleksander Bruno Wawrzyniak, Krystyna Wawrzyniak, Thea Westreich & Ethan Wagner, Jan Verwoert, Asia Zielińska, and Joanka Zielińska;

As well as to the following galleries and museums: AKINCI Gallery, Amsterdam; Galerie Buchholz, Cologne/Berlin; Cabinet Gallery, London; Foksal Gallery Foundation, Warsaw; Goetz Collection; The Craig Robins Art Collection, Miami; Metro Pictures, New York; Museum of Modern Art in Warsaw; Muzeum Sztuki in Łodź; National Museum in Krakow; Galerie Neu, Berlin; Simon Lee Gallery, London/Hong Kong.

Photo Credits
Artist's Archive: p. 148mm/mb, 151m; Stuart Bailey: p. 151mt; Yael Bartana: p. 41; Julieta Cervantes/The Museum of Modern Art: p. 160mt; Peter Cox: p. 154lb; Waldek Czapor: p. 42, 43; Alan Dimmick: p. 149lm/lb, 150mm; Justyna Gryglewicz: p. 130–131; Zygmunt K. Jagodziński: p. 112t; Werner Kaligofsky: p. 31; Kacper Kasprzyk: p. 152 mt; Anke Kempkes: p. 150mt; Zuzanna Krajewska: p. 149lt; P. Krassowski: p. 112b; Achim Kukulies: p. 38–39; Natalia Lipińska: p. 148lt, 149rt, 149rm, 150lm; Thomas Manneke: p. 150lt; Thomas Müller: p. 20–23; Paulina Olowska: p. 147mt, 151rt; Jerzy Ostrowski: p. 83 ; Stephen Parise: 148rt; Joanna Piotrkowska; p. 133; Ilya Rabinovich: p. 149mm; Mateusz Romaszkan: p. 42, 43, 73, 134, 135; M. Sadowski: p. 159mb; J. Sieroslawski: p. 68m; Wolfgang Silveri: p. 113 ; Jens Ziehe: p. 102–103, 104–105, 106–107, 108, 109; Jasper Zoova: p. 148rm

Courtesy
AKINCI Gallery, Amsterdam: p. 16, 17, 18, 19; Galerie Buchholz, Berlin/Cologne: p. 24–25, 26, 27, 30, 32, 33, 35, 36, 37, 84, 96, 97, 98, 99, 100–101, 110–111, 126–129, 136, 157rt, 160lb; Foksal Gallery Foundation, Warsaw: p. 3, 10–11, 14–15, 40, 42–43, 132, 137, 151m, 159mt; Simon Lee Gallery, London & Hong Kong: p. 4, 79, 139, 141, 142, 143, 144, 148rb; Ryszard Gajewski: p. 90, 92r; Robert Jarosz & Trasa W-Z Archive: p. 94; Metro Pictures, New York: p. 5b, 56, 57, 58, 59, 60, 61, 62, 63, 64, 74, 89, 114, 115, 116, 117, 118, 119, 120, 121, 122, 123, 124, 125, 157l; The Artist & Bonnie Camplin, and Wiels Contemporary Art Centre, Brussels: p. 54–55; The Artist & Bonnie Camplin, and Tate Modern, London: p. 156mb; The Artist & Lucy McKenzie: p. 12–13; Wieslaw Sliwinski & Sopockie Korzenie Foundation: p. 92l; Michal Szymanski: p. 91; The Artist: p. 5t, 146, 147, 149mb; The Artist and Metro Pictures, New York: p. 160mb; The Artist and Kasia Kay: p. 28–29

Color Separation & Print
Musumeci S.p.A., Quart (Aosta)

The publication has received generous support from:

Galerie Buchholz
Neven-Dumont Strasse 17
Cologne – Germany
Fasanenstrasse 30
Berlin – Germany
www.galeriebuchholz.de

Foksal Gallery Foundation
Ul. Gorskiego 1A
Warsaw – Poland
www.fgf.com.pl

Simon Lee Gallery
12 Berkeley Street
London – United Kingdom
304, 3F The Pedder Building, 12 Pedder Street
Hong Kong
www.simonleegallery.com

Metro Pictures
519 W 24th Street
New York – USA
www.metropicturesgallery.com

Printed in Europe

Published by

JRP|Ringier
Limmatstrasse 270
CH–8005 Zurich
T +41 (0) 43 311 27 50
F +41 (0) 43 311 27 51
E info@jrp-ringier.com
www.jrp-ringier.com

ISBN 978-3-03764-287-0

JRP|Ringier books are available internationally at selected bookstores and from the following distribution partners:

Switzerland
AVA Verlagsauslieferung AG
Centralweg 16, CH-8910 Affoltern a.A.
verlagsservice@ava.ch, www.ava.ch

France
Les presses du reel
35 rue Colson, F-21000 Dijon
info@lespressesdureel.com
www.lespressesdureel.com

Germany and Austria
Vice Versa Distribution GmbH
Immanuelkirchstrasse 12, D–10405 Berlin
info@vice-versa-vertrieb.de
www.vice-versa-distribution.com

UK and other European countries
Cornerhouse Publications
70 Oxford Street, UK-Manchester M1 5NH
publications@cornerhouse.org
www.cornerhouse.org/books

USA, Canada, Asia, and Australia
ARTBOOK|D.A.P.
155 Sixth Avenue, 2nd Floor
USA-New York, NY 10013
dap@dapinc.com, www.artbook.com

For a list of our partner bookshops or for any general questions, please contact JRP|Ringier directly at info@jrp-ringier.com, or visit our homepage www.jrp-ringier.com for further information about our program.